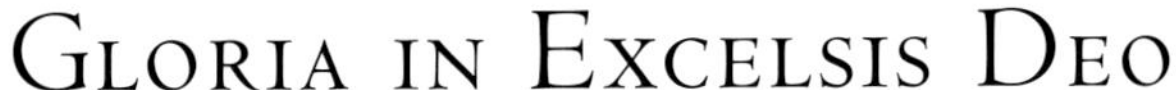

Gloria in Excelsis Deo

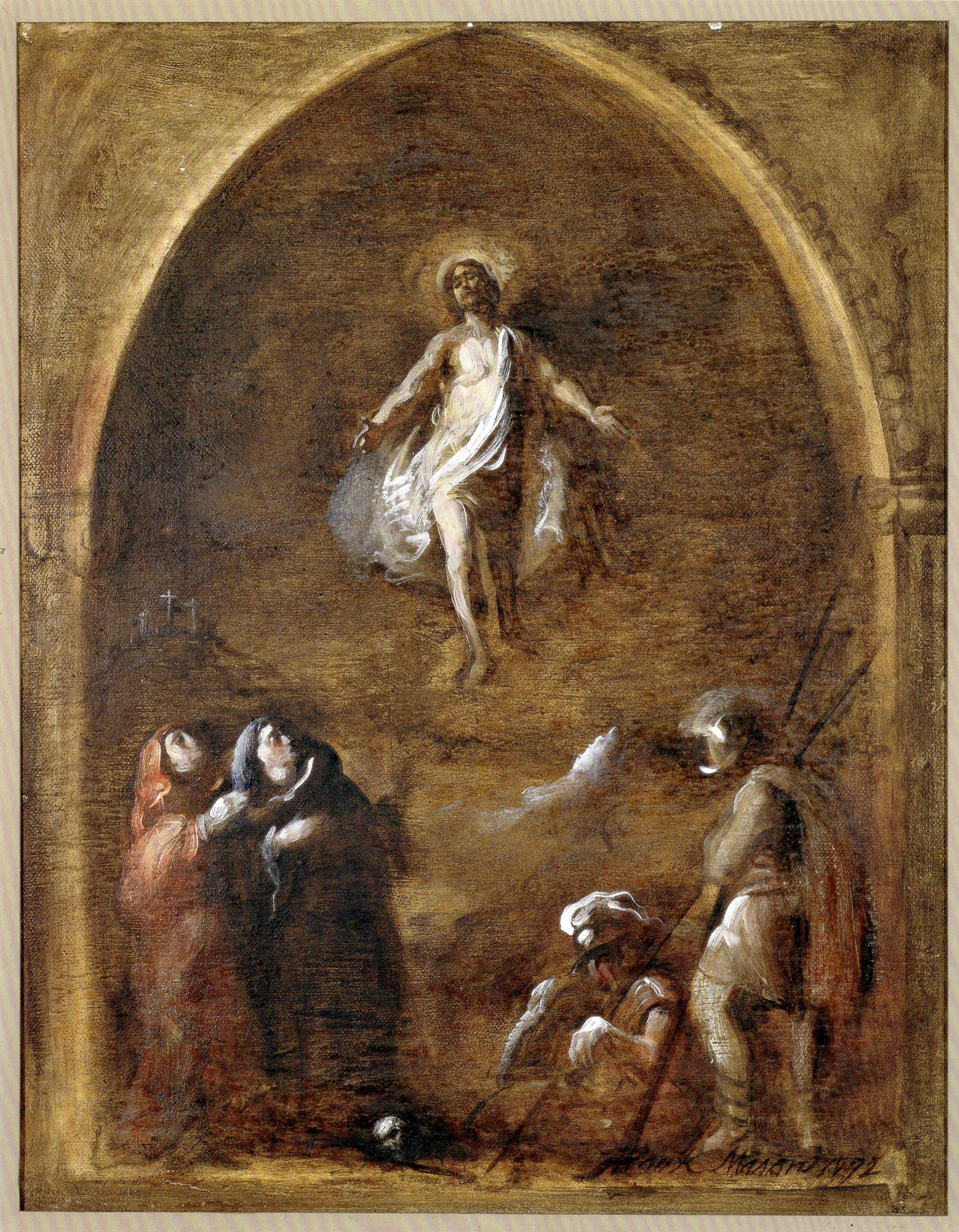

Gloria in Excelsis Deo
Frank Mason's Life of Christ

Introduction by James F. Cooper

Chameleon Books, Massachusetts

www.frankmason.org

Published by Chameleon Books, 2009
P.O. Box 445
31 Smith Road
Chesterfield, MA 01012
chambooks@earthlink.net

Distributed in the United States of America and in Canada by
ACC Distribution
6 West 18th Street (4th floor)
New York, NY 10011

Phone: (800) 252 5231 or (212) 645 1111
Fax: (212) 989 3205
Email: sales@antiquecc.com
www.accdistribution.com

10-digit ISBN: 0-915829-79-7
13-digit ISBN: 978-0-915829-79-8

Design: Arnold Skolnick
Production: Chameleon Books
Design Assistance: KC Scott, Robert Aller
Copy Editor: Jamie Nan Thaman

Printed in China

Frontispiece: *The Resurrection of Christ with the Two Marys*, 1972
Oil on panel, 32 x 26 inches, Collection of the Artist

Dedication

To my dear wife, Anne Mason, always the light of my life and inspiration.
And to my friend and publisher, Arnold Skolnick, with gratitude for his guidance.

Introduction
by James F. Cooper

In making his Christian faith the focus of his artistic skills, Frank Mason has turned to drawing, the oldest and most direct form of visual communication. Cave drawings discovered at Lascaux date back 25,000 years, when early man sought to evoke magical forces of nature in his favor. The sophisticated language of a finished painting—in terms of craft, iconography and formal aesthetic—requires a long process of education and practice. Drawing, however, whether with a stone or bone on a cave wall or a Conté crayon on Arches paper, comes directly from the soul. It is a way of seeing and divining meaning. This handsomely designed volume has sidestepped the formality of finished artistic style, which each century cultivates through its various academies and institutions, to better focus directly on its artistic and religious themes. The intuitive movement of Mason's hand, as it guides the pencil, brush and pen, reveals the rhythm of his soul, in febrile traceries of delicate line and clouded washes. Gloria in Excelsis Deo: Frank Mason's Life of Christ, then, is as much about artistic beauty as it is about the greatest story ever told. This collection—mostly drawings in ink, chalk, pencil and oil—reminds us that, in most of the civilizations that have flourished during the last 5,000 years of recorded history, art and the spiritual were inseparable. It is when the artist is fully engaged with the subject that he is most likely to create works of high aesthetic quality.

The Old and New Testaments became a primary source of inspiration for the greatest artists of Western civilization. In Mason's drawings, the majority of them studies for commissioned and non-commissioned religious paintings, we glimpse qualities we usually associate with drawings by Rembrandt, Raphael, Michelangelo, Tiepolo and Titian. Following the discipline of that tradition, Mason draws from the posed model for the purpose of study and composition. Like drawings by the old masters, Mason's studies were not meant to be exhibited. Yet, like the drawings we admire in museums, they have a direct eloquence often absent from more "finished" works. A few lines etched by Rembrandt with a stylus or a pen contain an entire world. Mason's *Study after Christ Healing the Man with the Withered Hand* (2003) juxtaposes, on the same sheet, a brown-ink wash study of a man with a black-chalk study of two figures. An old master sheet or an engraver's print often combined disparate images. Consciously or unconsciously, the artist would arrange these studies so they cohere on the page into a perfectly balanced composition. As he sketched a figure for a finished painting, the artist simultaneously created an aesthetically sophisticated composition that might have nothing to do with the appearence of the final work. The beautiful drawings by Mason carefully selected for this book, like those by Michelangelo and Rembrandt, are sometimes superior to the finished fresco or oil painting.

If Mason's skill reminds us of the old masters, however, he faces a very different universe of ideas. The world inhabited by Michelangelo and Rembrandt was far more unified in terms of cosmology than the world we inhabit. Their understanding of the life of Christ may not differ substantially from ours, but they had the benefit of a communal iconography endorsed by society. Religious art today is treated with suspicion. Is the artist being ironic or simply naïve? Bible illustration was a living tradition for over a millennium, from medieval manuscripts to Rembrandt to Gustave Doré. But in secular times, the genre can descend into mediocrity and kitsch. Today, even those inspired by genuine spiritual feeling often find it difficult to avoid, either by commission or omission, postmodernism's subtle nihilist chill. In contrast, Mason's pen-and-ink series *Angels* (1971–72) has a fluid electricity reminiscent of Rembrandt drawings, not because he is consciously copying the Dutch master, but because he is in touch with the same inner resources possessed by other great draftsmen. As Ruskin observed, in the museums of Europe, one will never find a childish or feeble drawing by one of the great masters. Unlike paintings, which are public performances, drawings can realize a fragment of life. A finished painting has many components which must be synthesized into a cohesive formal structure if it is to be successful. In a drawing, the artist is working only to please himself. There is no one looking over his shoulder. Mason pursues his personal narrative of the life of Christ with courage and grace, combining rigorous standards of formal excellence and genuine religious feeling. His achievement could be compared to the 300-drawing *New Testament* of Domenico Tiepolo (1727–1804), best known for his Venetian carnival images, and to J. James Tissot's 1899 *Bible in Pictures,* which marked the spiritual awakening of a previously worldly society painter. But Mason brings his own power to this enterprise in a particularly difficult era.

Frank Herbert Mason was born in Cleveland in 1921. His mother, a violinist and pianist, and his father, a Shakespearean actor, both painted, and Frank's talent as an artist was encouraged. When the family moved to New York City in 1932, he was selected to be among the first pupils to attend an experimental new Music and Arts High School. At age 16, he was granted a scholarship to study with the classicist Frank Vincent Dumond at the Art Students League. Their close association lasted until 1951, when Mason was appointed his successor. In 1962, Mason received a major commission from the Sovereign Military Order of Malta to paint a series of eight large paintings depicting the life of Saint Anthony of Padua. These paintings are now installed in the Church of San

Giovanni di Malta, in Venice. The Order of Malta subsequently conferred the Cross of Merit, *Prima Classe,* upon Mason, an honor last awarded for painting to Caravaggio.

The designer of this volume has wisely decided to include many of the beautiful studies and preparatory drawings, rather than focusing exclusively on the finished paintings Mason has done over the last fifty years. The looseness and inventiveness of these drawings reveal the hand of a master draftsman. The different mediums he uses, the subtle colors, the variety of surfaces he works with add greatly to the visual beauty and design of the book. Also reproduced are several finished oil paintings of major events in the life of Christ, from his birth in the manger to Gethsemene, the trial, crucifixion and resurrection. But it is the Renaissance quality of the drawings that most seduce the eye. Mason's red- and black-chalk study *Shepherd, Back View* (1970) stands in contrast to his brown-ink study *Center Shepherd for Gloria* (1972). Beautiful and sensitive, the first might have been sketched by Raphael. The latter, with its vigorous strong ink lines, resembles the sharp analysis of Albrecht Dürer.

In selecting the works to illustrate Gloria in Excelsis Deo, Mason has been guided by his life-long commitment to beauty and excellence, the same path chosen by his predecessors Fra Angelico, Memling, Michelangelo, Raphael and Bouguereau. Gloria in Excelsis Deo is inspired by the artist's deep Christian faith. It is also an expression of the artist's deep faith in art. In much of the Western tradition, for the faithful, the Word is everything, but visual beauty—the gift of the artist—has the power to bring us closer to nature and the universe by which we know God. The arts are mankind's feeble attempt to match the Creator's beauty. This is Frank Mason's offering.

—Newington-Cropsey Foundation
Hastings-on-Hudson, New York, 2009

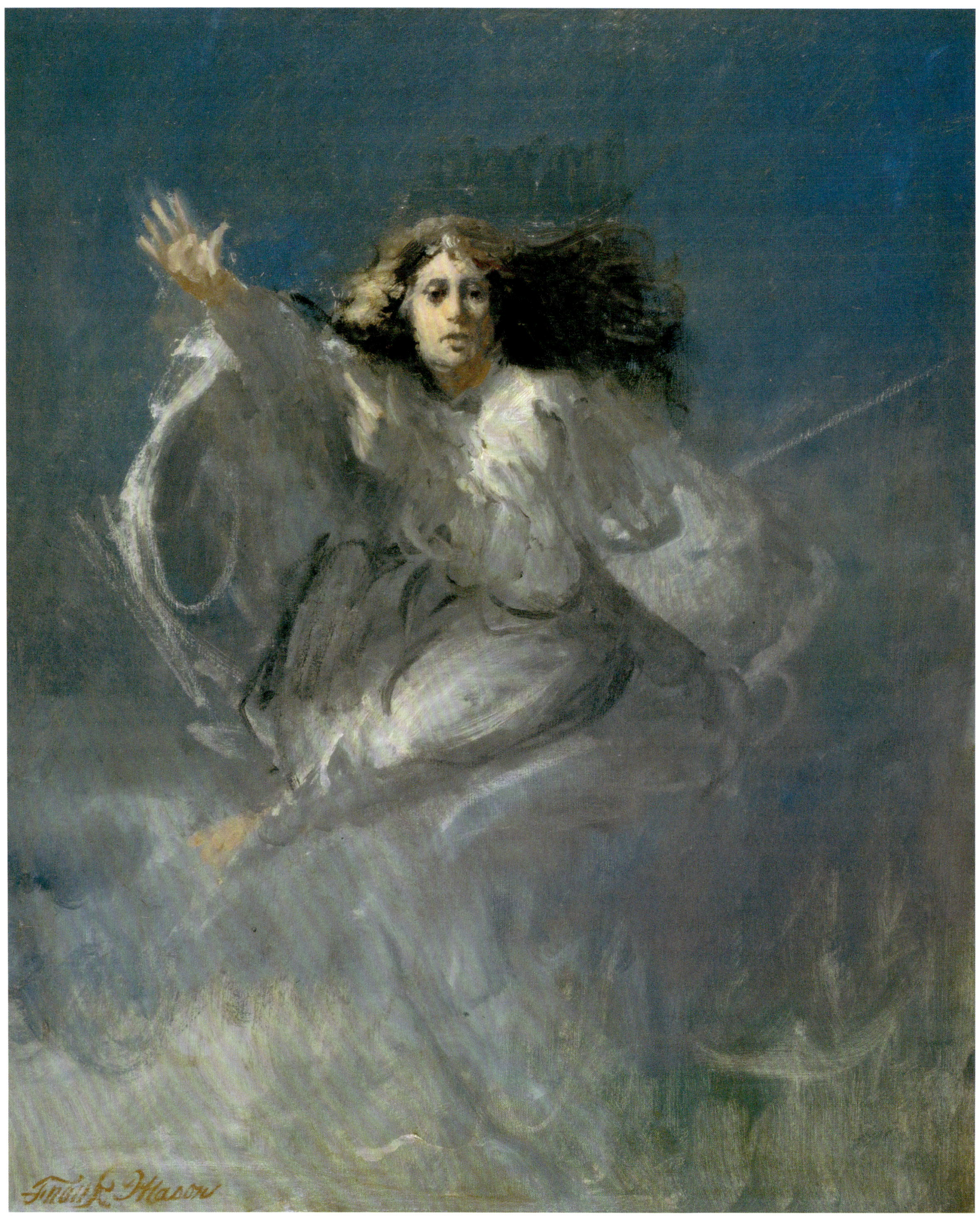

The Angel Gabriel, 1953
Oil on canvas, 30 x 25 in.

Young Mary Receiving the Holy Ghost, 2003
Oil on panel, 14 x 18 in.

The Annunciation

. . . . The angel Gabriel was sent from God unto a city of Galilee, named Nazareth, to a virgin espoused to a man whose name was Joseph. . . .And the virgin's name was Mary. . . .And the angel said unto her, Fear not, Mary: for thou hast found favour with God. . . .Thou shalt conceive in thy womb, and bring forth a son, and shalt call his name Jesus. . . .And of his kingdom there shall be no end. . . .The Holy Ghost shall come upon thee. . .that holy thing which shall be born of thee shall be called the Son of God. . . .For with God nothing shall be impossible. —Luke I : 26, 27, 30, 31, 33, 35, 37

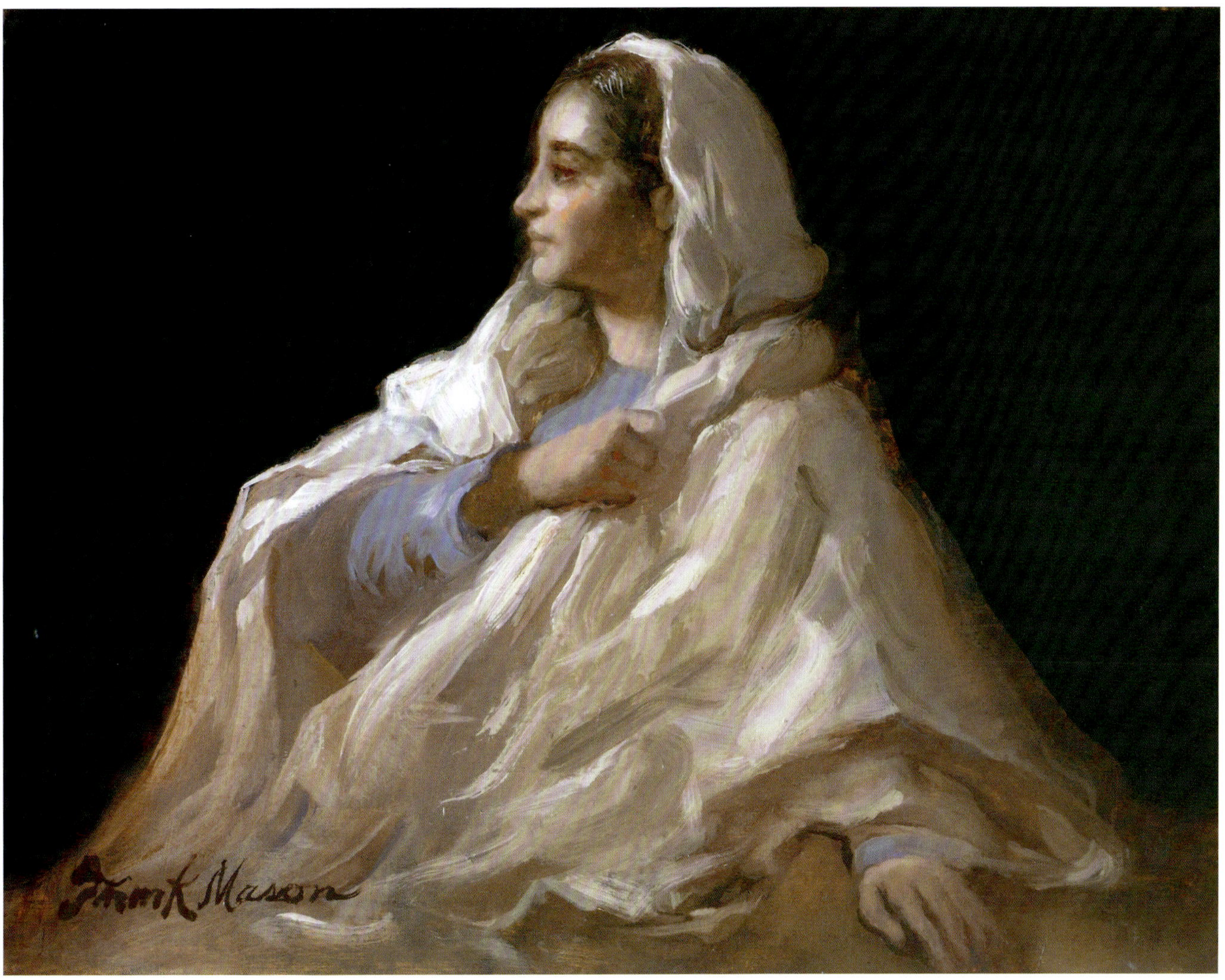

Many years ago, shortly after the death of my mother in the 1950s, I had a dream. In the brilliantly colored vision I saw a magnificent angel. I asked, "Who are you?" The angel replied, "I am the angel of death." "But you are beautiful," I said. Before disappearing, the angel answered, "I am beautiful." I could never possibly show you in paint the incredible beauty that I saw. I have used this imagery for the angel Gabriel appearing to Mary. The angel is coming forth to announce to Mary the blessing she will receive as the mother of Jesus, the Son of God. These two paintings were created a half century apart. In my mind there was no time. I was able to see my earlier vision of the angel in relationship to Mary as I began to paint her in the present. It is a vast privilege to be involved in the creative process which allows a bridging between past and present.

Gloria in Excelsis Deo

AND THERE WERE IN THE SAME COUNTRY SHEPHERDS ABIDING IN THE FIELD, KEEPING WATCH OVER THEIR FLOCK BY NIGHT. AND, LO, THE ANGEL OF THE LORD CAME UPON THEM, AND THE GLORY OF THE LORD SHONE ROUND ABOUT THEM: AND THEY WERE SORE AFRAID. AND THE ANGEL SAID UNTO THEM, FEAR NOT: FOR, BEHOLD, I BRING YOU GOOD TIDINGS OF GREAT JOY, WHICH SHALL BE TO ALL PEOPLE. FOR UNTO YOU IS BORN THIS DAY IN THE CITY OF DAVID A SAVIOUR, WHICH IS CHRIST THE LORD. AND THIS SHALL BE A SIGN UNTO YOU; YE SHALL FIND THE BABE WRAPPED IN SWADDLING CLOTHES, LYING IN A MANGER. AND SUDDENLY THERE WAS WITH THE ANGEL A MULTITUDE OF THE HEAVENLY HOST PRAISING GOD, AND SAYING, GLORY TO GOD IN THE HIGHEST, AND ON EARTH PEACE, GOOD WILL TOWARD MEN. —LUKE 2: 8–14

This painting deals with one of the great moments of the New Testament— the moment when the angel appeared in the heavens to the shepherds to announce the birth of Christ. It's the moment we all celebrate at the Christmas Eve service, and from the time I was a choir boy, I have been moved by the words and the image they evoke. The glorious angel in the heavens. . .the shepherds falling back in terror. . .and the splendid reassurance of the words: FEAR NOT! The scene as I visualized it thrilled me way back then and stayed dormant in my mind for many years. I used it finally as a sepia ink sketch for a Christmas card and a larger rough study, but I always wanted to put it on canvas. Finally, in 1972, I had the opportunity. That year I had a sabbatical—a year off with pay—from my teaching duties at the Art Students League. So I stretched a huge canvas and got to work. It was ready for a show at the National Arts Club in November 1973. Of course, I continued to work on it for another twelve years. How did I know when it was finished? Well, I got up one morning and looked at it, and it looked pretty good. I knew it was time to move on to something else.

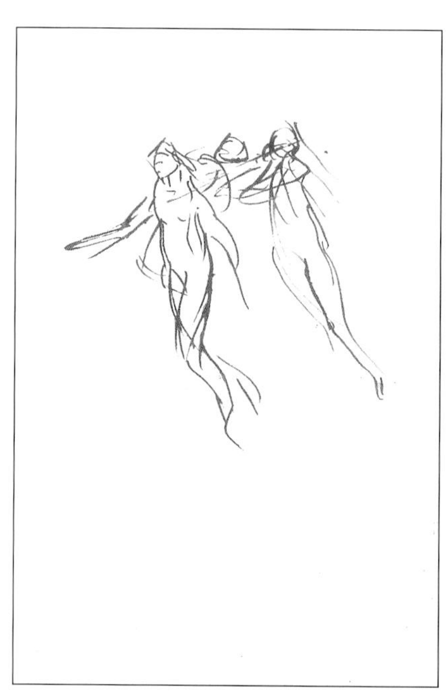

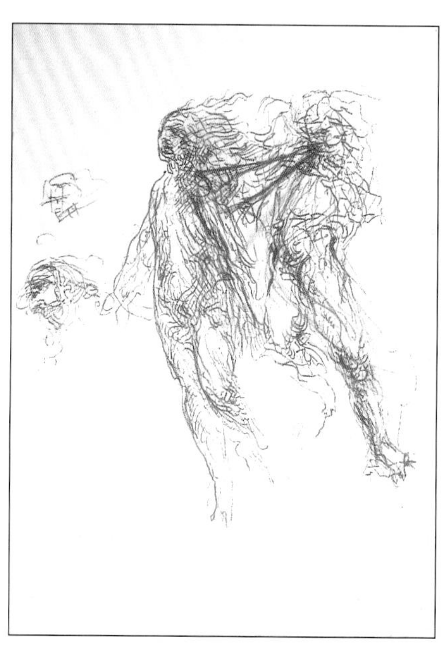

Angels, 1972
Pen and brown ink on cream paper
6 1/4 x 4 3/8 in.

Angels for Gloria in Excelsis Deo, 1971
Black ink on white paper
6 1/4 x 4 1/4 in.

(opposite)
Angel Appearing to the Shepherds, 1963
Oil on canvas, 20 x 16 in.

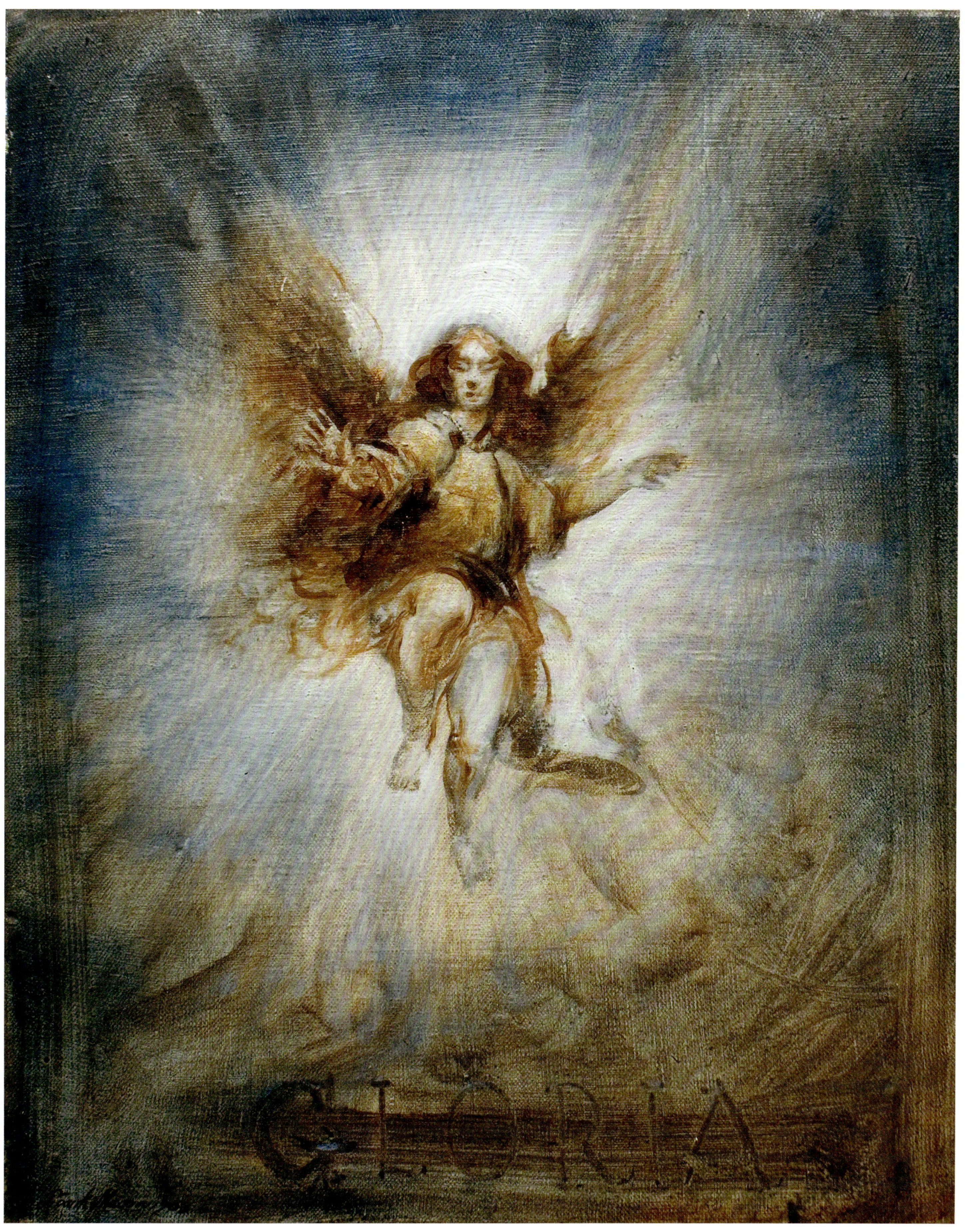
GLORIA

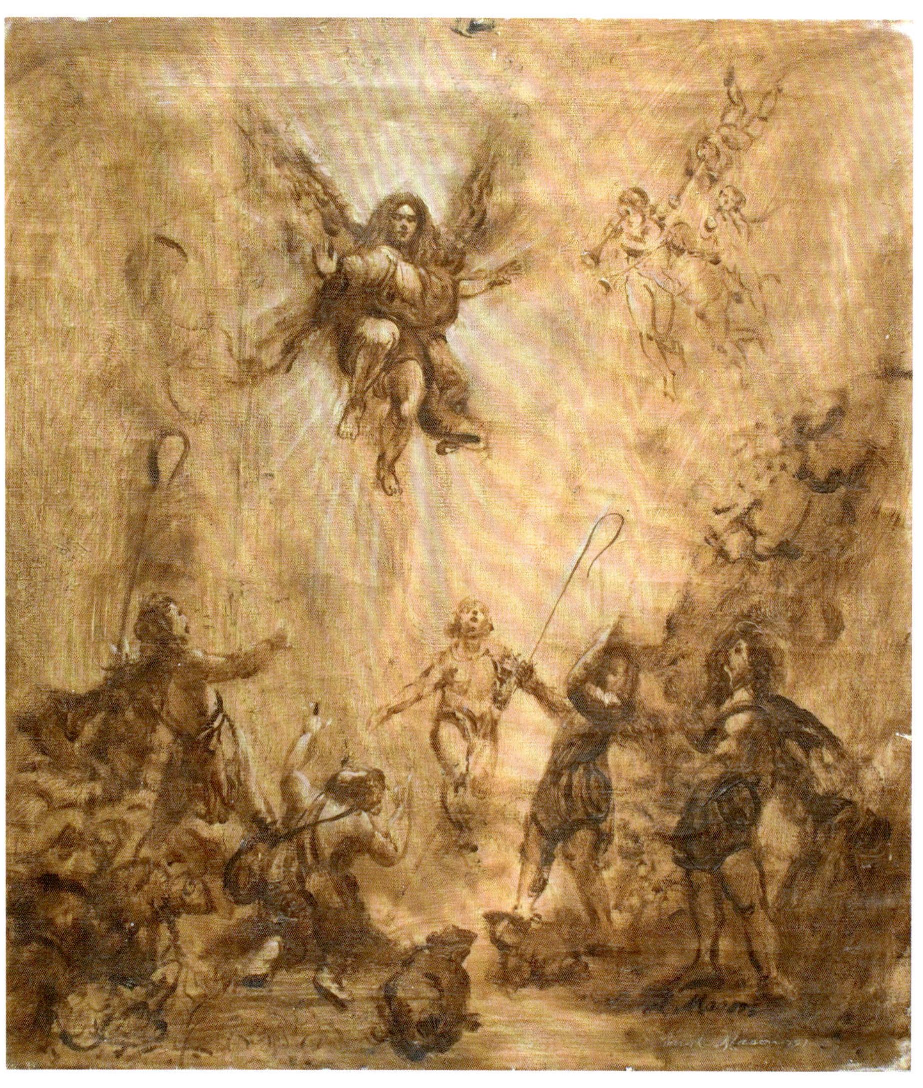

Original Bazzetto for Gloria in Excelsis Deo, 1957
Oil on canvas, 20 x 18 in.

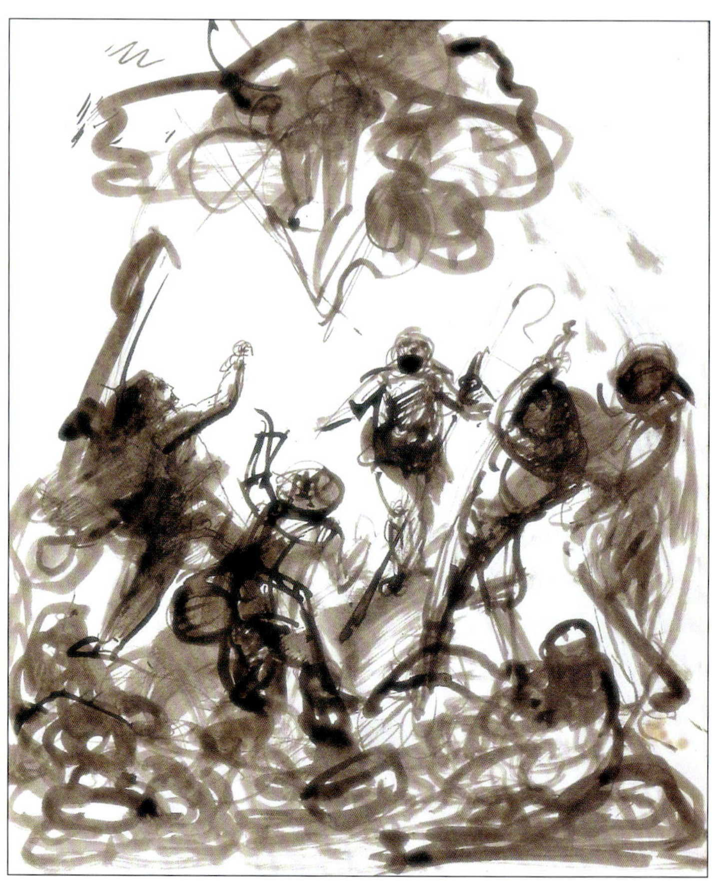

Shepherds and Angel for Gloria in Excelsis Deo, 1972
Pen and brown ink and wash on white paper
13 1/2 x 10 1/2 in.

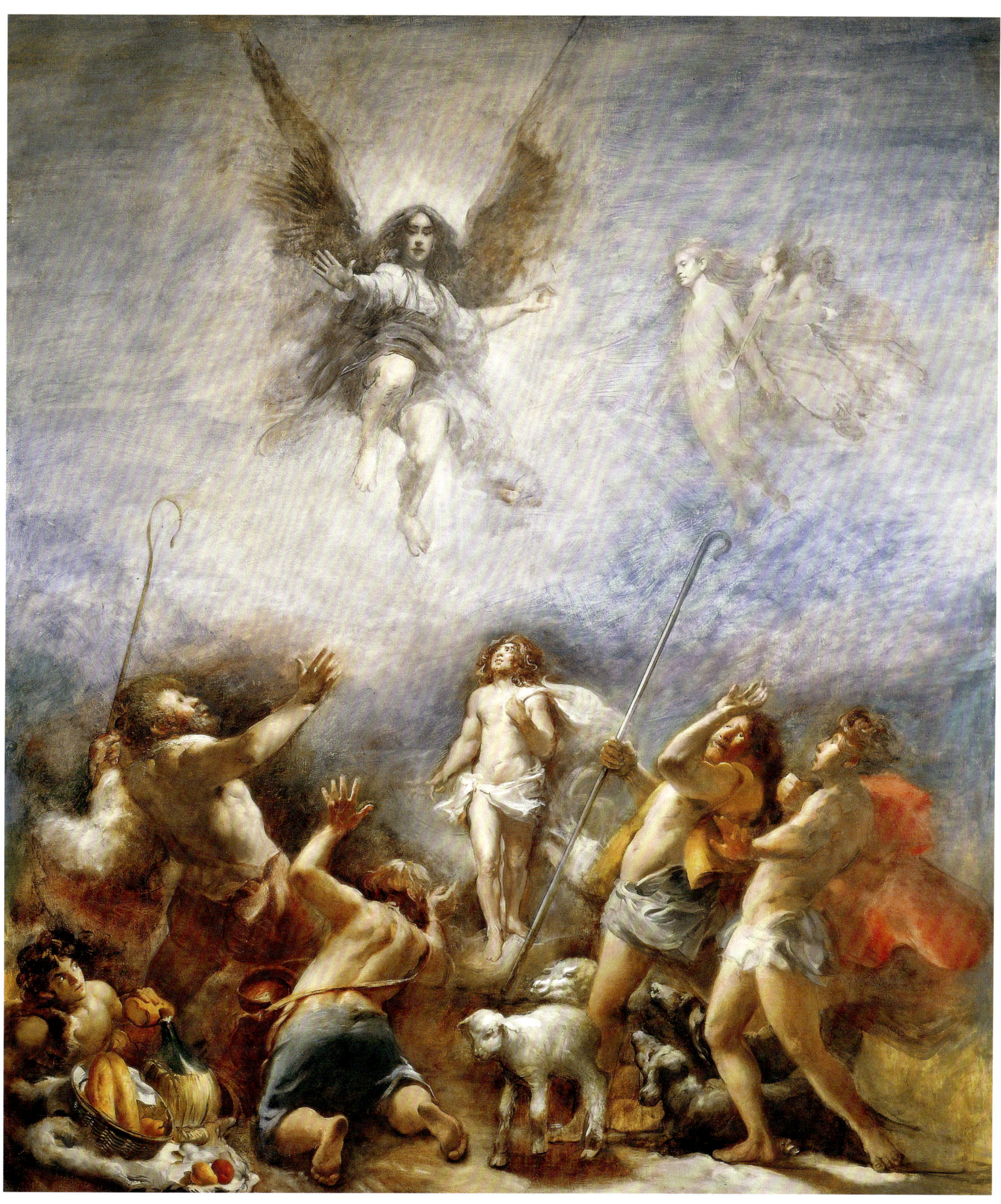

Gloria in Excelsis Deo, 1973
Oil on canvas, 142 in x 125 in.

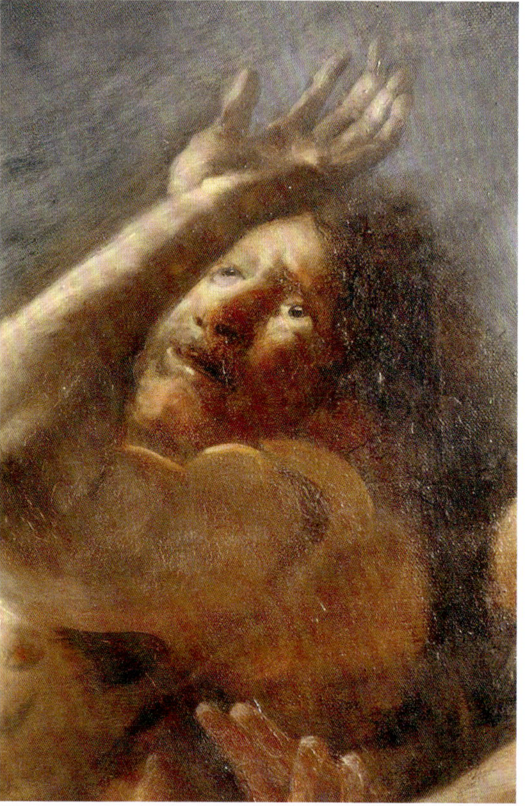

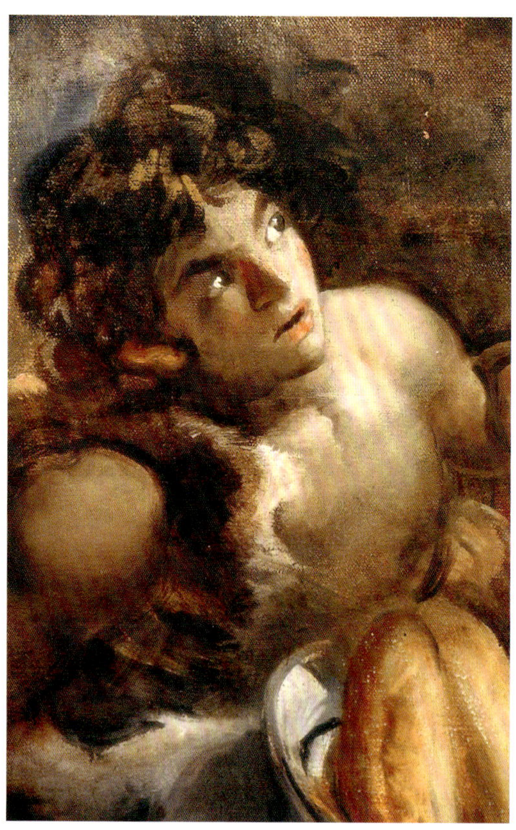

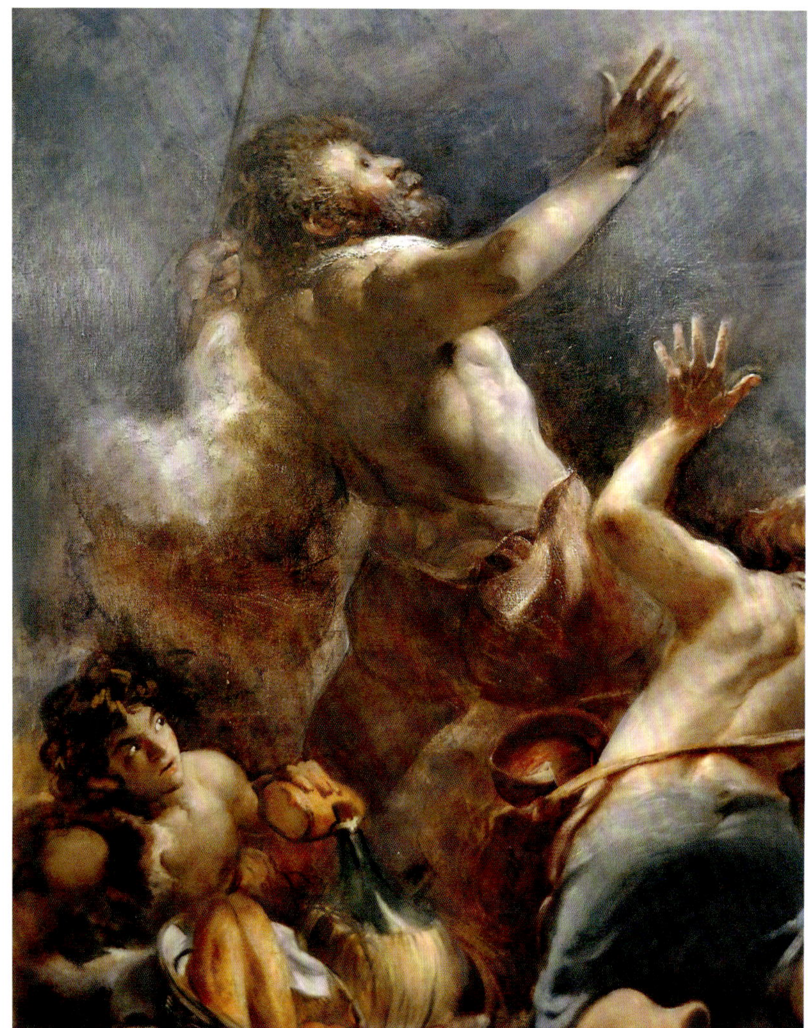

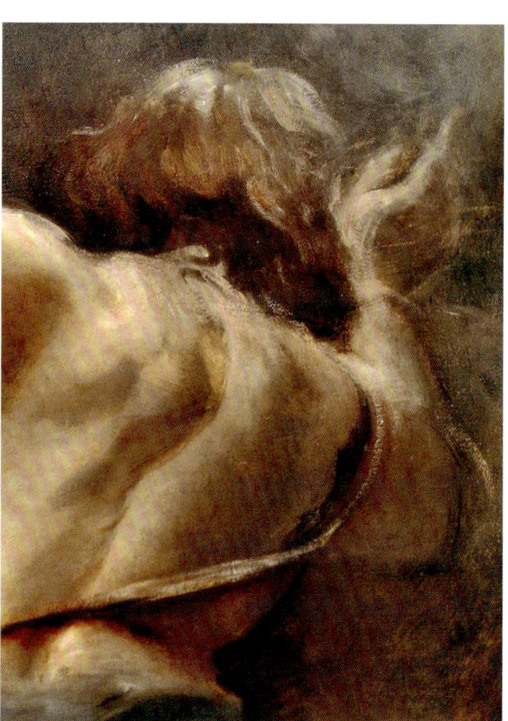

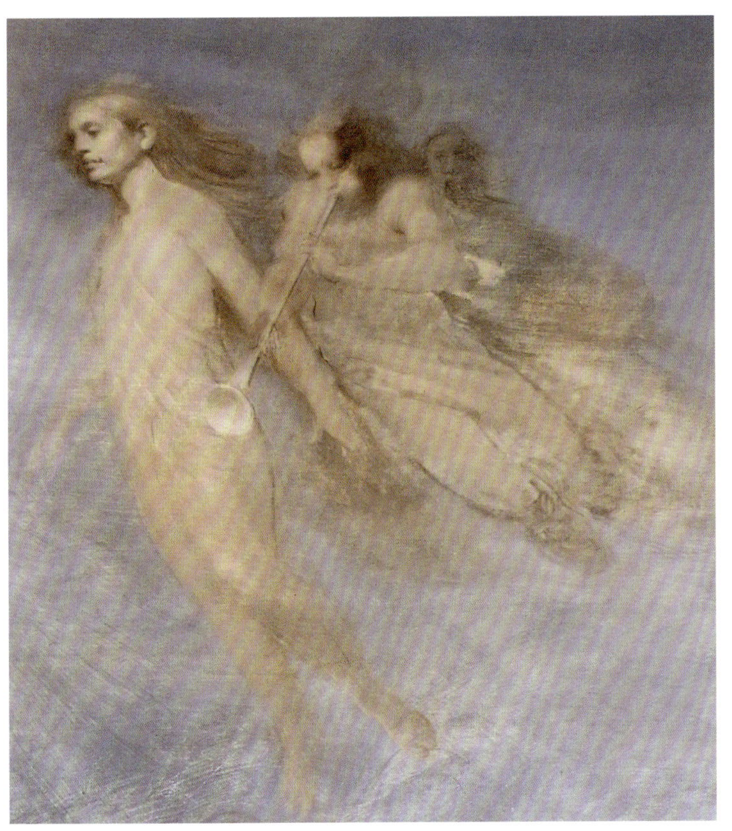

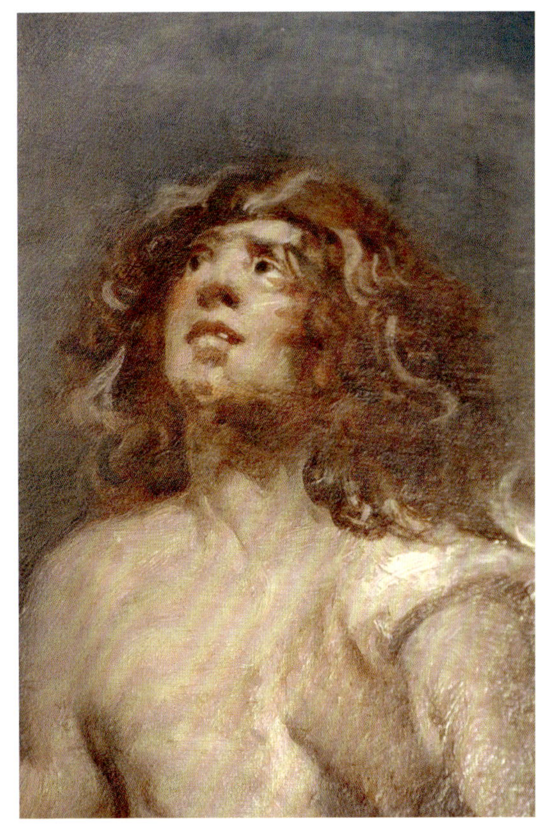

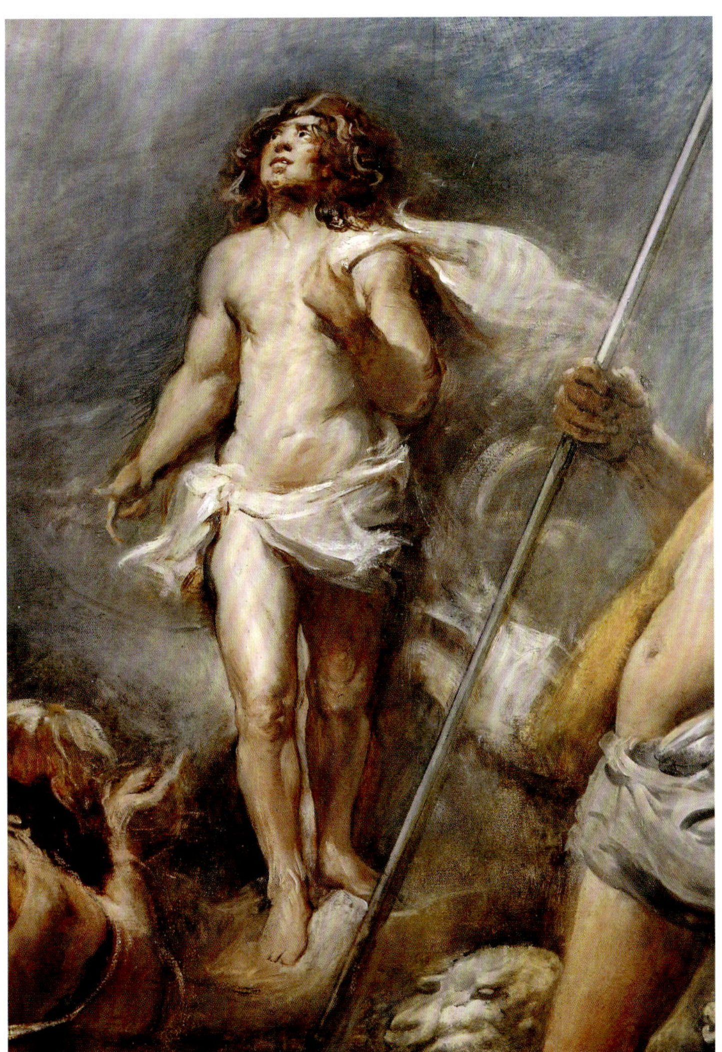

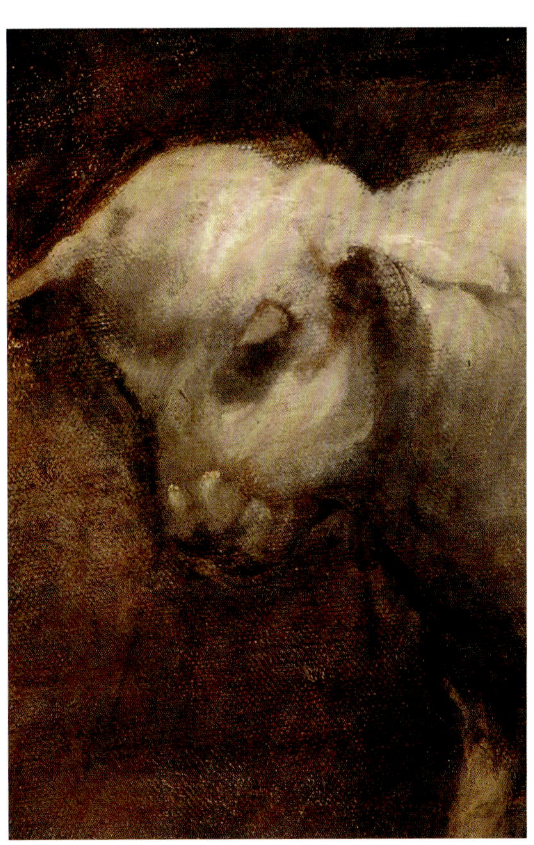

(Details)
Gloria in Excelsis Deo

Angel Heads, 1972
Graphite and pen and brown ink on cream paper, 6 1/4 x 4 3/8 in.

Head of Angel, 1972
Pen and brown ink on cream paper
6 1/4 x 4 3/8 in.

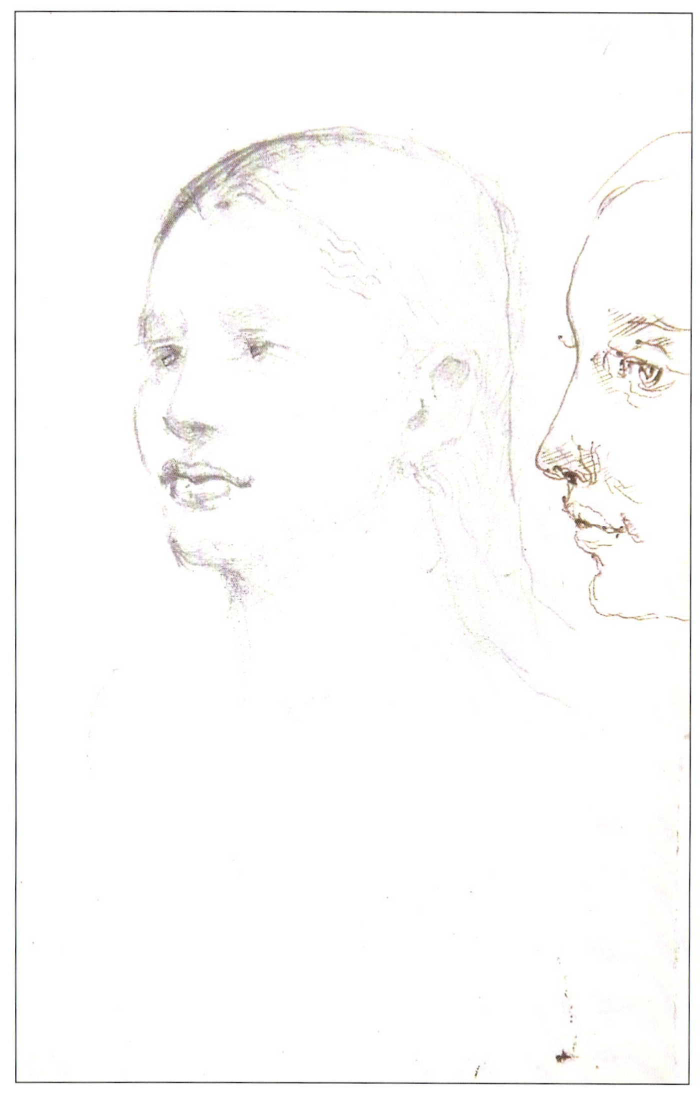

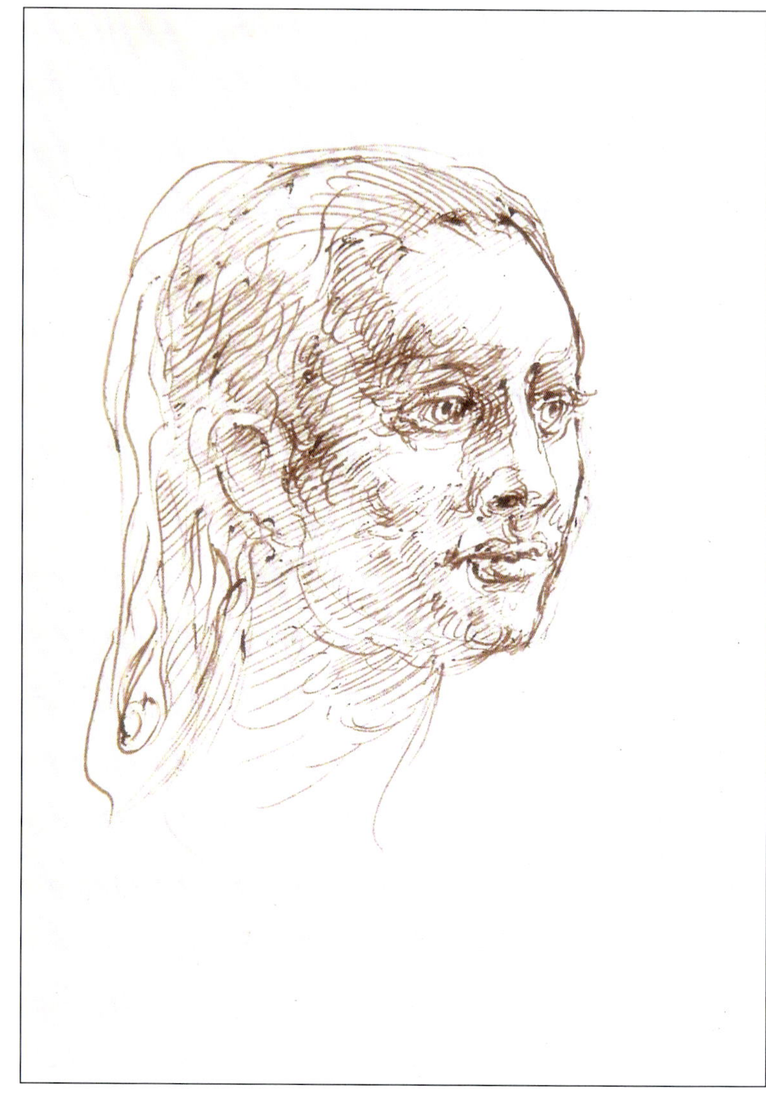

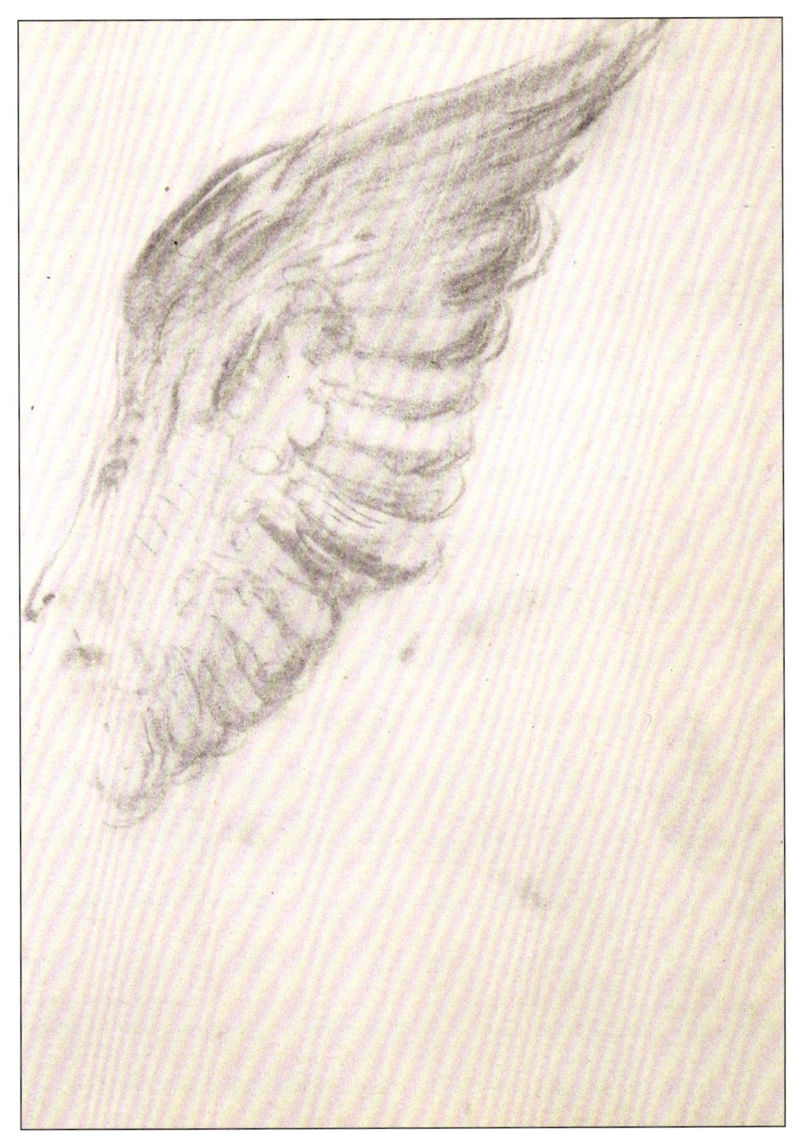

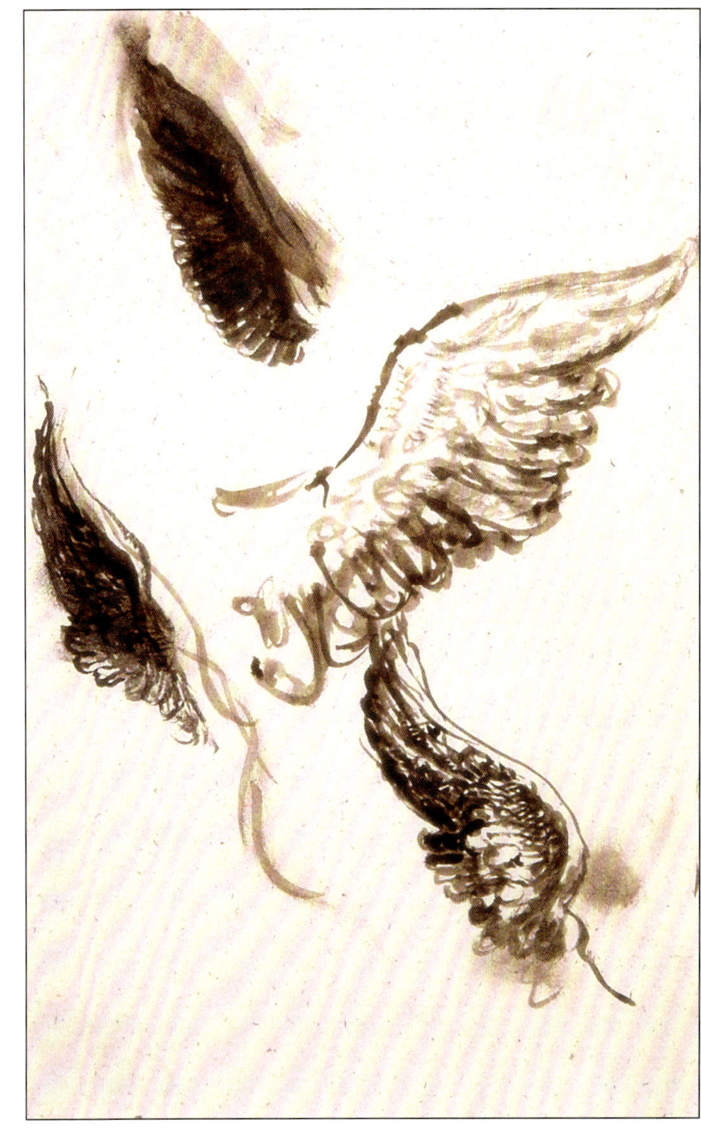

Angel Wing, 1971
Black chalk on cream paper
9 1/4 x 6 3/4 in.

Wings for Angel, 1972
Brown ink wash on buff paper
10 x 6 3/4 in.

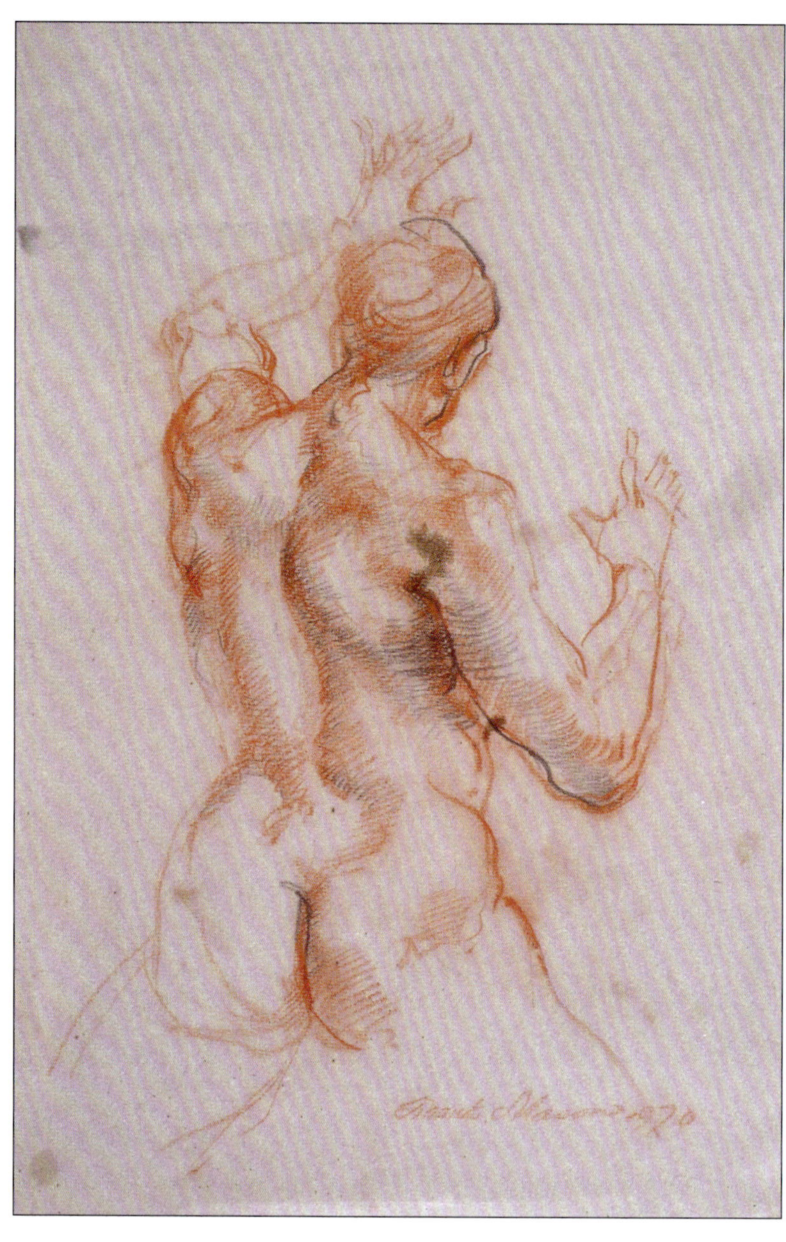

a.

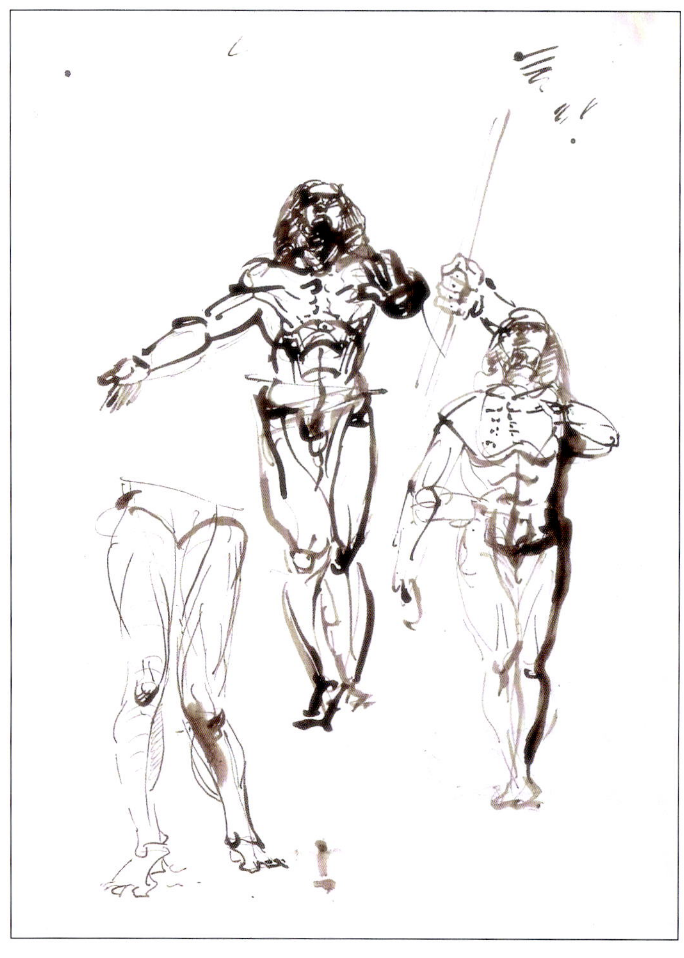

b.

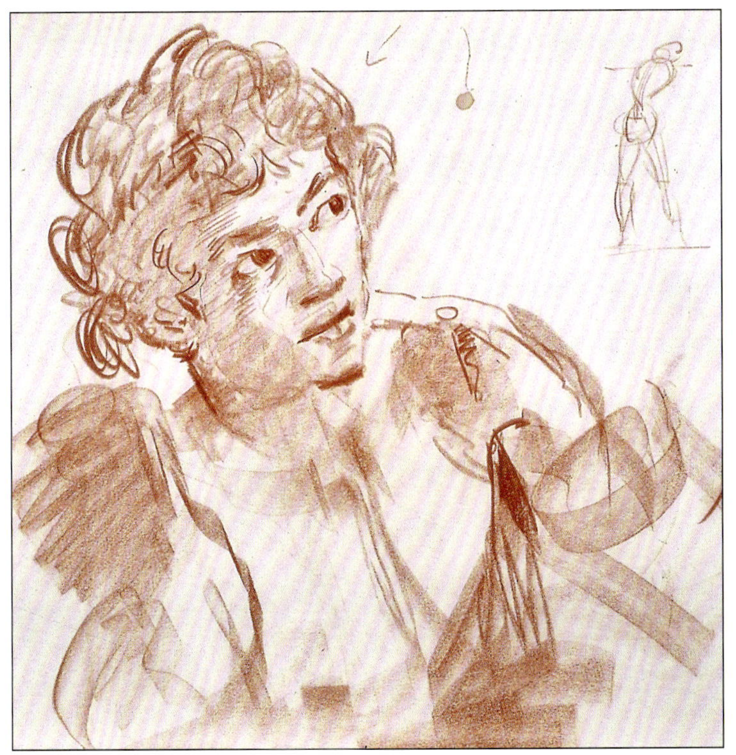

c.

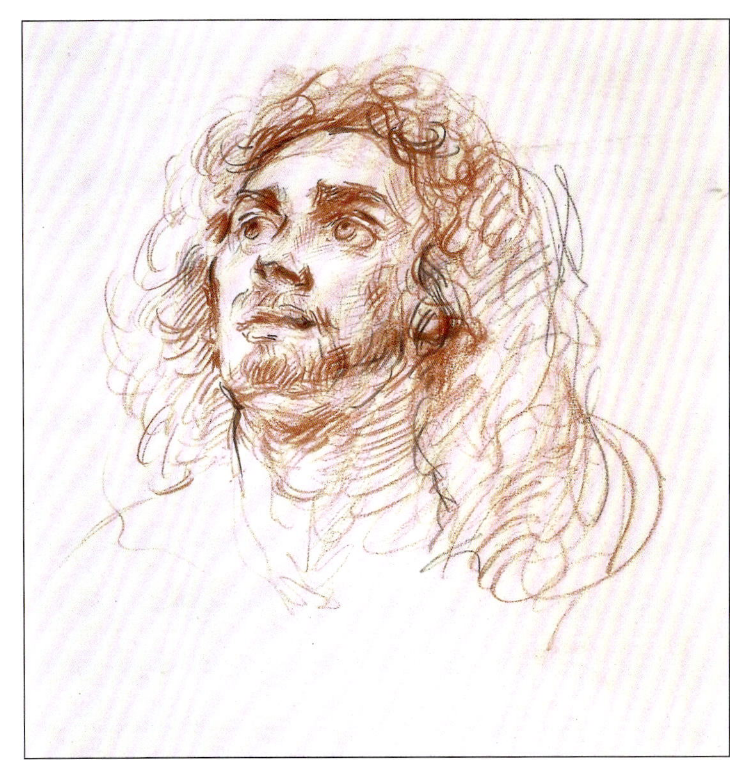

d.

e.

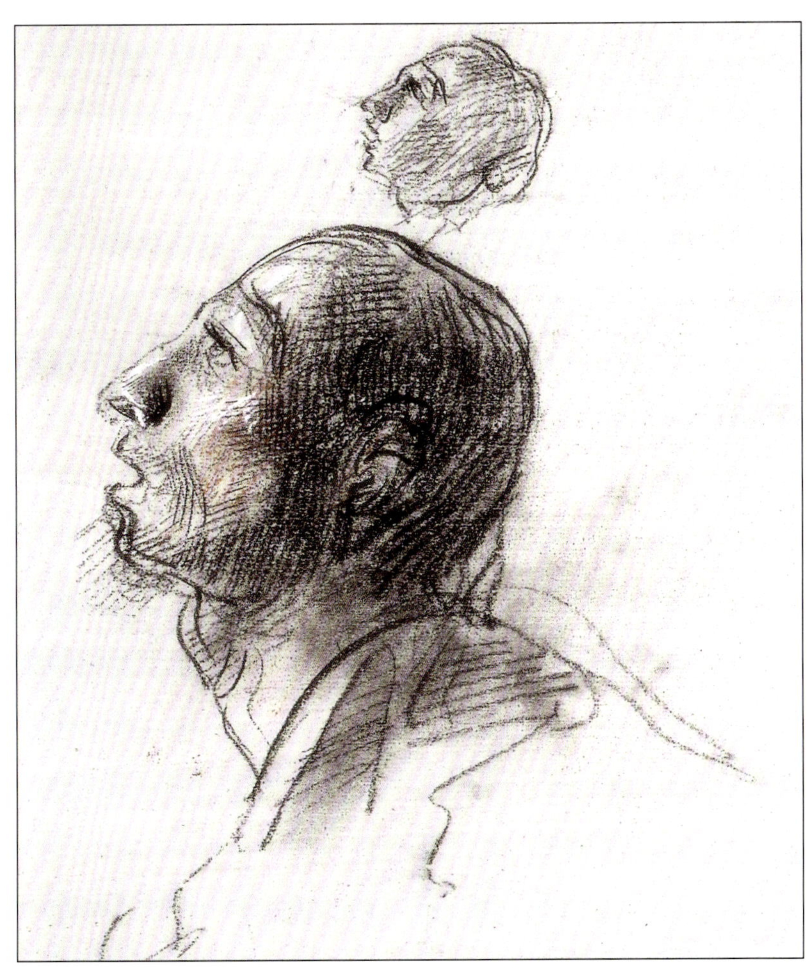

a. *Shepherd, Back View,* 1970
Red and black chalk on gray paper
17 1/4 x 12 in.

b. *Center Shepherd for Gloria,* 1972
Pen and brown ink on white paper
13 1/2 x 10 1/2 in.

c. *Arden Mason as Young Shepherd,* 1972
Red chalk on cream paper
16 x 16 1/2 in.

d. *Head of Shepherd,* 1972
Red and black chalk on cream paper
13 1/2 x 12 1/2 in.

e. *Shepherd in Profile,* 1972
Black, red and white chalk on gray prepared paper
11 x 9 3/4 in.

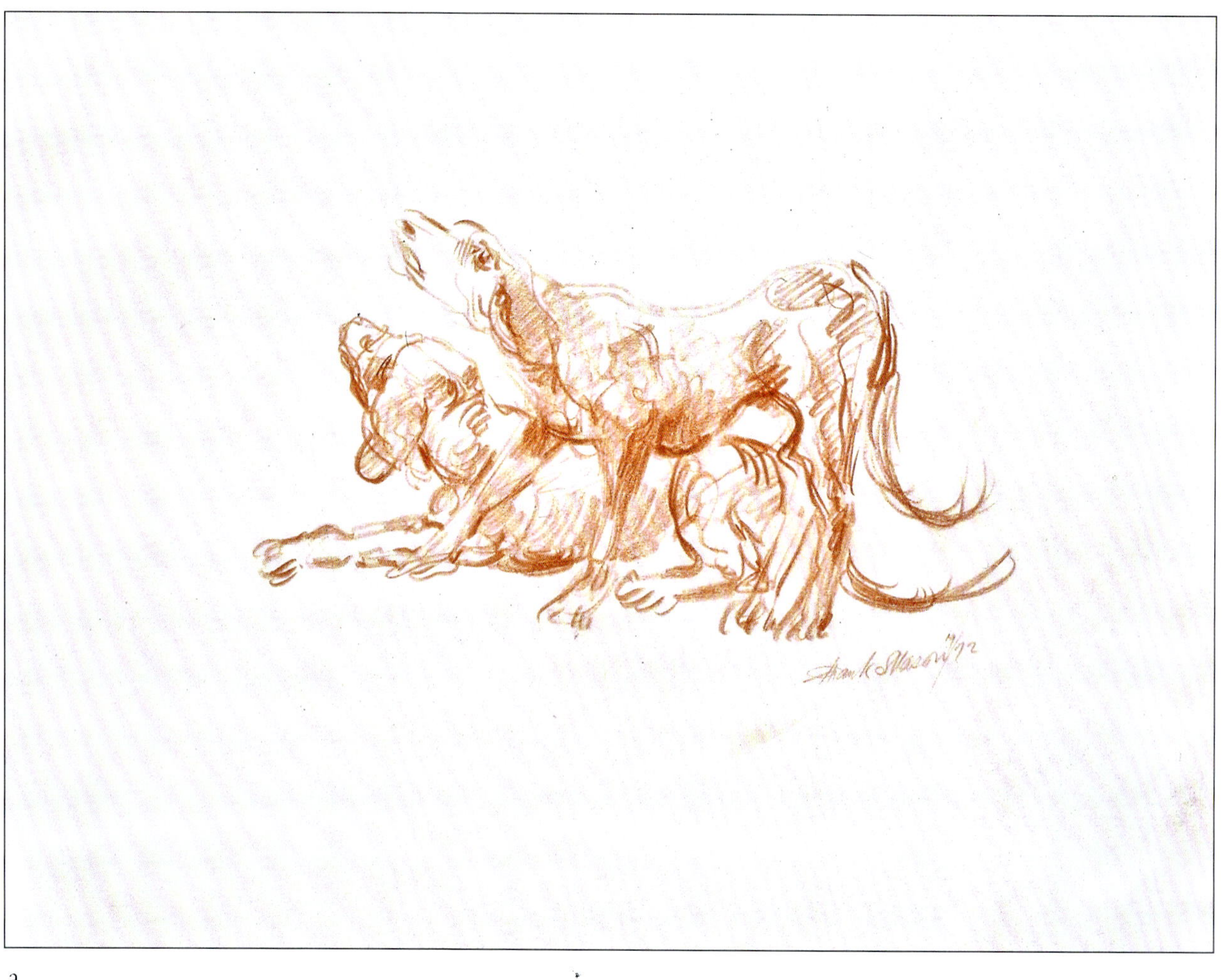

a.

b.

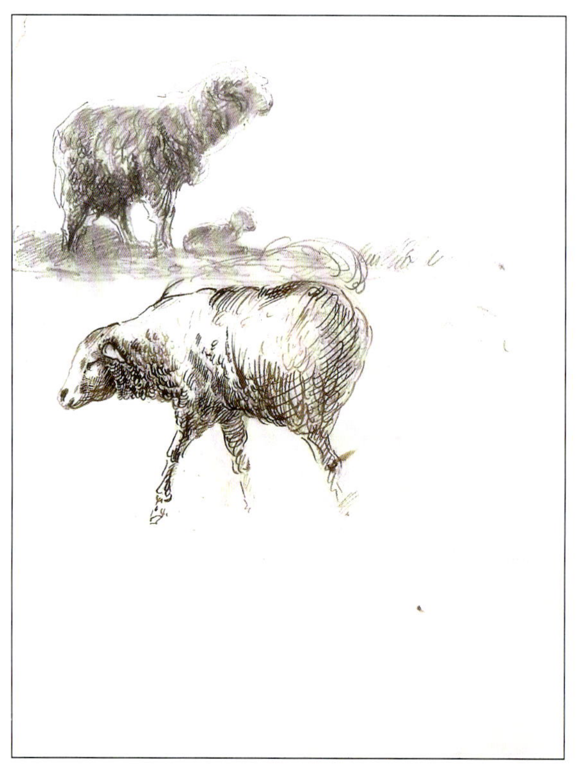

c.

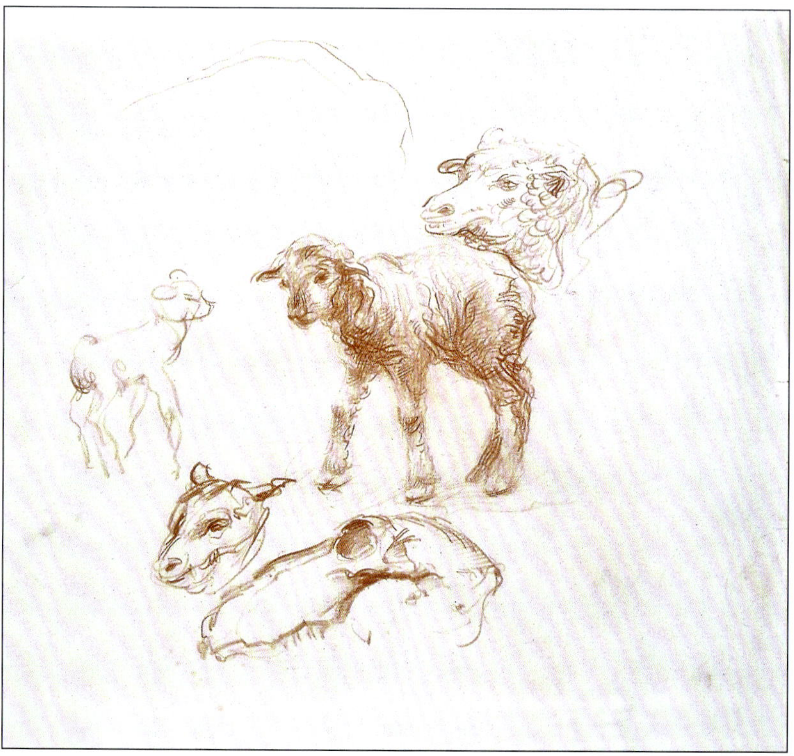

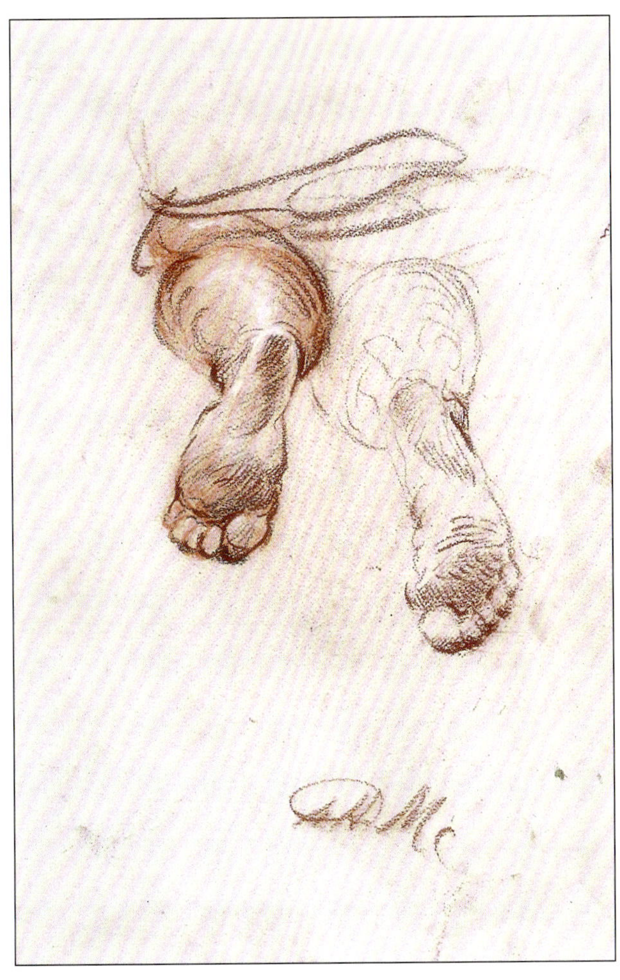

d.

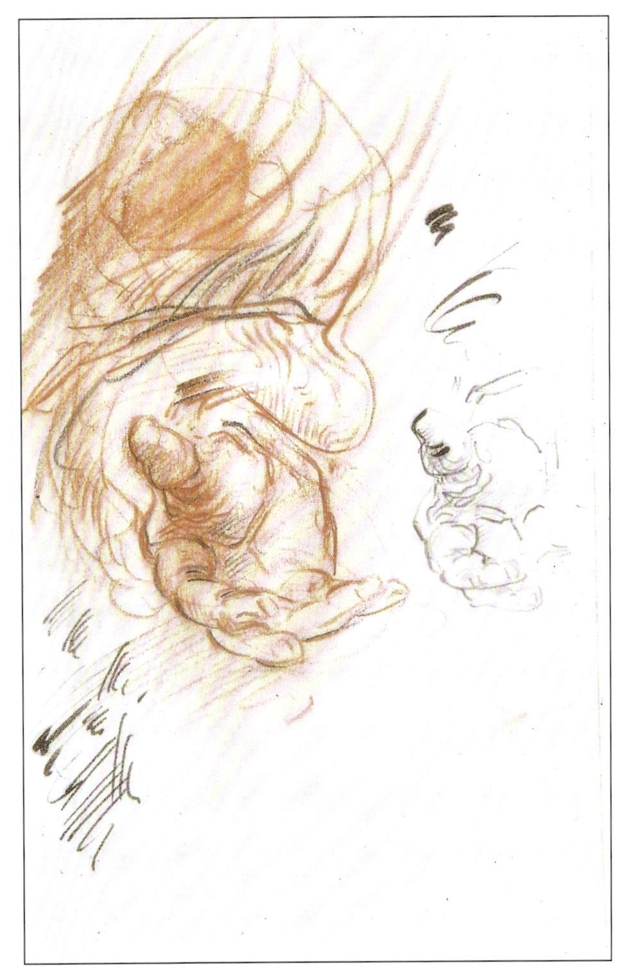

e.

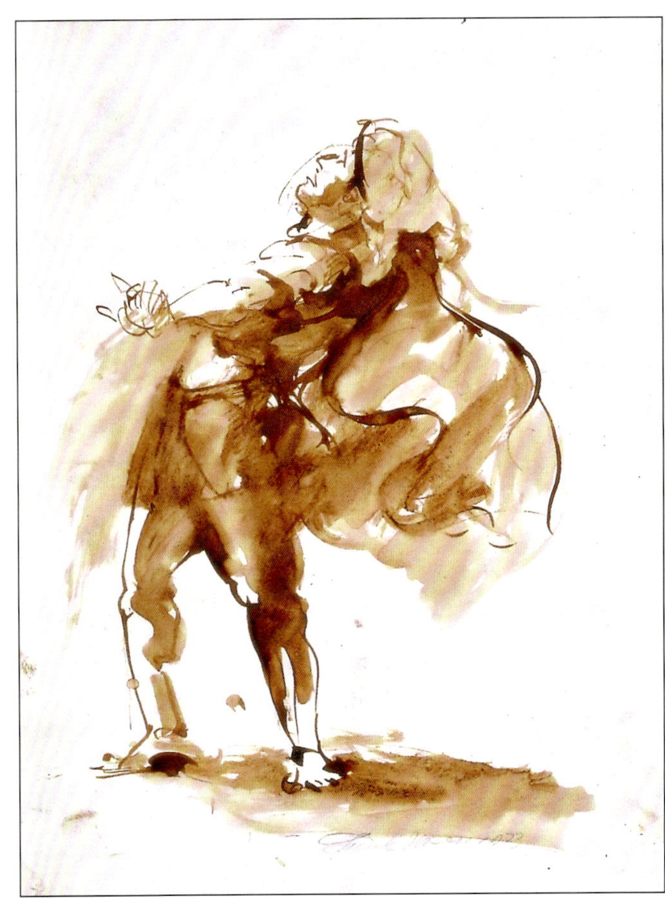

f.

a. *Dog Study,* 1972
Red chalk on cream paper
16 x 16 1/2 in.

b. *Study of Sheep for Gloria in Excelsis Deo,* 1970
Pen and brown ink and graphite on white paper
13 1/2 x 10 1/2 in.

c. *Sheep,* 1972
Red chalk on cream paper
16 x 16 1/2 in.

d. *Feet of Shepherd,* 1972
Red and black chalk on cream paper
15 1/2 x 11 1/2 in.

e. *Hand Study for Gloria in Excelsis Deo,* 1971
Red chalk and graphite on white paper
9 1/2 x 5 in.

f. *Shepherd,* 1973
Pen and brown ink and wash on white paper
10 x 7 in.

Adoration of the Magi

Now when Jesus was born in Bethlehem of Judaea in the days of Herod the king, behold, there came wise men from the east to Jerusalem, Saying, Where is he that is born King of the Jews? for we have seen his star in the east, and are come to worship him. When Herod the king had heard these things, he was troubled. . .And he sent them to Bethlehem, and said, Go and search diligently for the young child; and when ye have found him, bring me word again, that I may come and worship him also. . .And when they were come into the house, they saw the young child with Mary his mother, and fell down, and worshipped him: and when they had opened their treasures, they presented unto him gifts; gold, and frankincense, and myrrh. And being warned of God in a dream that they should not return to Herod, they departed into their own country another way.
—Matthew 2: 1–3, 8, 11, 12

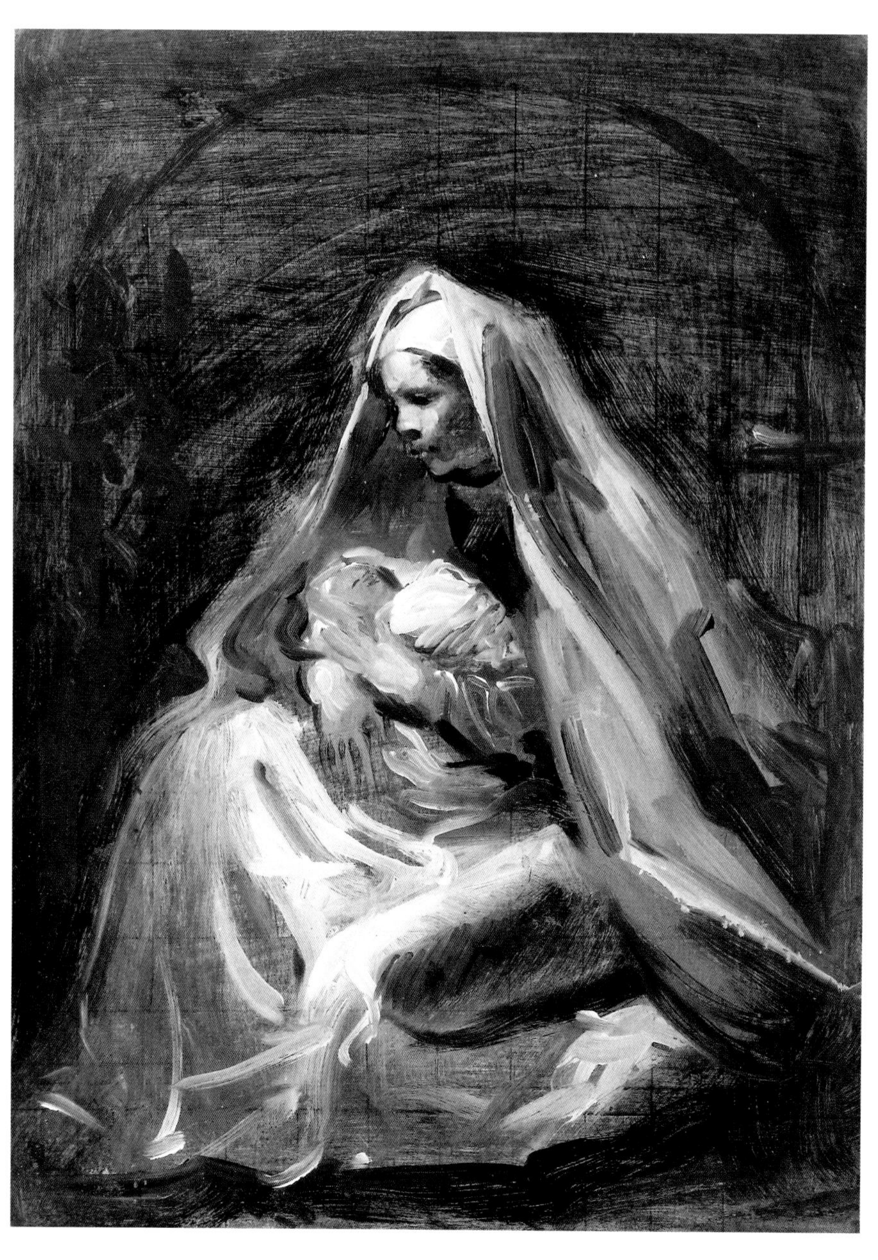

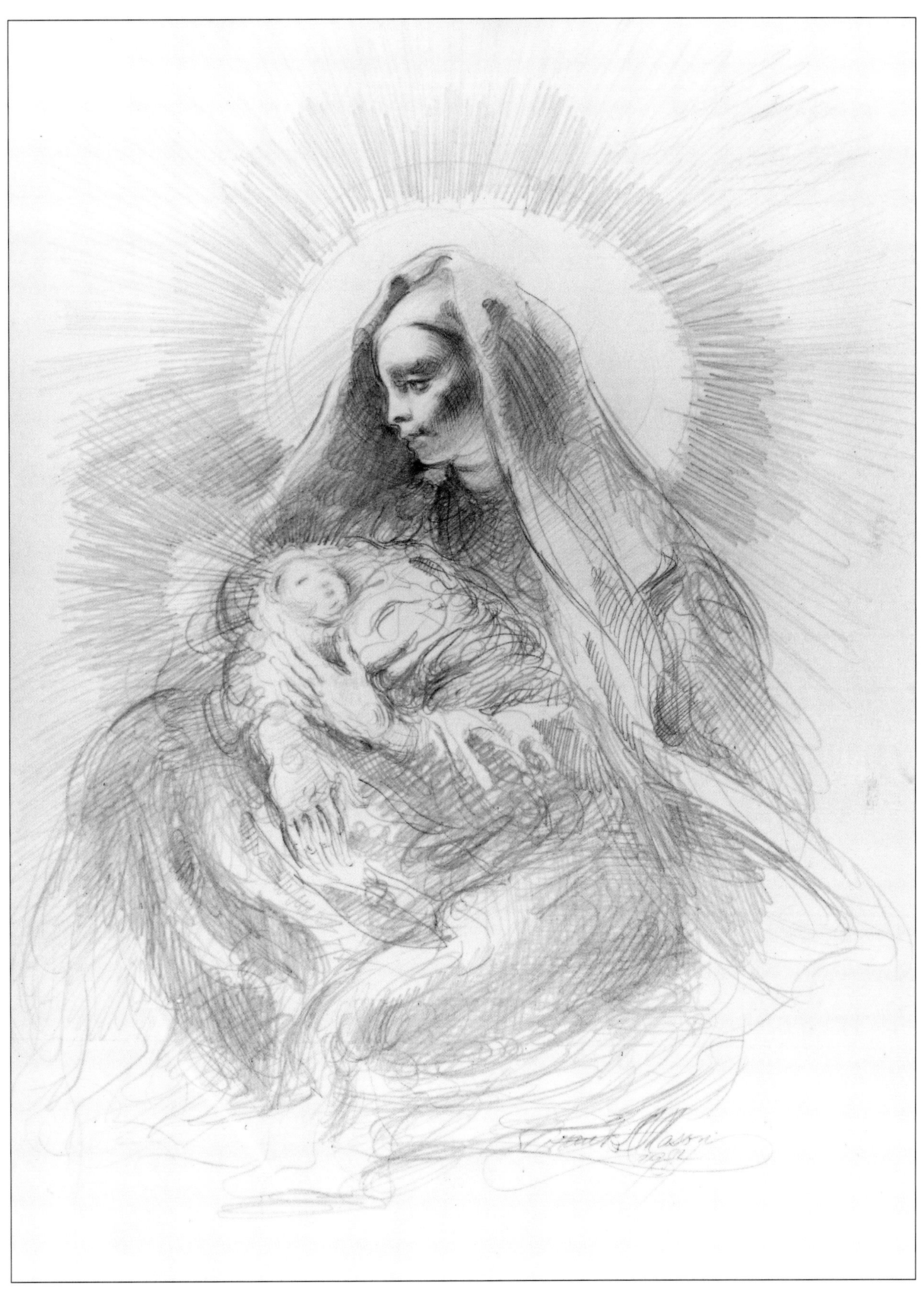

Madonna and Child, 1962
Oil on panel, 12 x 9 in.

Madonna and Child, 1984
Pencil on cream paper, 12 x 9 in.

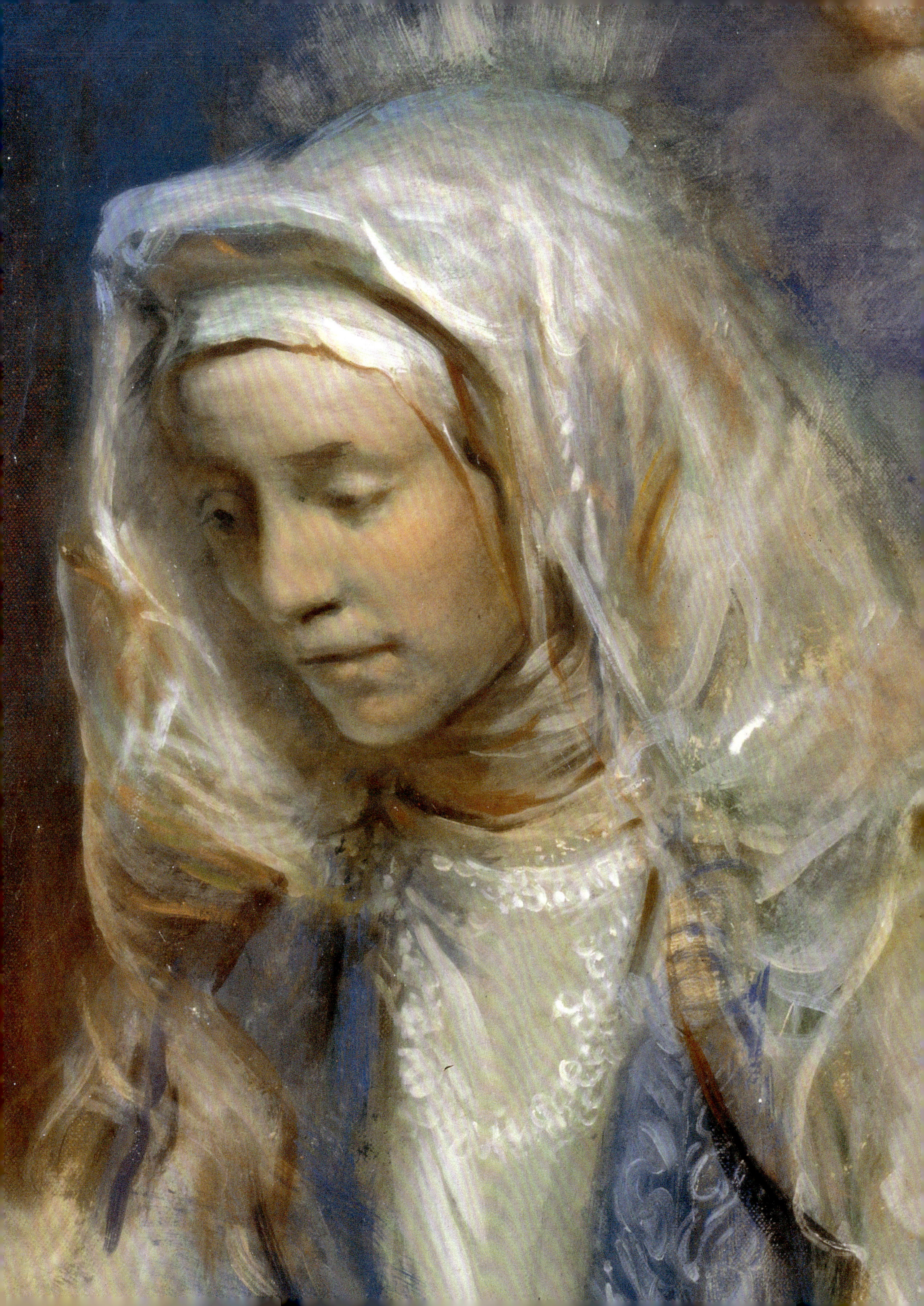

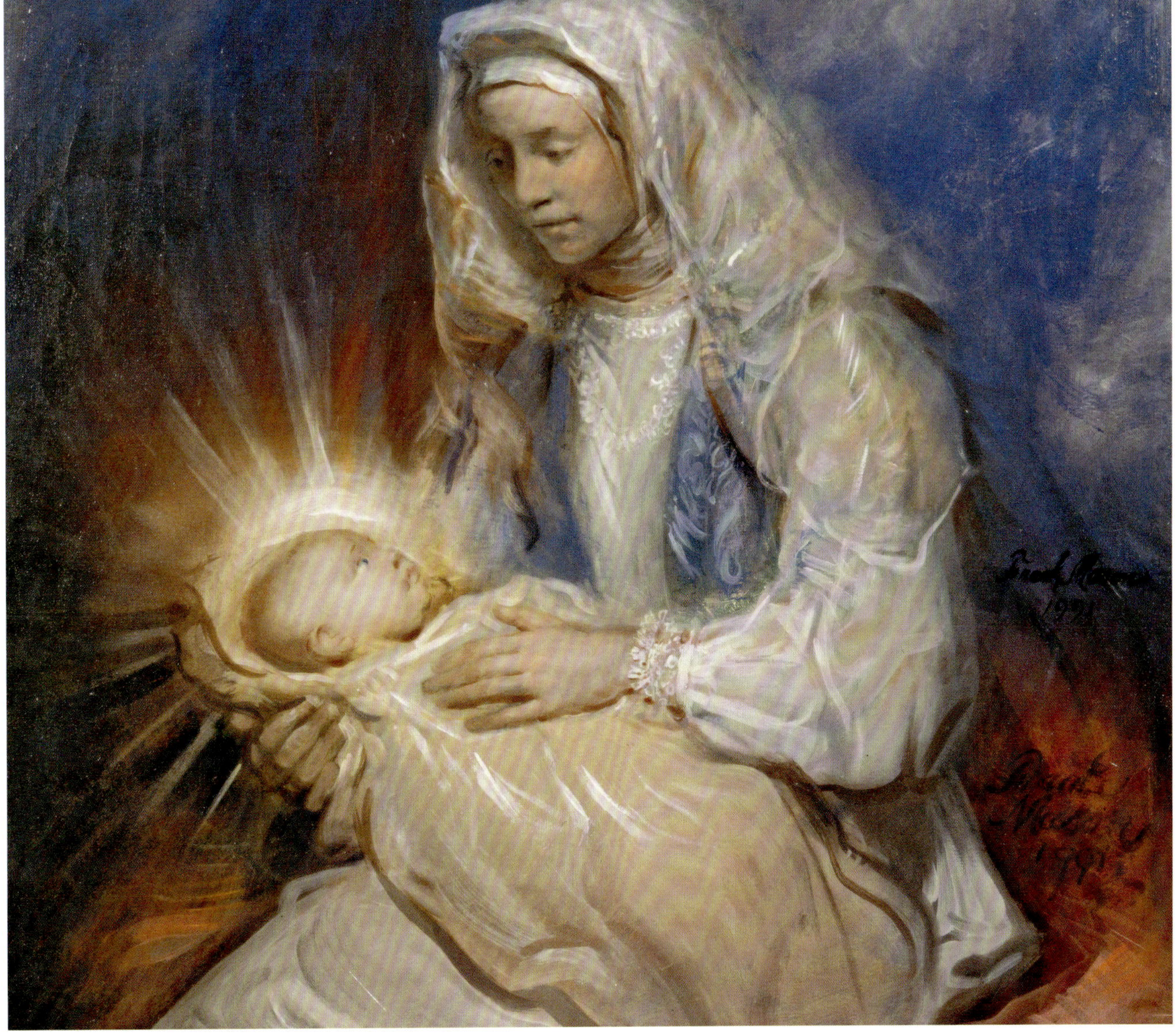

Madonna and Child, 1992
Oil on canvas, 40 x 36 in.

No wonder the Nativity scene has appealed to artists throughout the centuries; it's full of homely little components—the humble stable, the Babe in His lowly cradle, the shepherds and a sheep or two. Here, too, we find the Wise Men with their costly gifts, and the young mother taking the adulation of all these people for her Child quite for granted, as merely His due. But to me it is much more than that. Here we have the three kings, powerful men, coming from afar to find the

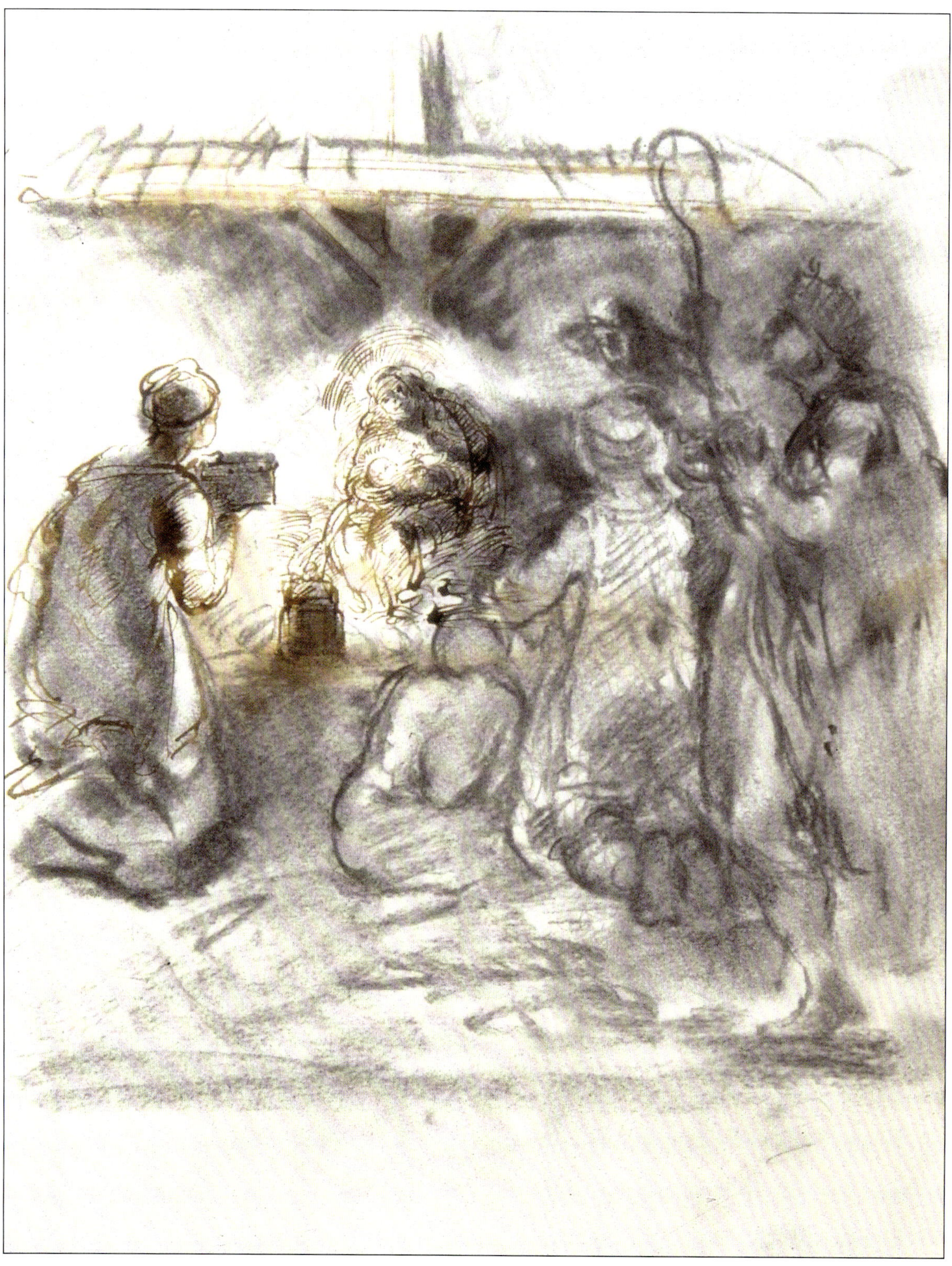

Adoration of the Magi, 1997
Pen and brown ink and charcoal and graphite on cream paper, 13 3/4 x 10 3/4 in.

Nativity, 1957
Pen and black ink on beige paper
17 1/2 x 14 in.

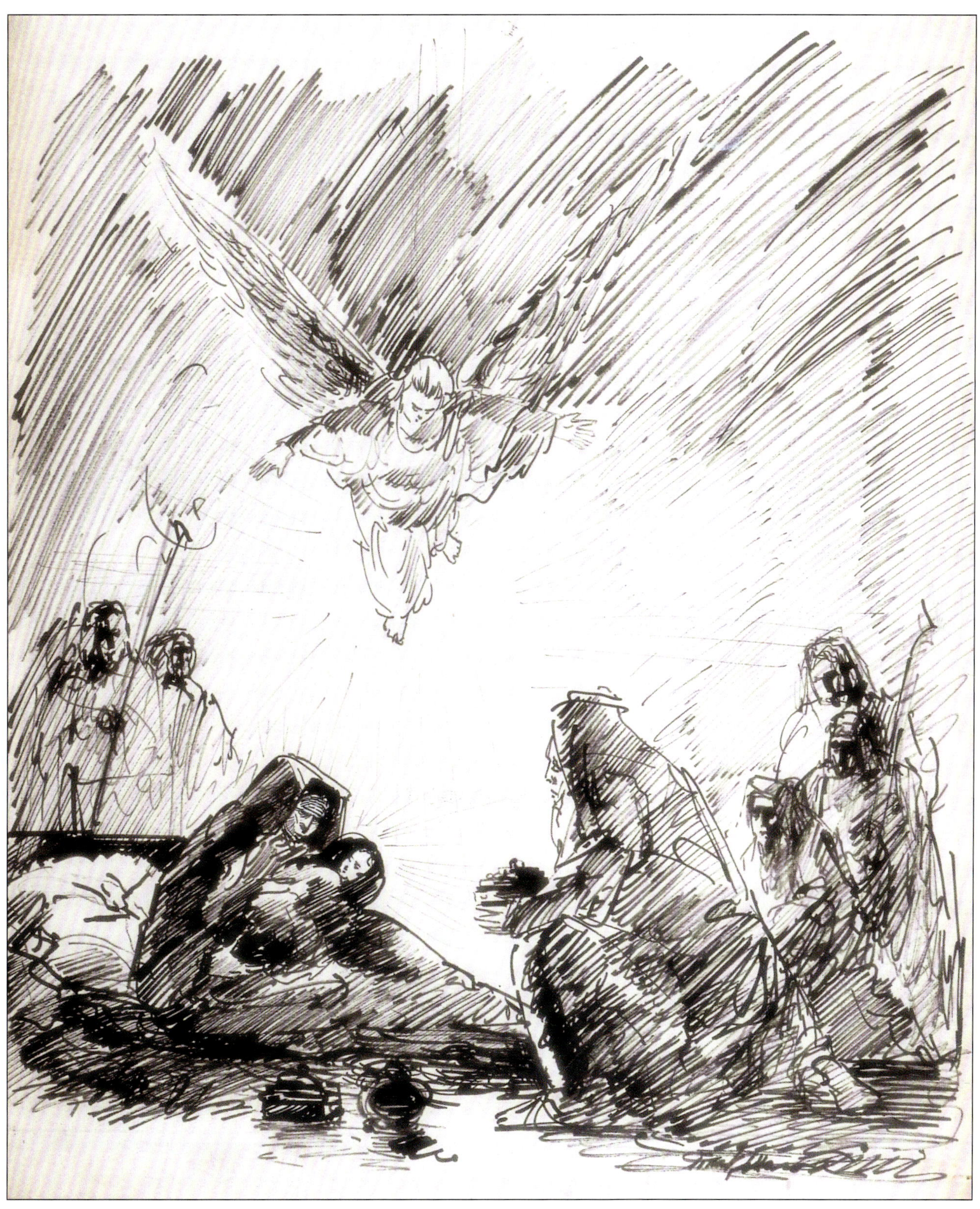

Christ child. How did they know about Him? What impelled them to follow the star? They came from all corners of the known world to worship Him, to celebrate the miracle of His birth. As they pass through the Holy Land, they stop to see King Herod—to present their diplomatic credentials, as it were —and ask for directions. Their inquiry terrifies Herod and "all Jerusalem with him." From here on, the story is fraught with portent. We know Herod is up to no good, and the Wise Men catch on to this, too. I read somewhere that traditionally in every painting of the Nativity there is somewhere the shadow of the cross. I included it quite unwittingly in the stable rafters of this drawing and the painting of the Adoration of the Magi.

Head of Mary, 1999
Oil on wood panel
12 x 9 in.

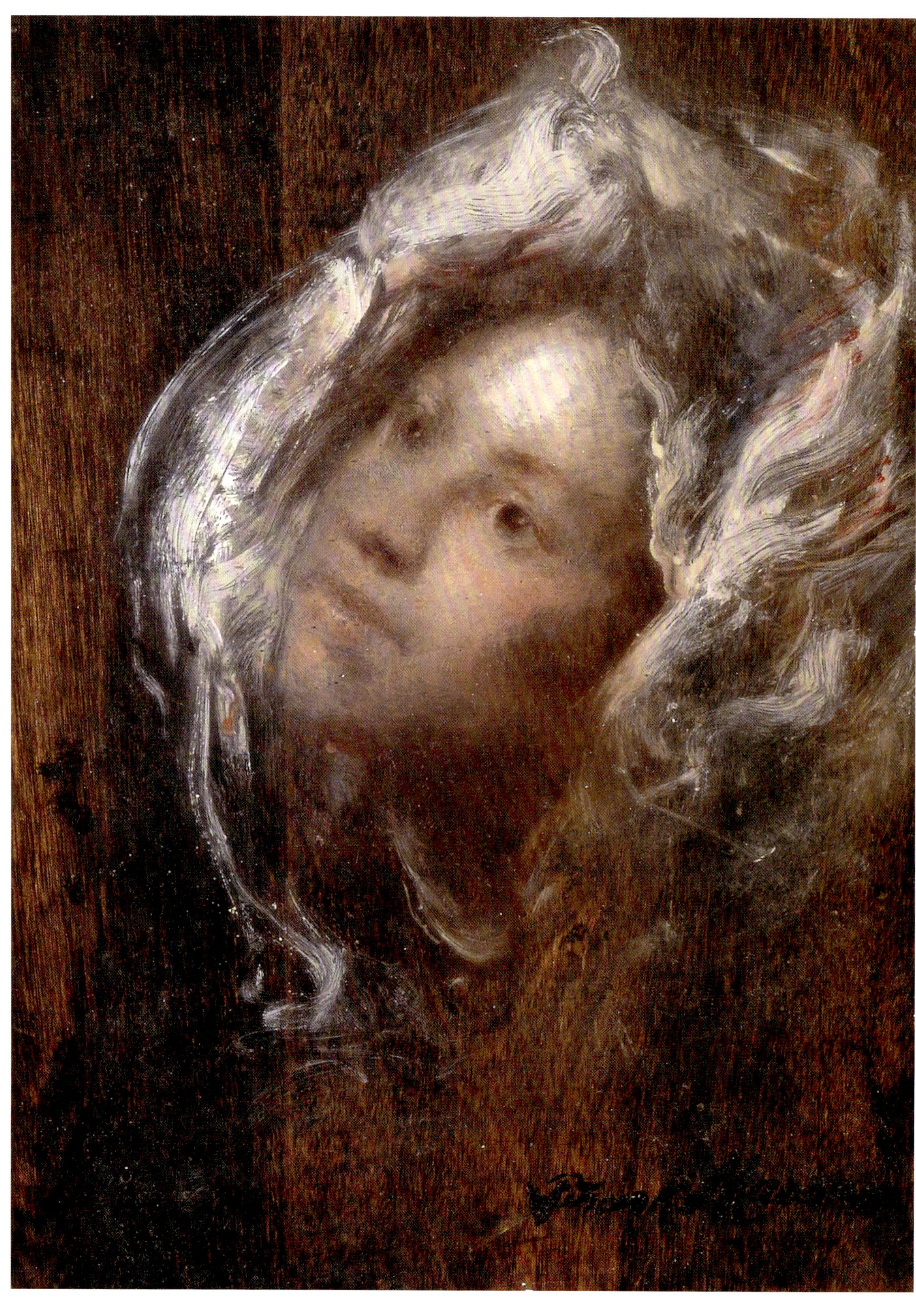

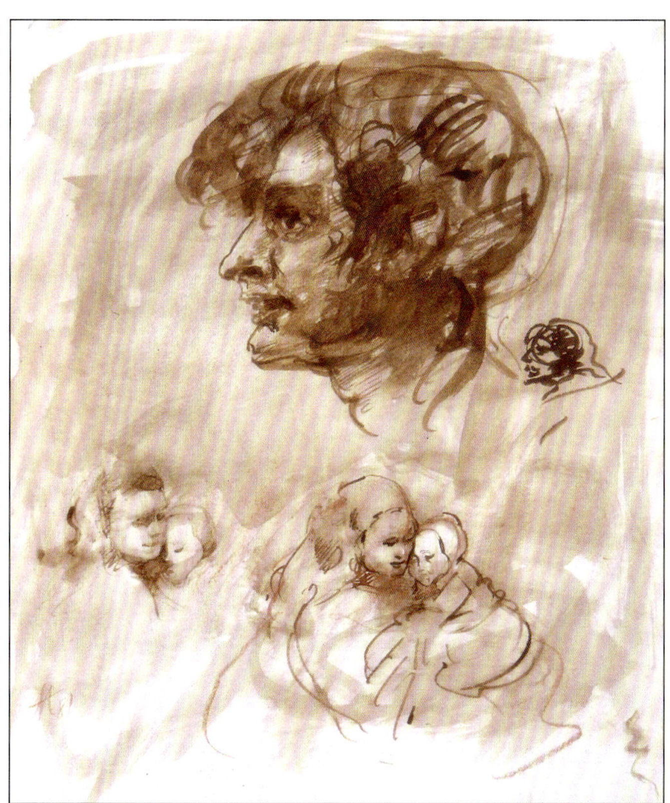

Joseph, Mother and Child, 1981
Pen and brown ink and wash and red chalk on cream paper, 14 3/4 x 12 1/2 in.

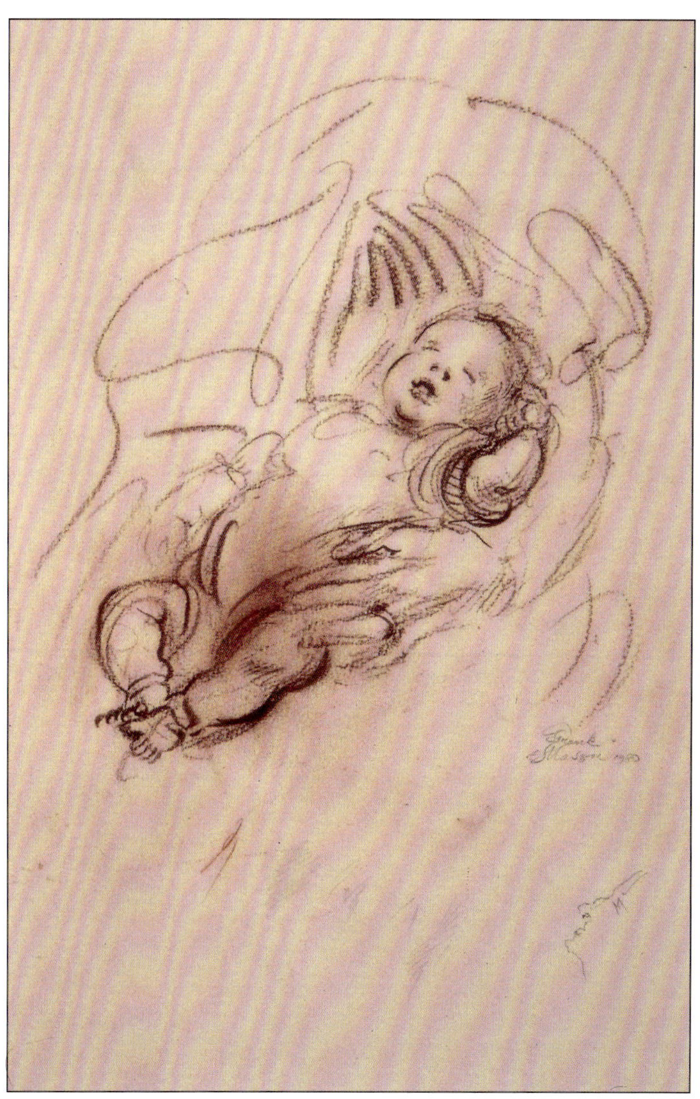

Infant Jesus, 1980
Red chalk on beige paper
14 7/8 x 10 5/8 in.

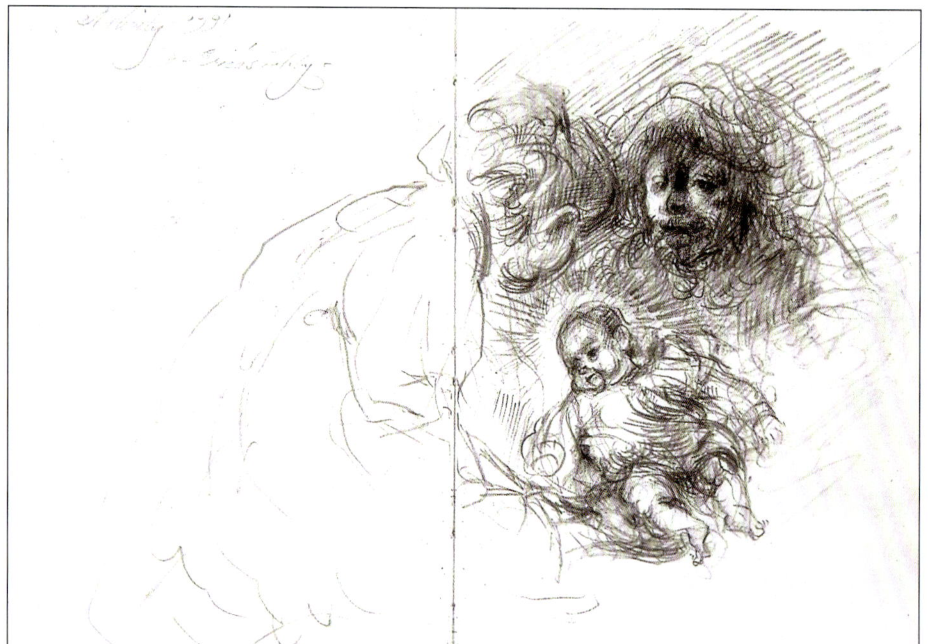

a.

b.

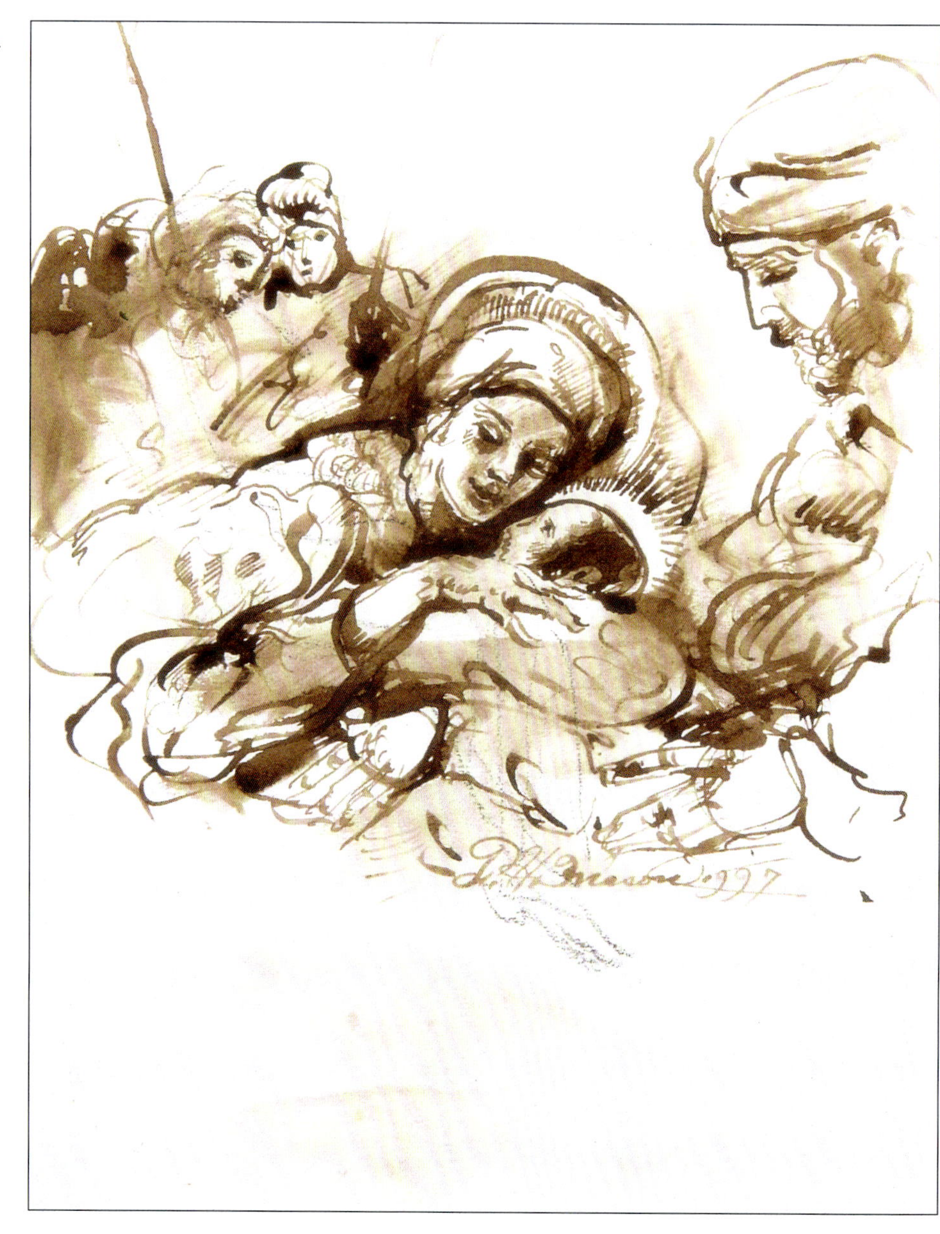

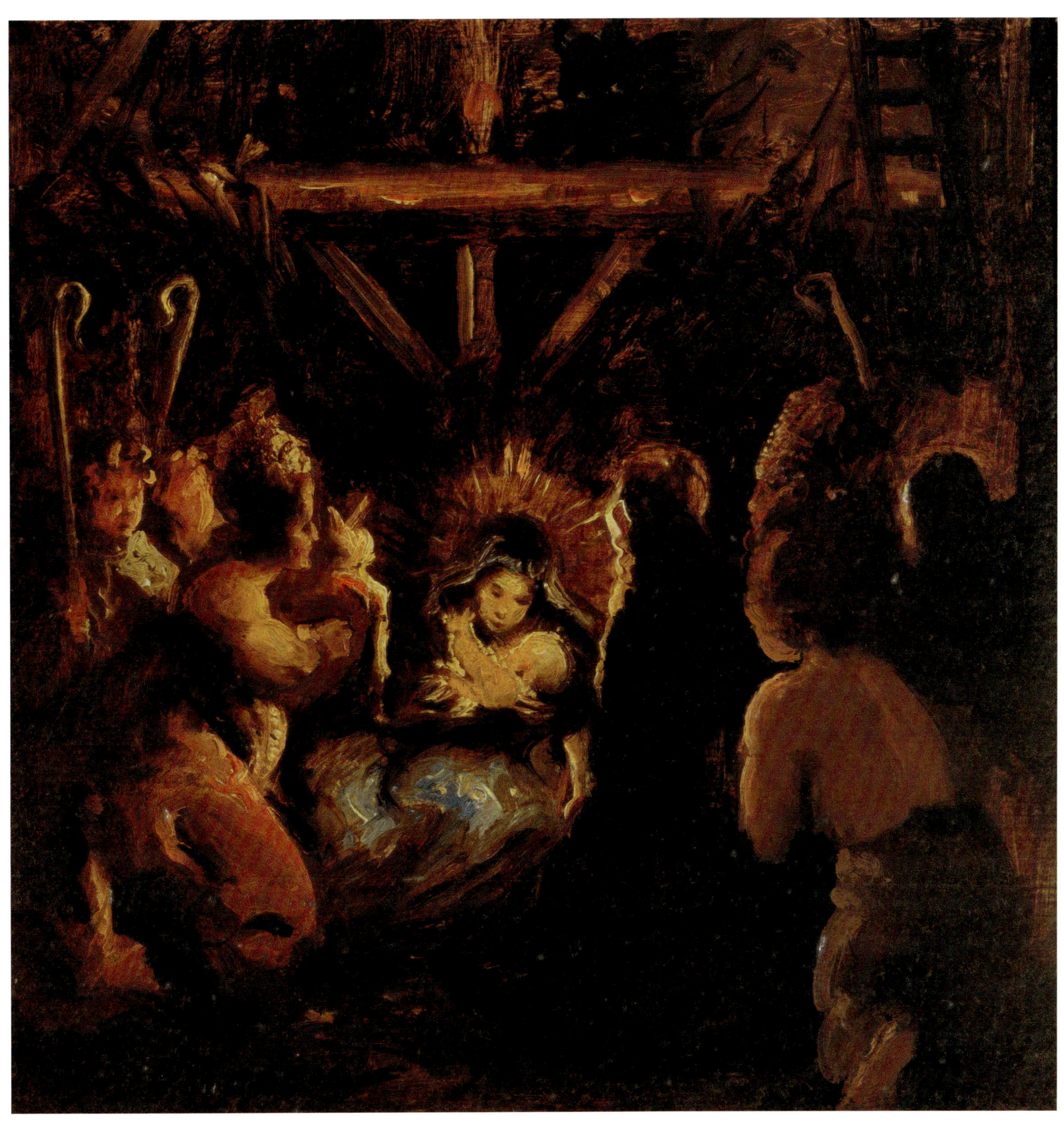

c.

a. *Jesus, Mary and Joseph,* 1991
Black chalk on white paper, 7 1/2 x 10 in.

b. *Jesus, Mary, Joseph and Shepherds,* 1997
Brown ink wash on cream paper, 12 x 9 in.

c. *Adoration of the Magi,* 1959
Oil on panel, 10 1/2 x 11 in.

THE FLIGHT INTO EGYPT

AND WHEN THEY WERE DEPARTED, BEHOLD, THE ANGEL OF THE LORD APPEARETH TO JOSEPH IN A DREAM, SAYING, ARISE, AND TAKE THE YOUNG CHILD AND HIS MOTHER, AND FLEE INTO EGYPT, AND BE THOU THERE UNTIL I BRING THEE WORD: FOR HEROD WILL SEEK THE YOUNG CHILD TO DESTROY HIM. WHEN HE AROSE, HE TOOK THE YOUNG CHILD AND HIS MOTHER BY NIGHT, AND DEPARTED INTO EGYPT: AND WAS THERE UNTIL THE DEATH OF HEROD: THAT IT MIGHT BE FULFILLED WHICH WAS SPOKEN OF THE LORD BY THE PROPHET, SAYING, OUT OF EGYPT HAVE I CALLED MY SON. —MATTHEW 2: 13–15

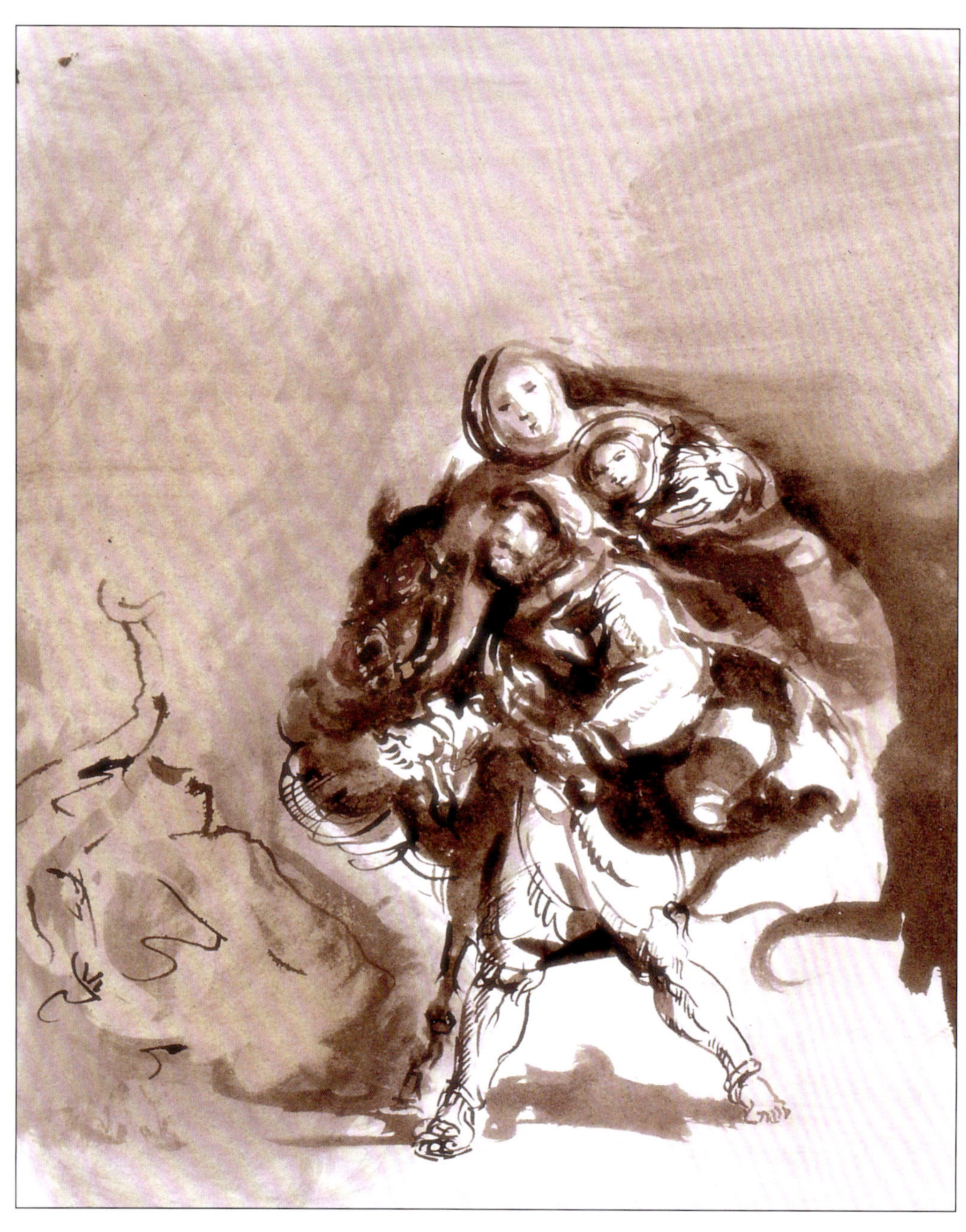

Study for The Flight into Egypt, 1995
Pen and brown ink and wash
on white paper, 13 5/8 x 12 1/2 in.

The Flight into Egypt, 1995
Oil on canvas, 35 x 24 in.

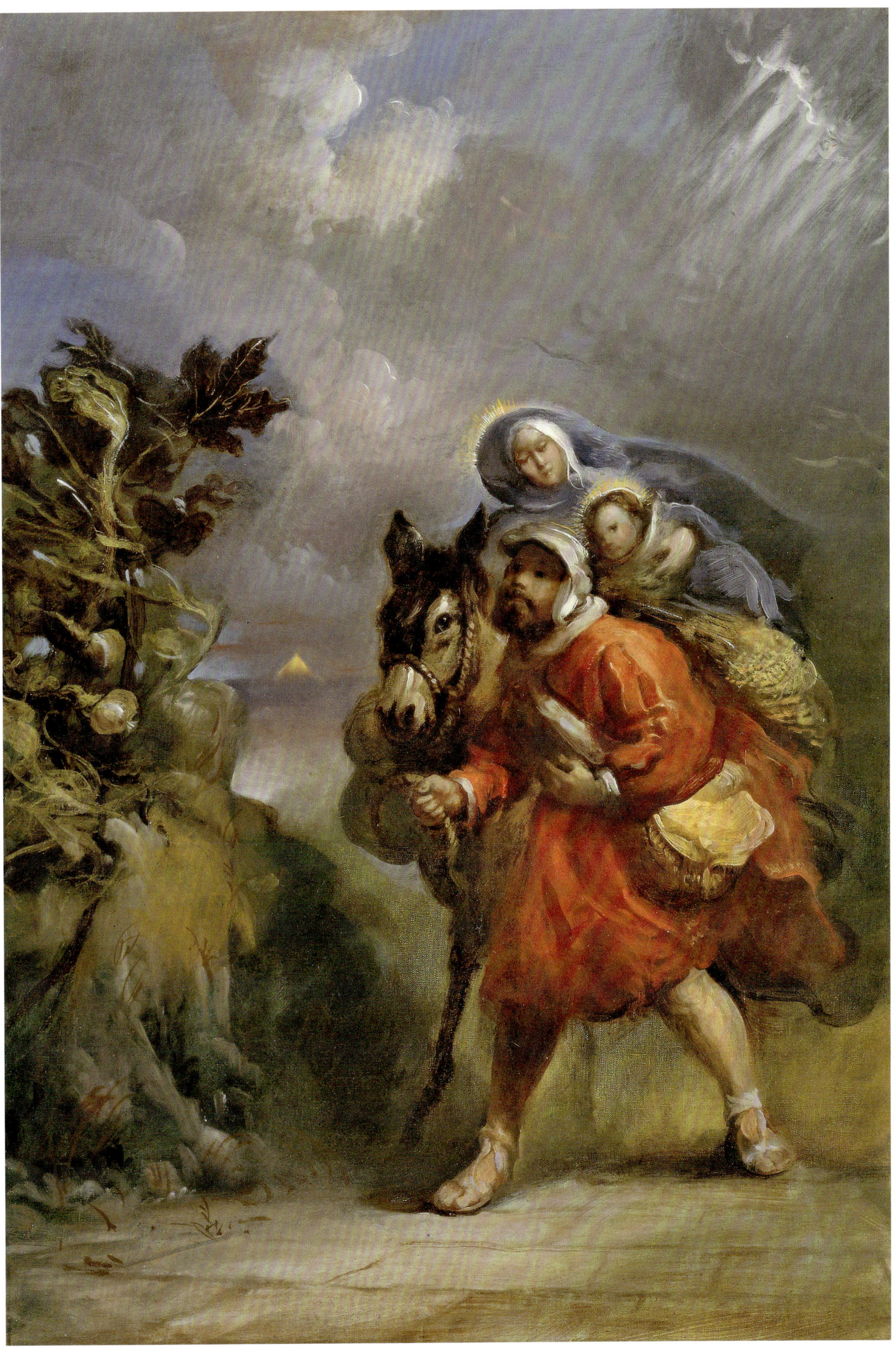

After the visit of the three kings, Herod is desperately afraid of losing his kingdom to the child who is prophesied to become "king of the Jews." He knows the child must be destroyed, and he asks the kings to let him know where to find him. The three kings disobey Herod and do not return but go home by another way. Realizing this, Herod throws a kingly tantrum and issues a terrible decree: all male children two years and under shall be slain. Matthew tells this story very tersely, making no mention of which minions of the king would carry out this grim task or how they might feel about it. But all is well with the Christ child. Joseph is warned in a dream to take the child and His mother and flee into Egypt. He obeys at once, rousing Mary and the Child in the middle of the night. Here we see them in the just-before-dawn darkness on the Roman road to Egypt, a route frequently traveled in those days and a safe, if arduous, journey. You can imagine their apprehension and anxiety; and you can feel Joseph's determination to move quickly and to put as much distance as he can between his family and Herod. They are probably headed for the Hebrew community in Cairo, where they will stay for several years until they hear of the death of Herod and decide that it is safe to return to Israel. Incidentally, I painted the donkey from a sketch I made in Aticoli Corrado, Italy, several years ago of a very amiable colt. He brayed loudly every time I walked past the stable and ignored all other passers-by. We had a special rapport, and I was glad to have an opportunity to give him a role in *The Flight into Egypt.*

Study for The Flight into Egypt, 1995
Pen and brown ink and wash on panel, 14 x 10 in.

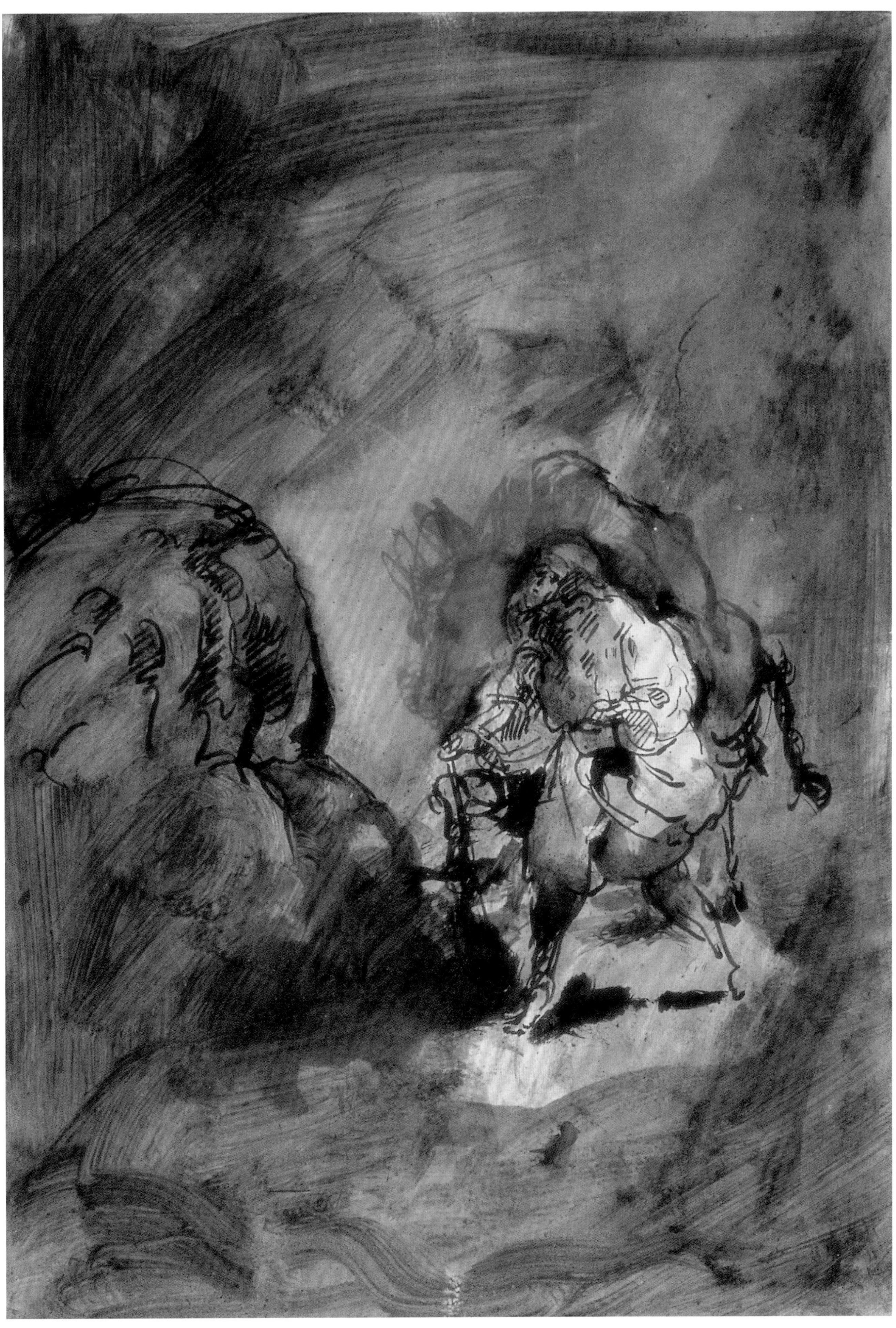

Studies for The Flight into Egypt, 1967
Graphite and red chalk on cream paper
13 1/4 x 17 1/2 in.

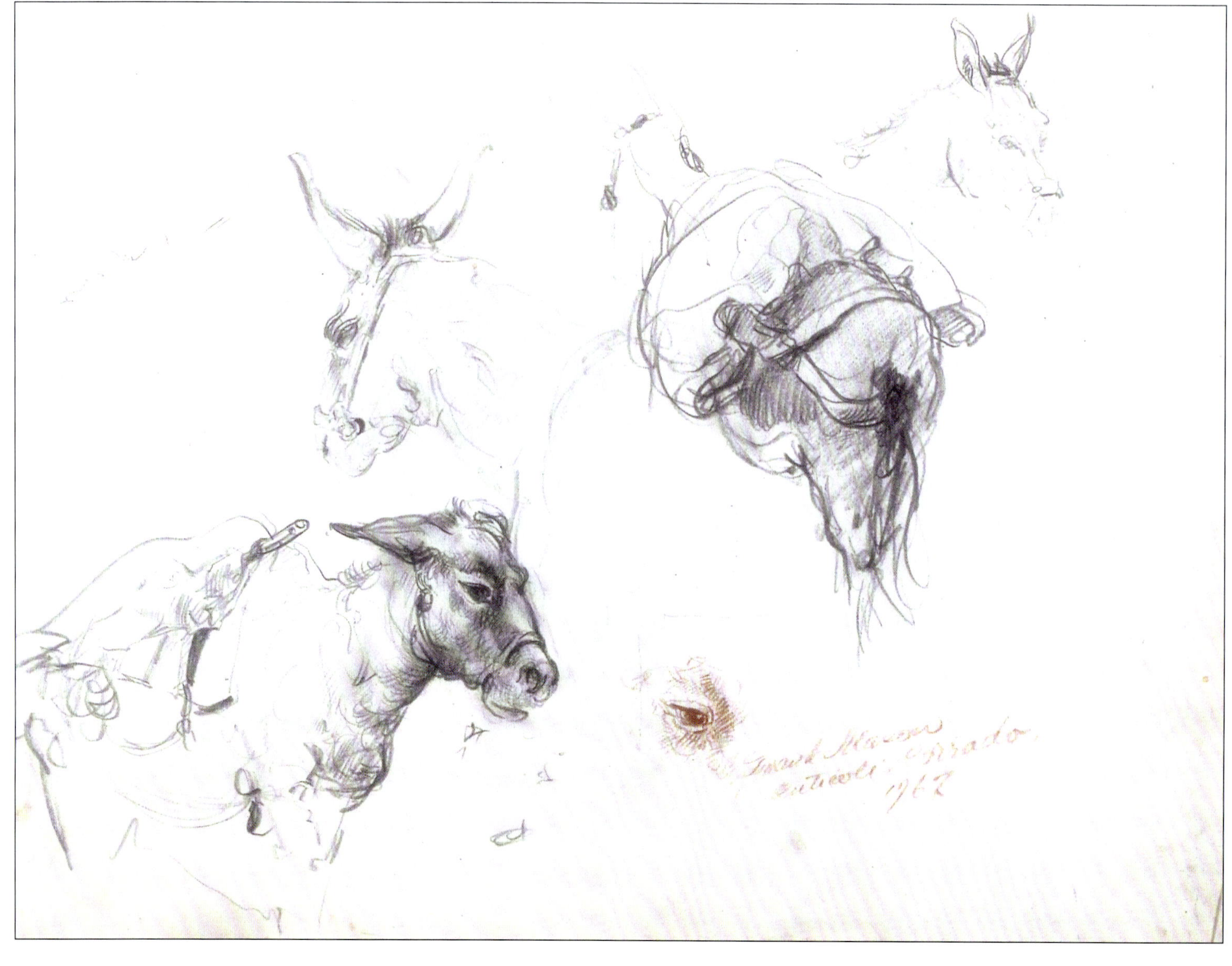

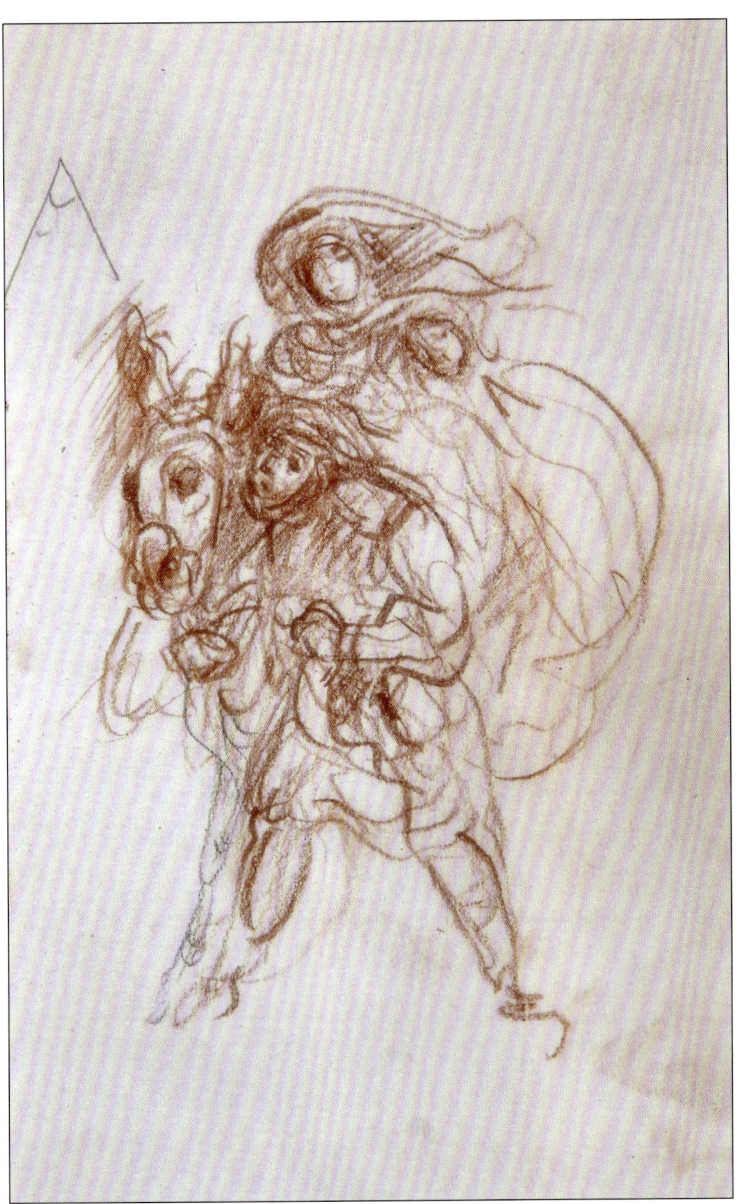

Study for The Flight into Egypt, 1995
Red chalk on white paper, 7 1/2 x 5 in.

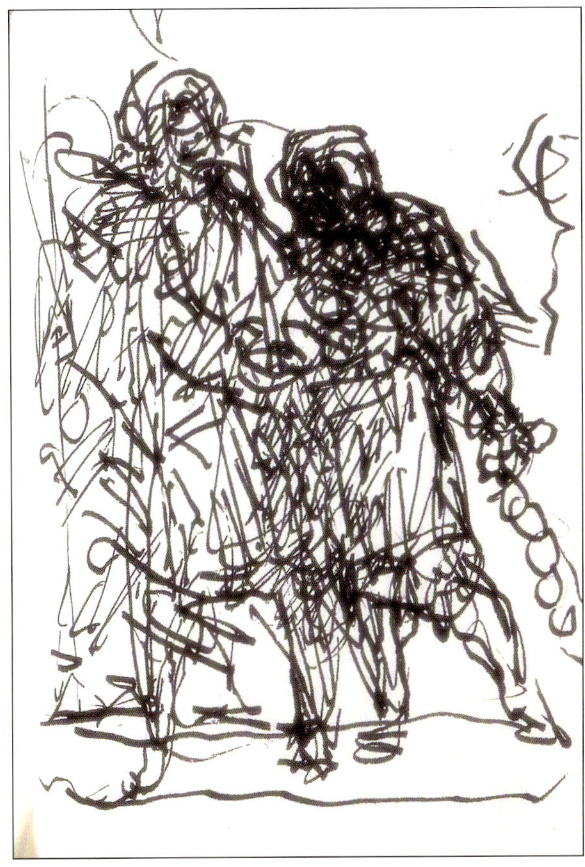

Study for The Flight into Egypt, 1995
Pen and black ink on white paper, 3 1/2 x 5 in.

Jesus Confounding the Elders

NOW HIS PARENTS WENT TO JERUSALEM EVERY YEAR AT THE FEAST OF THE PASSOVER. AND WHEN HE WAS TWELVE YEARS OLD, THEY WENT UP TO JERUSALEM AFTER THE CUSTOM OF THE FEAST. AND WHEN THEY HAD FULFILLED THE DAYS, AS THEY RETURNED, THE CHILD JESUS TARRIED BEHIND IN JERUSALEM; AND JOSEPH AND HIS MOTHER KNEW NOT OF IT. . . .AND IT CAME TO PASS, THAT AFTER THREE DAYS THEY FOUND HIM IN THE TEMPLE, SITTING IN THE MIDST OF THE DOCTORS, BOTH HEARING THEM, AND ASKING THEM QUESTIONS. AND ALL THAT HEARD HIM WERE ASTONISHED AT HIS UNDERSTANDING AND ANSWERS. AND WHEN THEY SAW HIM, THEY WERE AMAZED: AND HIS MOTHER SAID UNTO HIM, SON, WHY HAST THOU THUS DEALT WITH US? BEHOLD, THY FATHER AND I HAVE SOUGHT THEE SORROWING. AND HE SAID UNTO THEM, HOW IS IT THAT YE SOUGHT ME? WIST YE NOT THAT I MUST BE ABOUT MY FATHER'S BUSINESS? –LUKE 2: 41–43, 46–49

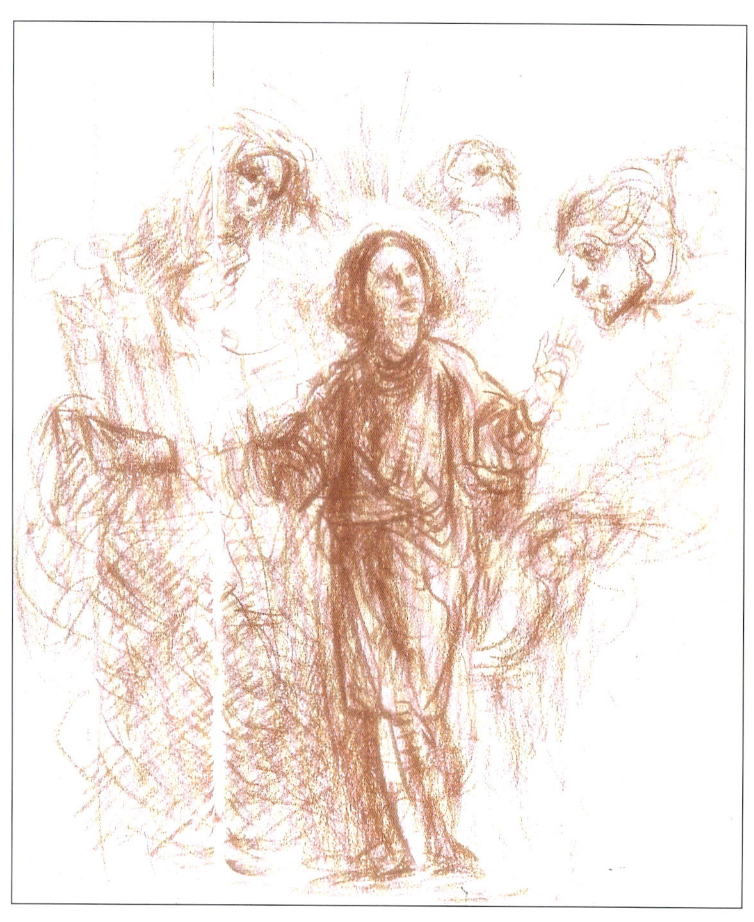

Jesus and Elders in the Temple, 1996
Red chalk on white paper
7 1/2 x 6 3/4 in.

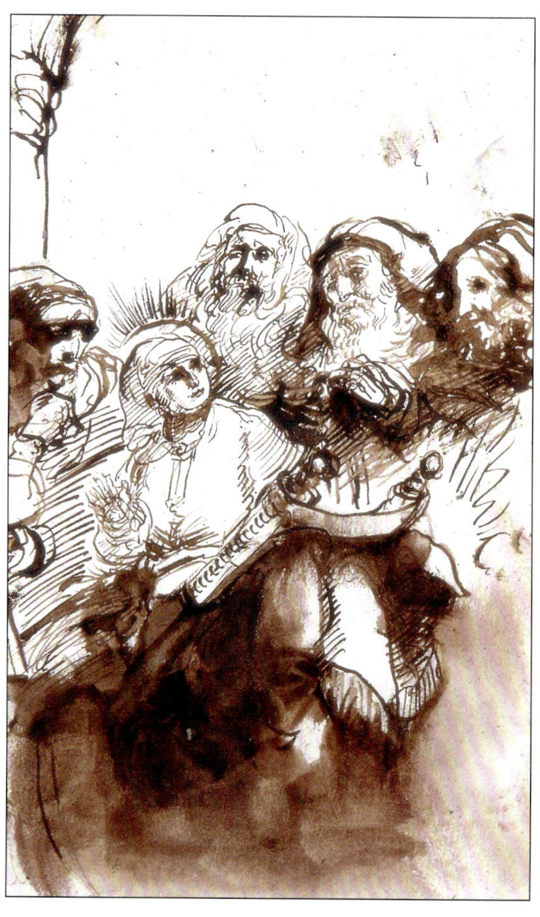

Jesus and Elders, ca. 1996
Pen and brown ink on beige paper
10 x 6 3/4 in.

Jesus Confounding the Elders, 1996
Oil on canvas, 35 x 24 in.

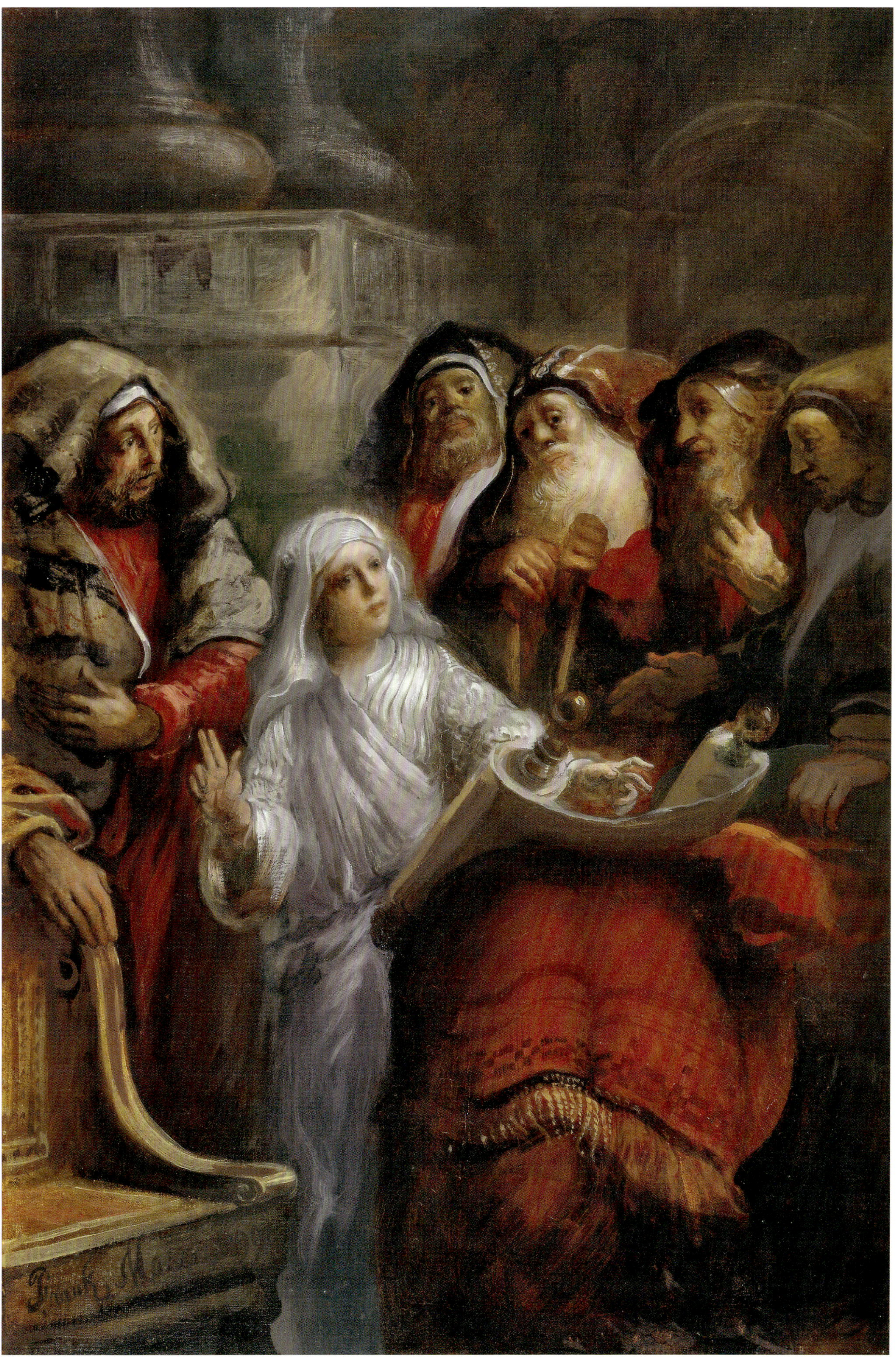

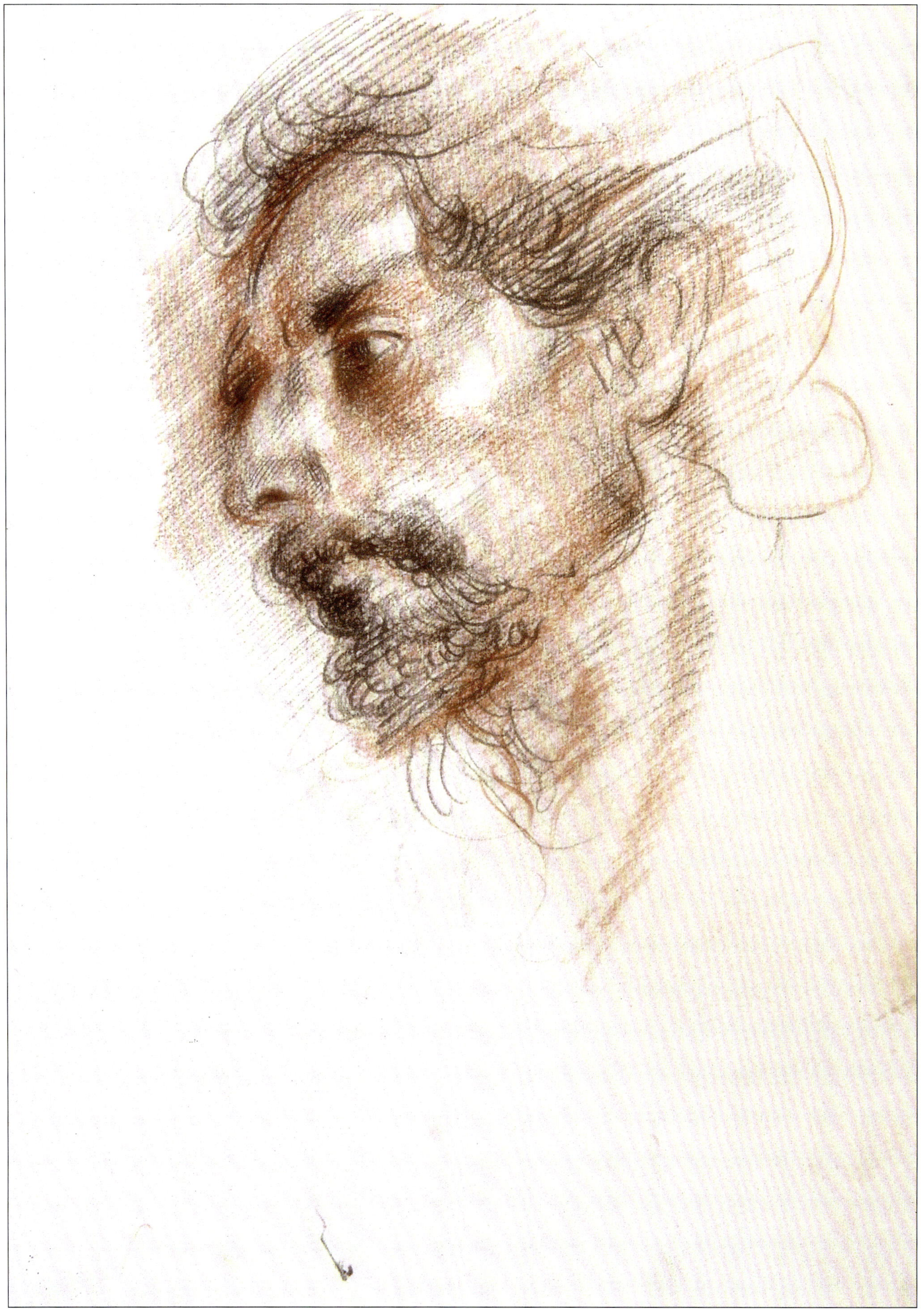

a.

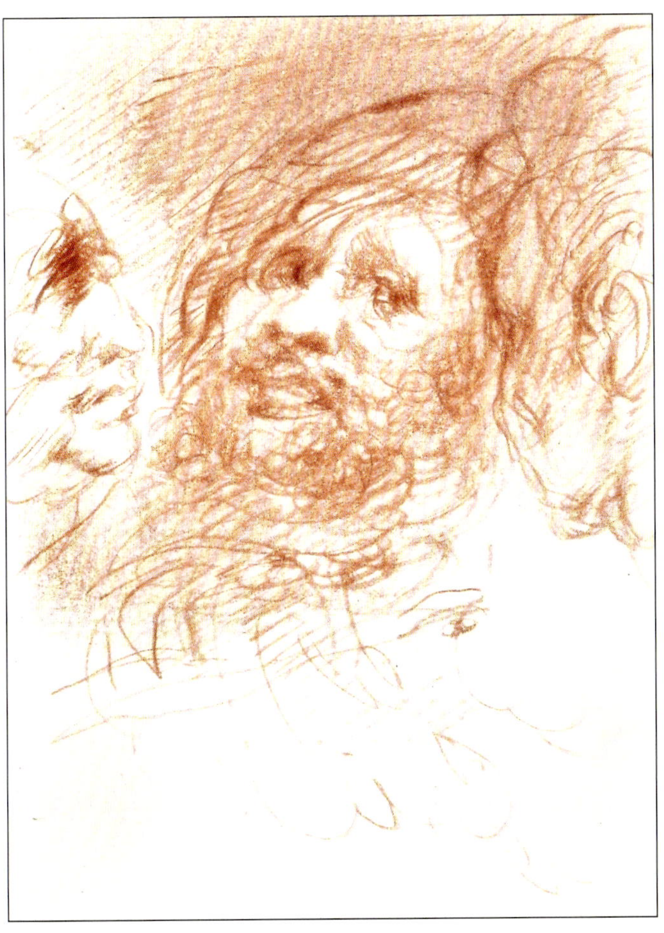

b.

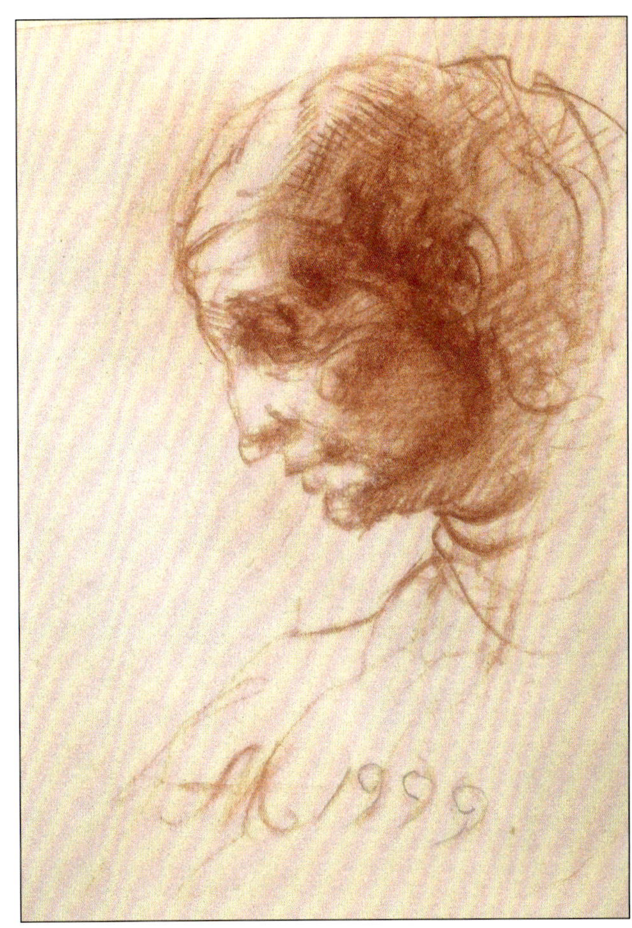

c.

Throughout the New Testament, there is an ongoing confirmation of Christ's divinity. One instance is the familiar story of Christ preaching to the Elders in the Temple. The Holy Family has been in Jerusalem for the Passover Feast, and they are on their way home, traveling with a caravan made up of many members of their extended family. All of the youngsters are in a group of their own. Joseph and Mary travel for a day before they realize that Jesus is not with them. They return to Jerusalem to look for Him, and they find Him at last in the Temple. We see Him there in the midst of patriarchs, His youth contrasting sharply with the age of His interrogators. His white costume stands out against the backdrop of the scholars' hand-woven, earth-colored robes. The men are obviously astonished at the wisdom and understanding of one so young, and their wonder shows in their faces. Plenty of proof here of His divinity, but we have more in His reply to His parents: "Wist ye not that I must be about my Father's business?" This is the first statement of His mission in the world.

a. *Head of Elder*, 1994
Red and black chalk on cream paper
14 7/8 x 10 5/8 in.

b. *Study of Elders*, 1996
Red chalk on cream paper
4 x 3 in.

c. *Head of Elder*, 1999
Red chalk on cream paper
4 x 3 in.

The Baptism of Christ

In those days came John the Baptist, preaching in the wilderness of Judaea, and saying, Repent ye: for the kingdom of heaven is at hand. . . . I indeed baptize you with water unto repentance: but he that cometh after me is mightier than I, whose shoes I am not worthy to bear: he shall baptize you with the Holy Ghost, and with fire. . . .Then cometh Jesus from Galilee to Jordan unto John, to be baptized of him. But John forbad him, saying, I have need to be baptized of thee, and comest thou to me? . . .And Jesus, when he was baptized, went up straightway out of the water: and, lo, the heavens were opened unto him, and he saw the Spirit of God descending like a dove, and lighting upon him: and lo a voice from heaven, saying, This is my beloved Son, in whom I am well pleased. —Matthew 3: 1, 2, 11, 13, 14, 16, 17

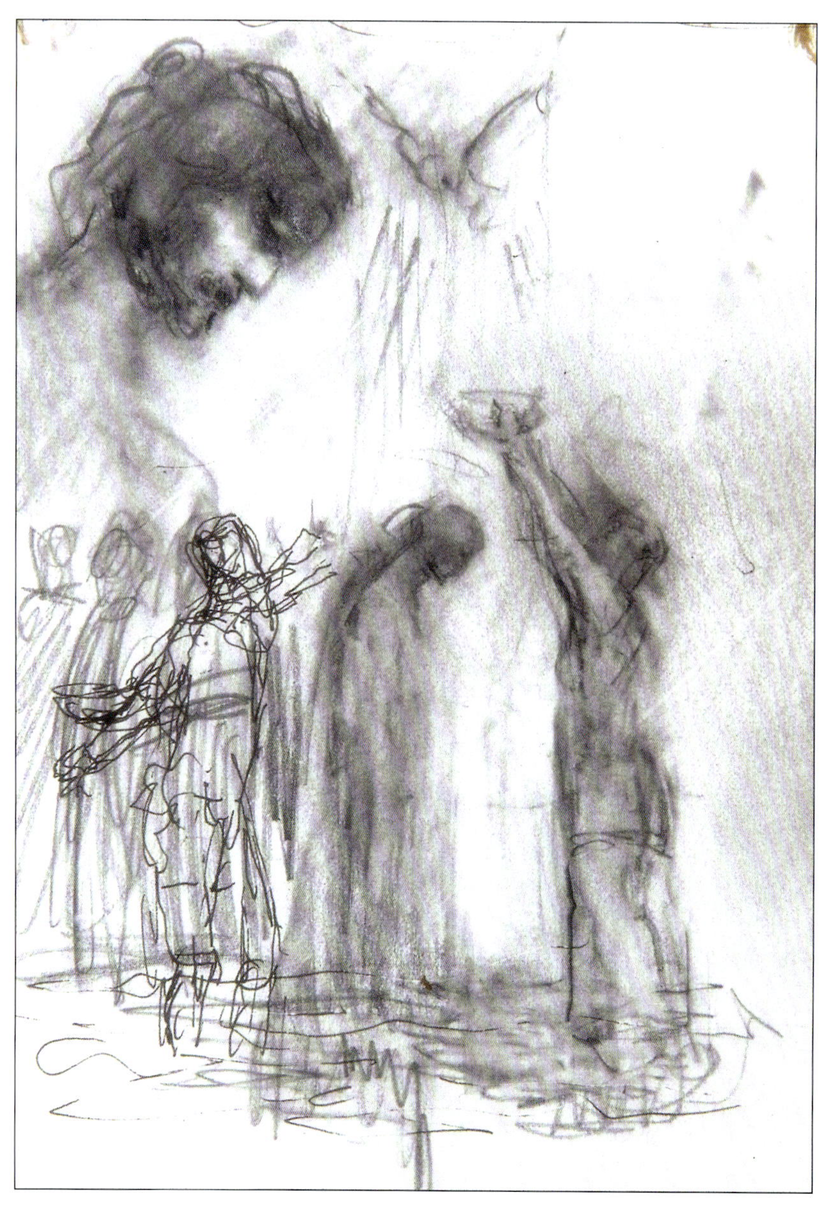

Study for the Baptism of Christ, 1997
Graphite on white paper, 6 5/8 x 5 in.

The Baptism of Christ, 1997
Oil on canvas, 35 x 24 in.

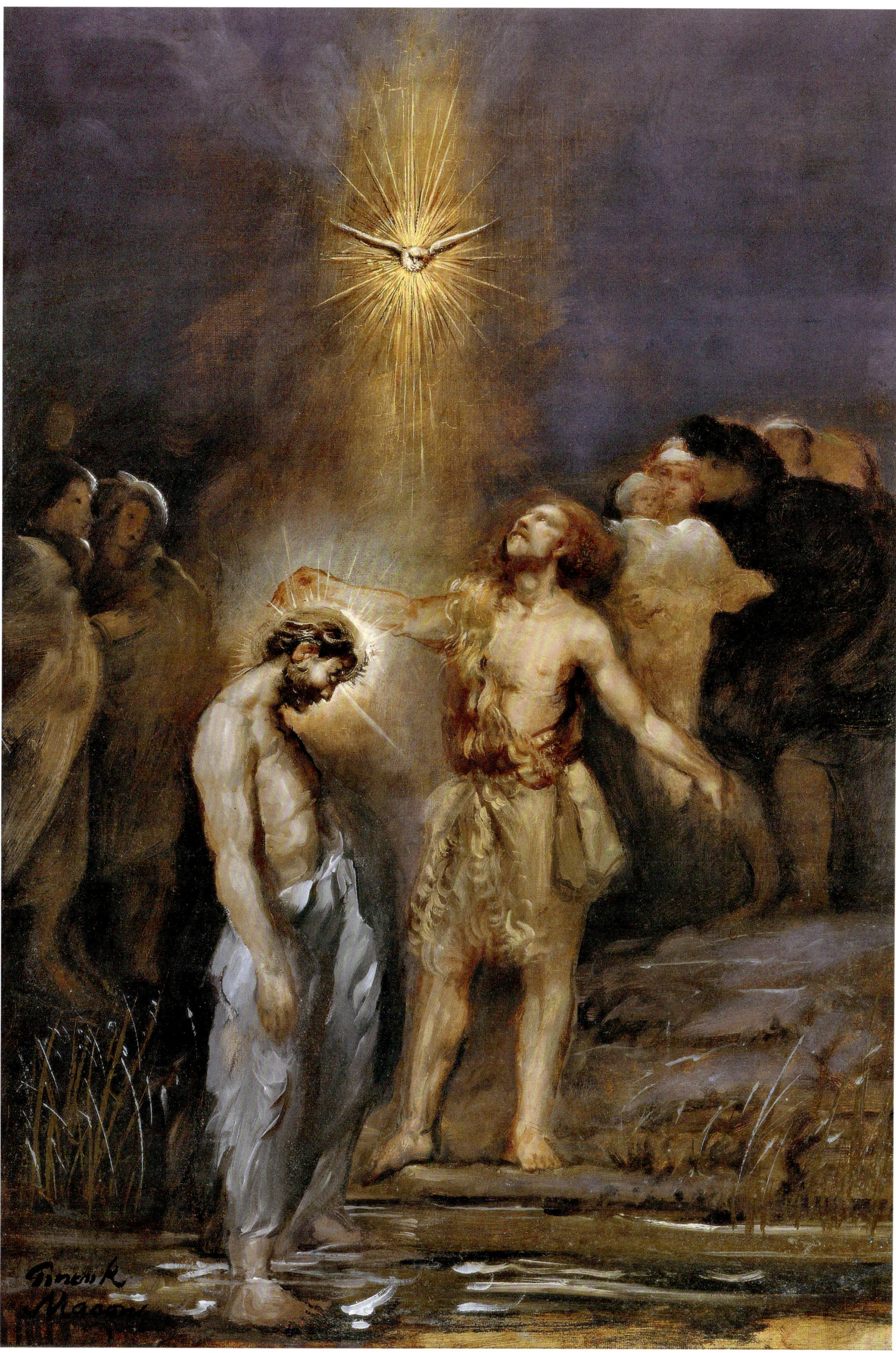

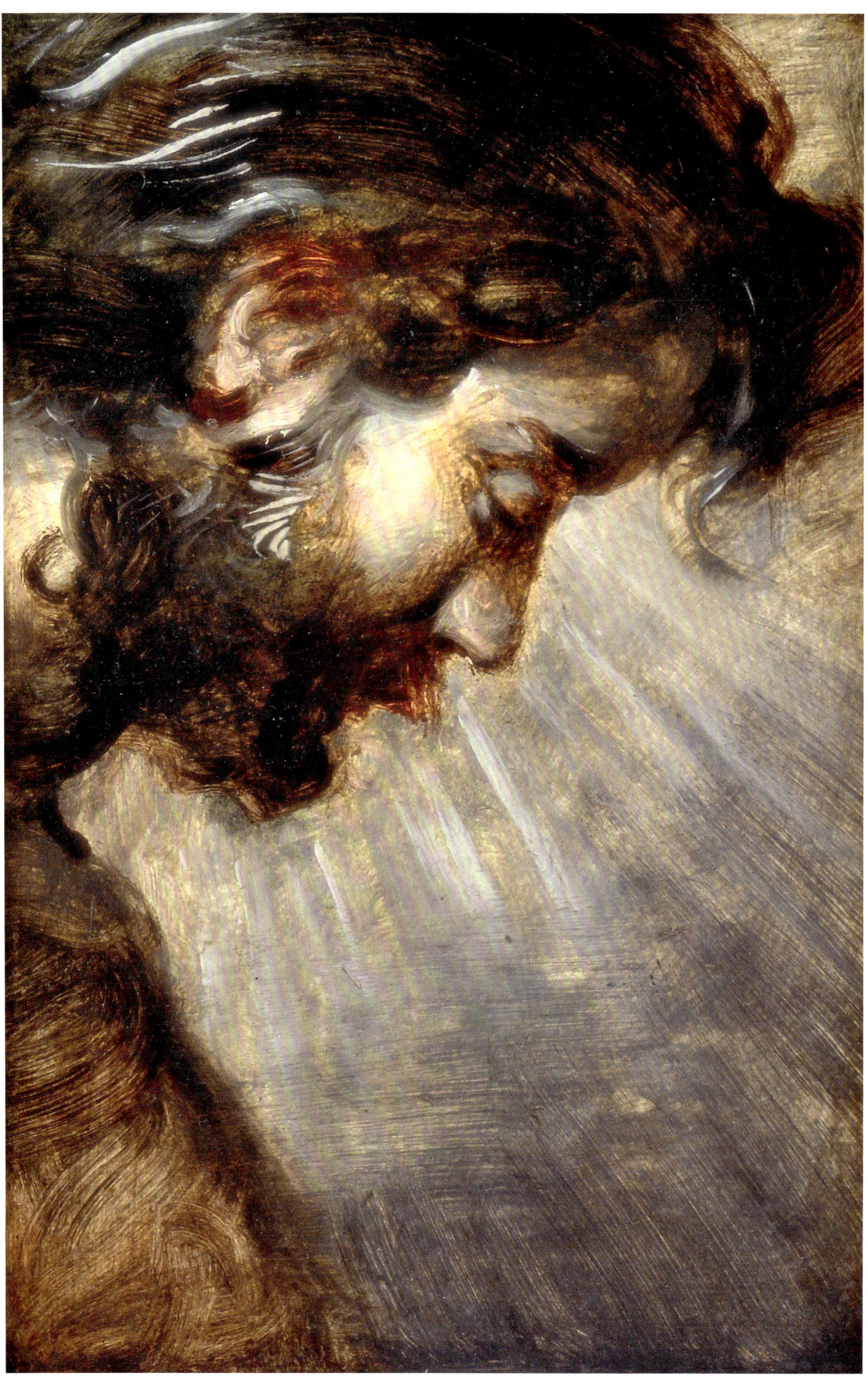

Here we have another instance of the ongoing confirmation of Christ's divinity. . .the dove descending from Heaven and the Voice of God identifying Christ as His beloved Son. The sky has suddenly darkened with wind-driven clouds, the reeds on the river-bank bend, the people watching shiver in the unexpected chill. Christ stands in the shallows of the river, His head bowed in reverence and humility. I often use students from the Art Students League as models but for this painting I posed Antonio Giangrande, a young actor, as Christ. I found him in the Easter Passion Play at the Cathedral of St. John the Divine, where he was cast in the same role. Because he could pose only on weekends, the work went slowly. Finally he urged me to hurry a little; he really needed to shave his beard in order to audition for certain roles. He was a good model, and I hope he has good luck on Broadway. My son Arden, who often poses for me, appears in *The Baptism of Christ* as St. John. He is also Peter, in *Peter's Denial.* Another good model was my father, who posed in *The Man with the Withered Hand.* And, of course, my wife Anne is a great model; she's the centurion with the plumed helmet in *Christ Healing the Sick.*

Head of Christ, 1997
Oil on panel
11 3/4 x 8 in.

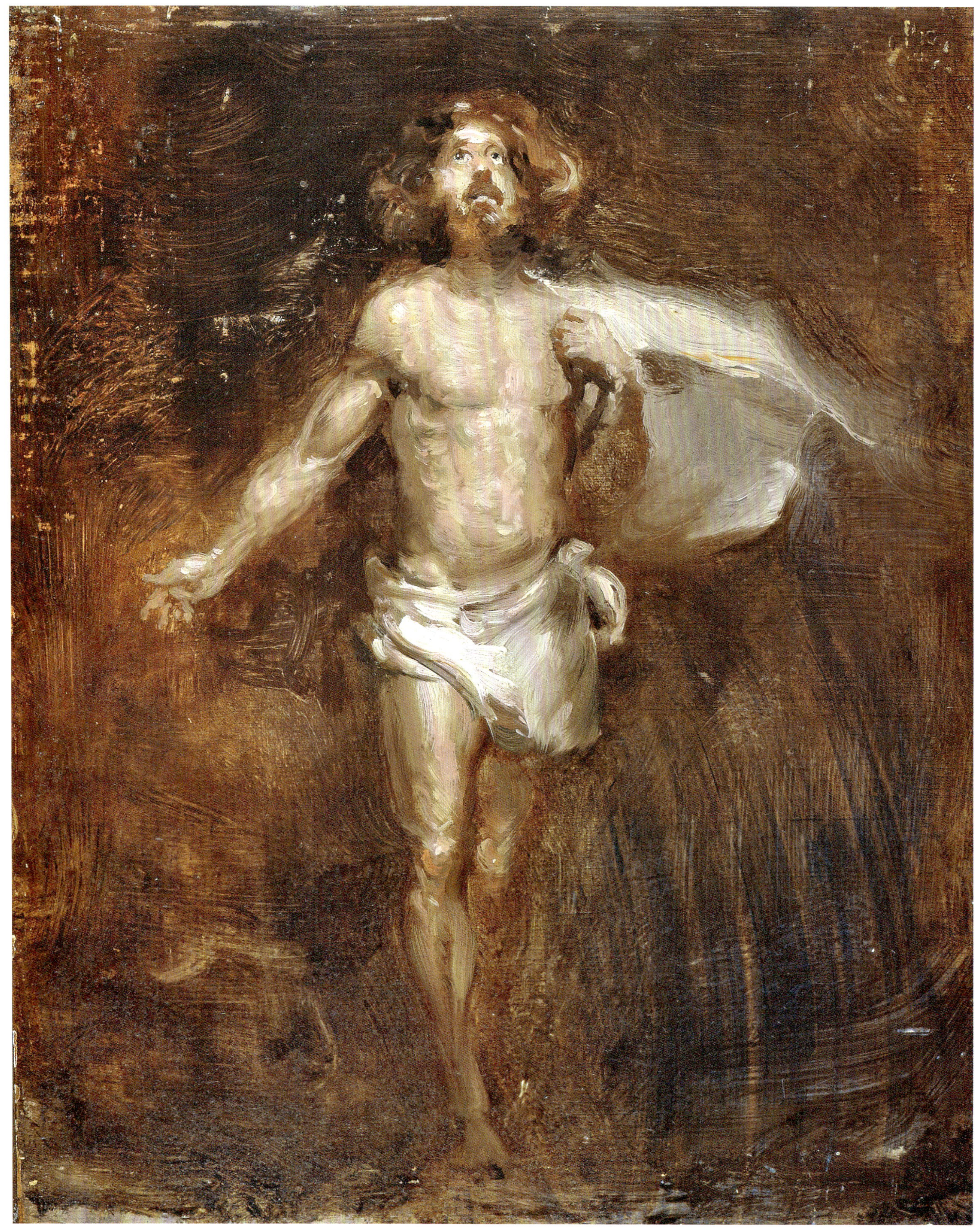

St. John in the Wilderness, 1972
Oil on panel, 22 x 18 in.

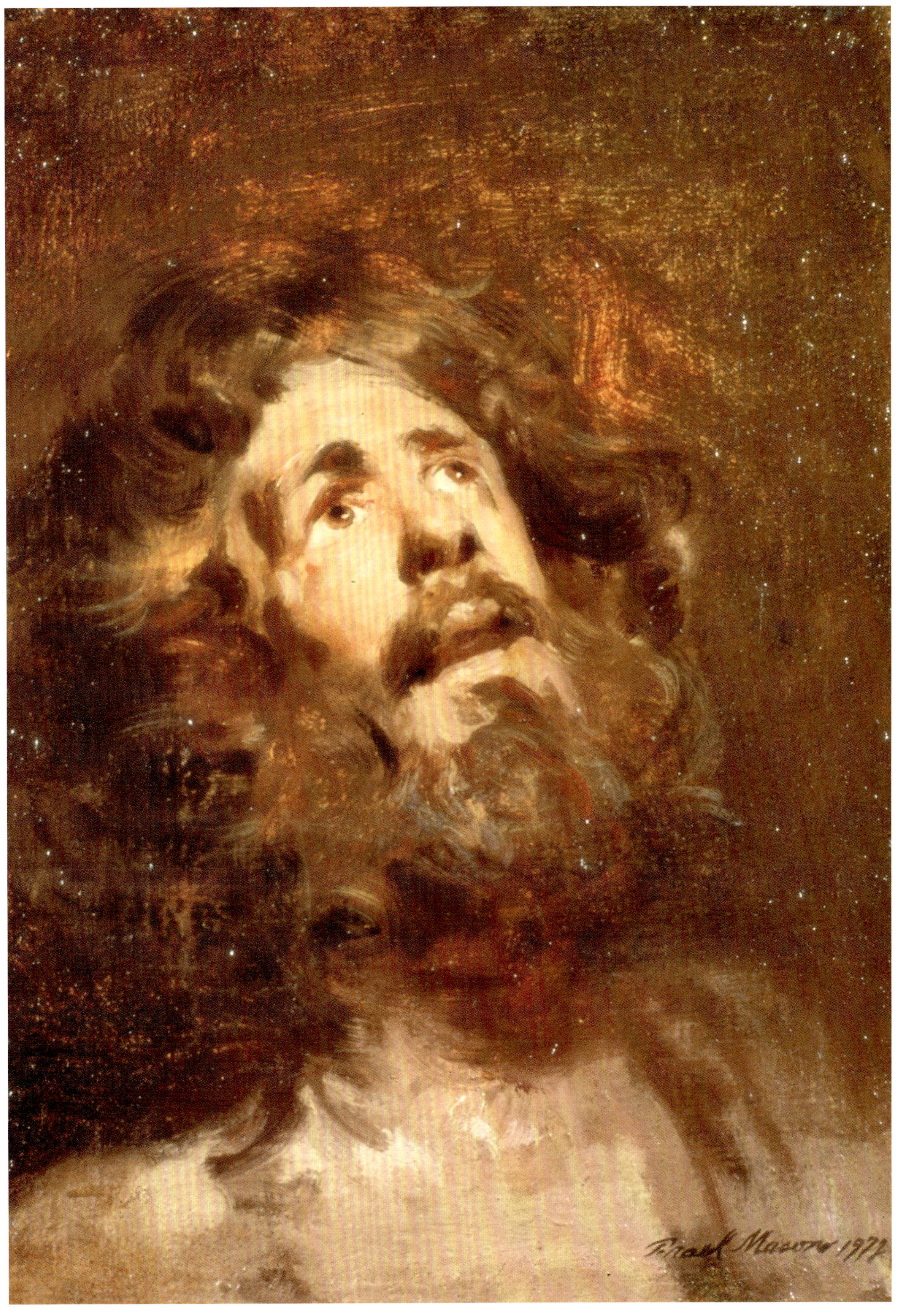

Head of St. John the Baptist, 1972
Oil on canvas, 20 x 16 in.

Woman of Samaria

HE LEFT JUDAEA, AND DEPARTED AGAIN INTO GALILEE. AND HE MUST NEEDS GO THROUGH SAMARIA. . .NOW JACOB'S WELL WAS THERE. JESUS THEREFORE, BEING WEARIED WITH HIS JOURNEY, SAT THUS ON THE WELL. . . .THERE COMETH A WOMAN OF SAMARIA TO DRAW WATER: JESUS SAITH UNTO HER, GIVE ME TO DRINK. . . .JESUS. . .SAID UNTO HER, WHOSOEVER DRINKETH OF THIS WATER SHALL THIRST AGAIN: BUT WHOSOEVER DRINKETH OF THE WATER THAT I SHALL GIVE HIM SHALL NEVER THIRST; BUT THE WATER THAT I SHALL GIVE HIM SHALL BE IN HIM A WELL OF WATER SPRINGING UP INTO EVERLASTING LIFE. . . .THE WOMAN SAITH UNTO HIM, I KNOW THAT MESSIAS COMETH, WHICH IS CALLED CHRIST: WHEN HE IS COME, HE WILL TELL US ALL THINGS. JESUS SAITH UNTO HER, I THAT SPEAK UNTO THEE AM HE. . . .THE WOMAN. . .WENT HER WAY INTO THE CITY, AND SAITH TO THE MEN, COME, SEE A MAN, WHICH TOLD ME ALL THINGS THAT EVER I DID: IS NOT THIS THE CHRIST? —JOHN 4: 3, 4, 6, 7, 13, 14, 25, 26, 28, 29

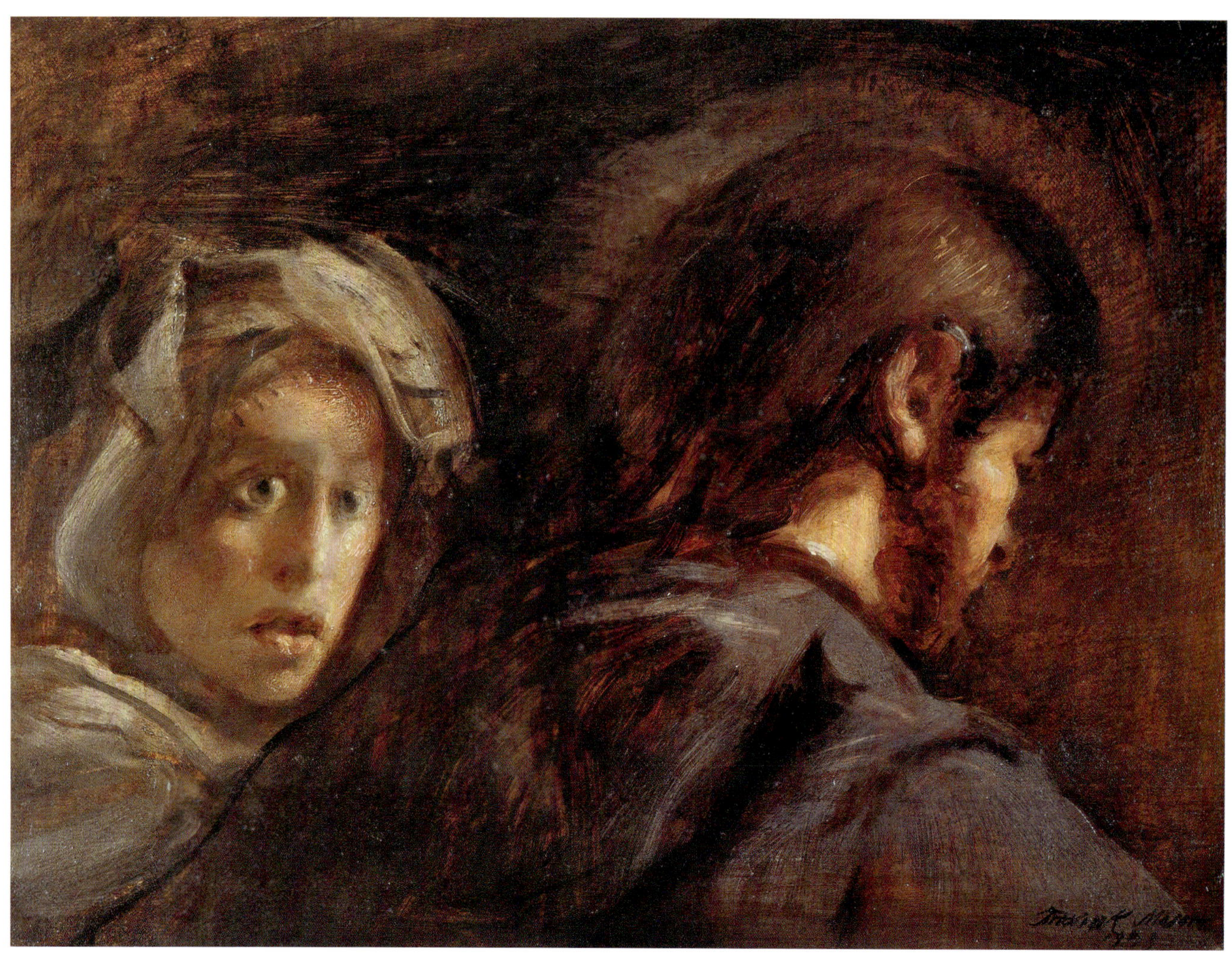

Christ and the Woman of Samaria, 1973
Oil on canvas, 18 x 24 in.

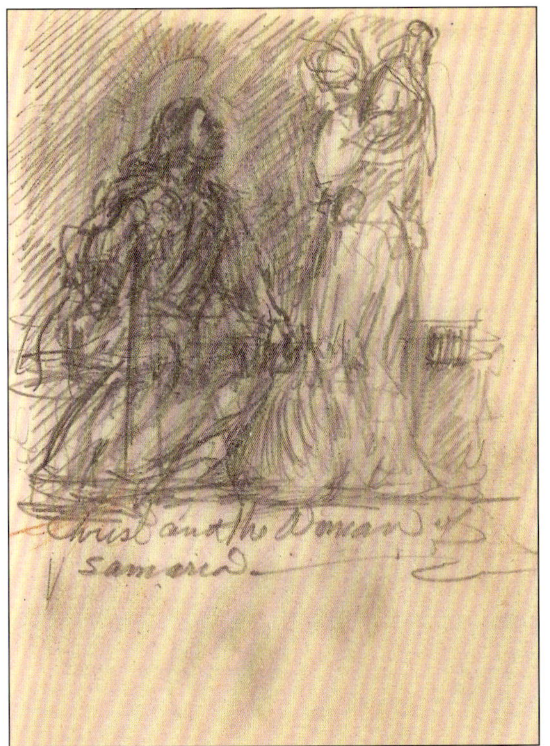

My grandmother probably would have described this woman as being "no better than she should be," by which she meant a woman very naughty indeed. Unprintably naughty, in fact, by my grandmother's standards. The woman's chance encounter with Christ at the well brings her to painful self-realization. We see her here with Christ as He tells her "all she has ever done." There are only the two figures in the scene, and the shadowy background provides an aura of privacy almost like that of the confessional. It is a moment of great personal revelation, and her tormented face reflects her pain as she faces the truth about her life. When He tells her that He is the Messiah, she takes Him at His word. This incident—private though it is—has far-reaching impact. Because of the woman's words to her fellow Samaritans, they, too, come to believe.

Christ and the Woman of Samaria, 1994
Graphite on cream paper, 4 x 3 in.

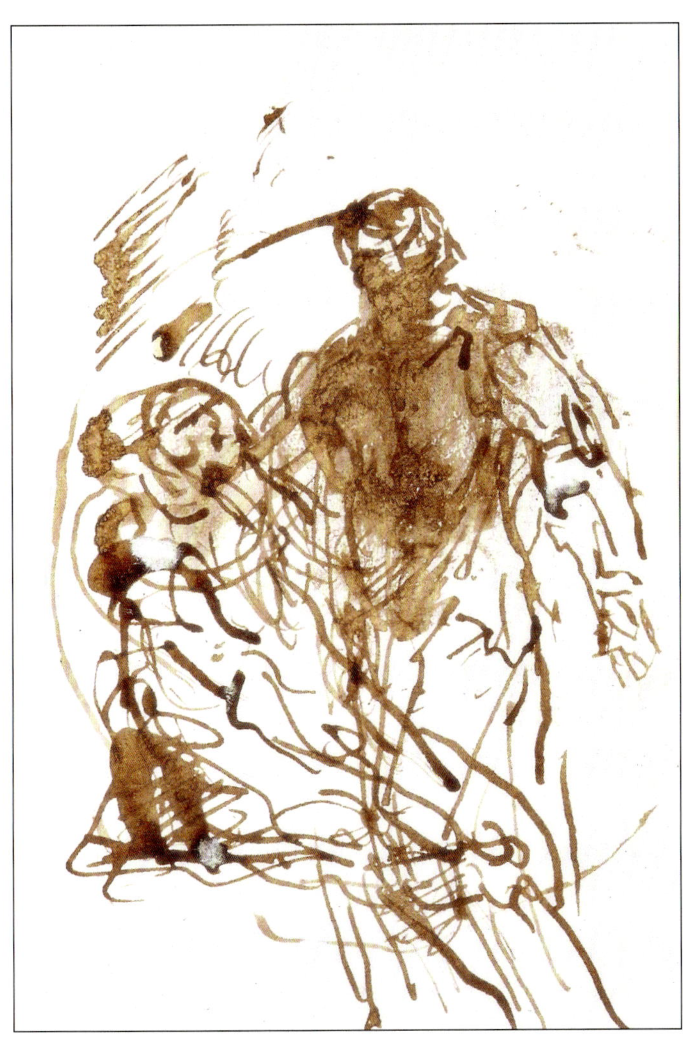

Woman at the Well, 2000
Pen and brown ink and wash
on beige paper, 5 x 3 1/2 in.

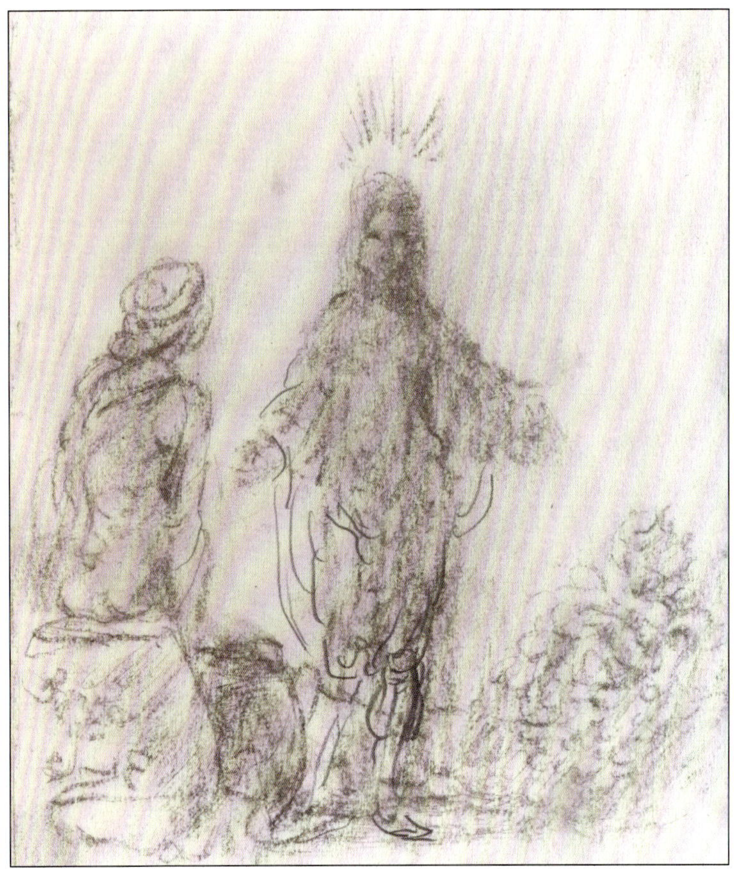

Christ with the Woman at the Well
Black chalk on white paper
6 x 5 1/4 in.

Christ Healing the Man with the Withered Hand

AND HE ENTERED AGAIN INTO THE SYNAGOGUE; AND THERE WAS A MAN THERE WHICH HAD A WITHERED HAND. AND THEY WATCHED HIM, WHETHER HE WOULD HEAL HIM ON THE SABBATH DAY; THAT THEY MIGHT ACCUSE HIM. AND HE SAITH UNTO THE MAN WHICH HAD THE WITHERED HAND, STAND FORTH. AND HE SAITH UNTO THEM, IS IT LAWFUL TO DO GOOD ON THE SABBATH DAYS, OR TO DO EVIL? TO SAVE LIFE, OR TO KILL? BUT THEY HELD THEIR PEACE. AND WHEN HE HAD LOOKED ROUND ABOUT ON THEM WITH ANGER, BEING GRIEVED FOR THE HARDNESS OF THEIR HEARTS, HE SAITH UNTO THE MAN, STRETCH FORTH THINE HAND. AND HE STRETCHED IT OUT: AND HIS HAND WAS RESTORED WHOLE AS THE OTHER. AND THE PHARISEES WENT FORTH, AND STRAIGHTWAY TOOK COUNSEL WITH THE HERODIANS AGAINST HIM, HOW THEY MIGHT DESTROY HIM. –MARK 3: 1–6

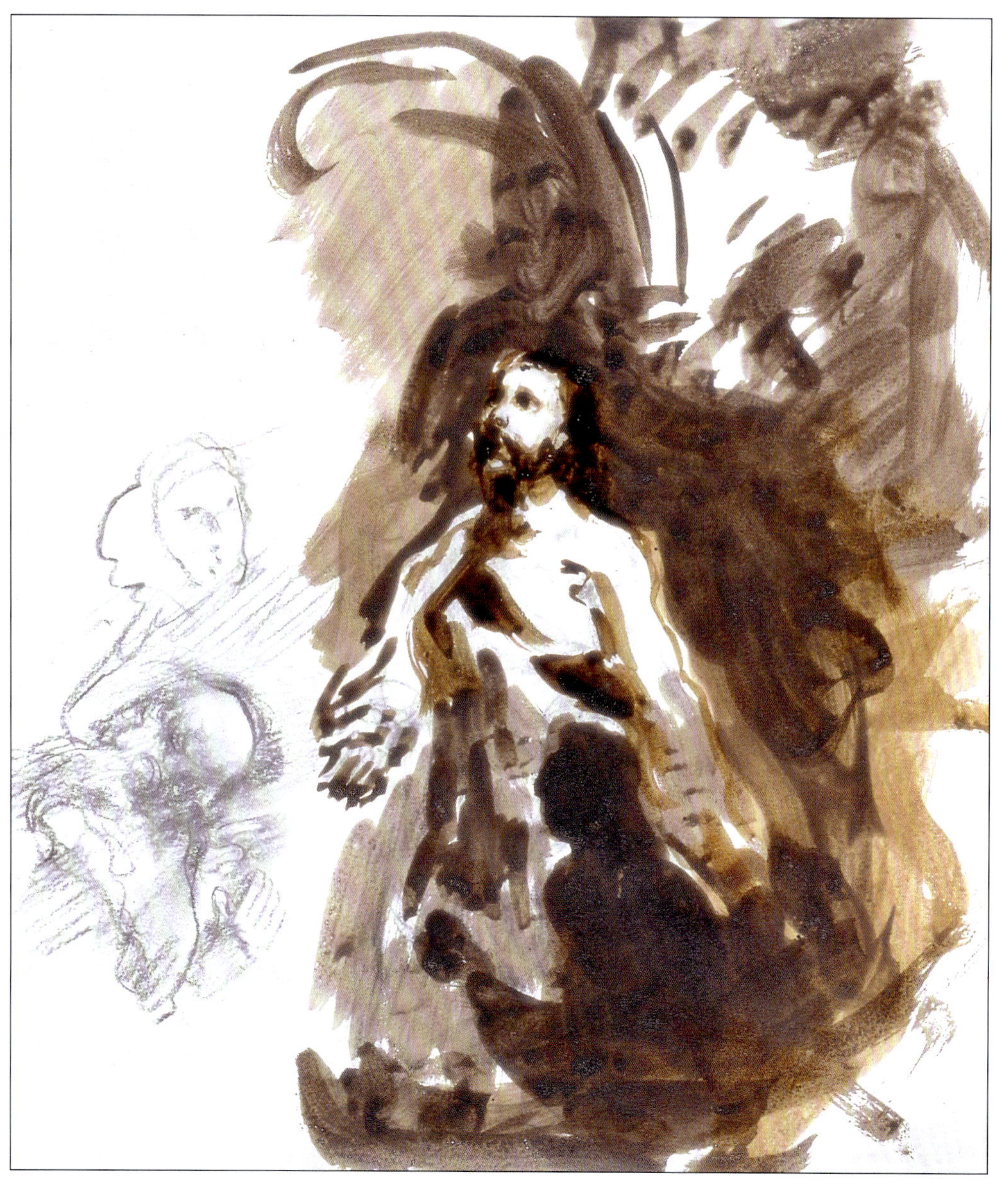

Study after Christ Healing the Man with the Withered Hand, 2003
Brown ink wash and black chalk on white paper, 13 1/2 x 12 1/2 in.

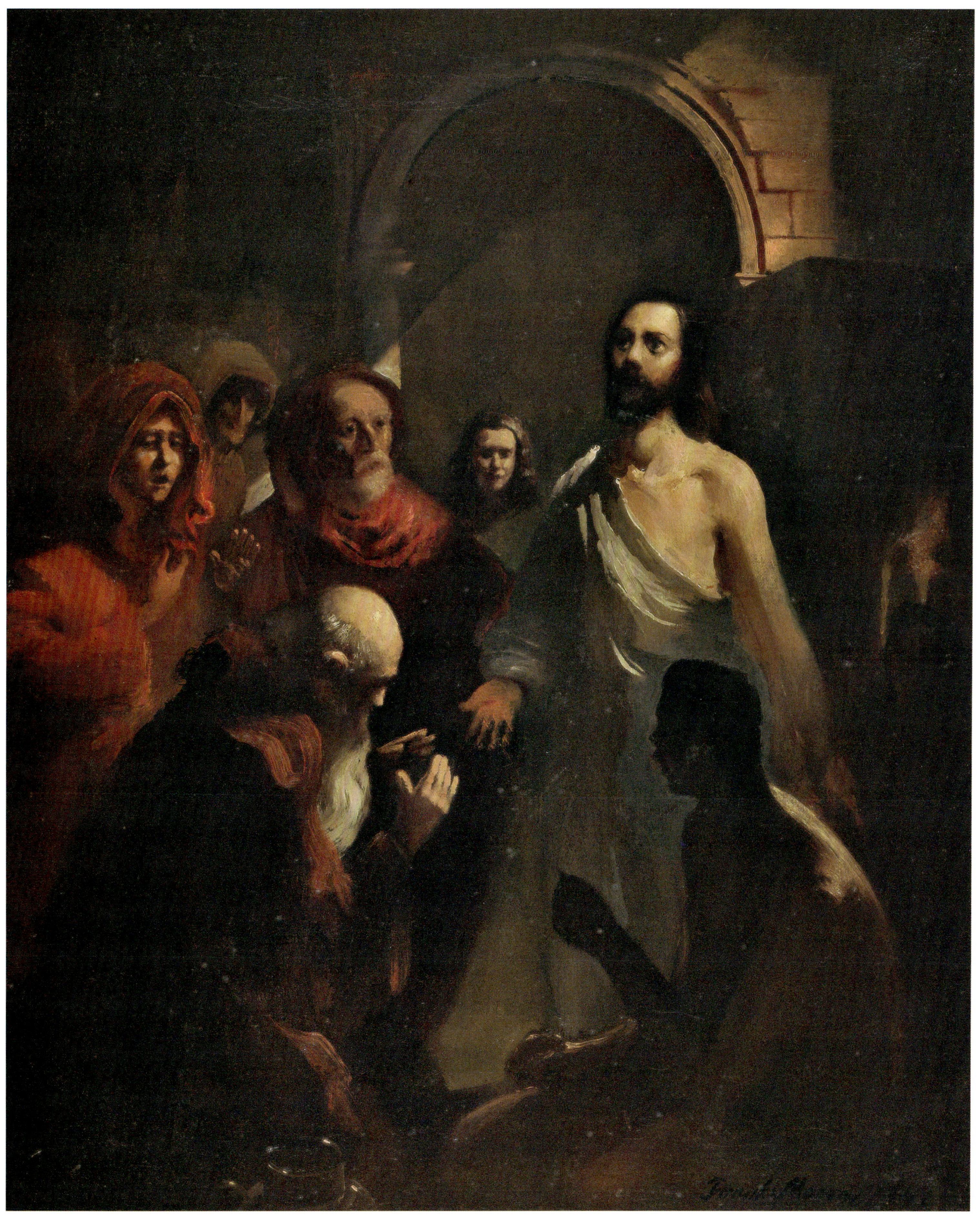

Christ Healing the Man with the Withered Hand, 1940
Oil on canvas, 24 x 20 in.

Mark tells this story with great economy of language. In the first verse we have the setting—the synagogue—and the two chief characters—Jesus and the man with the withered hand. By the end of the second verse, we have met the antagonists—the Pharisees. We are even given the gist of the plot, and the suspense is beginning to build: will Jesus heal the man on the Sabbath? Will they be able to accuse Him? All this in fewer than one hundred words! In spite of its brevity, the scene has always been very vivid to me. I wanted to show the shadowy interior of the synagogue with its thick stone walls and deeply recessed windows. One window serves almost as a spotlight illuminating the central action of Christ healing the white-bearded old man. Crowded around are some of His followers, casual bystanders in the temple, and of course the ever-present, ever-watchful Pharisees. I was nineteen years old when I painted this. My father posed for the old man with the withered hand.

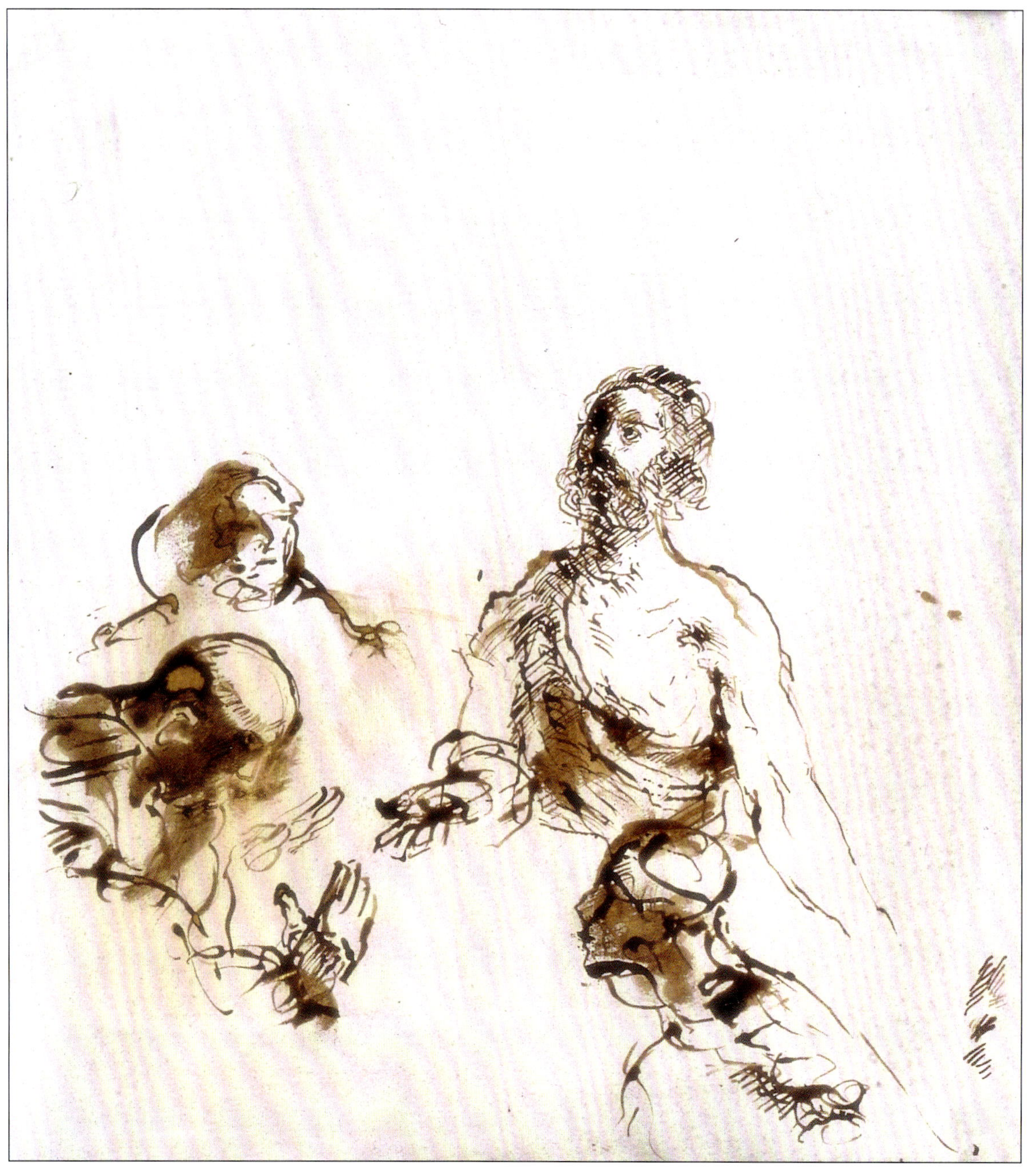

Study after Christ Healing the Man with the Withered Hand, 2003
Pen and brown ink and wash on gray prepared paper, 11 x 9 3/4 in.

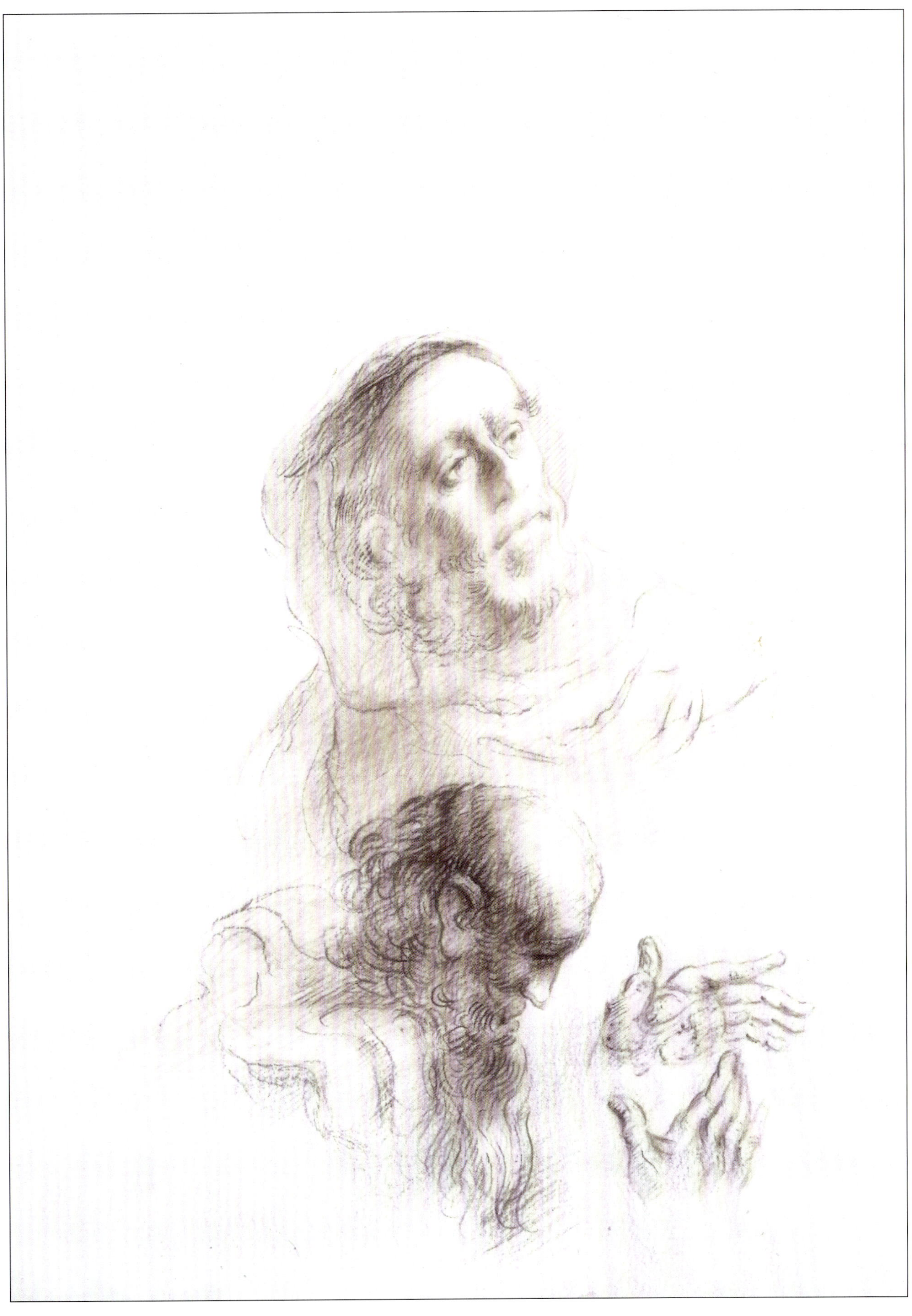

Studies after Christ Healing the Man with the Withered Hand, 2003
Black chalk on white paper, 14 x 11 in.

Christ Healing the Sick

And Jesus went about all Galilee, teaching in their synagogues, and preaching the gospel of the kingdom, and healing all manner of sickness and all manner of disease among the people. And his fame went throughout all Syria: and they brought unto him all sick people that were taken with divers diseases and torments, and those which were possessed with devils, and those which were lunatick, and those that had the palsy; and he healed them. —Matthew 4: 23, 24

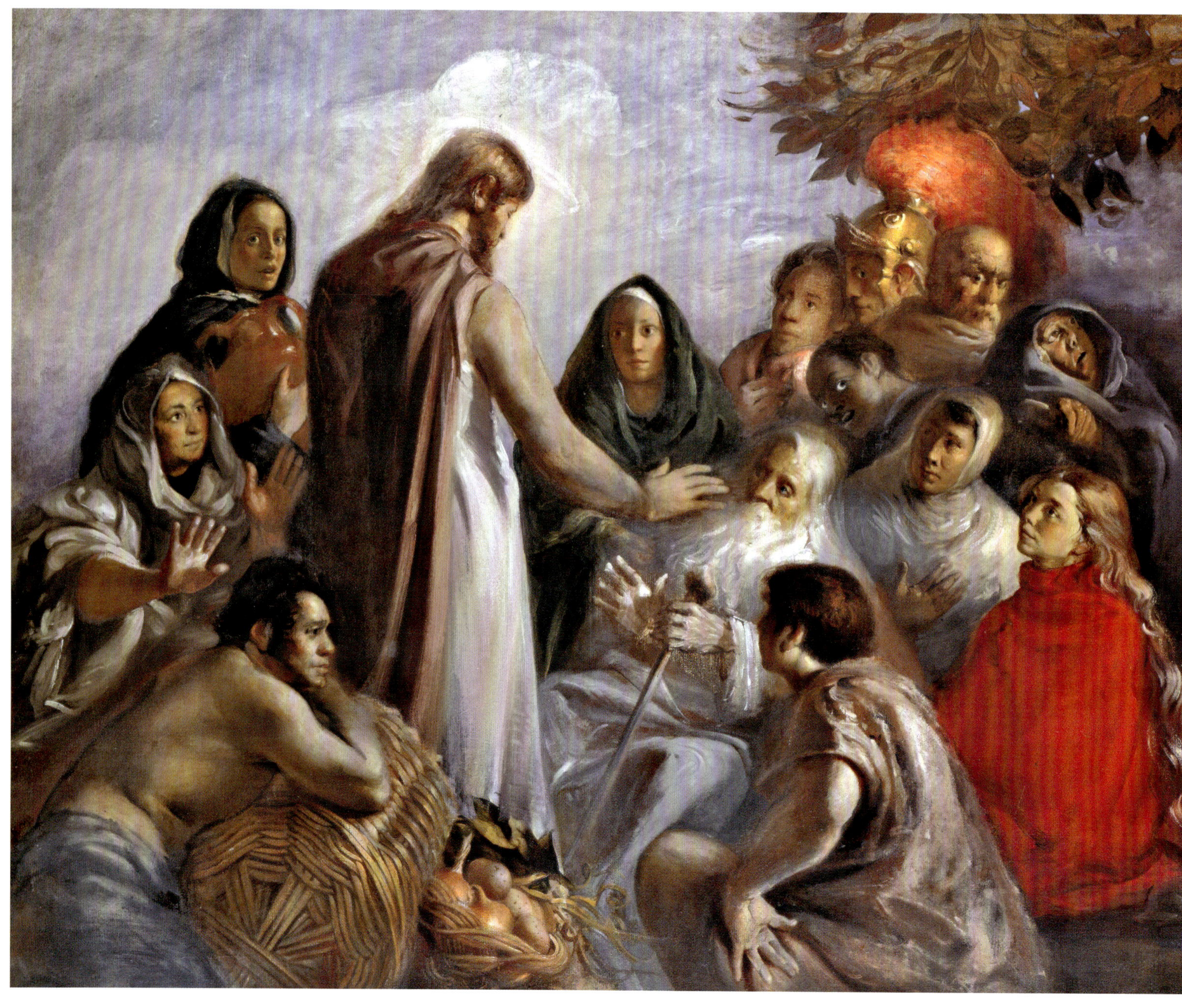

Christ Healing the Sick, 1973, oil on canvas, 72 x 120 in.

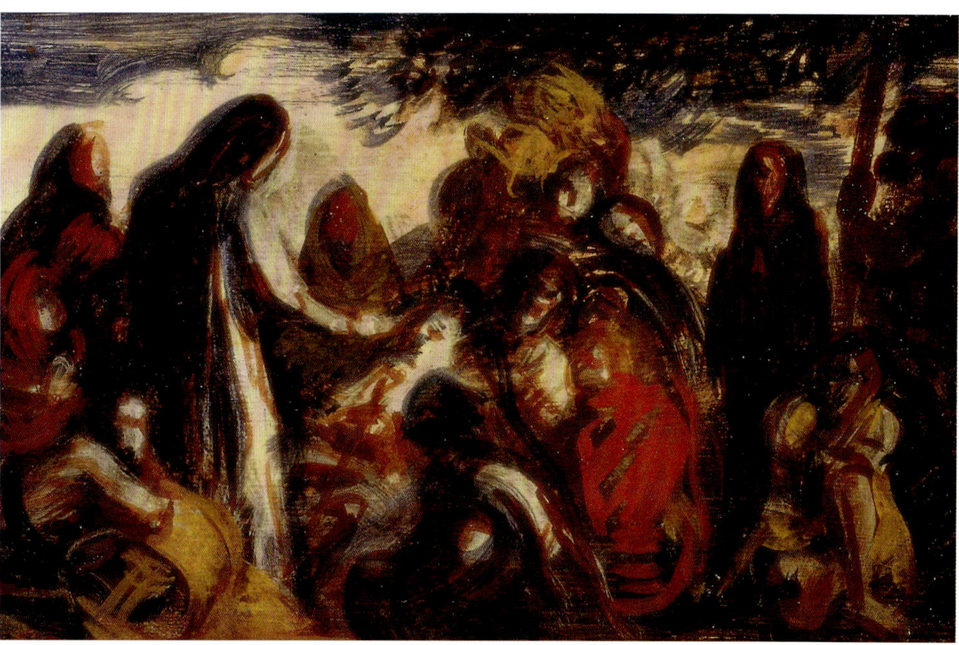

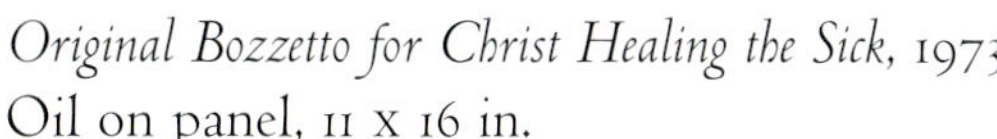

Original Bozzetto for Christ Healing the Sick, 1973
Oil on panel, 11 x 16 in.

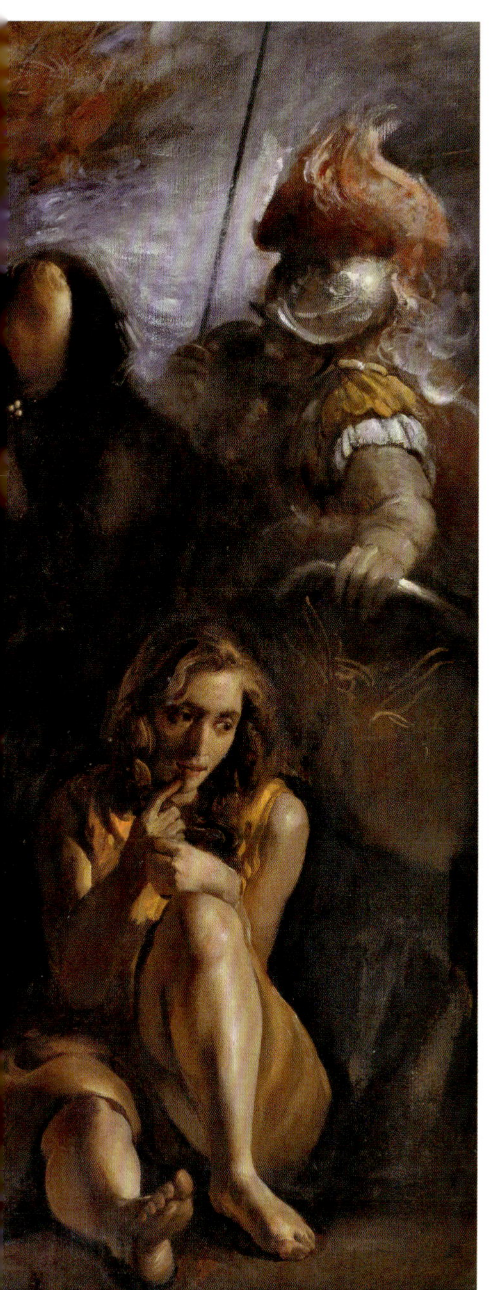

Ever since I painted the scene of Christ in the synagogue healing the man with the withered hand, I have been fascinated by the stories of the miraculous cures He performed throughout His ministry. I chose to present a synthesis of the healing miracles, a scene that would embody the motif common to all the stories: the confidence of the afflicted who sought Him out and the awe of bystanders who marveled at what He was doing. Here you see two young farmers on their way to market putting down their basket of onions to take in every detail of what is going on. Here, too, are Christ's followers who look on as a once-blind man, his sight restored, opens his eyes on a world he now can see. A woman reaching out to Him will be healed of a twelve-year illness as she touches His robe. Behind her is the woman in blue from Samaria whom Christ met at the well and who now proclaims He is the Messiah. A young woman with leprosy pushes into the crowd, defying strict quarantine and ignoring the man beside her who shrinks away in horror at her approach. The centurion in the center is the man who later on approaches Christ to ask help for a servant afflicted with palsy. The stories of the healing miracles always overwhelm me. As I read them, I see the lame, the halt, and the blind approaching Him with utter faith in His loving kindness. Their total trust in His power and their poignant hope for a happy solution to their afflictions fill me with wonder.

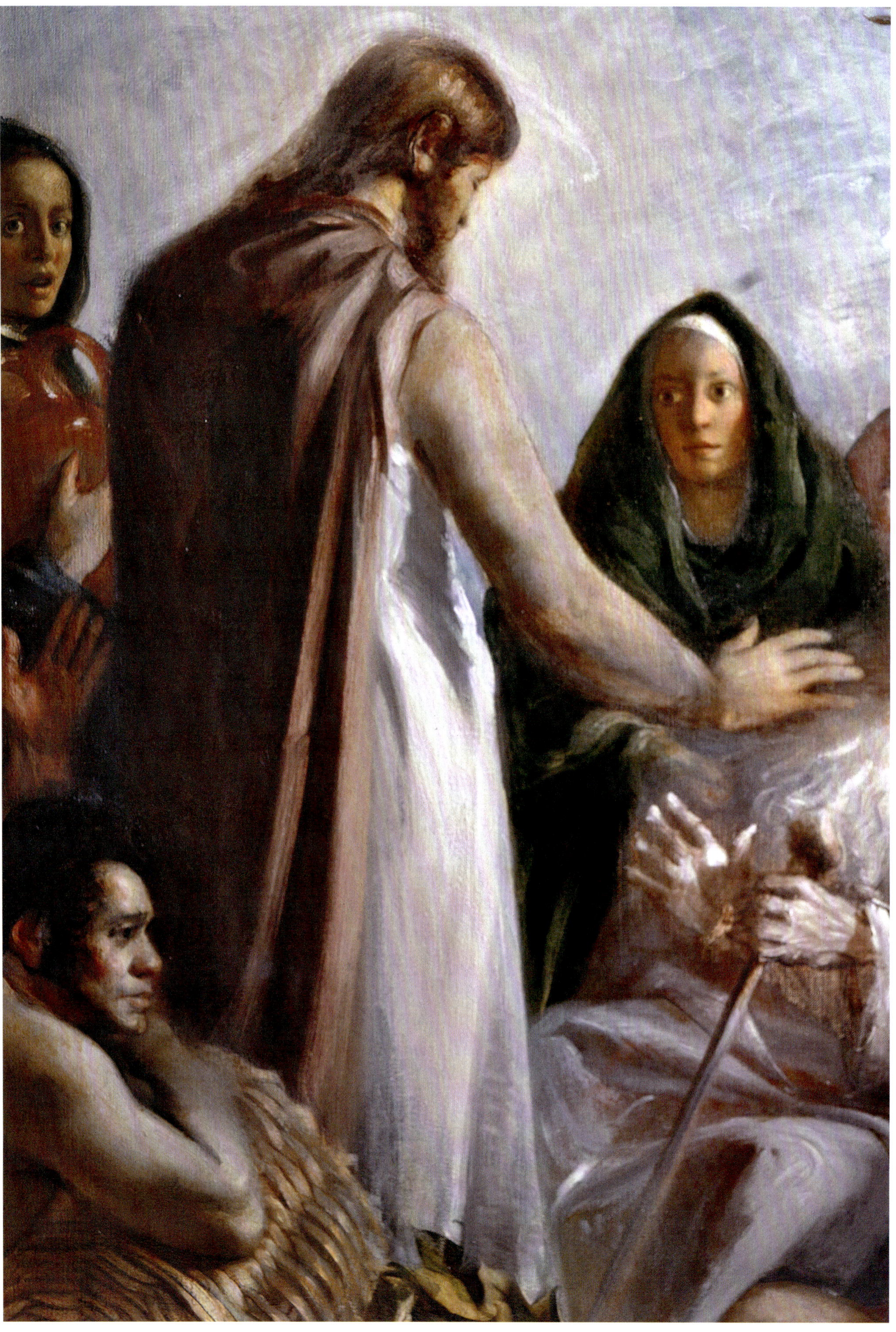

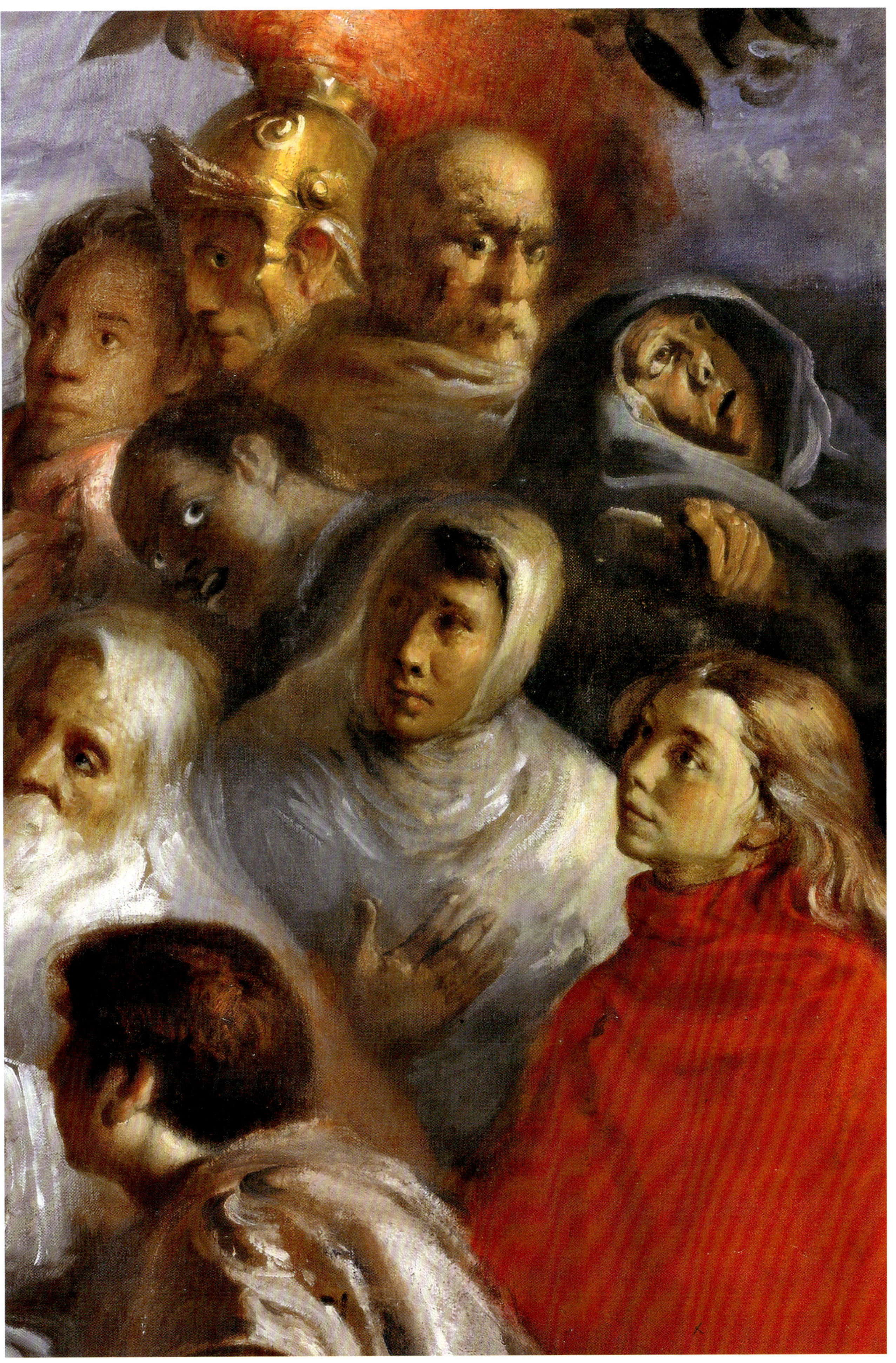

(Details) *Christ Healing the Sick*

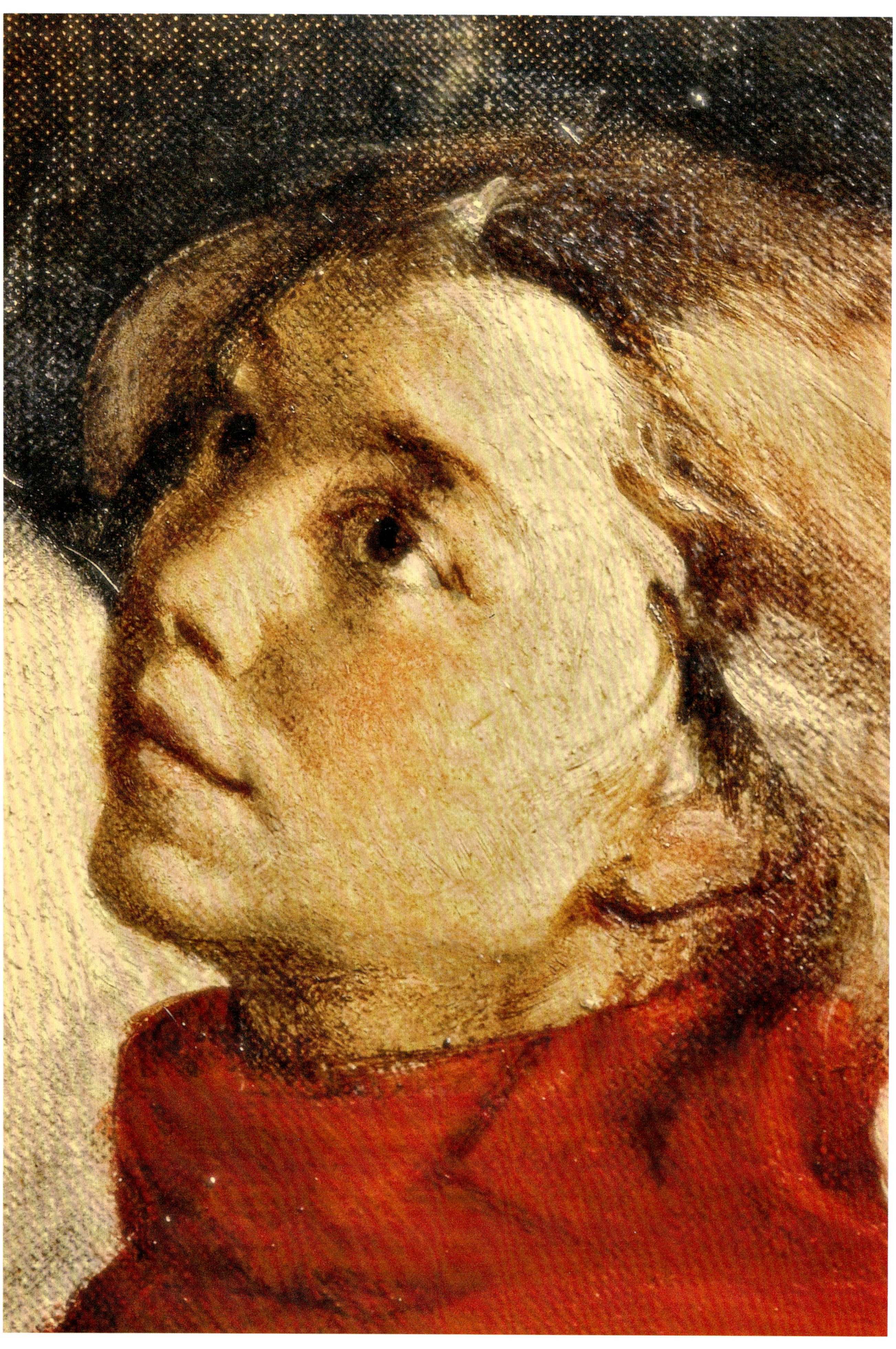

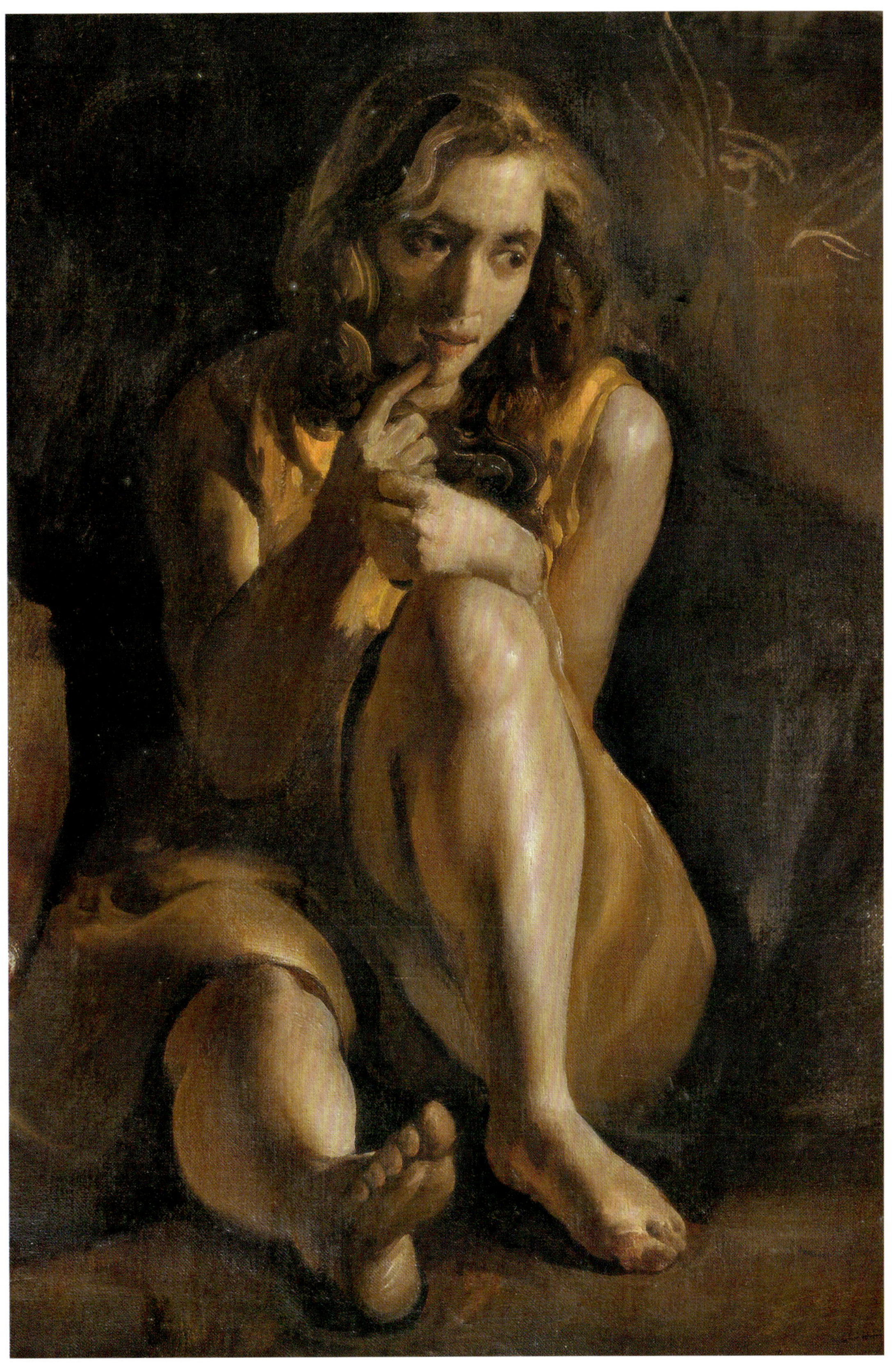

(Details) *Christ Healing the Sick*

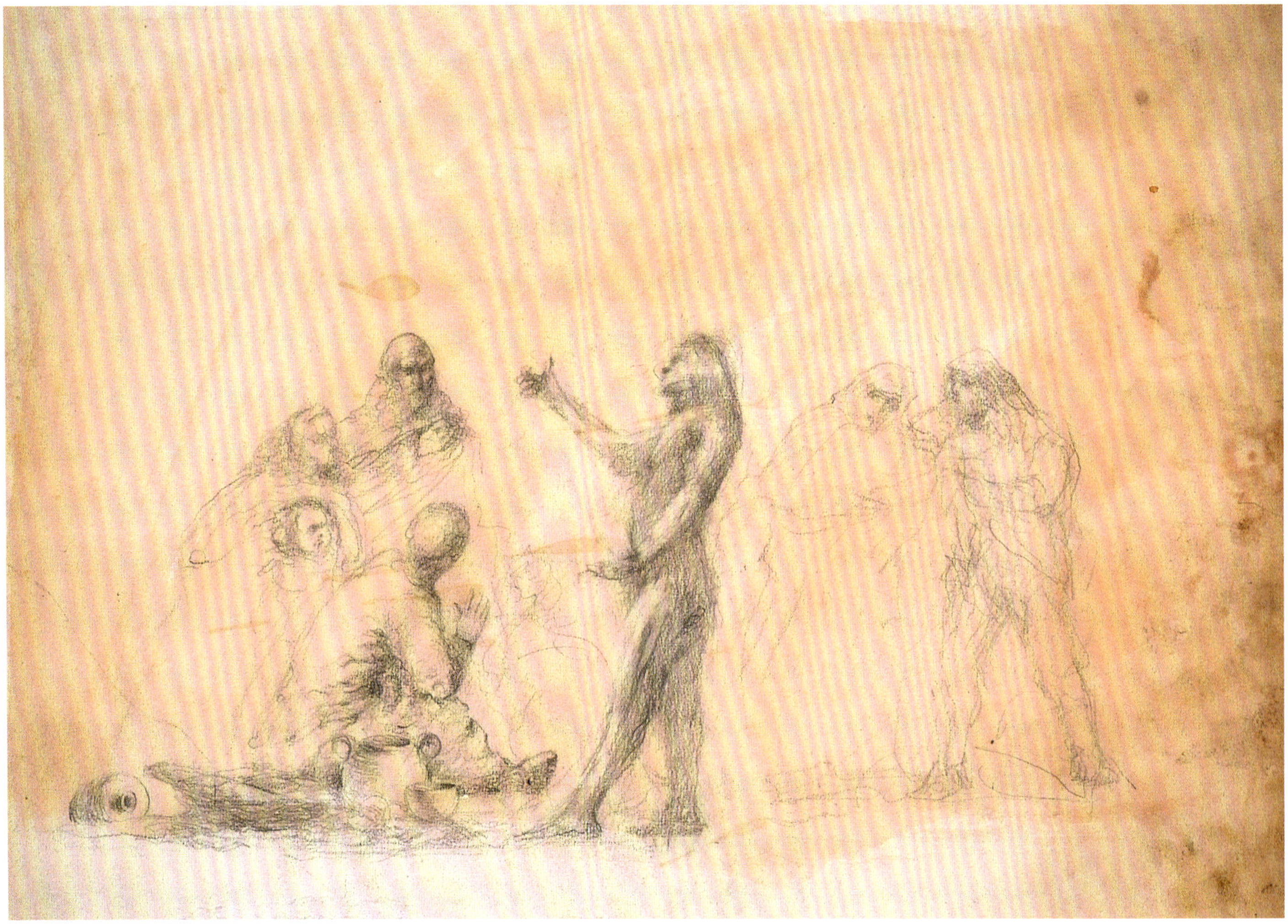

Christ Healing, ca. 1970
Pencil on pink prepared paper
9 x 11 1/2 in.

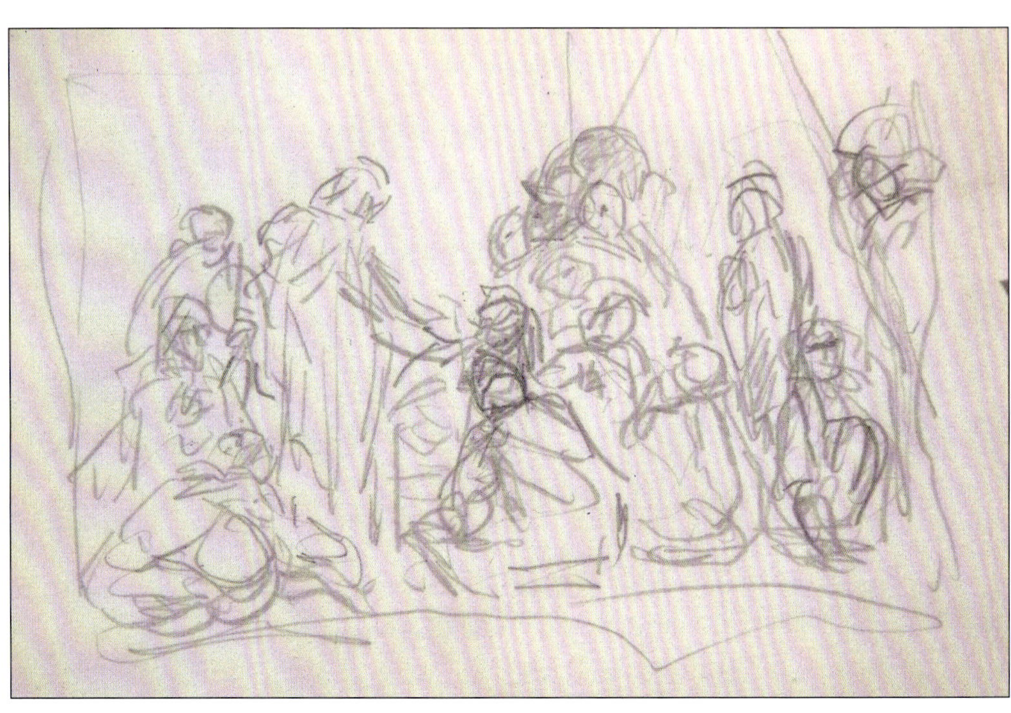

Christ Healing the Sick, 1972
Graphite on white paper
4 1/4 x 6 1/4 in.

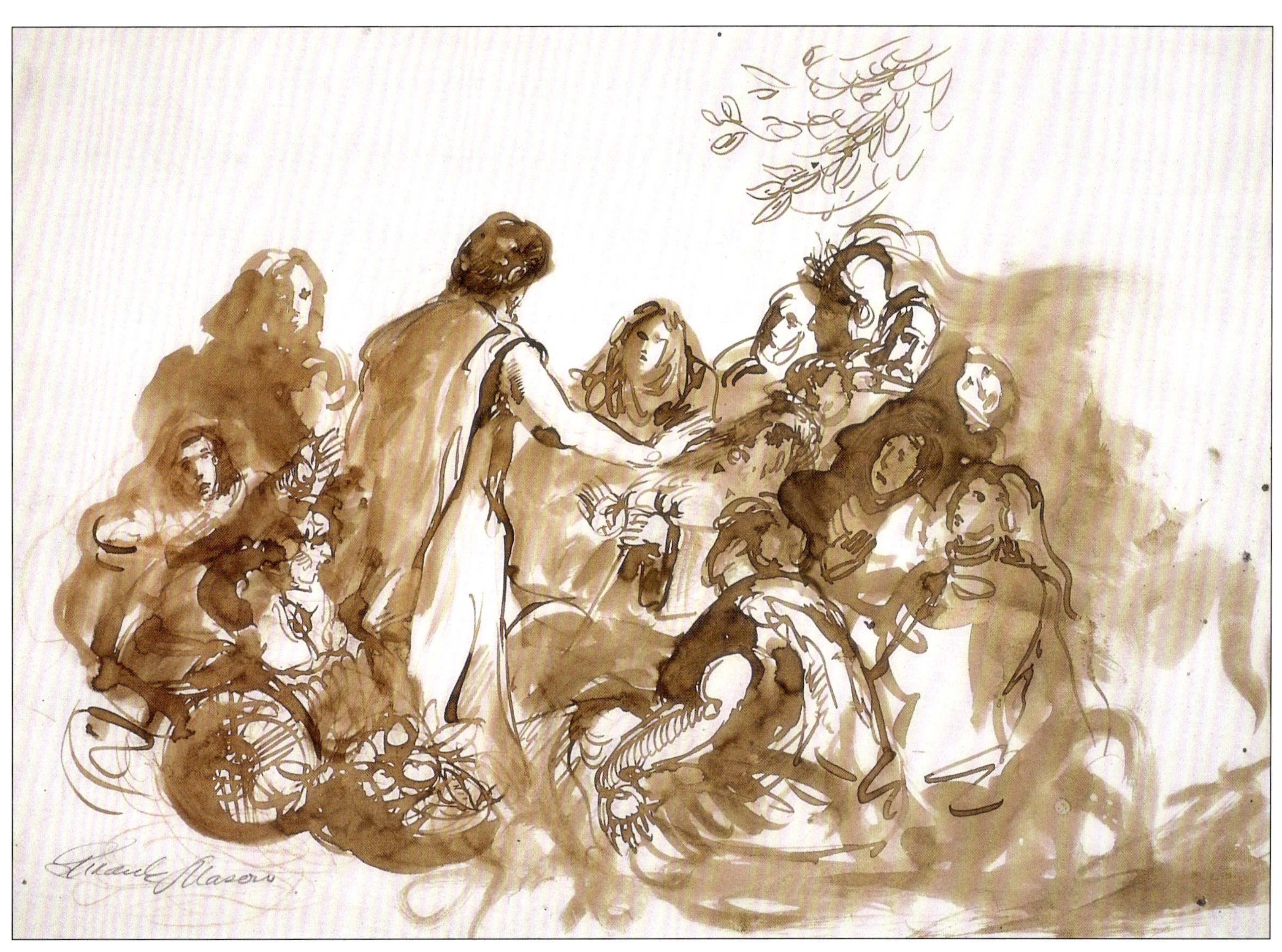

Christ Healing the Sick, 1982
Sepia wash on cream paper
11 x 15 in.

In one of the sketches here Christ is seen in profile, facing the crowd. I considered this composition but then put it aside for another view. It is often difficult to choose between many ideas that I have for a particular subject; there are endless possibilities. My final choice of composition was determined by the purpose of the painting which was to concentrate attention on a miracle in progress. The selected composition allows the central focus of the painting to be on the blind man at the moment when he is first able to see. In this painting the viewer is able to observe the expressions on the faces of the nearby witnesses who are present as the miracle occurs. In order to allow this view the figure of Christ had to be turned away from us to face the blind man who is seen looking up at Him.

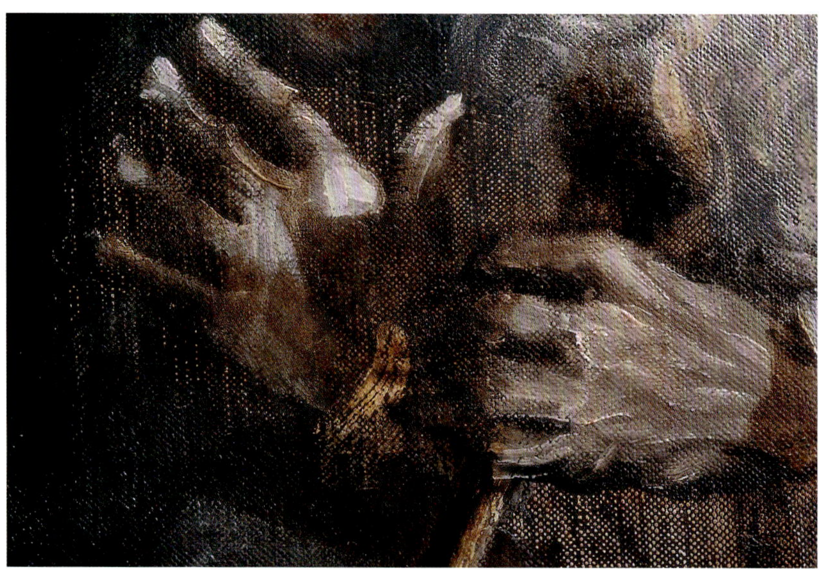

(Detail) *Christ Healing the Sick*

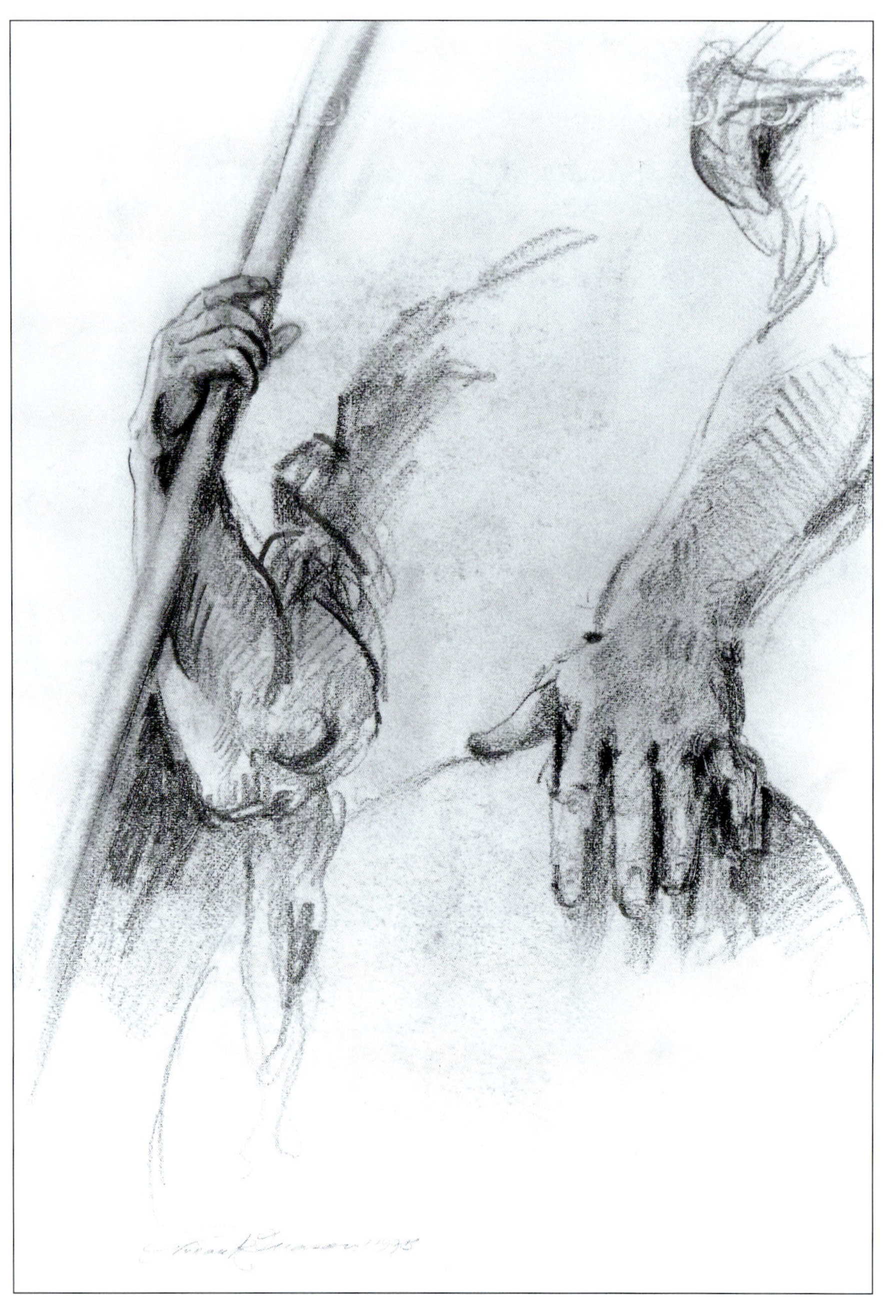

Roman Soldier with Spear, 1995
Graphite on white paper
12 1/2 x 8 3/4 in.

The Leper, 1972
Graphite on white paper
6 1/4 x 4 1/4 in.

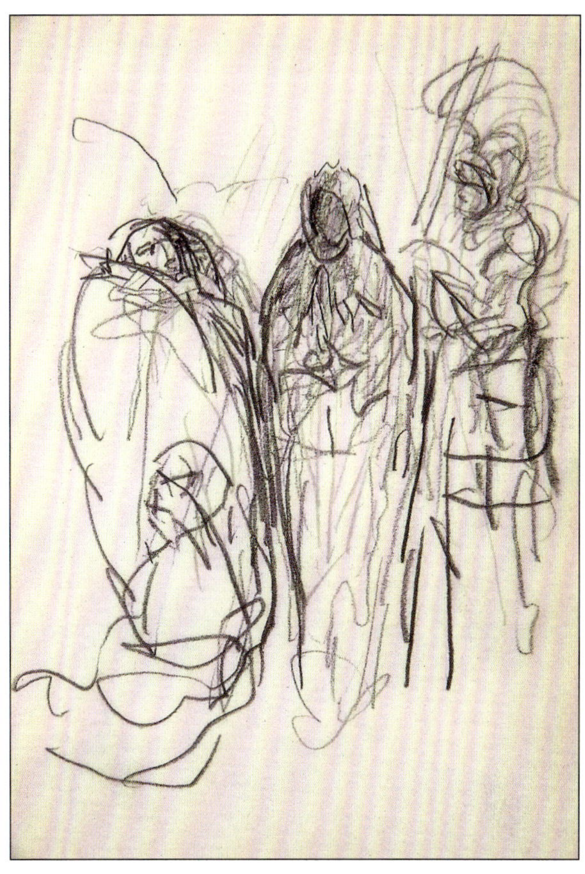

Christ Healing the Sick, 1958
Oil on panel, 16 x 24 in.

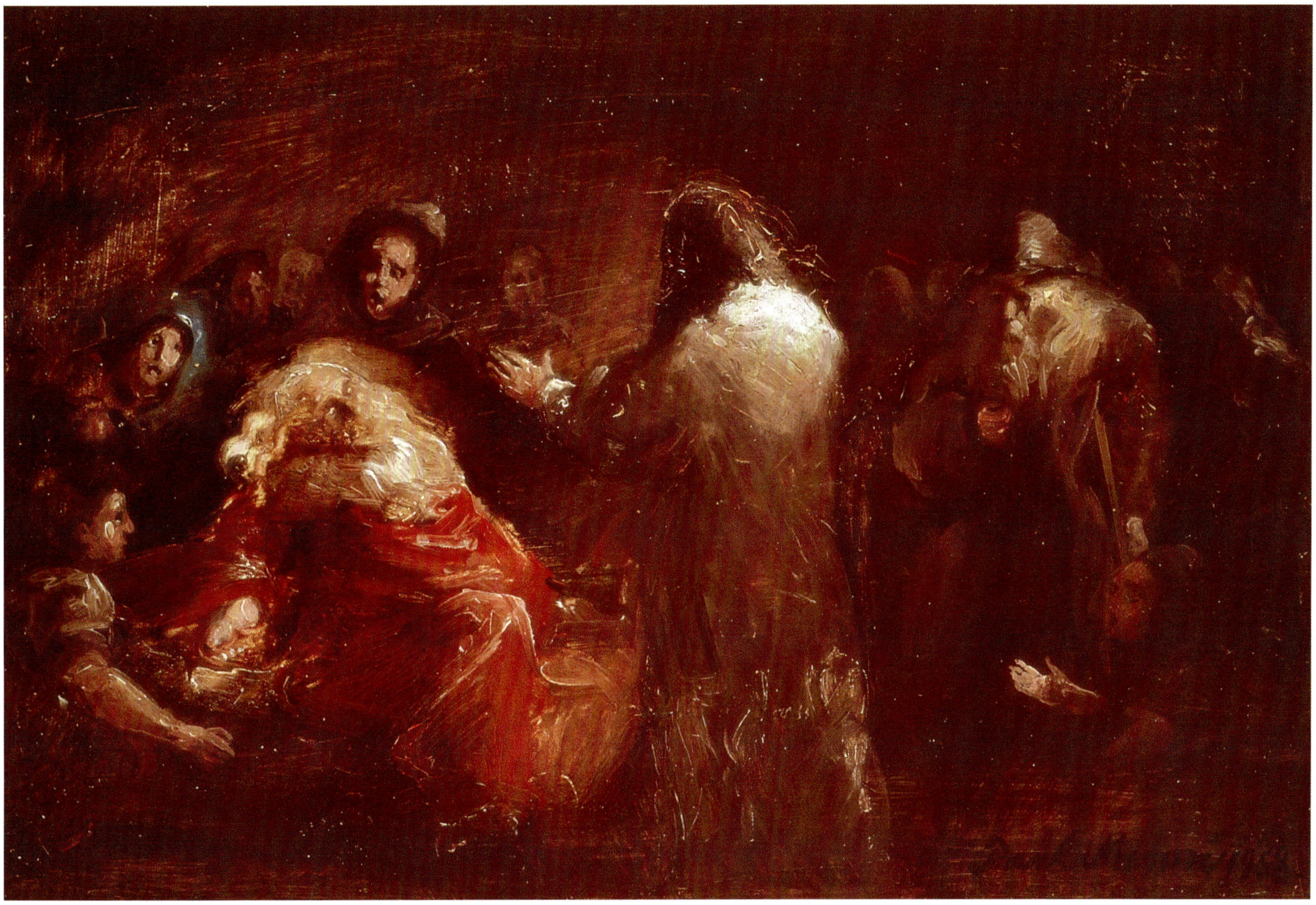

The Raising of Lazarus

Now a certain man was sick, named Lazarus. . . .His sisters sent unto him, saying, Lord, behold, he whom thou lovest is sick. When Jesus heard that, he said, This sickness is not unto death, but for the glory of God, that the Son of God might be glorified thereby. . . .He abode two days still in the same place where he was. . .Then said Jesus unto them plainly, Lazarus is dead. . .When Jesus came, . . . he had lain in the grave four days already. . .Said Martha unto Jesus, Lord, if thou hadst been here, my brother had not died. . . Jesus saith. . .Thy brother shall rise again. . .I am the resurrection, and the life: he that believeth in me, though he were dead, yet shall he live: And whosoever liveth and believeth in me shall never die. . . .Jesus said, Take ye away the stone. . .he cried with a loud voice, Lazareth, come forth. And he that was dead came forth, bound hand and foot with graveclothes. . .Jesus saith unto them, Loose him, and let him go. —John 11: 1, 3, 4, 6, 14, 17, 21, 23, 25, 26, 39, 43, 44

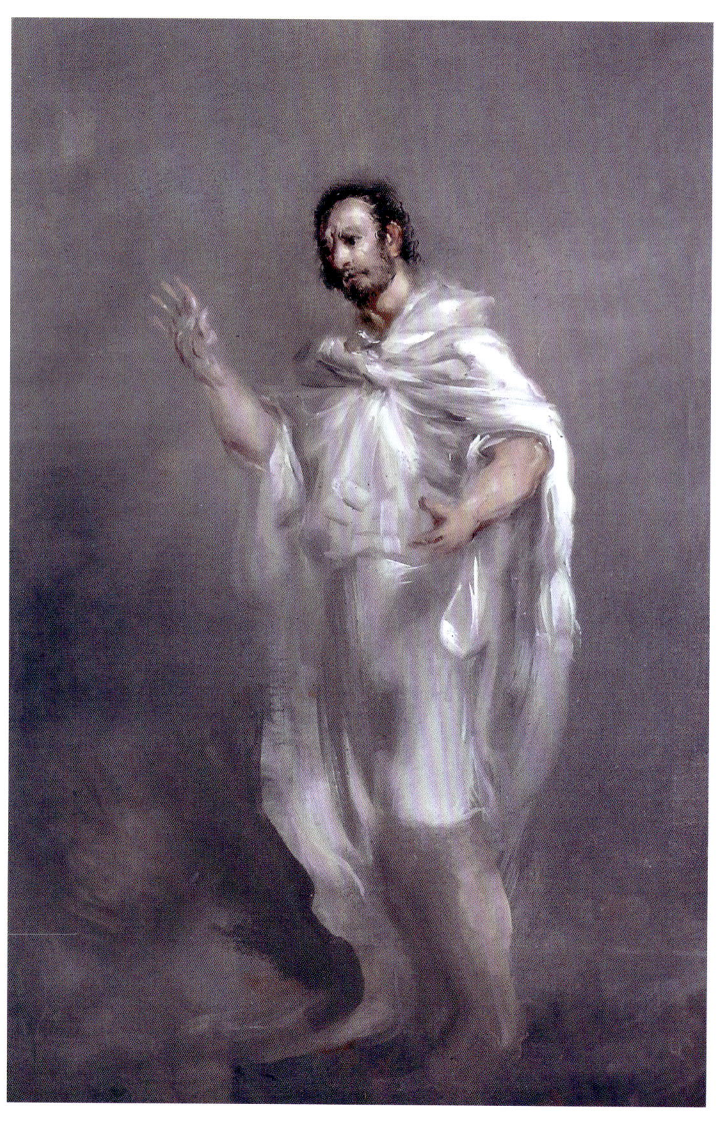

Study for The Raising of Lazarus, 2002, oil on canvas, 36 x 24 in.

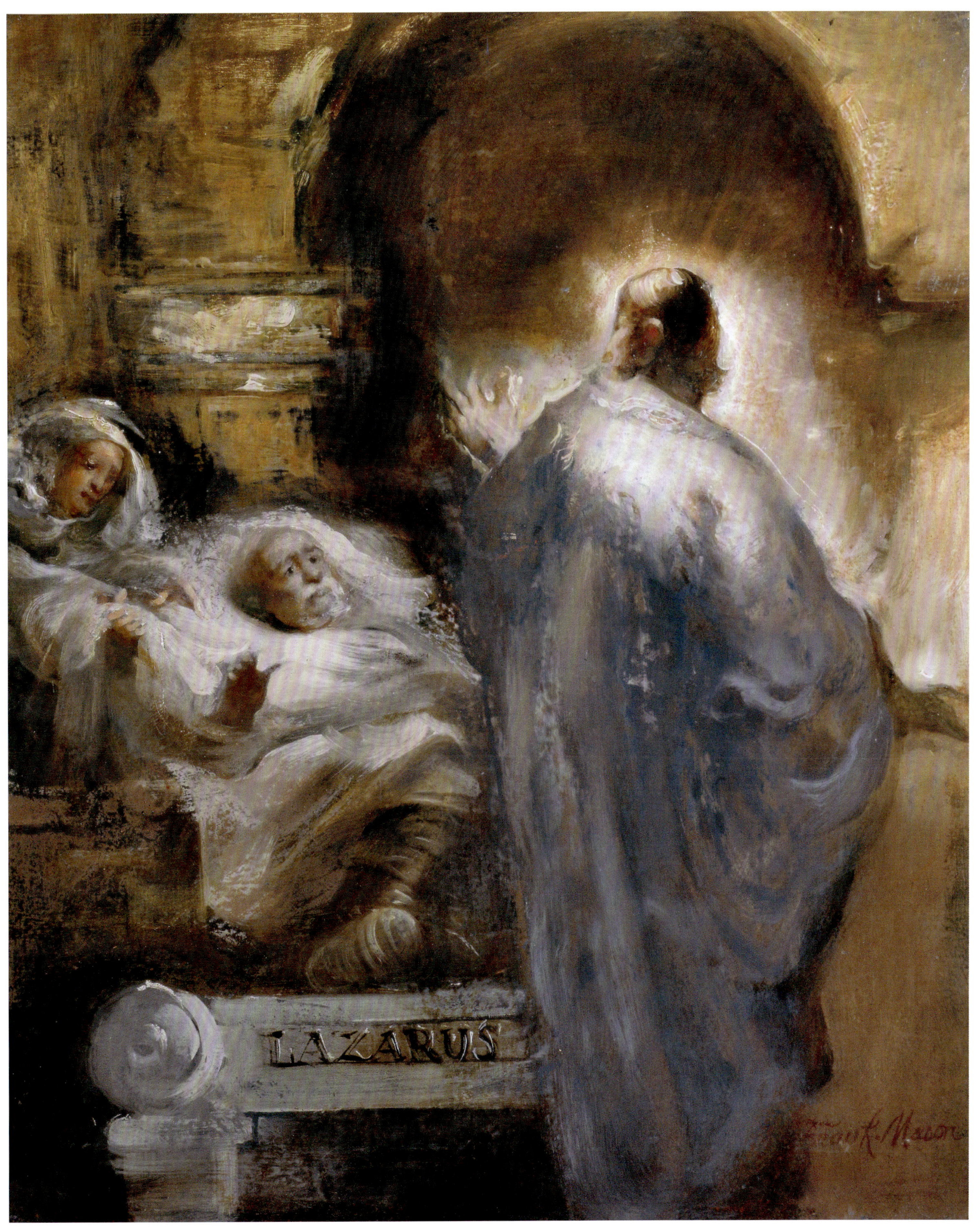

The Raising of Lazarus, 2003, oil on panel, 24 x 20 in.

Before going to Judea in response to the news of the death of Lazarus, Jesus is reminded by the disciples that He is already in danger of being stoned. He is fully aware of the danger. Jesus knows that this miracle will further enrage the Pharisees and confirm their determination to destroy Him. He also knows that this victory over death will be a precursor to His own resurrection. Great artists through history have been moved by the raising of Lazarus—a moment when Christ shows His full power over the living and the dead. When the priests of the Sanhedrin see Lazarus come forth, they are greatly terrified of this power that Jesus has revealed to the people. They fear an uprising that would bring down the fury and might of the Roman empire. The plan is laid forth to arrest Jesus. For these reasons I consider the raising of Lazarus the climactic event leading to the crucifixion of Jesus and to His resurrection from the dead.

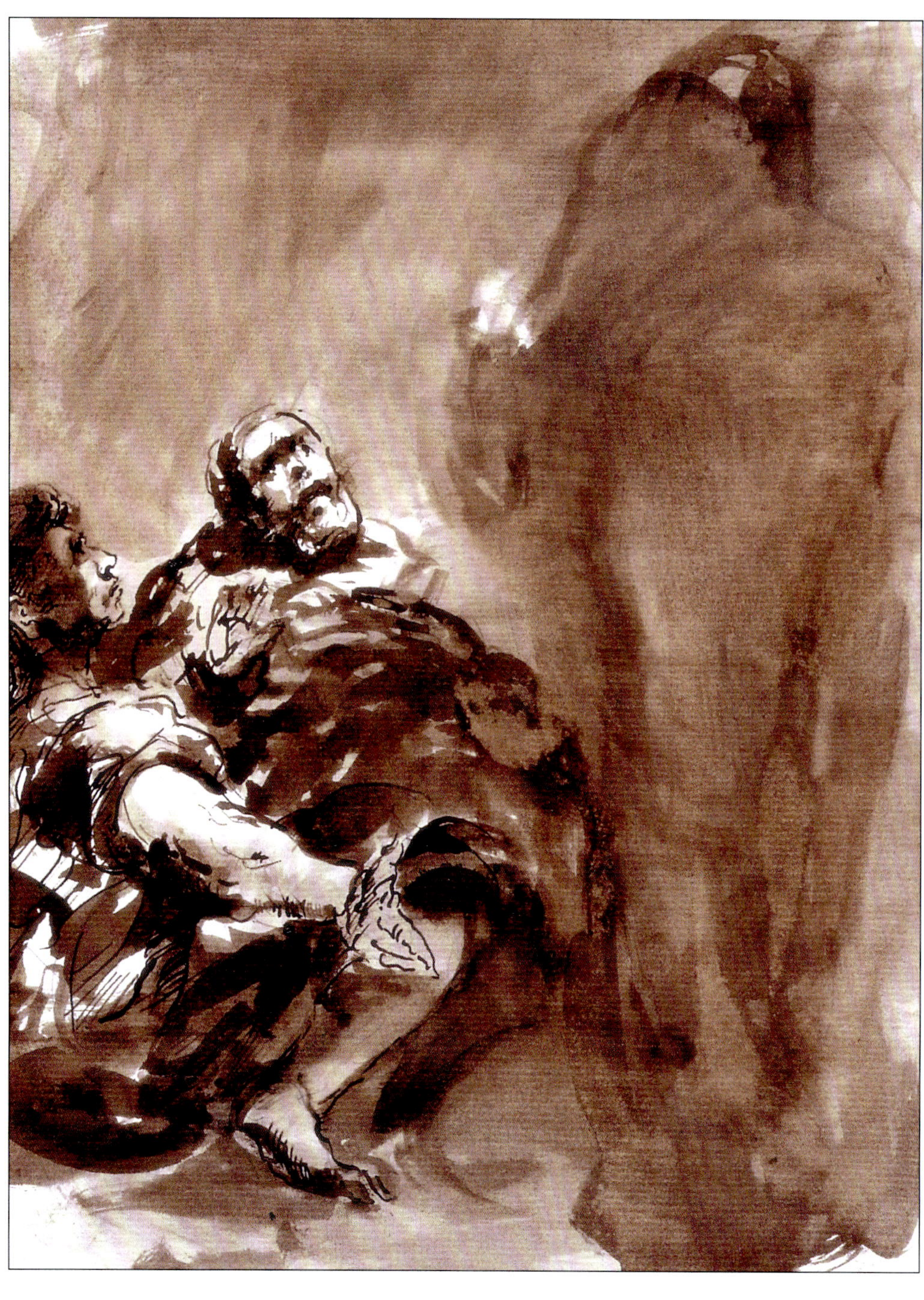

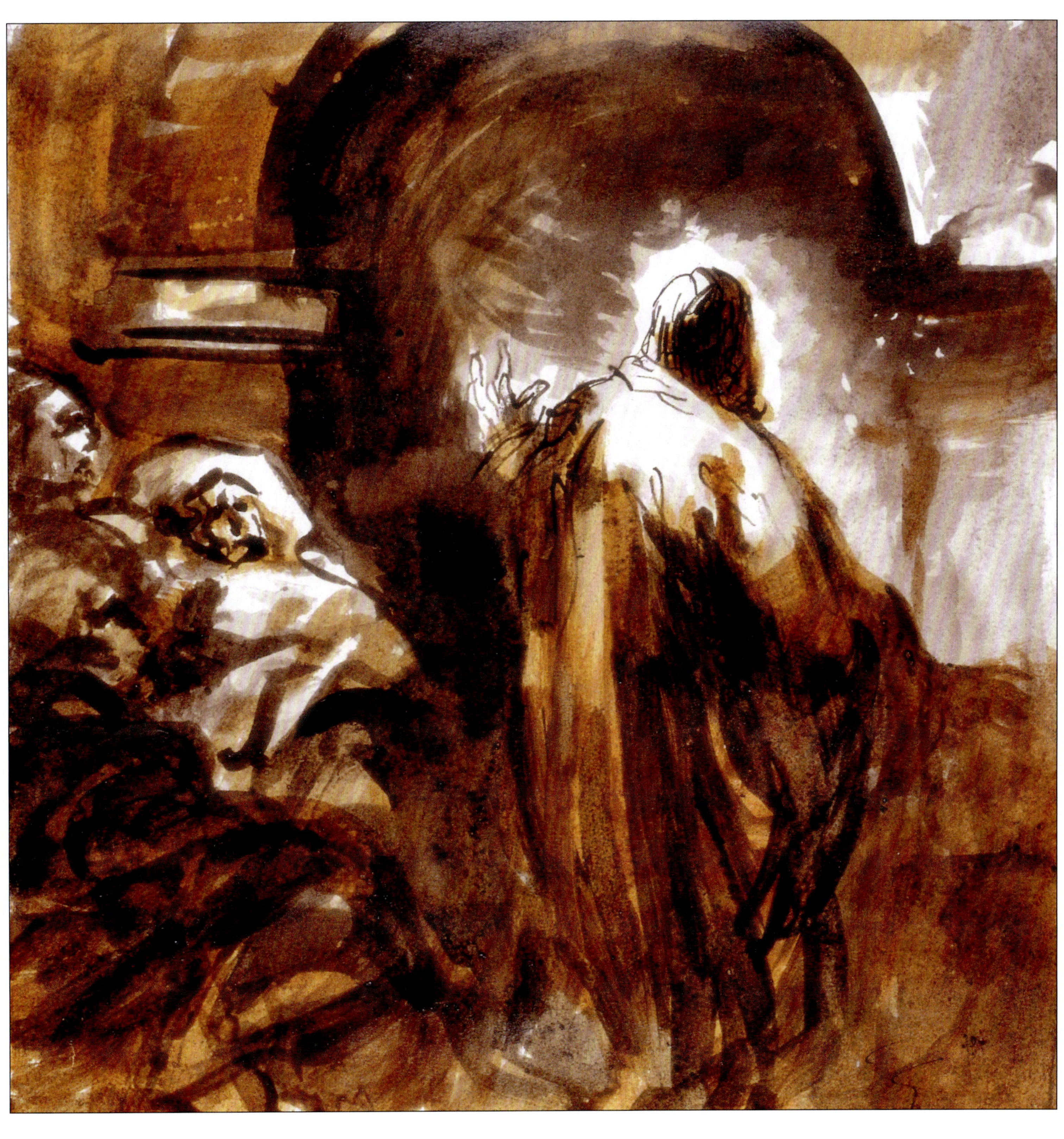

Christ Raising Lazarus, 2002
Pen and brown ink and wash
on white paper, 12 x 9 in.

Christ Raising Lazarus, 2003
Pen and brown ink and wash
on white paper, 13 1/2 x 12 1/2 in.

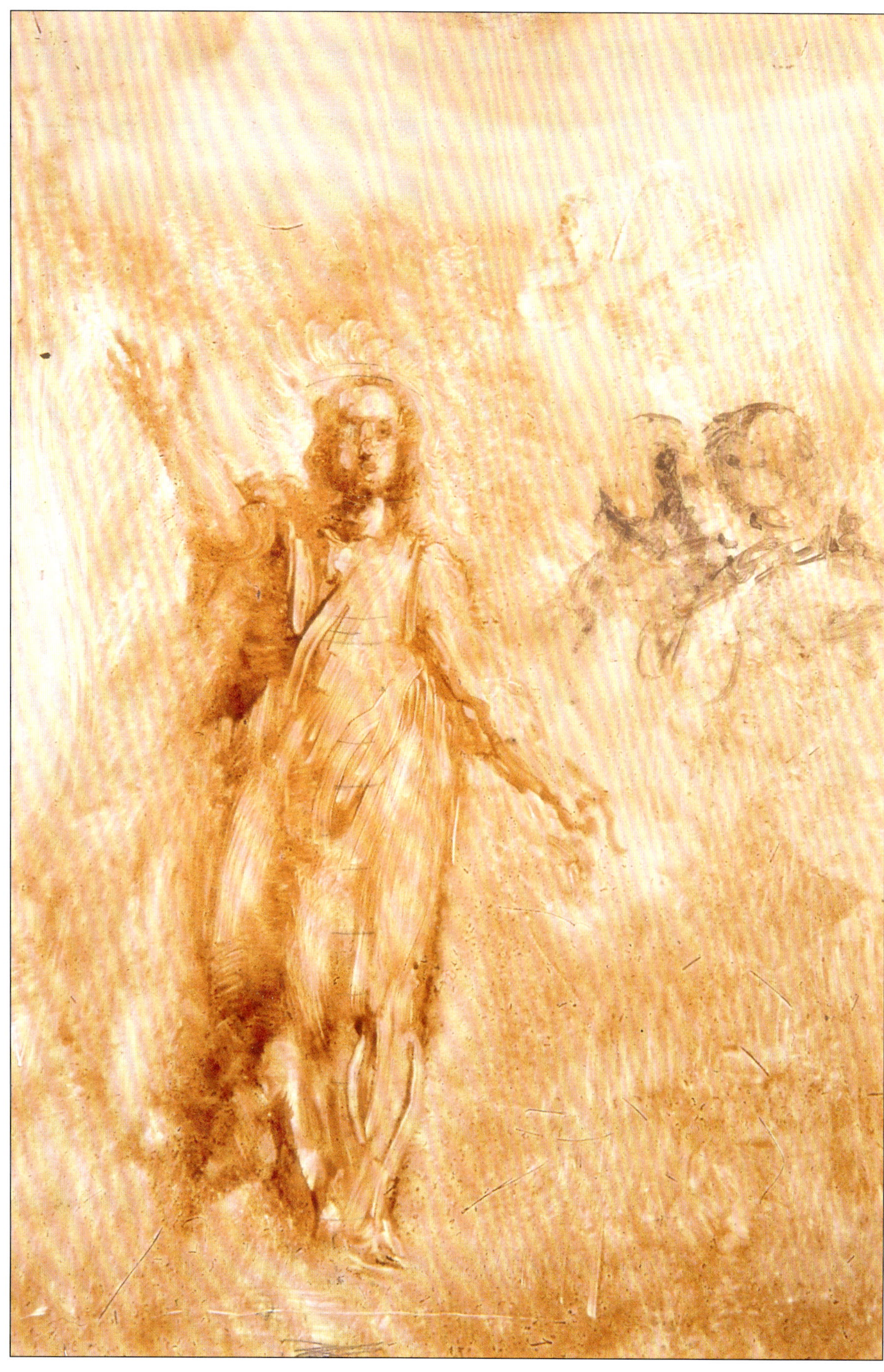

Christ Calling for Lazarus, 1999
Oil on panel, 14 x 10 in

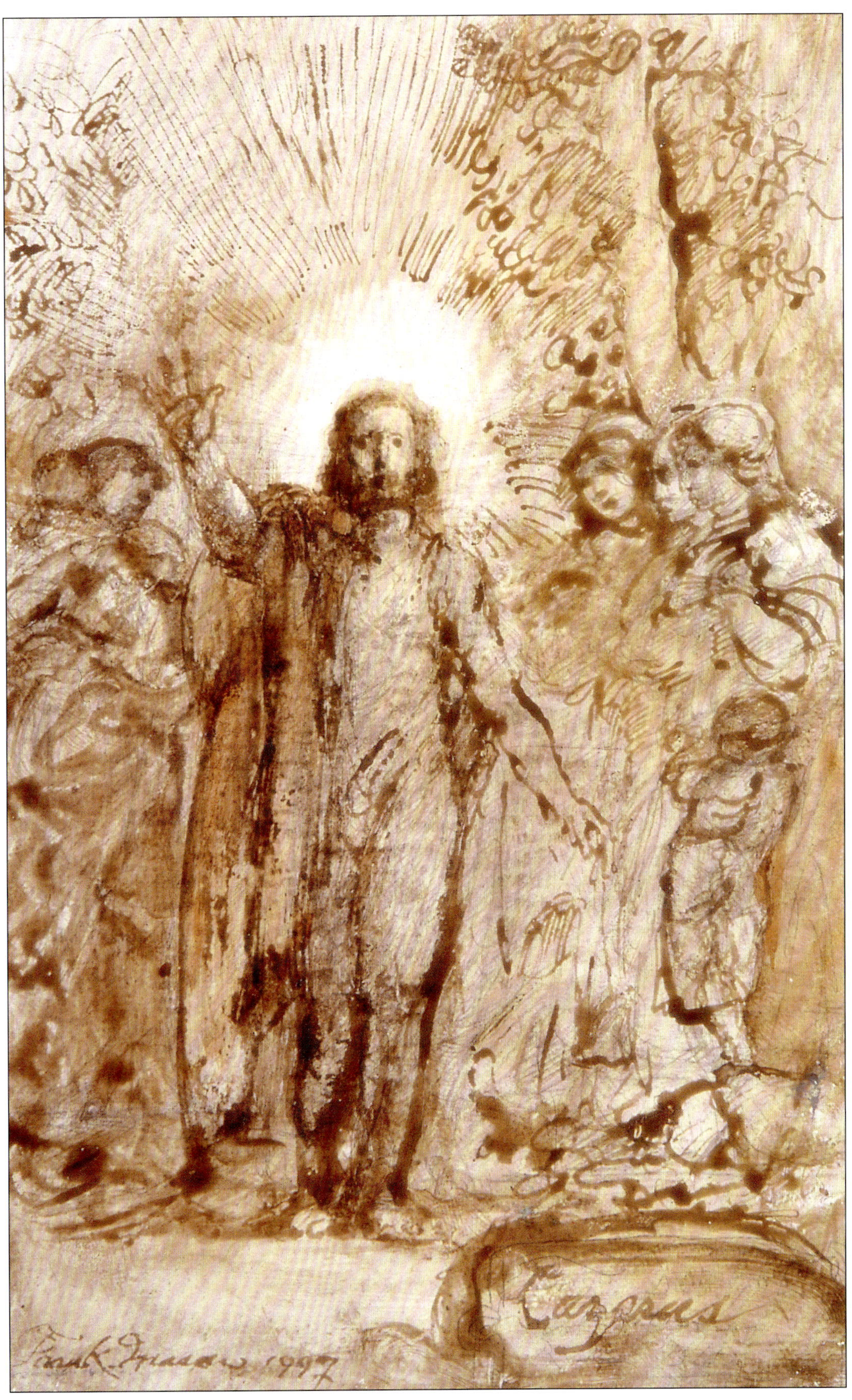

Christ Calling for Lazarus, 1997
Pen and brown ink and wash on panel, 12 x 8 in.

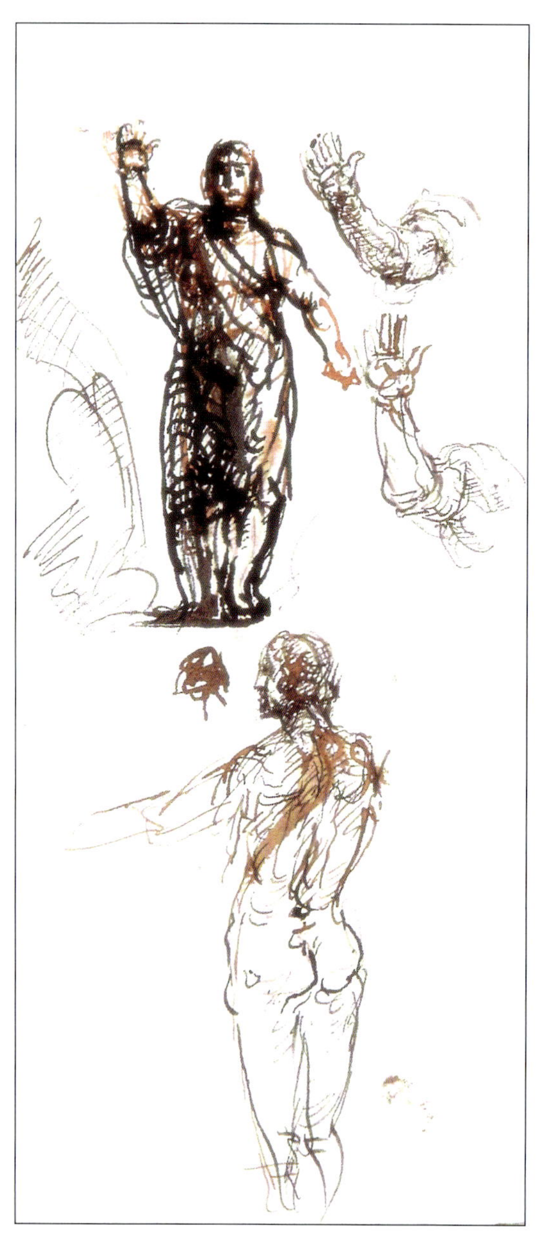

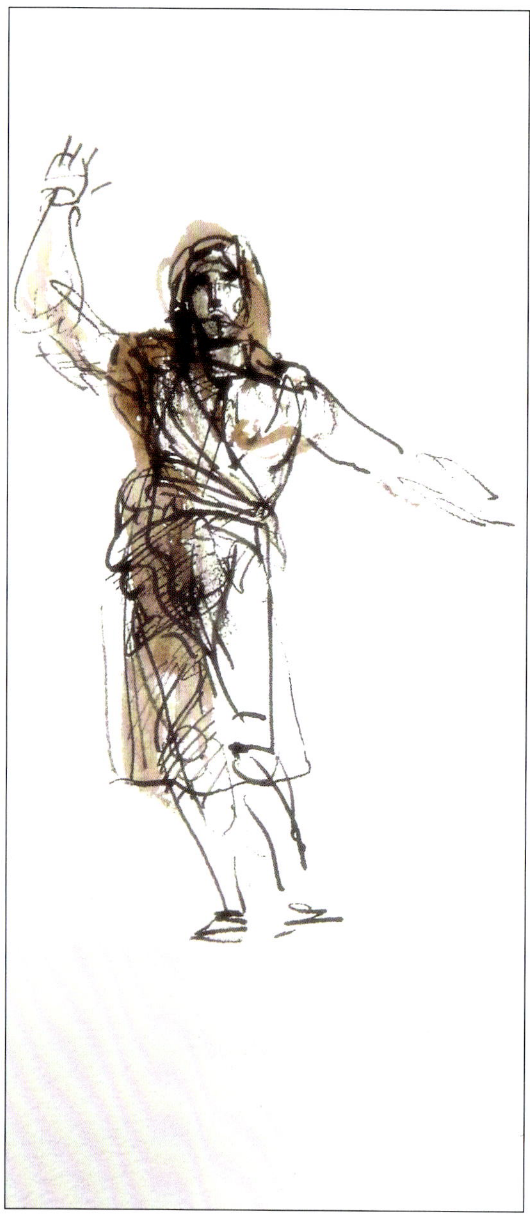

a. *Studies for Christ Raising Lazarus,* 1987, pen and black and red ink on white paper, 11 x 5 in.

b. *Study for Christ,* 1987
Pen and black and brown ink on white paper, 11 x 5 in.

c. *Lazarus, Come Forth—John 11:44,* 1995, red chalk on cream paper 4 x 3 in.

d. *Christ Calling Forth Lazarus,* 1995
Pen and black ink on cream paper, 4 x 3 in.

e. *Christ Raising Lazarus,* 1995
Black chalk and pen and brown ink and wash on white paper 11 7/8 x 9 in.

b.

a.

d.

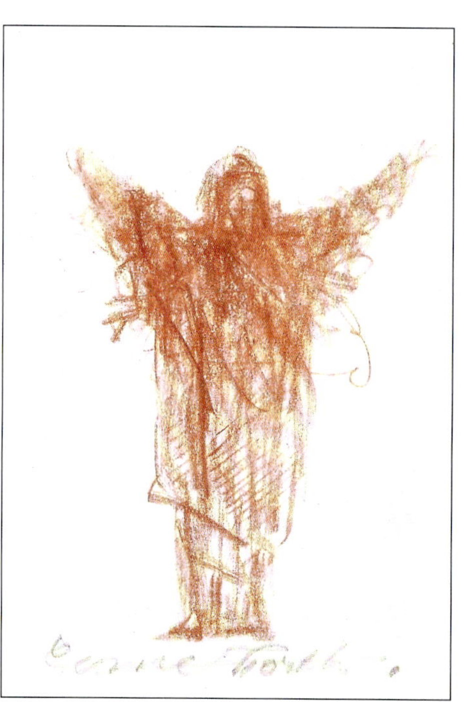

c.

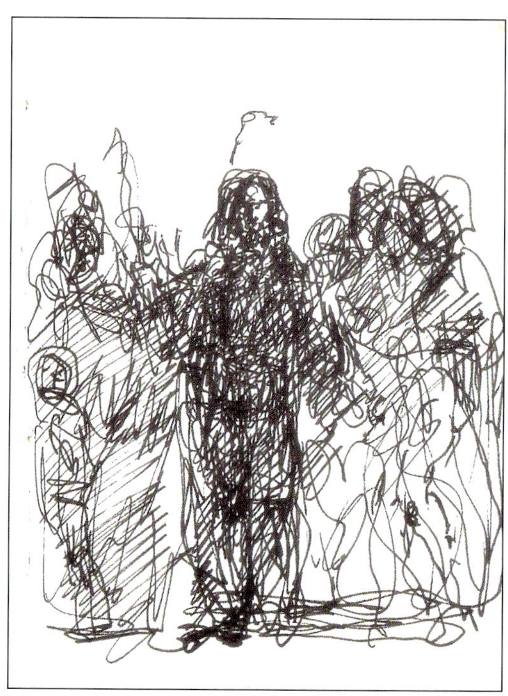

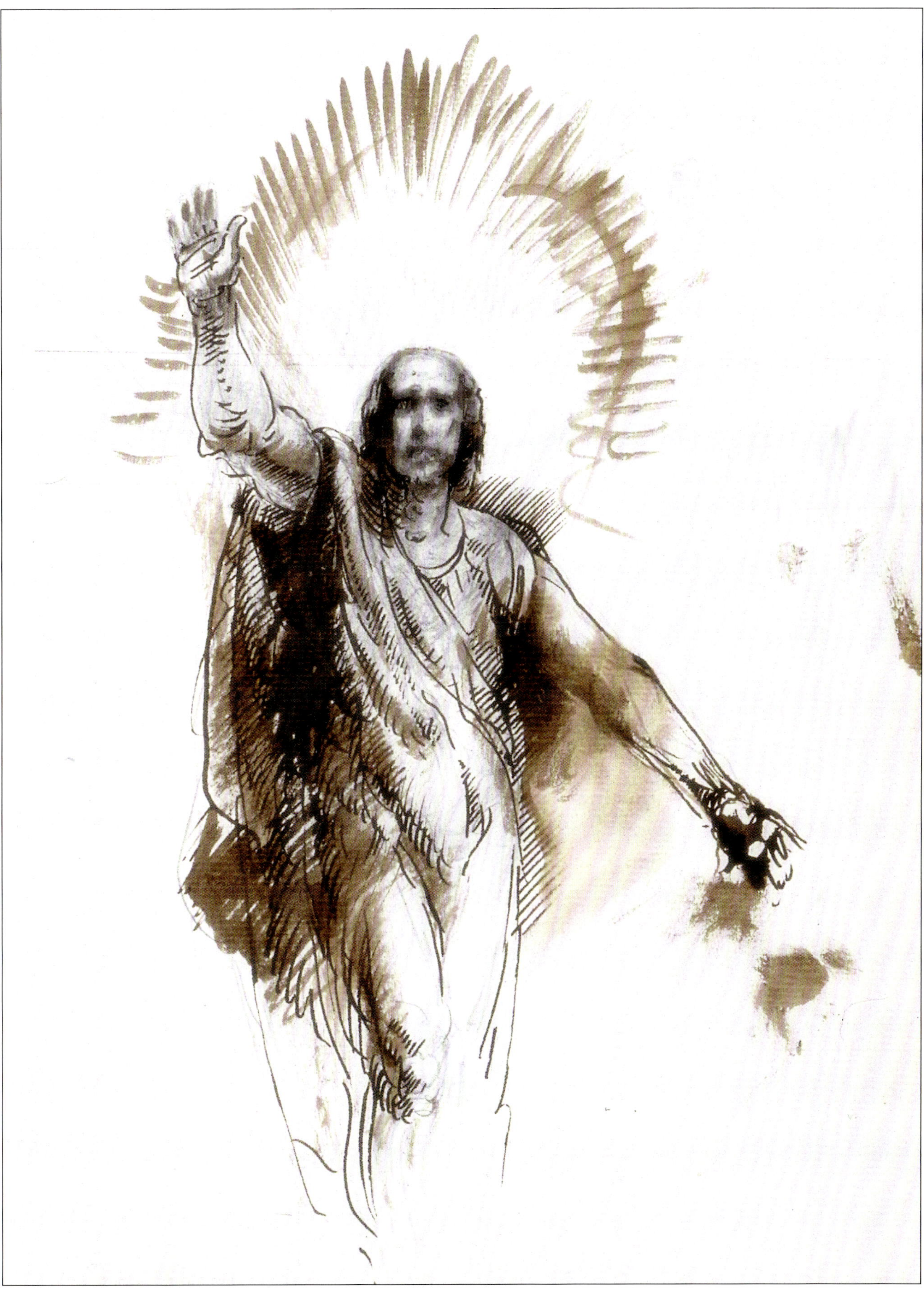

e.

Christ in the Garden of Gethsemane

. . . Jesus . . .went forth with his disciples over the brook Cedron, where was a garden, into the which he entered, and his disciples. . . . Judas then, having received a band of men and officers from the chief priests and Pharisees, cometh thither with lanterns and torches and weapons. Jesus therefore, knowing all things that should come upon him, went forth, and said unto them, Whom seek ye? They answered him, Jesus of Nazareth. Jesus saith unto them, I am he. And Judas also, which betrayed him, stood with them. . . .Then Simon Peter having a sword drew it, and smote the high priest's servant, and cut off his right ear. The servant's name was Malchus. Then said Jesus unto Peter, Put up thy sword into the sheath: the cup which my Father hath given me, shall I not drink it? Then the band and the captain and officers of the Jews took Jesus, and bound him. —John 18: 1, 3–5, 10–12

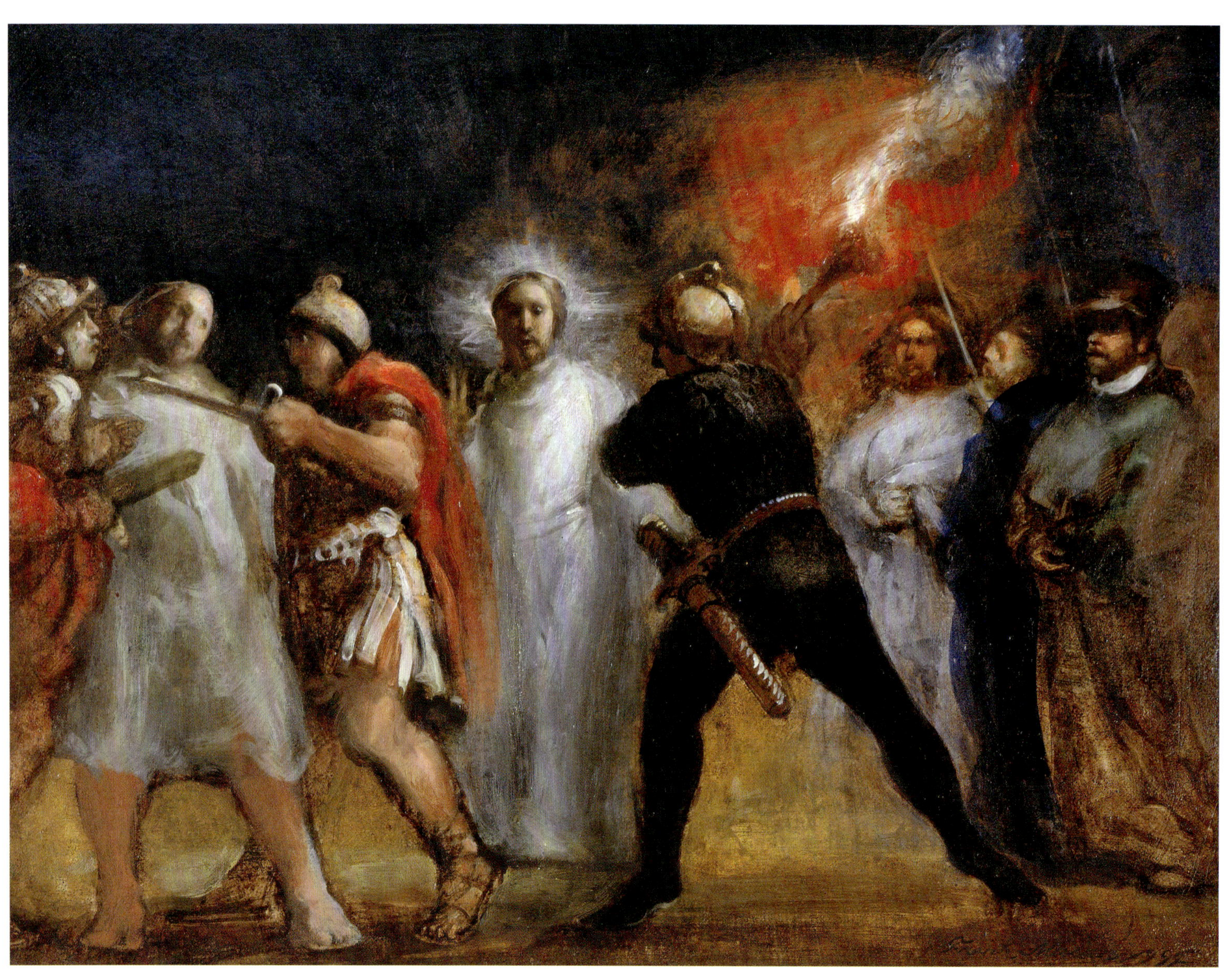

Christ in the Garden of Gethsemene, 1992
Oil on canvas, 18 x 24 in.

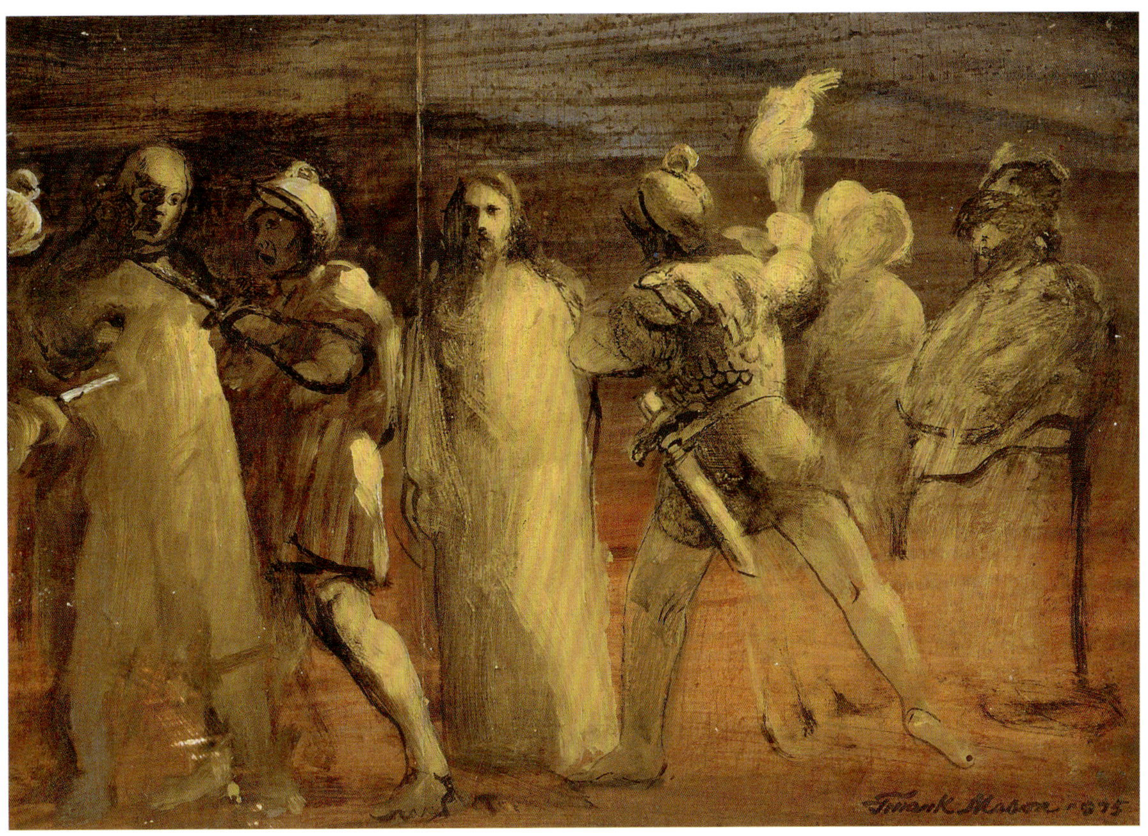

Garden of Gethsemene, 1975
Oil on panel, 8 x 11 in.

This story comprises one of the great moments of Christianity—the evening when Christ is betrayed by Judas in the Garden of Gethsemane and taken prisoner by the Temple guards. Knowing what is in store for Him, He has asked His followers to stay awake with Him and pray. Devoted as they are, they have fallen asleep not once but three times. So much for the human frailty of all of us. I wanted to capture the dramatic moment of exposure when the Temple guards burst into the dark, quiet garden with swords drawn and torches blazing. All the disciples except Peter fall back before the clangorous onslaught. But Peter—rash, impulsive Peter—springs to the defense of his Lord. In a spontaneous act of courage, he slashes off the ear of one Malchus, a servant of the high priest. The guardsmen are ready to cut Peter's throat in reprisal until Jesus orders him to put up his sword. In chapter 22, verse 51, of the Gospel of St. Luke we learn that Jesus touched the ear of this servant and healed him. The healing at even this moment of extreme duress is a dramatic demonstration to His disciples and to us that Jesus was able to forgive His enemies. Peter's courage does not sustain him for long. When the other disciples flee, he too abandons Christ.

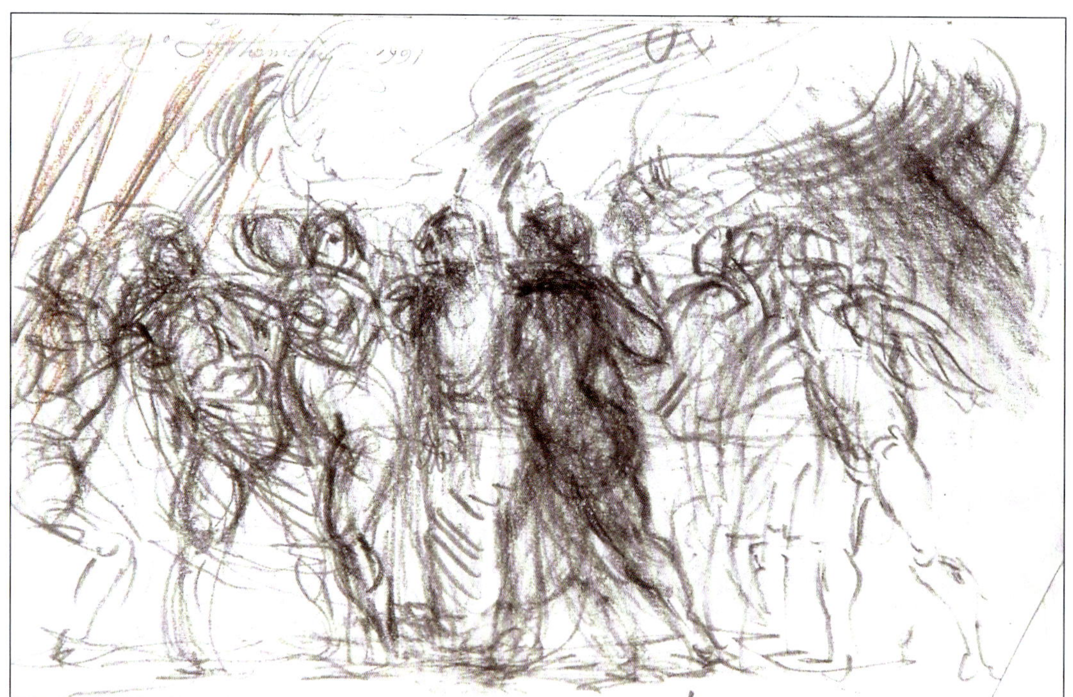

a.

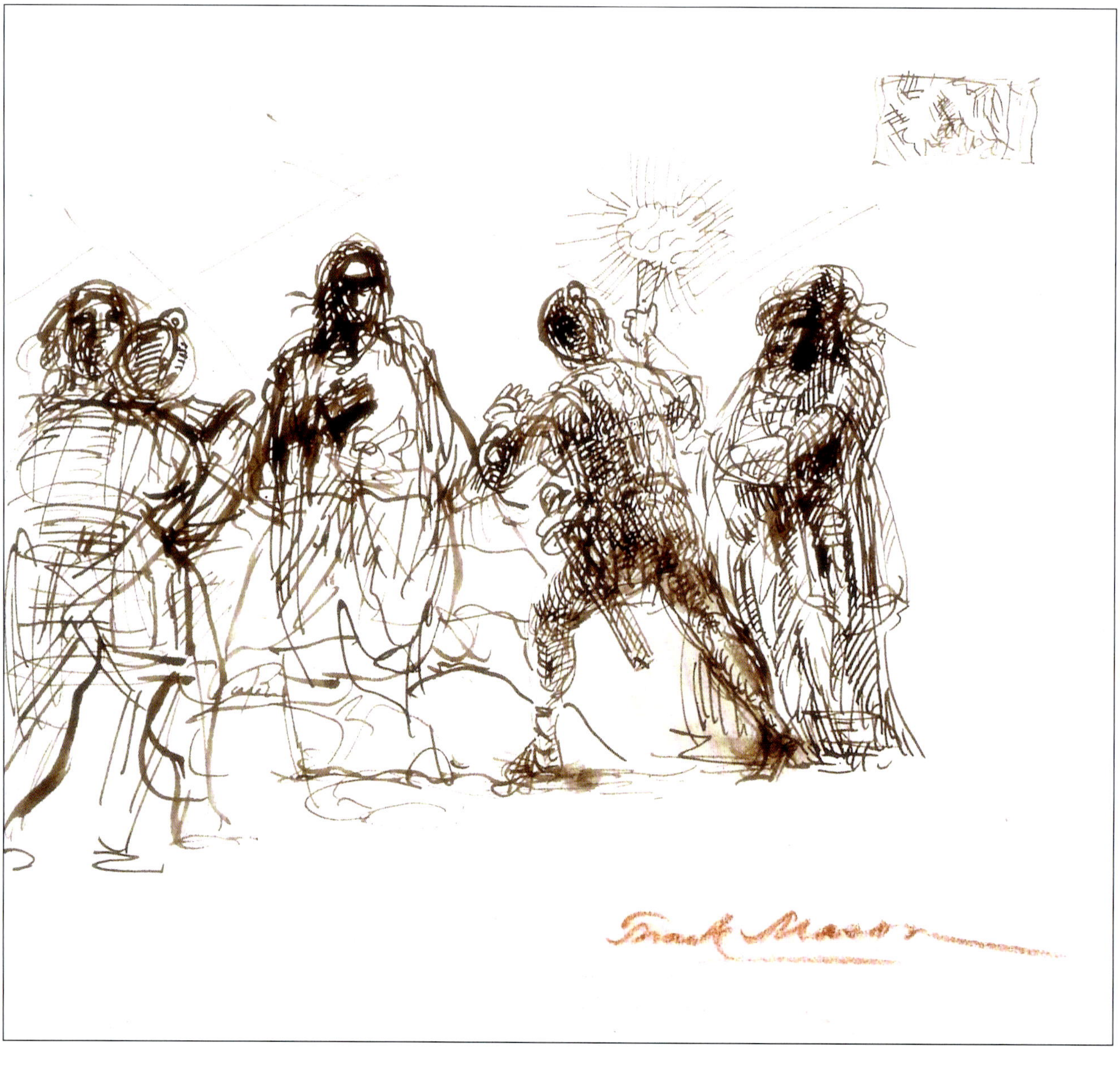

b.

c.

a. *Put Up Thy Sword into the Sheath,* 1991
Black and red chalk on white paper
5 x 7 1/2 in.

b. *The Taking of Christ in the Garden of Gethesemene,* 1975
Red chalk and pen and brown ink on cream paper
10 x 11 in.

c. *Head of Christ,* 1992
Black chalk on cream paper
9 3/8 x 7 in.

PETER'S DENIAL

THEN TOOK THEY HIM, AND LED HIM, AND BROUGHT HIM INTO THE HIGH PRIEST'S HOUSE. AND PETER FOLLOWED AFAR OFF. AND WHEN THEY HAD KINDLED A FIRE IN THE MIDST OF THE HALL, AND WERE SET DOWN TOGETHER, PETER SAT DOWN AMONG THEM. BUT A CERTAIN MAID BEHELD HIM AS HE SAT BY THE FIRE, AND EARNESTLY LOOKED UPON HIM, AND SAID, THIS MAN WAS ALSO WITH HIM. AND HE DENIED HIM, SAYING, WOMAN, I KNOW HIM NOT. AND AFTER A LITTLE WHILE ANOTHER SAW HIM, AND SAID, THOU ART ALSO OF THEM. AND PETER SAID, MAN, I AM NOT. AND ABOUT THE SPACE OF ONE HOUR AFTER ANOTHER CONFIDENTLY AFFIRMED, SAYING, OF A TRUTH THIS FELLOW ALSO WAS WITH HIM; FOR HE IS A GALILAEAN. AND PETER SAID, MAN, I KNOW NOT WHAT THOU SAYEST. AND IMMEDIATELY, WHILE HE YET SPAKE, THE COCK CREW. AND THE LORD TURNED, AND LOOKED UPON PETER. AND PETER REMEMBERED THE WORD OF THE LORD, HOW HE HAD SAID UNTO HIM, BEFORE THE COCK CROW, THOU SHALT DENY ME THRICE. AND PETER WENT OUT AND WEPT BITTERLY.
—LUKE 22: 54–62

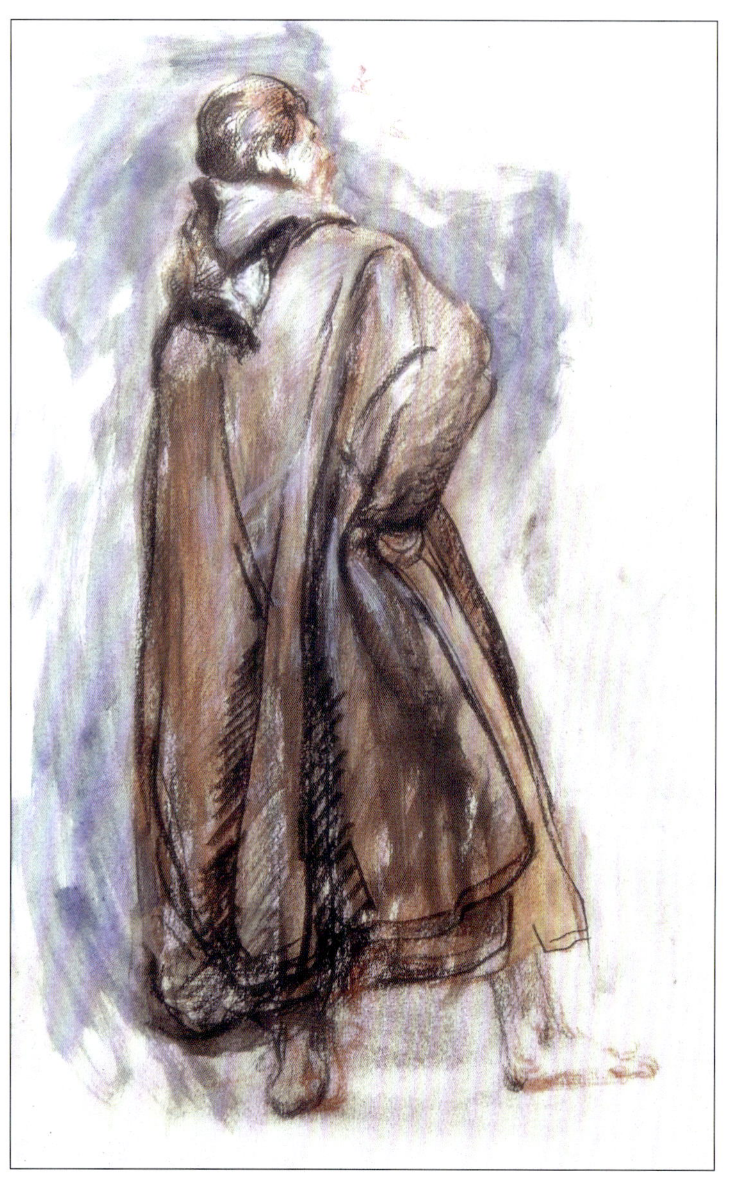

Back View of a Priest, 1984
Black, red, and white chalk and blue watercolor on white paper
14 1/2 x 12 in.

Peter's Denial, 1984
Oil on panel
24 x 30 in.

Having followed Jesus and his captors, Peter joins the group around the fire. A serving maid recognizes him as one of Christ's disciples. Here we see Peter shrinking back against a pillar as if trying to hide. Peter denies all knowledge of Jesus three times in the course of the evening, just as Jesus had predicted. When the cock crows, Peter realizes what he has done and weeps bitterly. In this act of contrition for his own weakness, Peter recognizes his human fallibility and takes the first step toward fulfilling his potential as a human being. Only in this way can he become the man he is destined to be: the rock on which Christ will build His church.

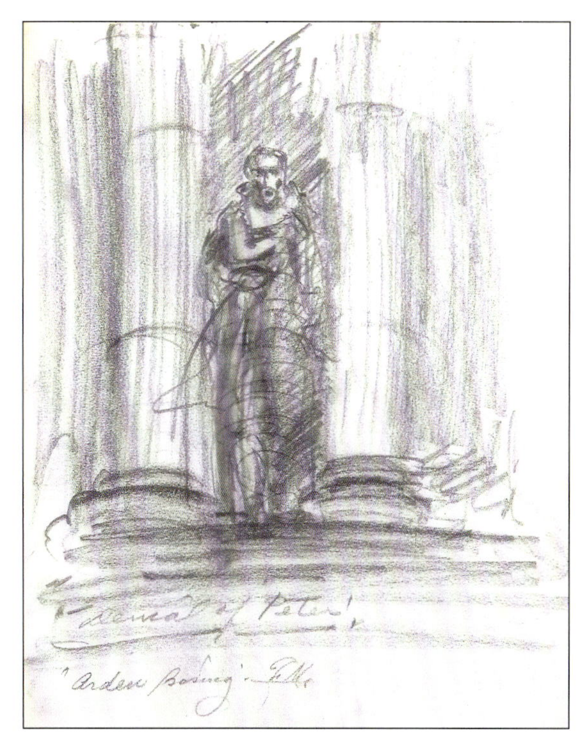

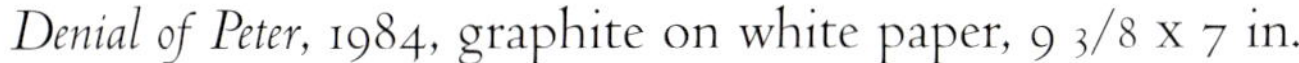

Denial of Peter, 1984, graphite on white paper, 9 3/8 x 7 in.

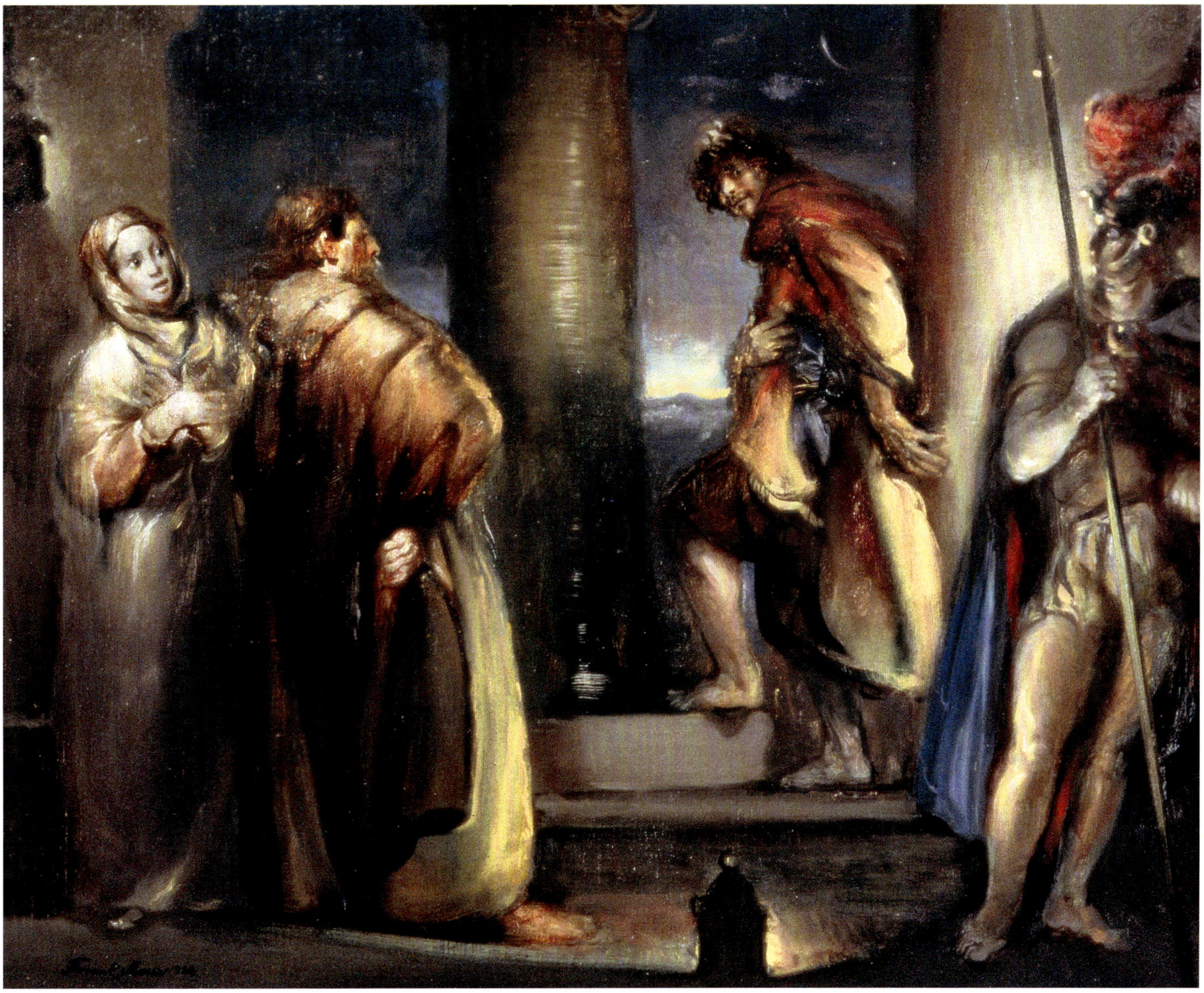

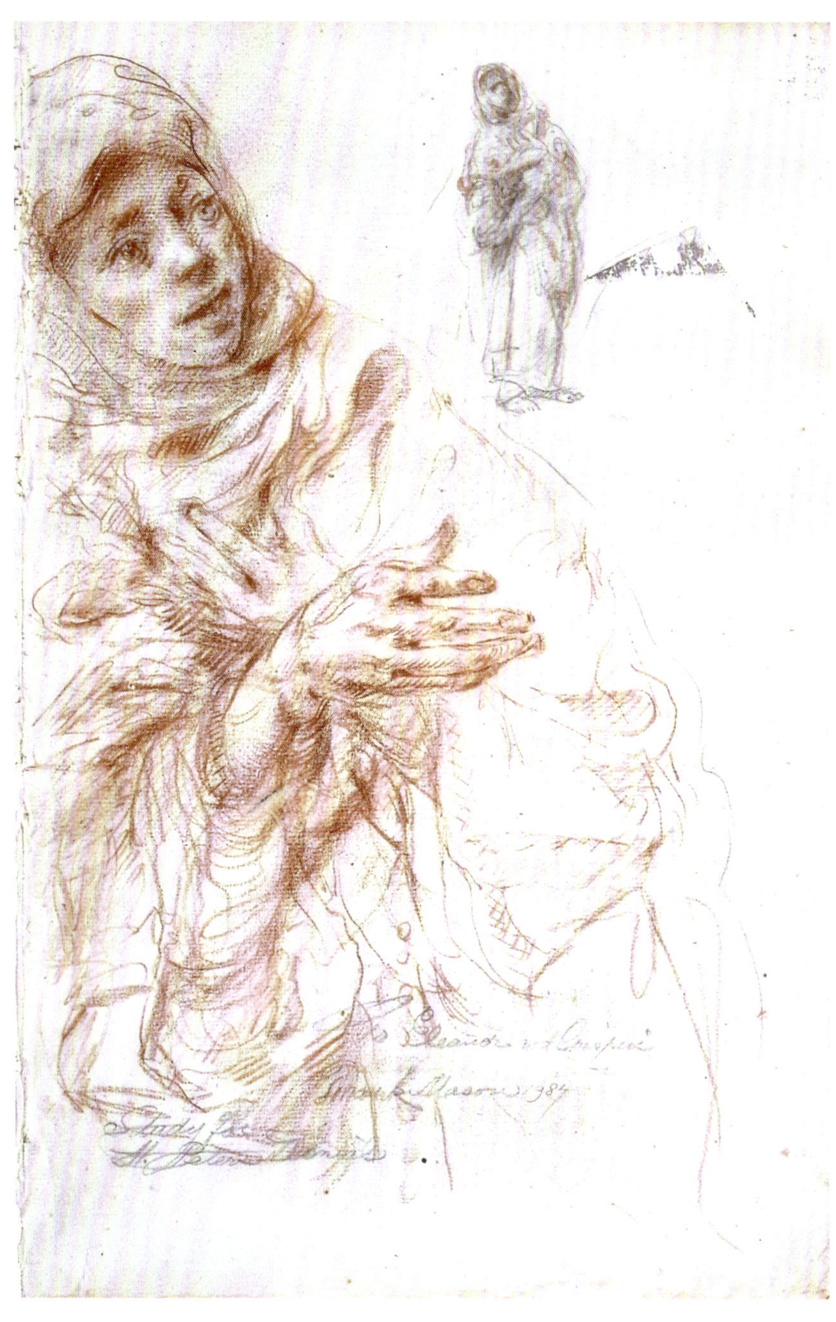

Study for Witness, Peter's Denial, 1984
Red chalk and graphite on white paper
12 1/2 x 8 1/2 in.

Witness, Peter's Denial, 1985
Oil on canvas, 24 x 16 in.

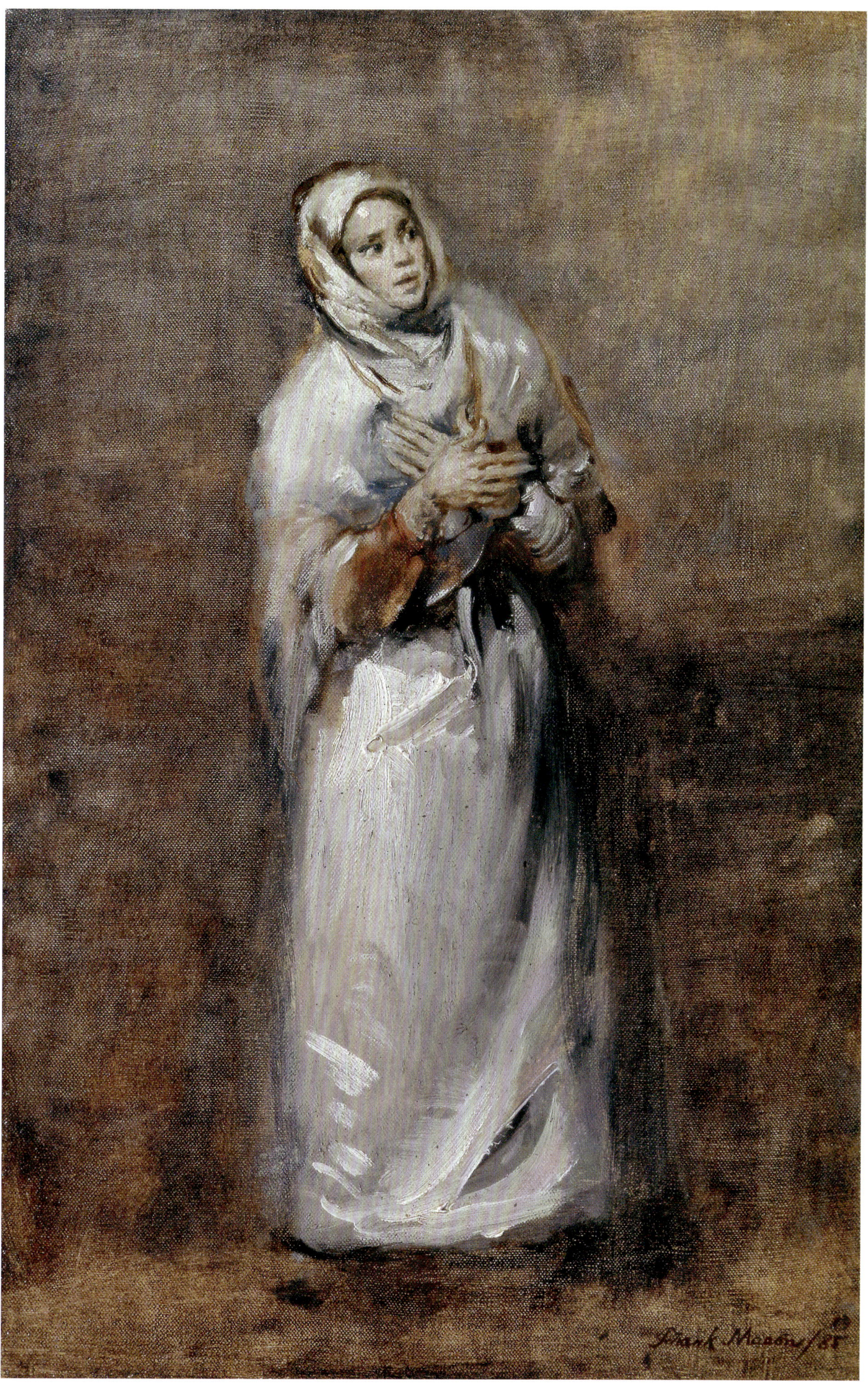
Frank Mason /85

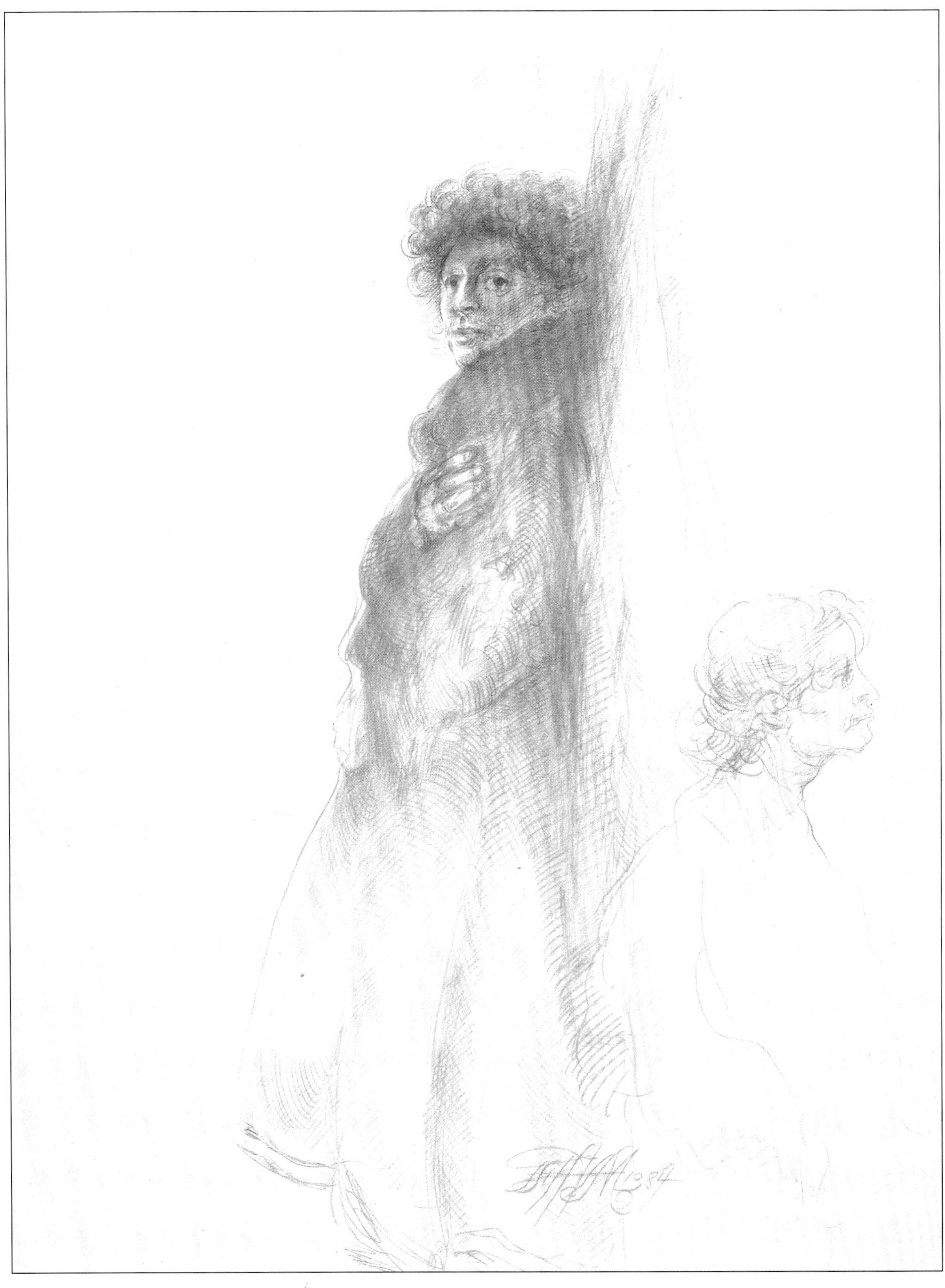

Arden as Peter and Head of Witness, 1984
Silverpoint on white paper, 12 x 9 1/2 in.

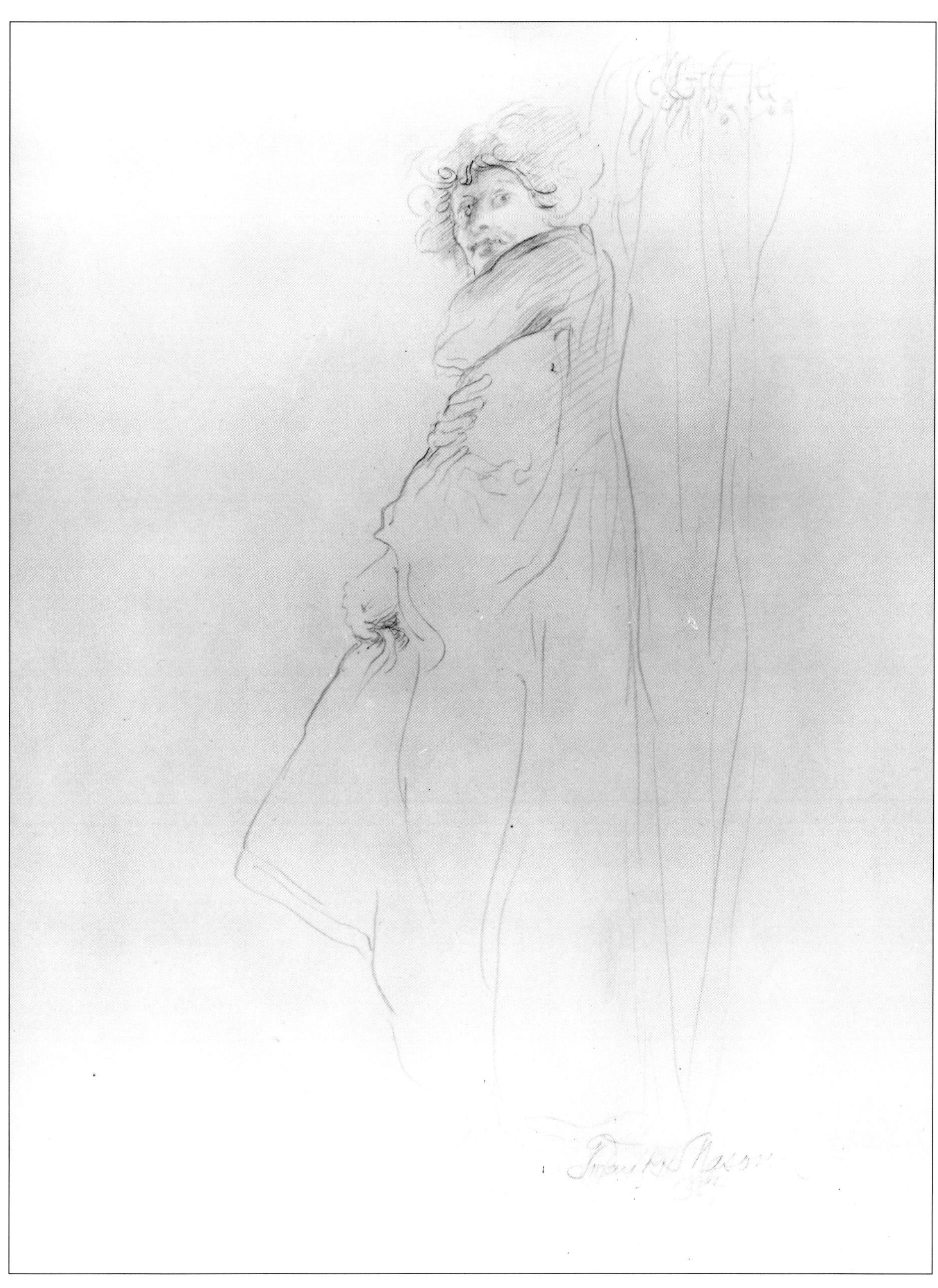

Arden as Peter, 1984
Silverpoint on white paper
12 x 9 1/2 in.

Christ Before Pilate

AND THE WHOLE MULTITUDE OF THEM AROSE, AND LED HIM UNTO PILATE. AND THEY BEGAN TO ACCUSE HIM, SAYING, WE FOUND THIS FELLOW PERVERTING THE NATION, AND FORBIDDING TO GIVE TRIBUTE TO CAESAR, SAYING THAT HE HIMSELF IS CHRIST A KING. AND PILATE ASKED HIM, SAYING, ART THOU THE KING OF THE JEWS? AND HE ANSWERED HIM AND SAID, THOU SAYEST IT. THEN SAID PILATE TO THE CHIEF PRIESTS AND TO THE PEOPLE, I FIND NO FAULT IN THIS MAN. AND THEY WERE THE MORE FIERCE, SAYING, HE STIRRETH UP THE PEOPLE, TEACHING THROUGHOUT ALL JEWRY, BEGINNING FROM GALILEE TO THIS PLACE. . . .PILATE THEREFORE, WILLING TO RELEASE JESUS, SPAKE AGAIN TO THEM. BUT THEY CRIED, SAYING, CRUCIFY HIM, CRUCIFY HIM. . . .AND PILATE GAVE SENTENCE THAT IT SHOULD BE AS THEY REQUIRED. –LUKE 23: 1–5, 20, 21, 24

Pilate is usually depicted as a commanding personage, sitting on a throne-like chair and fixing a steely eye on the accused person who has been brought before him. All eyes in the courtroom are on him. He is the governor! But what about the man himself? What is he like? Here he is—a highly placed civil servant somewhat reluctantly doing his duty as governor of a province he doesn't much like. The hot climate doesn't agree with him. His wife misses the busy social life of Rome. He doesn't understand the contentious people of Jerusalem. To make matters worse, the intransigent Pharisees have forced him into a dilemma. He wants to do the right thing and be fair to the accused person, Jesus. But the Pharisees are out for blood. When Pilate says mildly that he finds no fault with Jesus, the Pharisees become even more angry. Pilate can't risk an uproar in Jerusalem that will be heard in Rome to his discredit. He is a man in a tough position, and he gives in. Perhaps that's why I painted the reverse of the usual scene. Seated in a simple chair, Pilate is looking up at the accused. I have denuded him of all his Roman pomp and panoply. He even has a bald spot, that common denominator of male middle age. I've always felt a little sorry for him.

Christ Before Pilate, 1992
Oil on panel, 24 x 20 in.

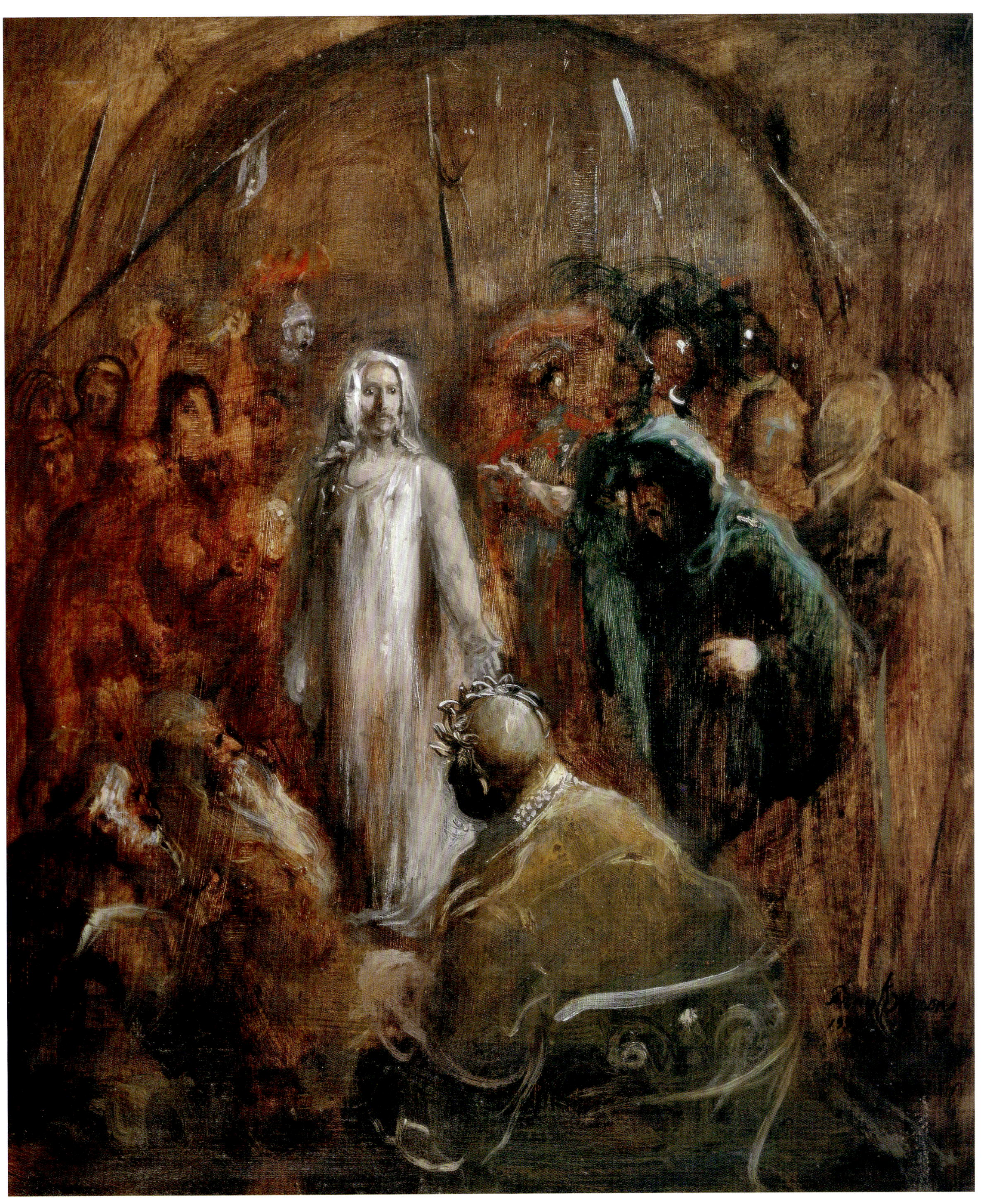

The Crucifixion

THEN DELIVERED HE HIM THEREFORE UNTO THEM TO BE CRUCIFIED. AND THEY TOOK JESUS, AND LED HIM AWAY. AND HE BEARING HIS CROSS WENT FORTH INTO A PLACE CALLED THE PLACE OF A SKULL, WHICH IS CALLED IN THE HEBREW GOLGOTHA. . . .WHEN JESUS THEREFORE SAW HIS MOTHER, AND THE DISCIPLE STANDING BY, WHOM HE LOVED, HE SAITH UNTO HIS MOTHER, WOMAN, BEHOLD THY SON! THEN SAITH HE TO THE DISCIPLE, BEHOLD THY MOTHER! AND FROM THAT HOUR THAT DISCIPLE TOOK HER UNTO HIS OWN HOME. . . .AND WHEN THEY HAD CRUCIFIED HIM, THEY PARTED HIS GARMENTS, CASTING LOTS UPON THEM, WHAT EVERY MAN SHOULD TAKE. AND IT WAS THE THIRD HOUR. . . .
—JOHN 19: 16, 17, 26, 27, AND MARK 15: 24, 25

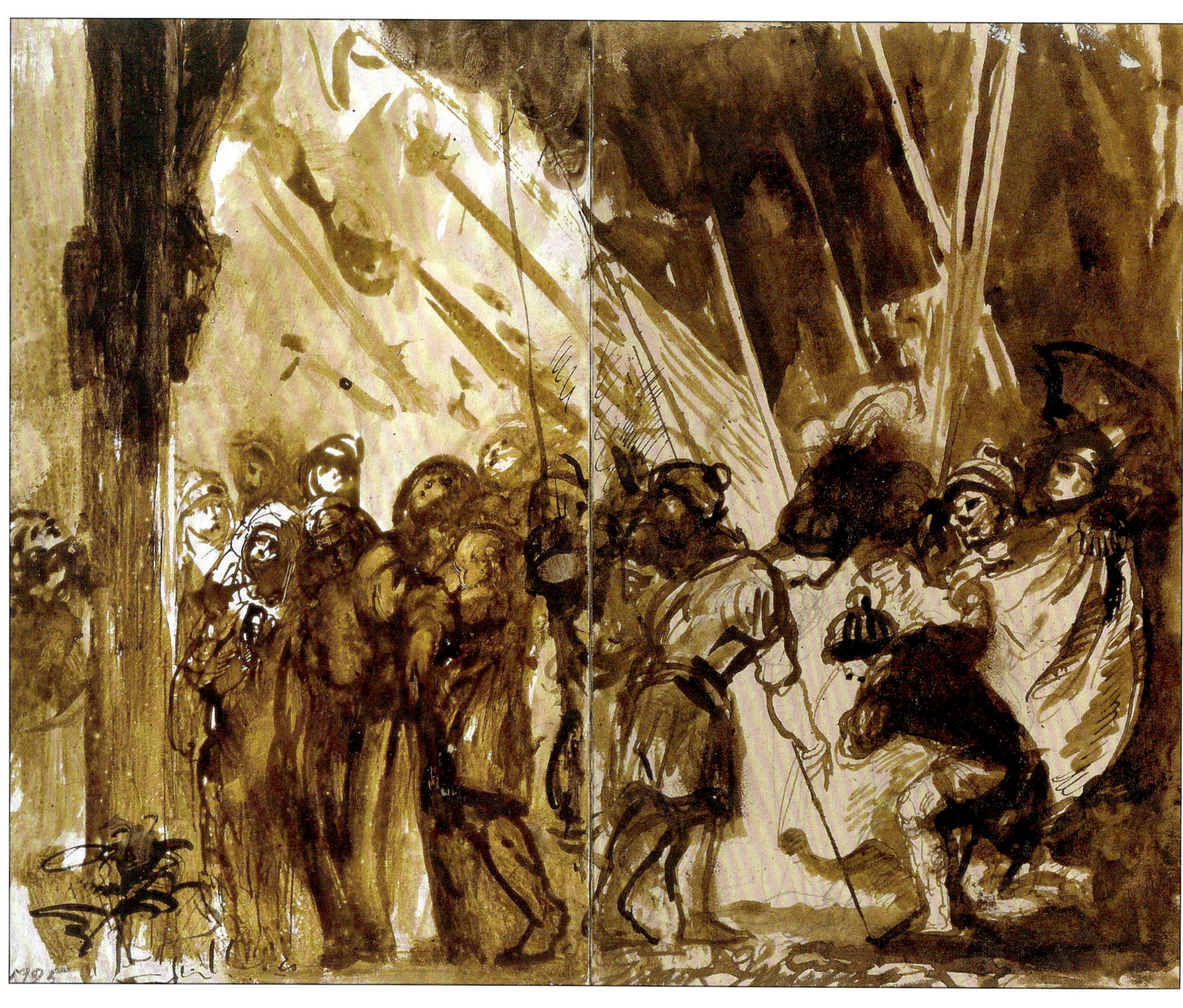

Crucifixion—Mary and Soldiers Gambling, 1995
Pen and brown ink and wash and graphite on tan paper, 9 7/8 x 13 in.

(opposite above)
The Crucifixion, 1998
Oil on panel, 24 x 34 in.

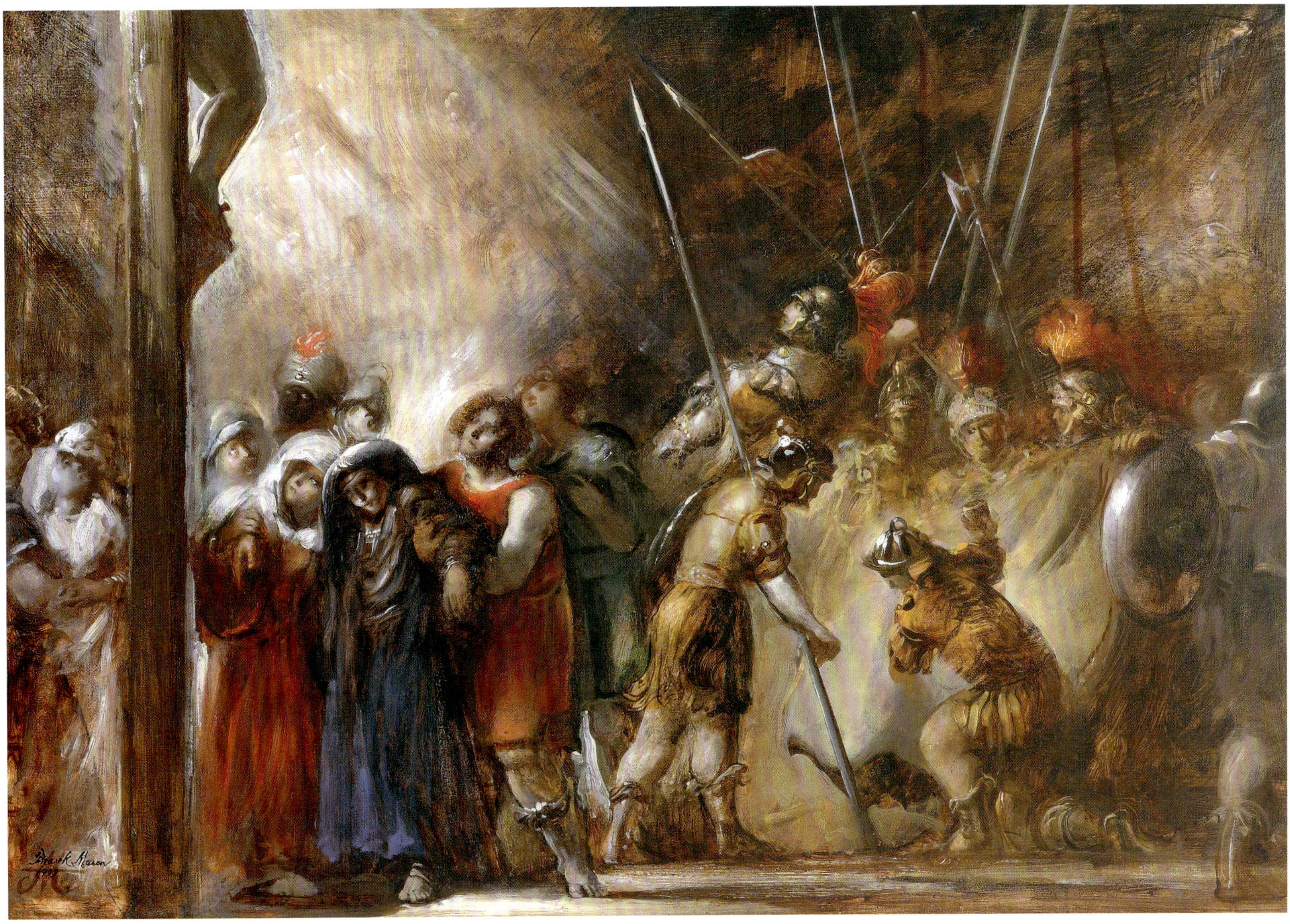

Artists throughout the centuries have painted their versions of the Crucifixion, and I too wanted to make my own statement about this momentous occurrence. But the emotional impact of the story has always overwhelmed me. Somehow I could not face in my mind that figure on the Cross and transfer the scene to canvas. Then one day a friend suggested that I do the scene from behind the Cross, concentrating on the reactions of the people who watched as He died. I tried a few sketches and then a canvas. Many of the spectators—evil men whose power and position He threatened, who mocked Him as He hung on the cross—have long since left the scene, frightened by the darkening sky and the tremors presaging the earthquake to come. But His grieving mother is there and so are a few faithful followers sorrowing with her. You see, as He did, the Roman soldiers indifferent to His suffering, casting lots for His robe. I added a note of hope, however. There is one man—the centurion on horseback—who looked at Jesus' face as He died and said, "Truly, this man was the Son of God."

Study for Crucifixion, 1998
Pen and black ink on cream paper, 3 1/2 x 5 in.

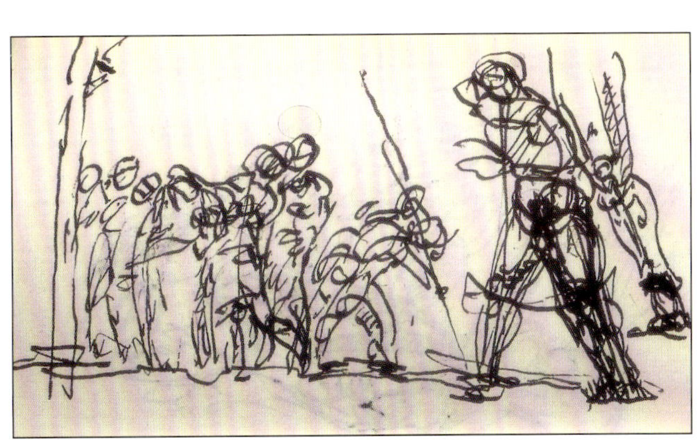

(overleaf)
The Crucifixion, 1998–2003
Oil on canvas, 96 x 144 in.

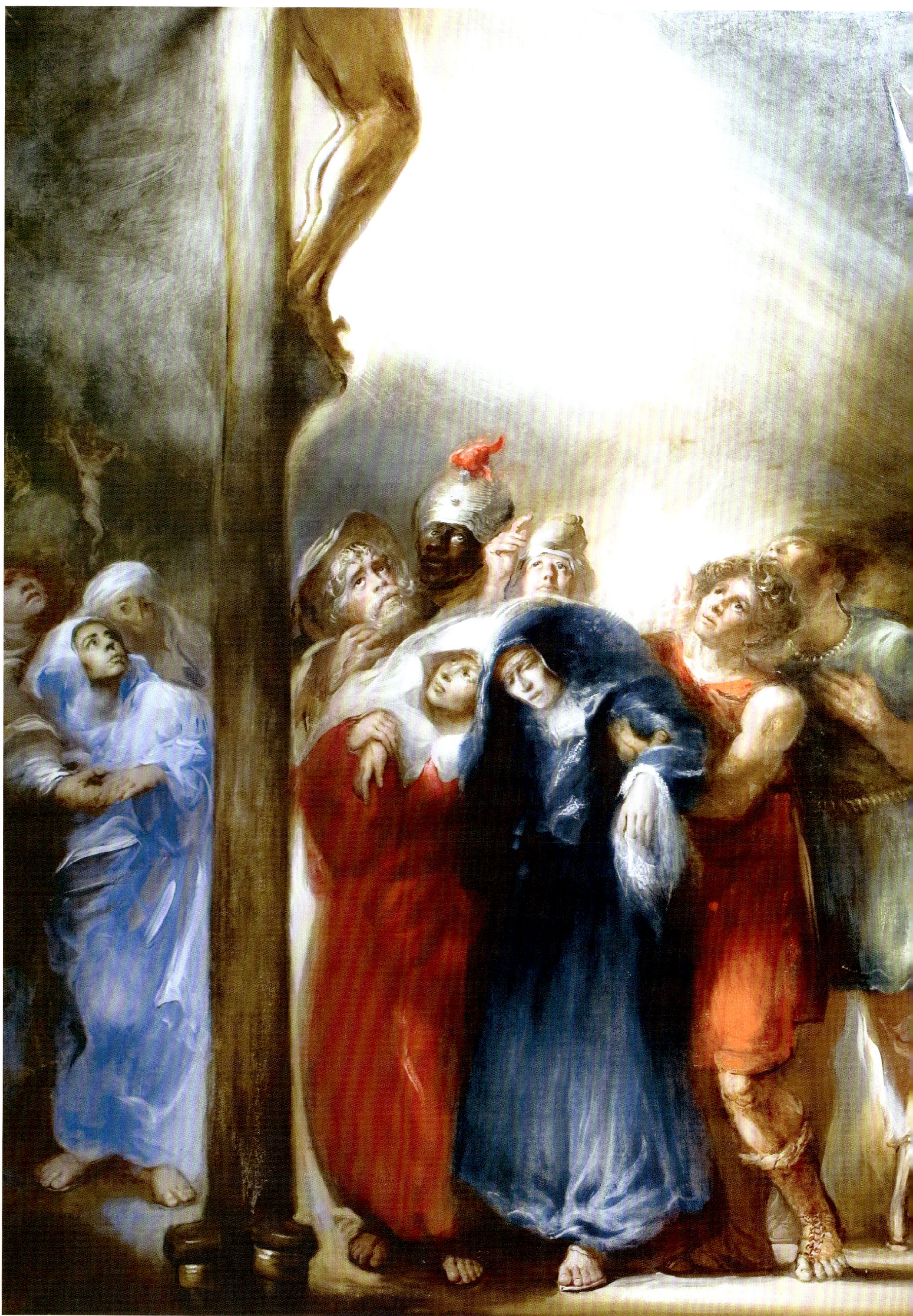

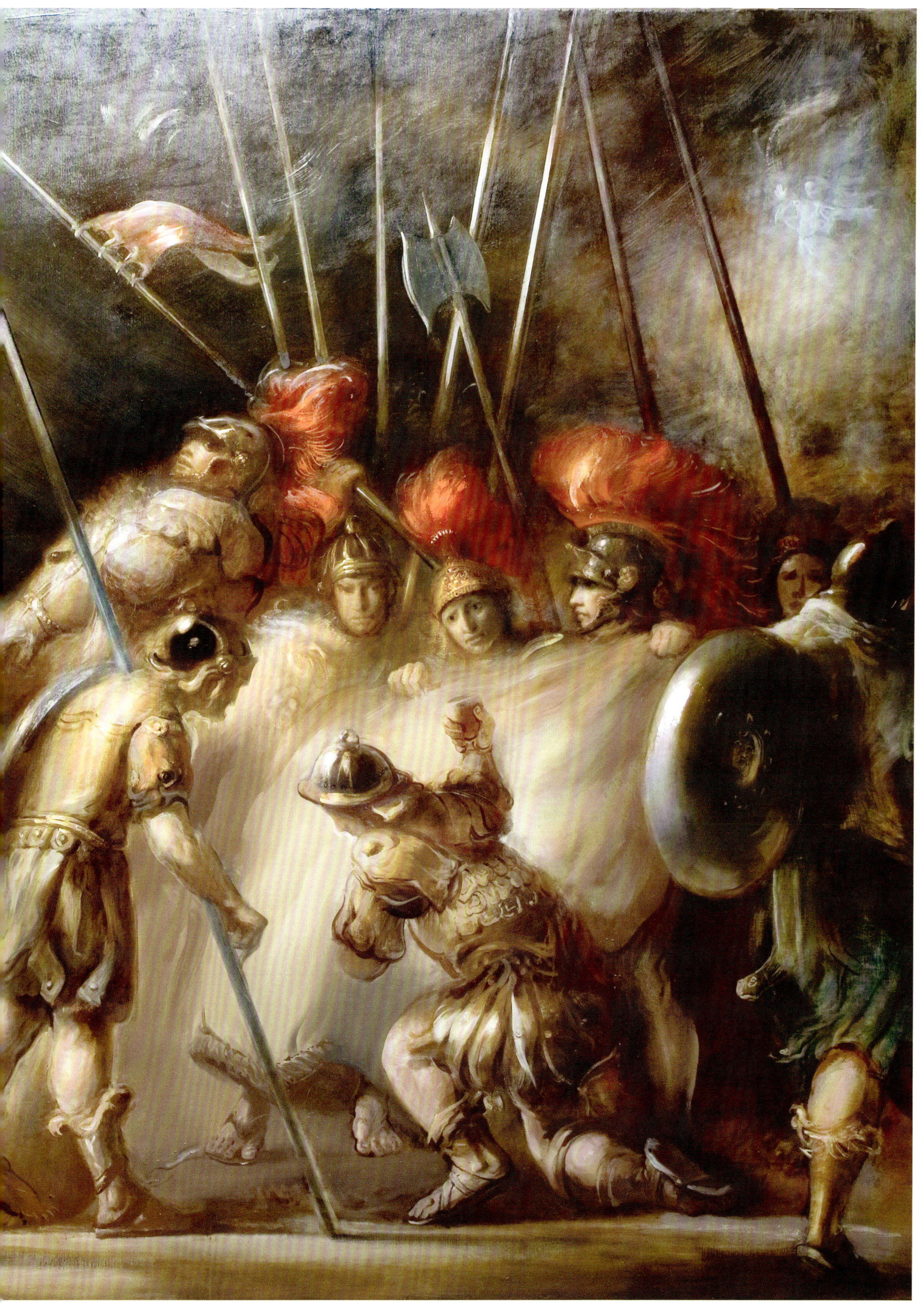

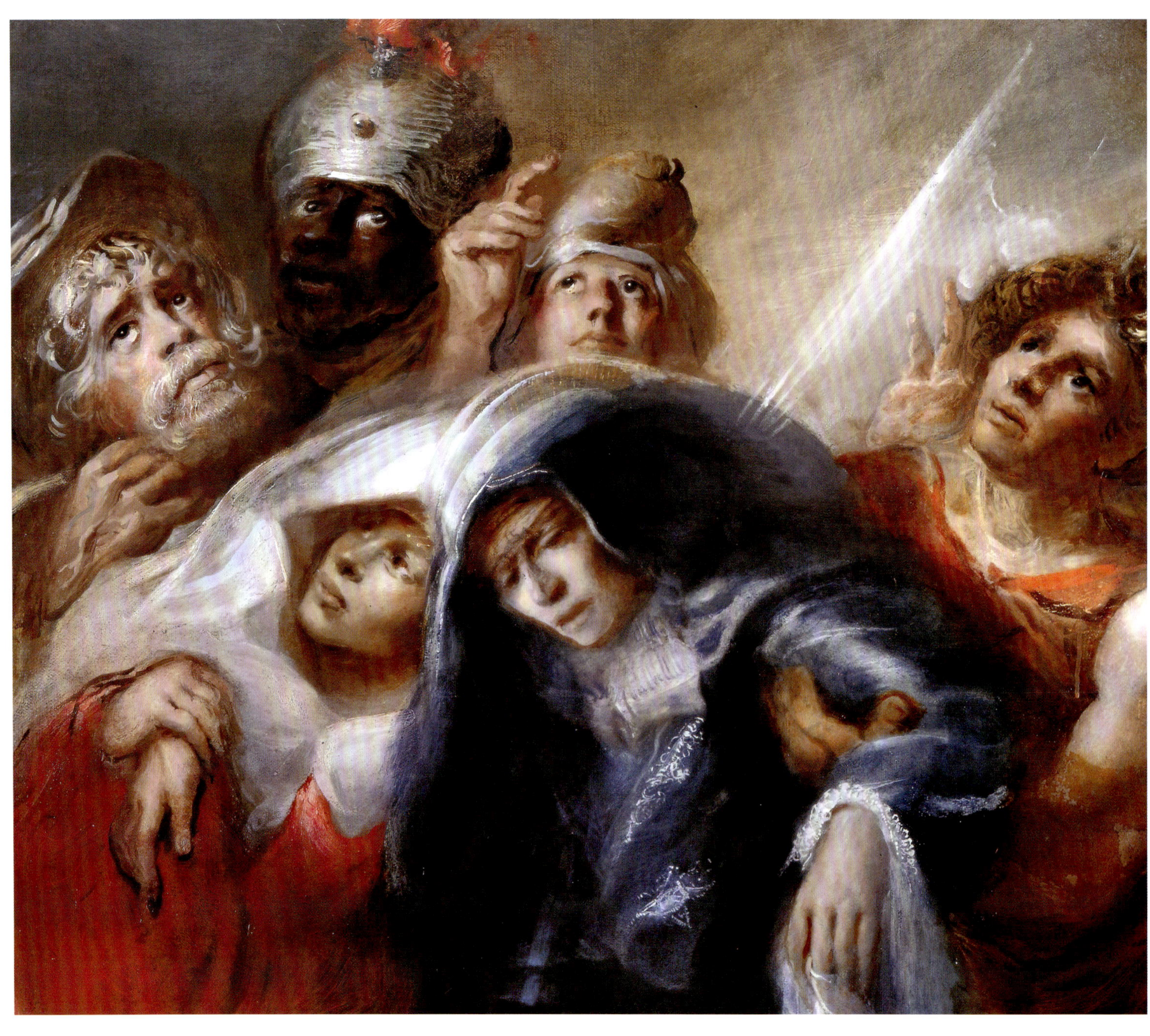

(Detail) *The Crucifixion*
Mary and followers of Jesus under the cross including Mary Magdalene, Joseph of Arimathaea, and John.

(Detail) *The Crucifixion*
Soldiers gambling for Christ's robe

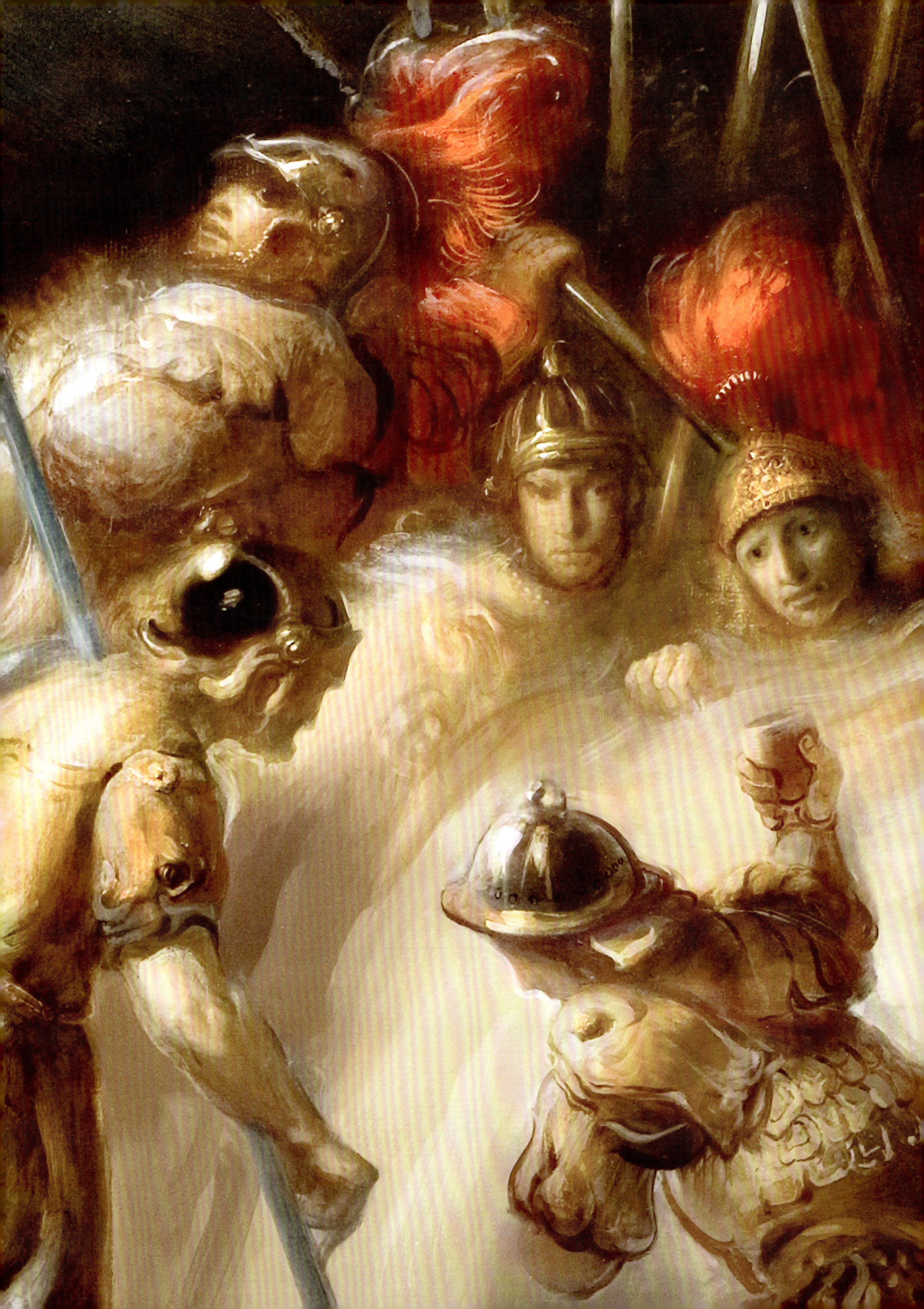

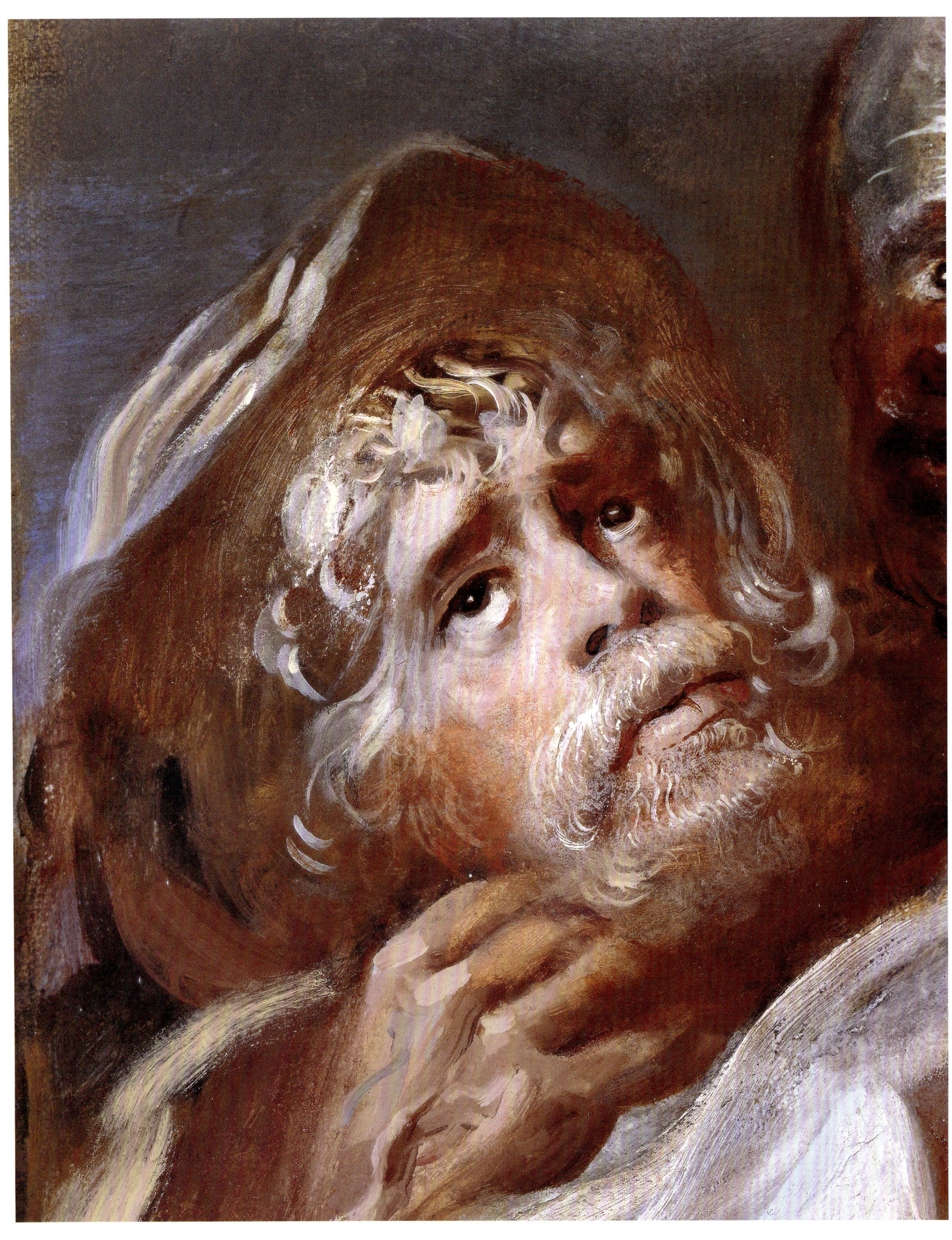

(Detail) *The Crucifixion*
Joseph of Arimathaea

(Detail) *The Crucifixion*
The disciple John

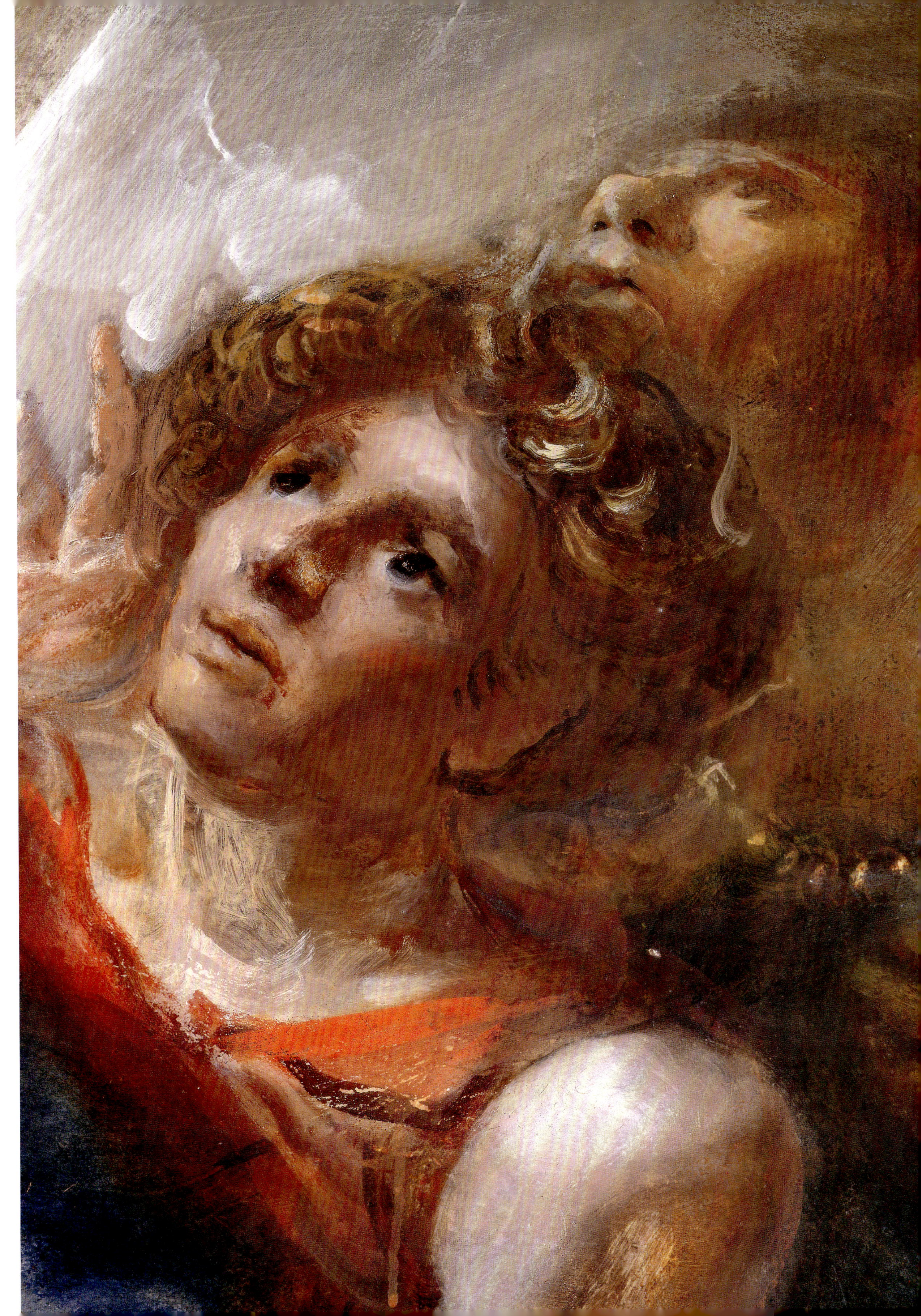

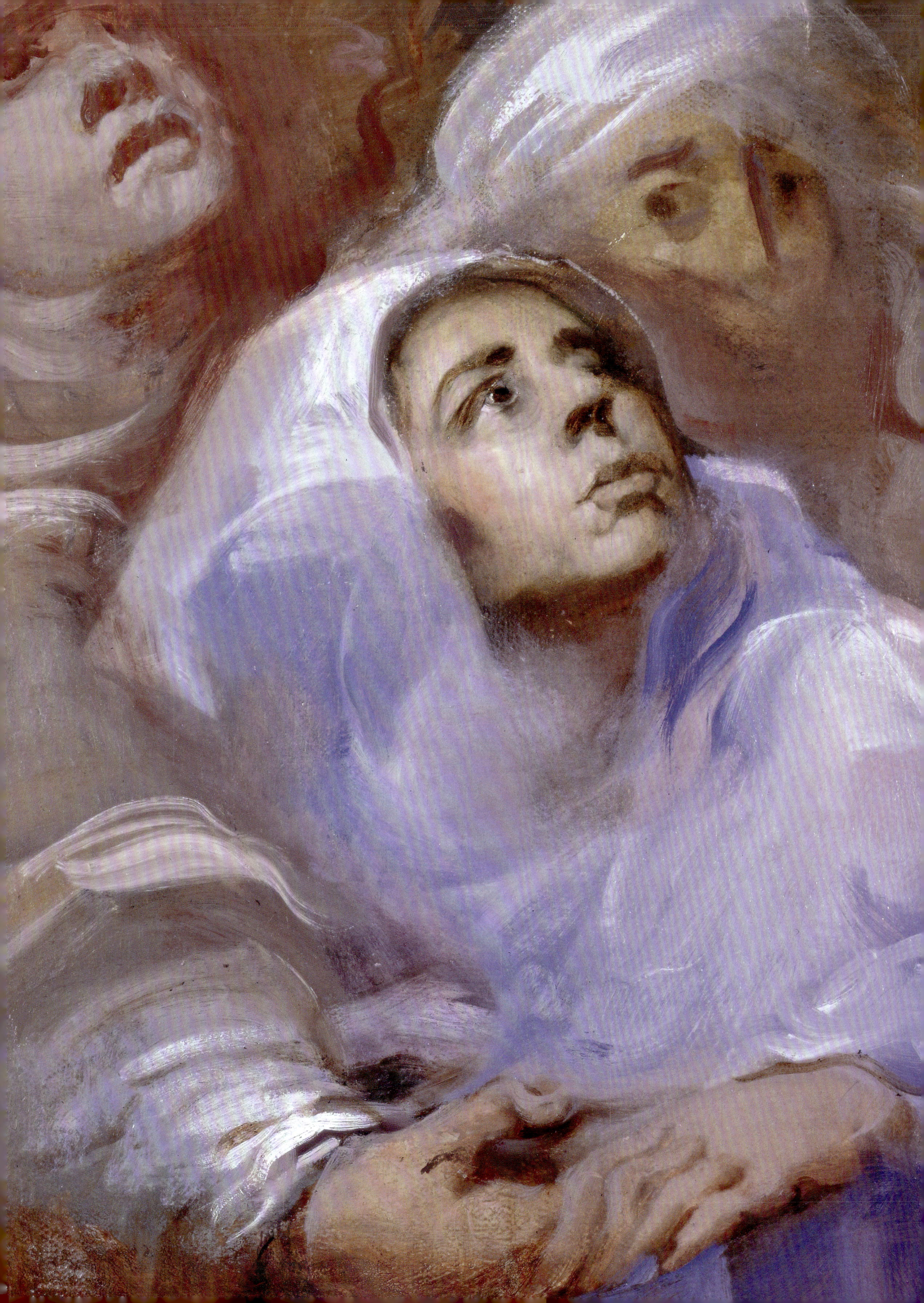

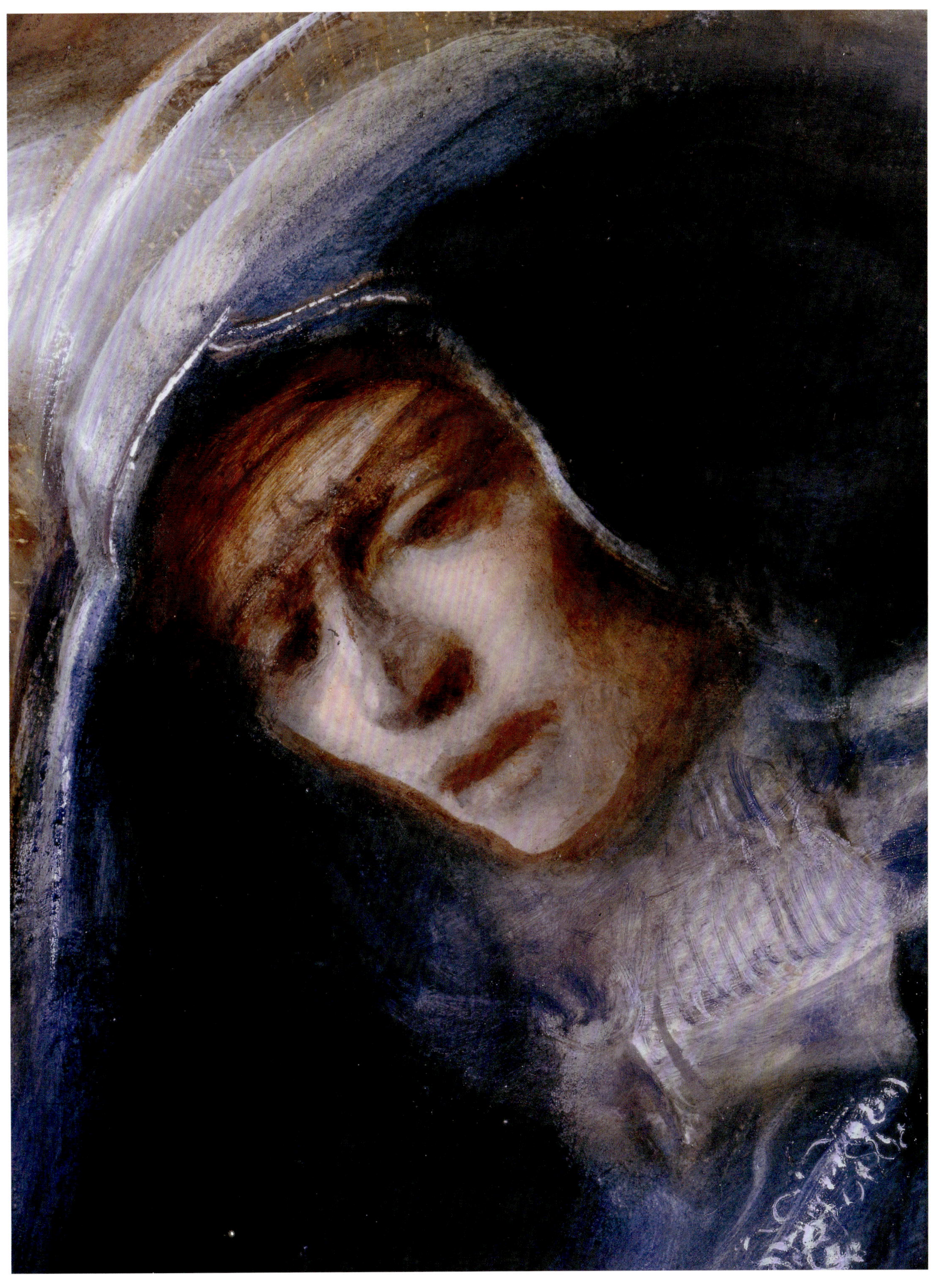

(Detail) *The Crucifixion*
Mary, mother of James

(Detail) *The Crucifixion*
Mary, mother of Jesus

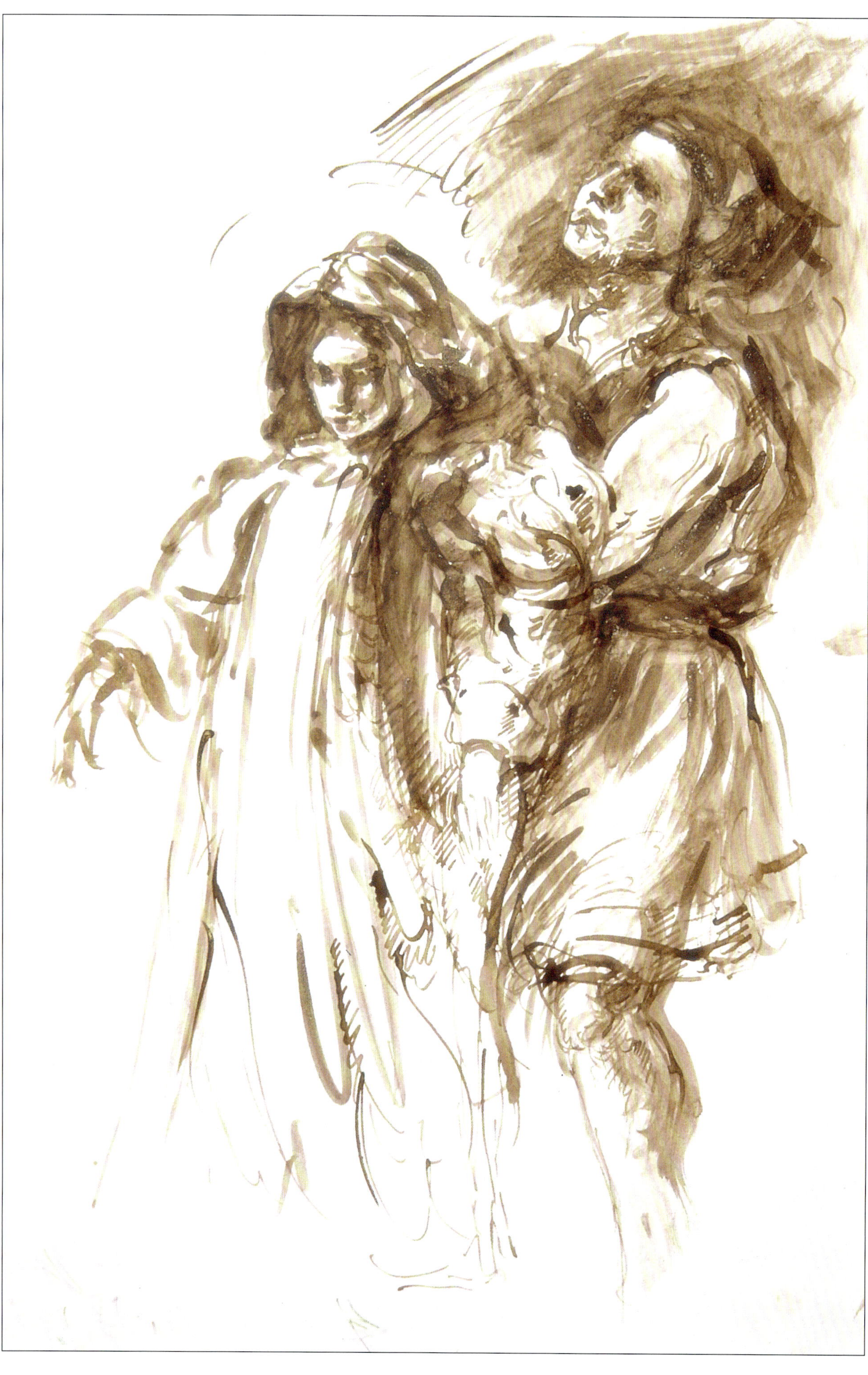

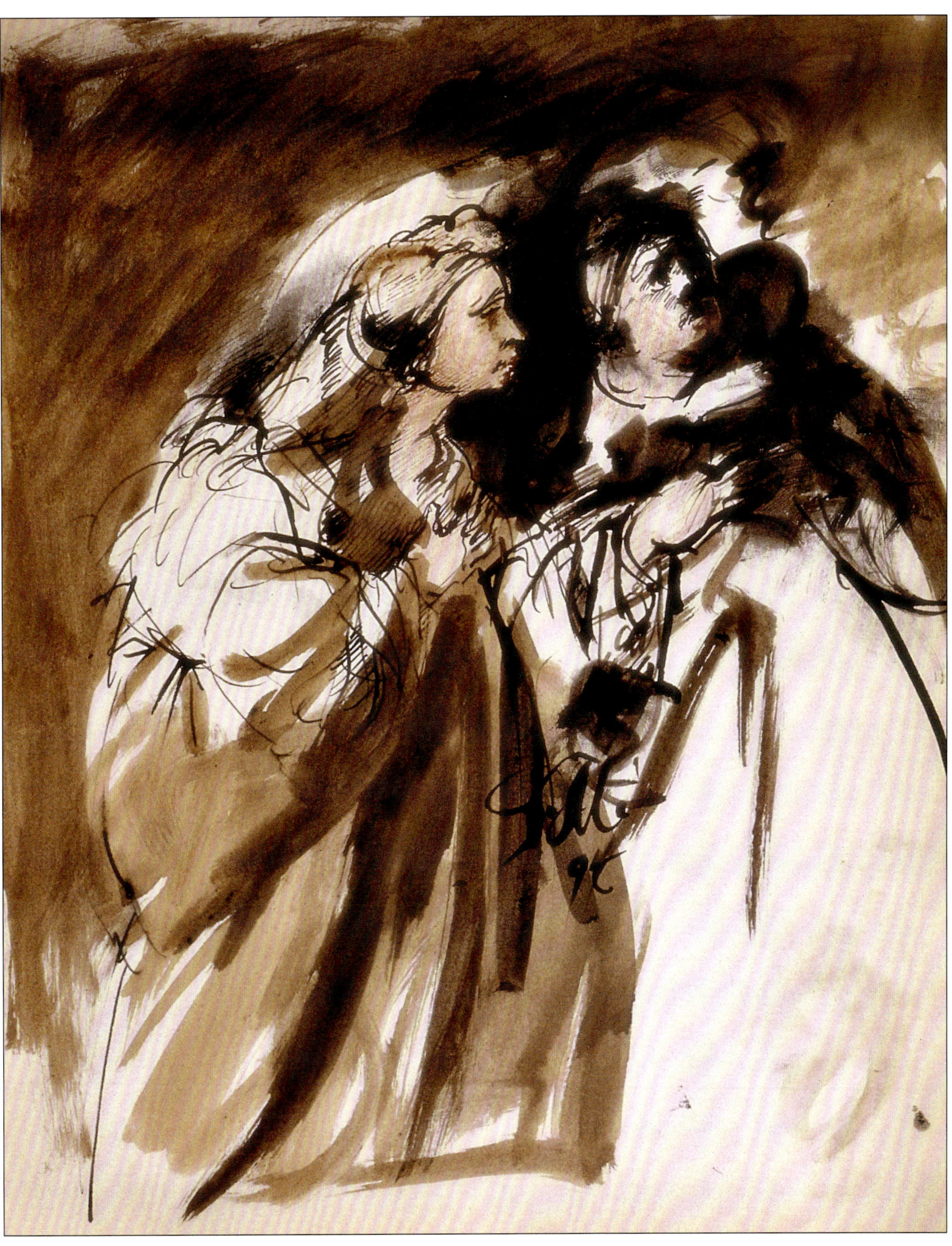

John Holding Mary, 1999
Brown ink wash on cream paper
16 1/4 x 11 in.

Two Marys under the Cross, 1994
Pen and brown ink and wash and watercolor on cream paper, 11 3/4 x 9 3/4 in.

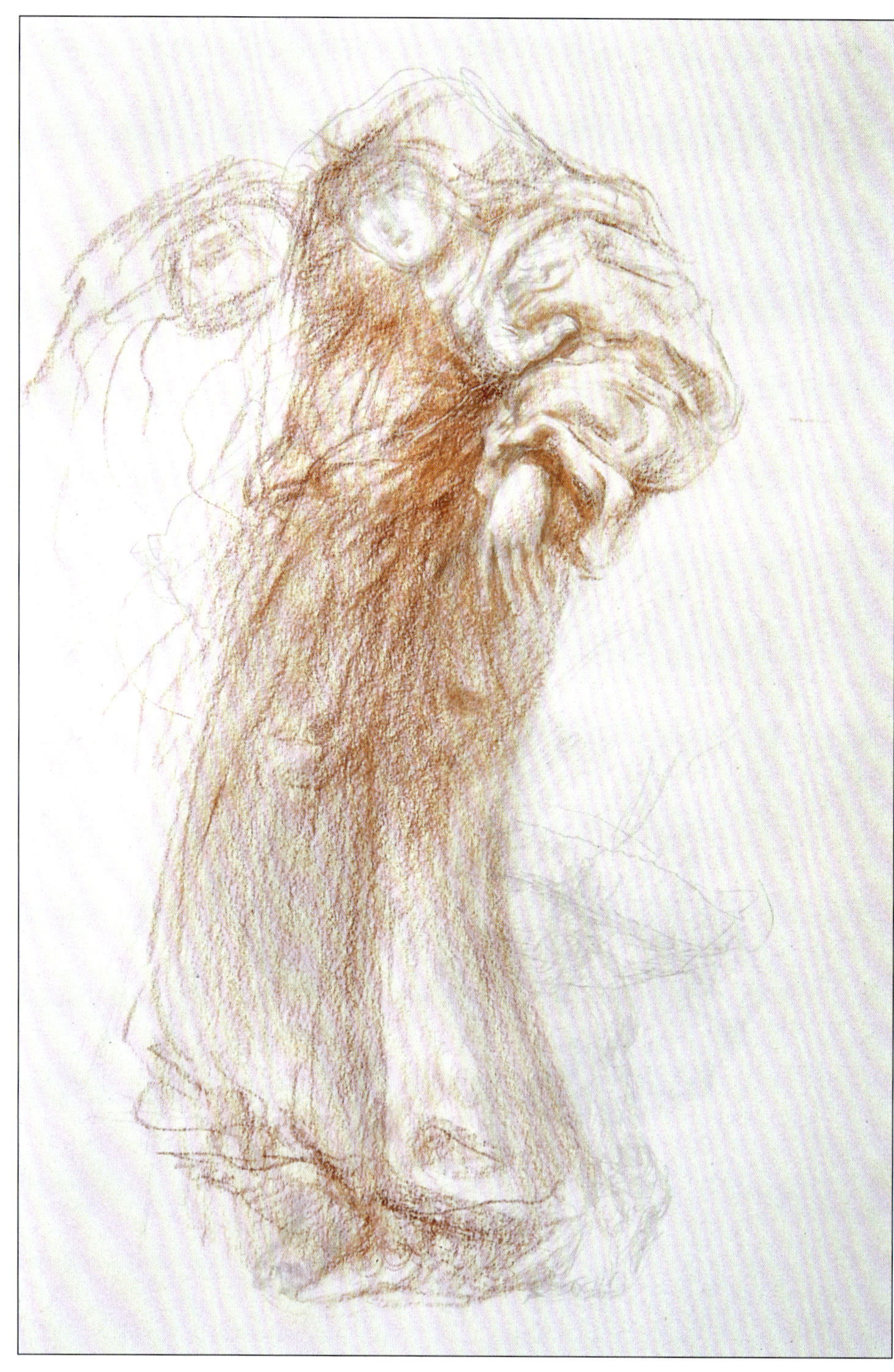

a.

a. *Mary Collapsing,* 1999
Red and black chalk on white paper
12 x 9 in.

b. *Mary under the Cross,* 1994
Pen and brown ink and wash on cream paper
11 3/4 x 9 3/4 in.

c. *Mary Supported by John,* 1995
Pen and ink and wash on tan paper
9 7/8 x 6 3/4 in.

d. *Beneath the Cross,* 1998
Pen and black ink on cream paper
5 x 3 1/2 in.

e. *John Drawn over Two Figures from Left of Cross,* 1998
Pen and black ink on cream paper
5 x 3 1/2 in.

f. *Group Beneath the Cross,* 1998
Pen and black ink on cream paper
5 x 3 1/2 in.

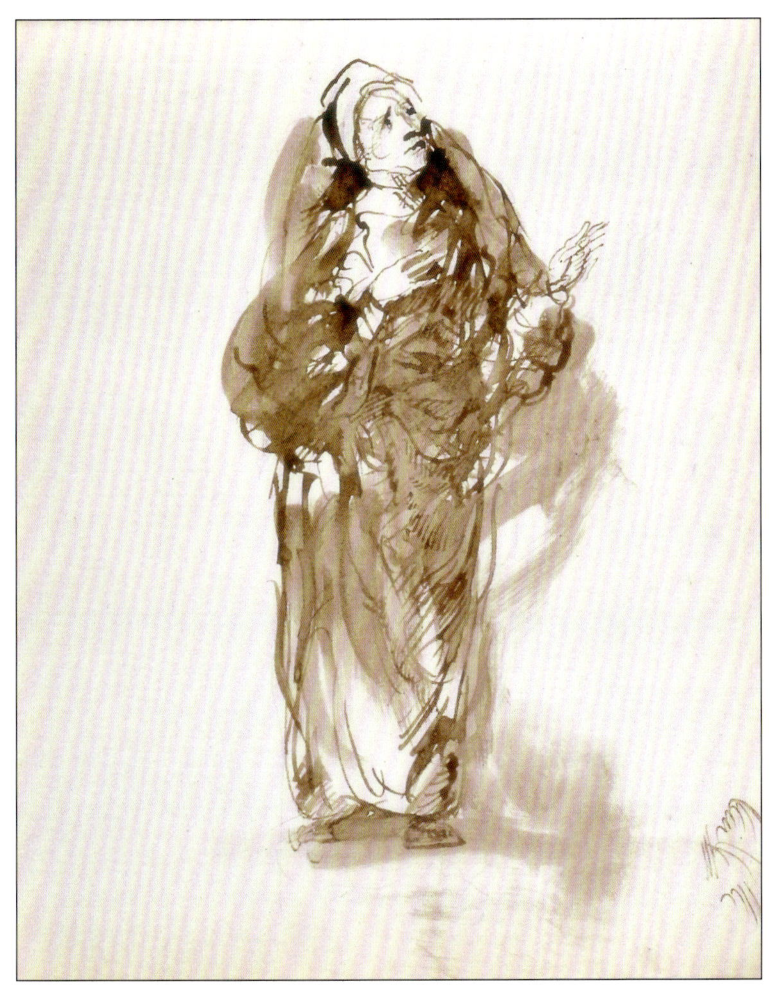

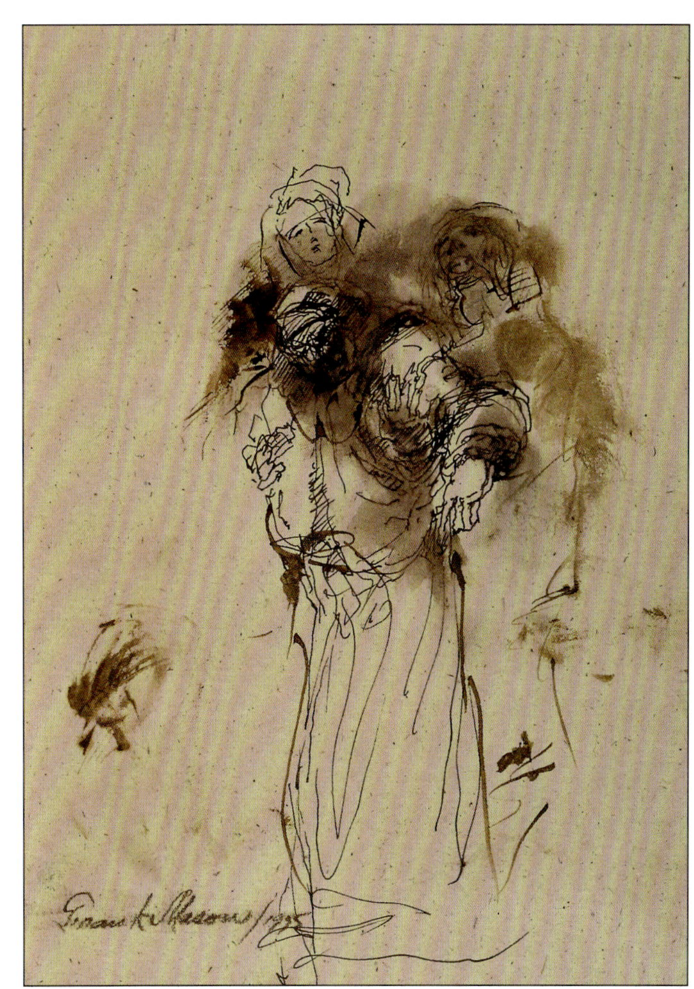

b. c.

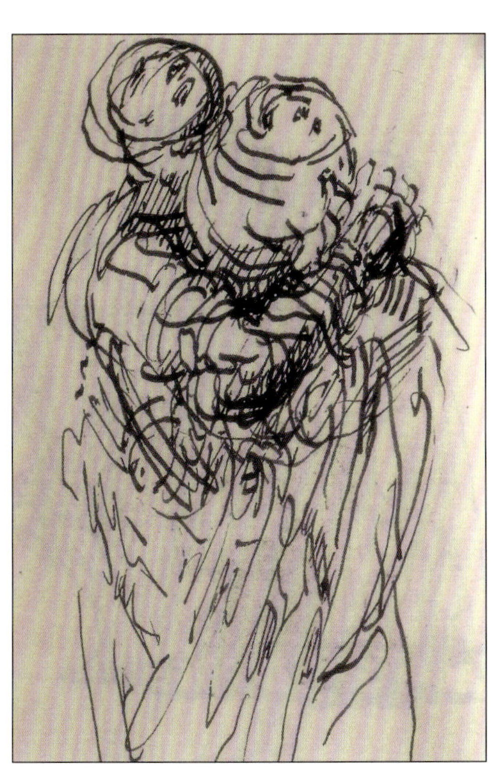

d.

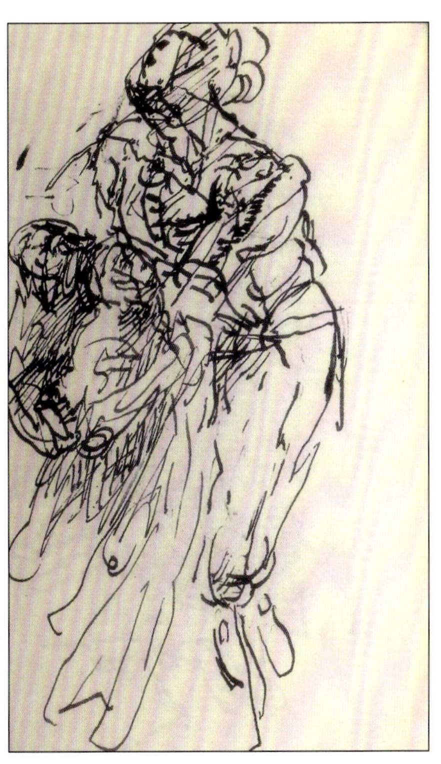

e.

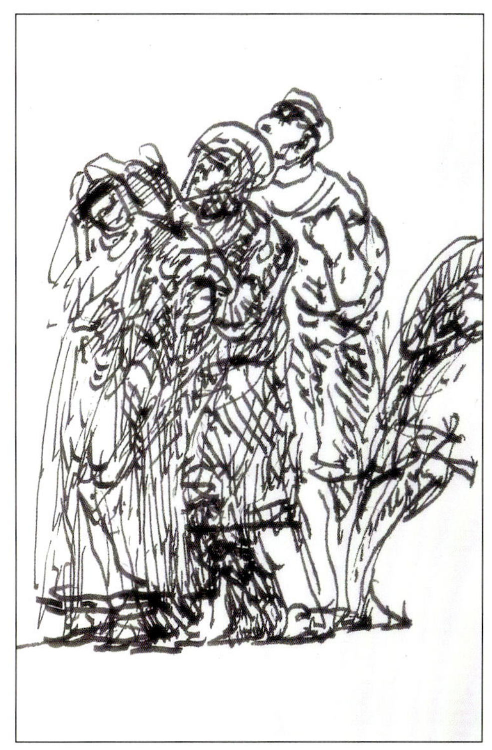

f.

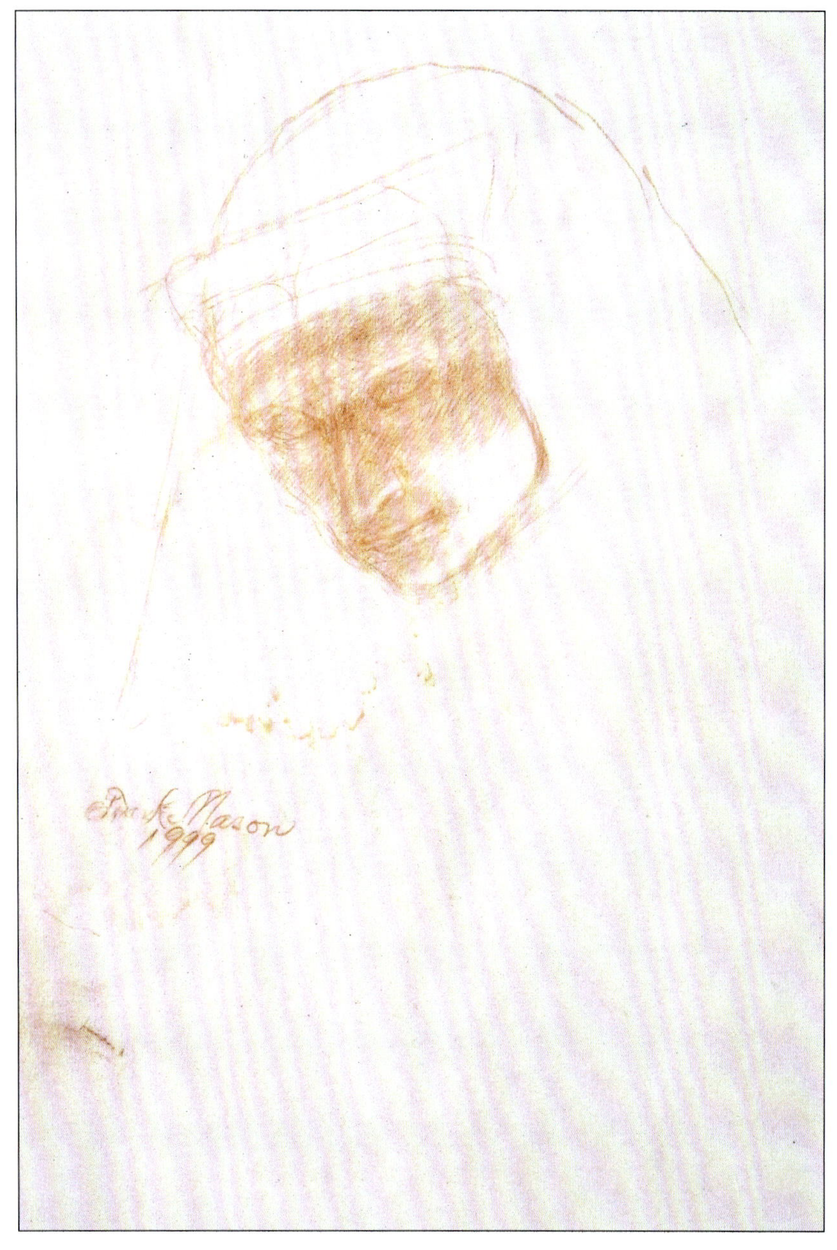

a.

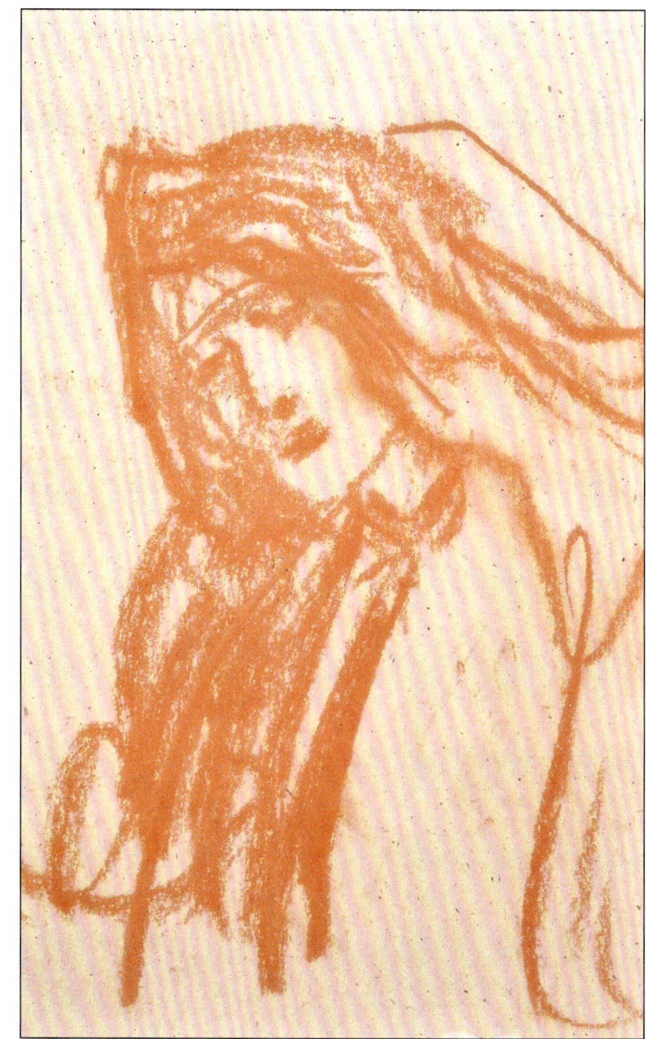

b.

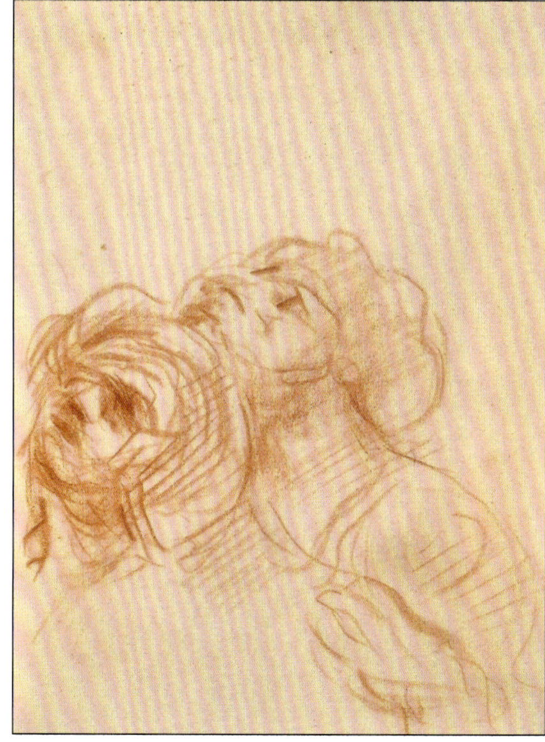

c.

a. *Mary,* 1999
Red chalk on white paper
12 x 9 in.

b. *Mary,* 1999
Red chalk on tan paper
10 x 6 3/4 in.

c. *John and Mary,* 1999
Red chalk on cream paper
4 x 3 in.

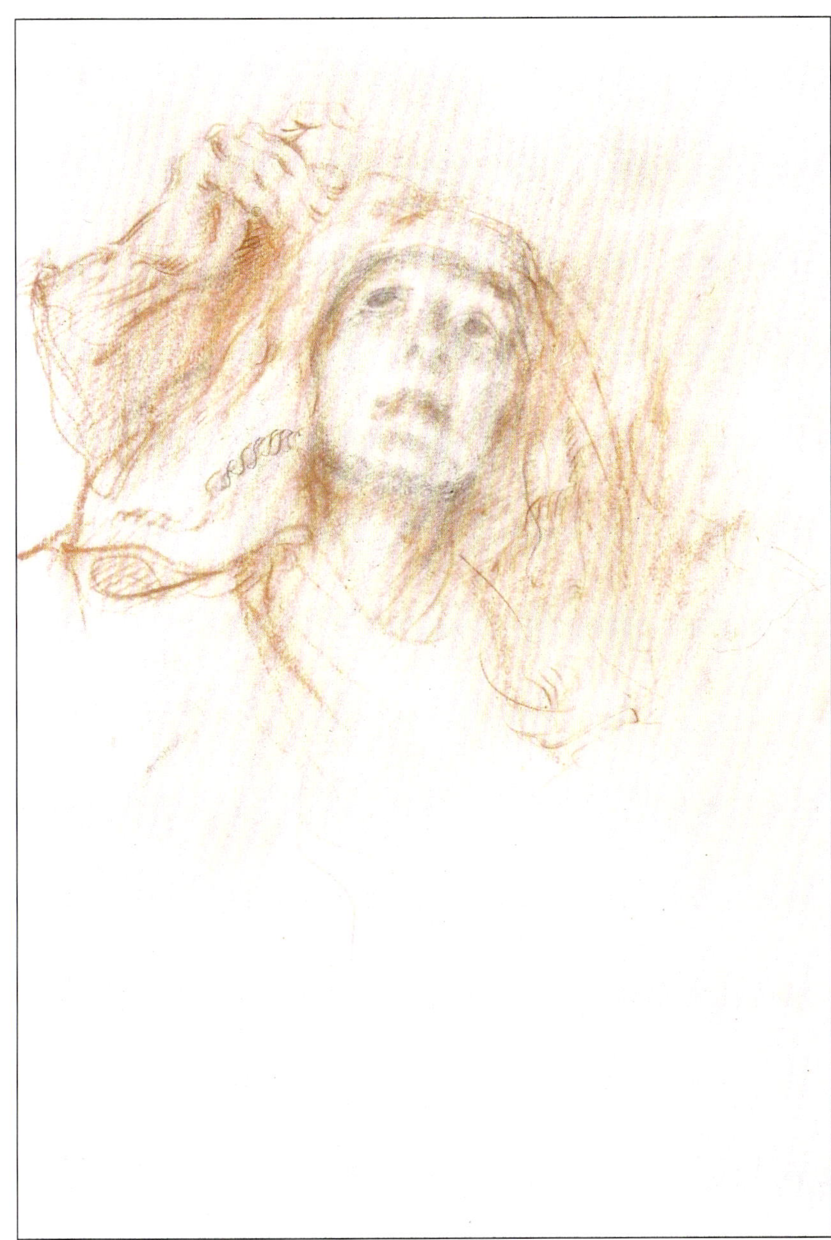

a.

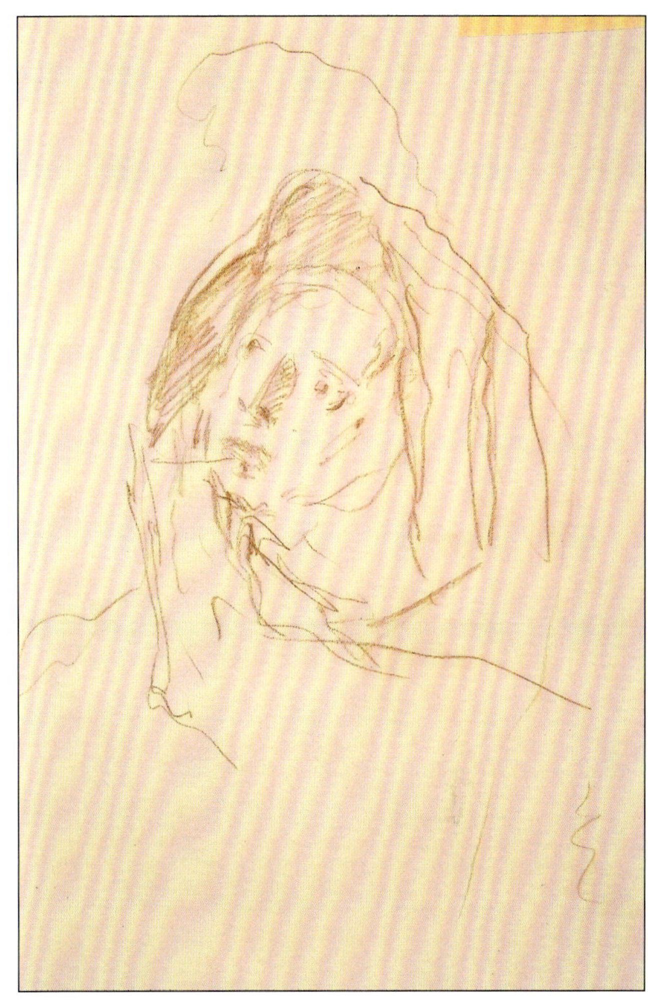

b.

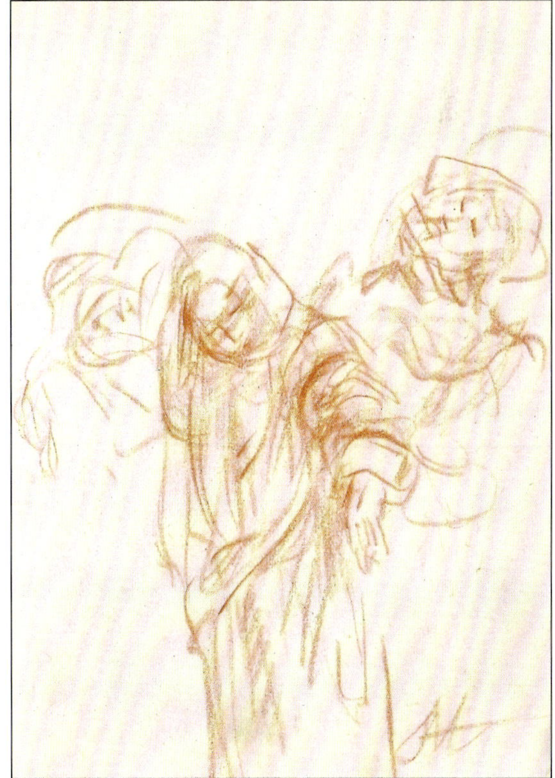

c.

a. *My Wife Anne as Figure under the Cross,* 1999
Red and black chalk on white paper
12 x 9 in.

b. *Mary Magdalene,* 1999
Red chalk on cream paper
16 1/4 x 11 in.

c. *Lamenting Mary,* 1999
Red chalk on cream paper
4 x 3 in.

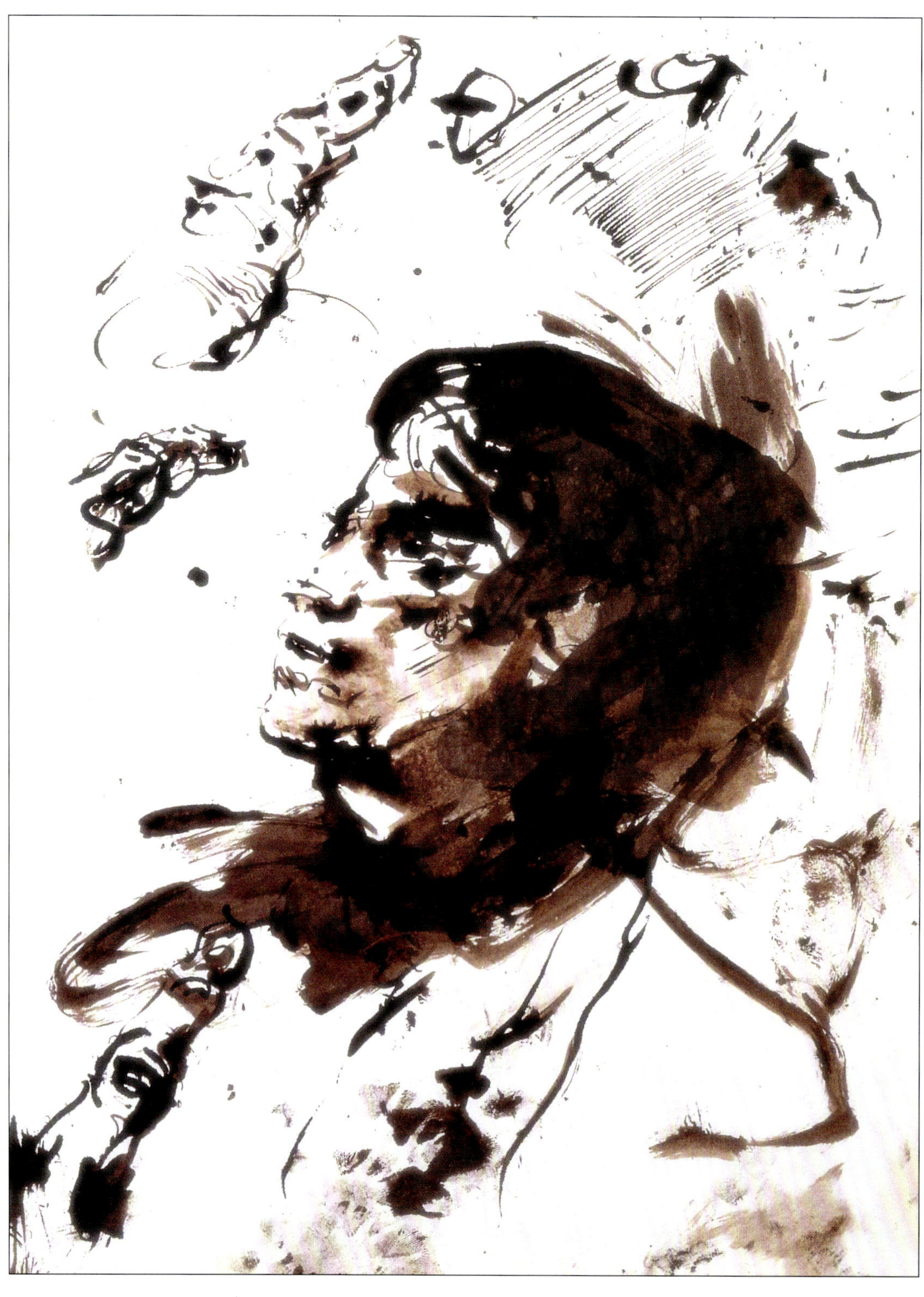

John, 1994
Brown ink wash on cream paper
13 5/8 x 11 in.

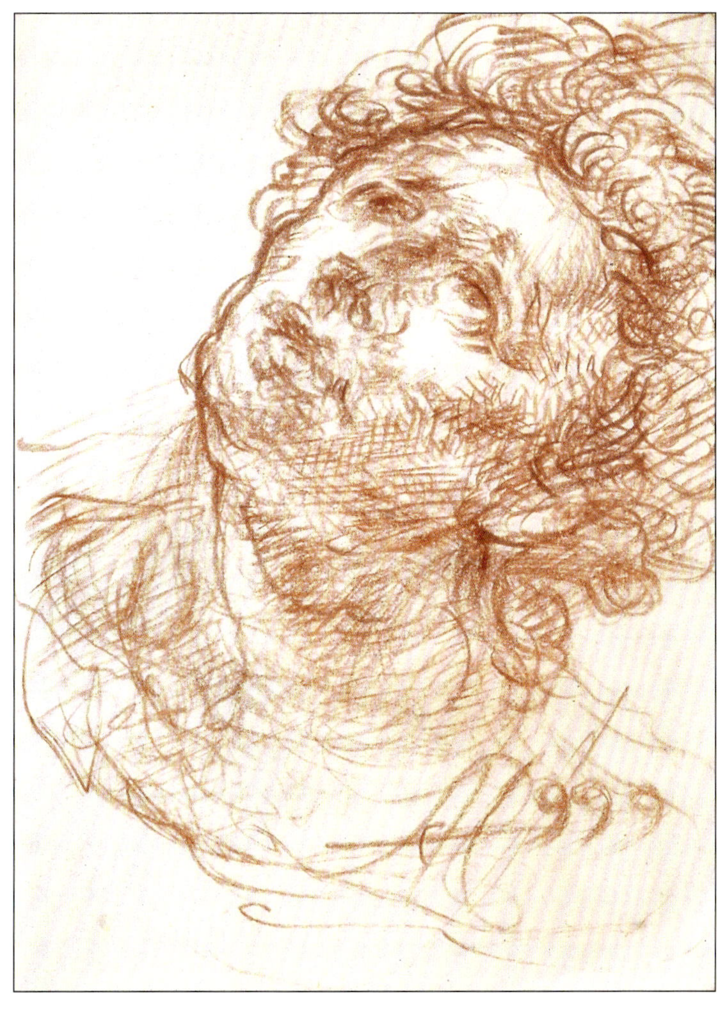

a.

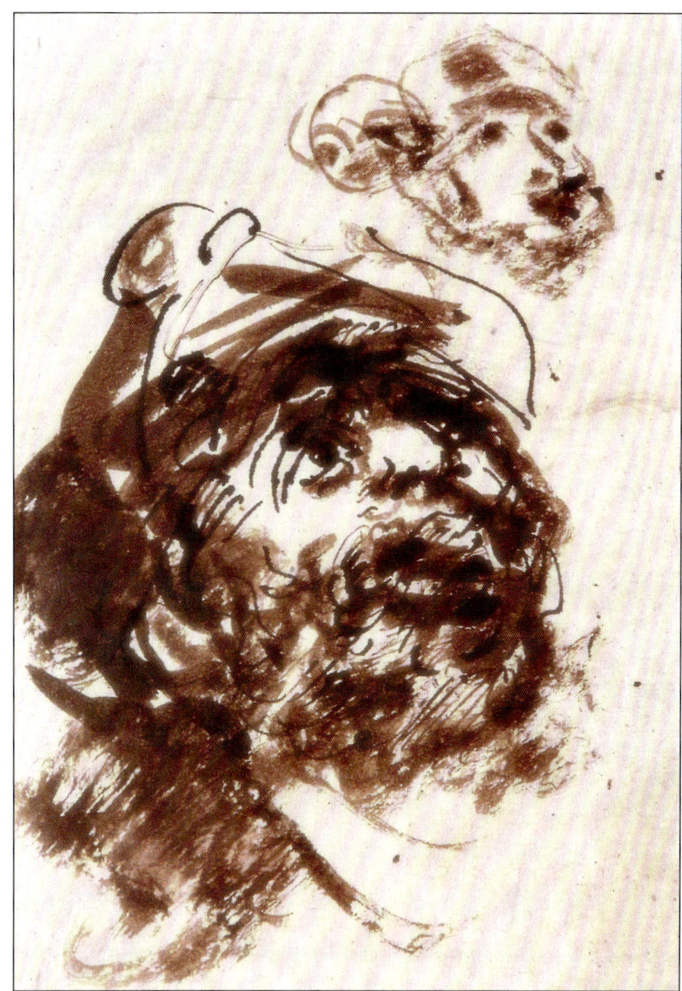

b.

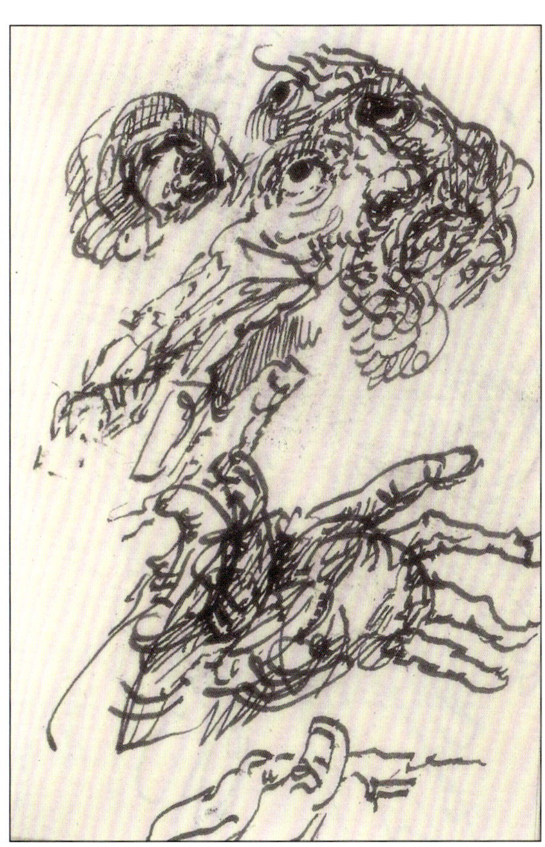

c.

a. *John,* 1999
Red chalk on cream paper
4 x 3 in.

b. *Study for Joseph of Arimathaea,* 1999
Pen and brown ink and wash on cream paper
7 x 5 in.

c. *Study for Joseph of Arimathaea,* 1998
Pen and black ink on cream paper
5 x 3 1/2 in.

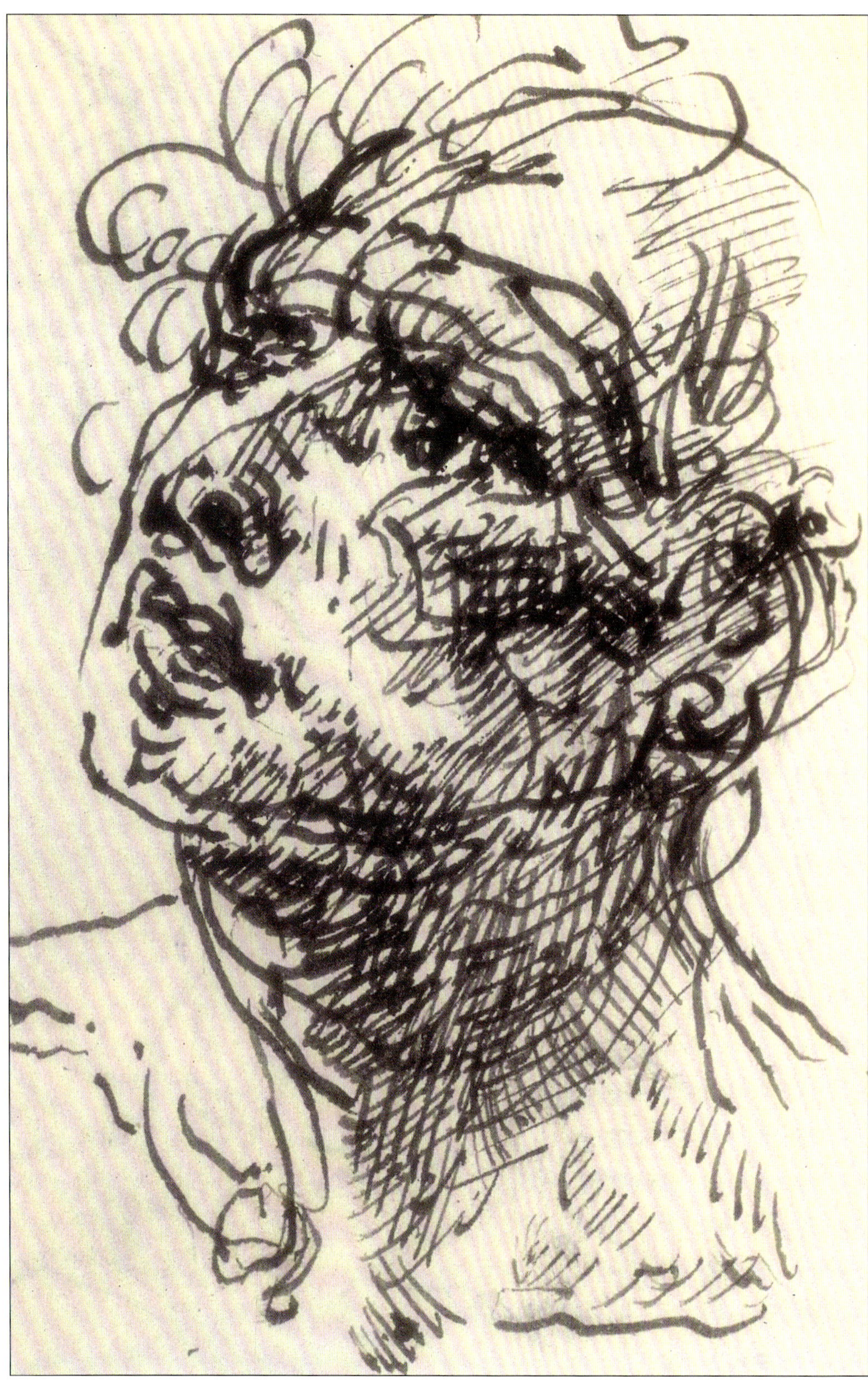

a.

a. *John,* 1998
Pen and black ink on cream paper, 5 x 3 1/2 in.

b. *Study for John,* 1998
Pen and black ink on cream paper, 5 x 3 1/2 in.

c. *Study for the Moor,* 1998
Pen and black ink on cream paper, 5 x 3 1/2 in.

d. *John Under Cross,* 1998
Pen and black ink on cream paper, 5 x 3 1/2 in.

e. *John, Two Studies,* 1998
Pen and black ink on cream paper, 5 x 3 1/2 in.

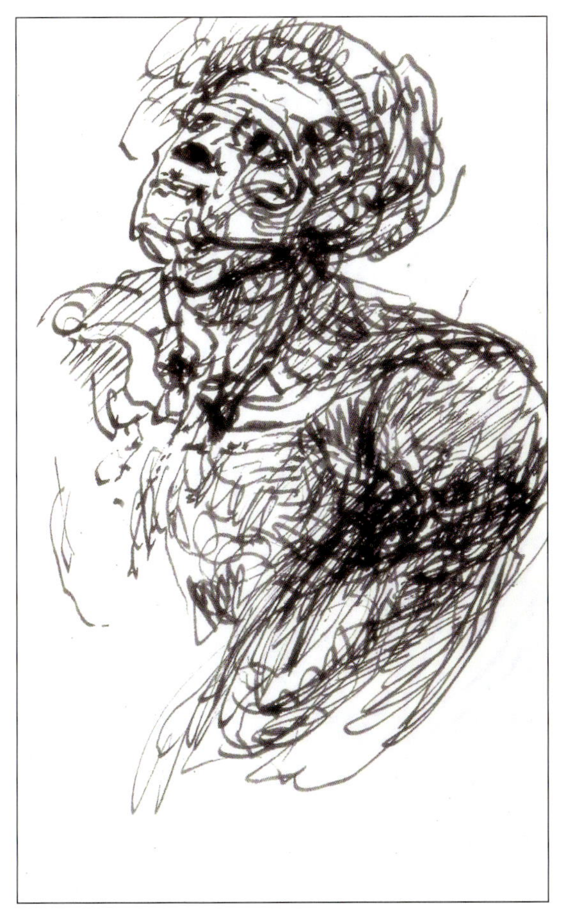
b.

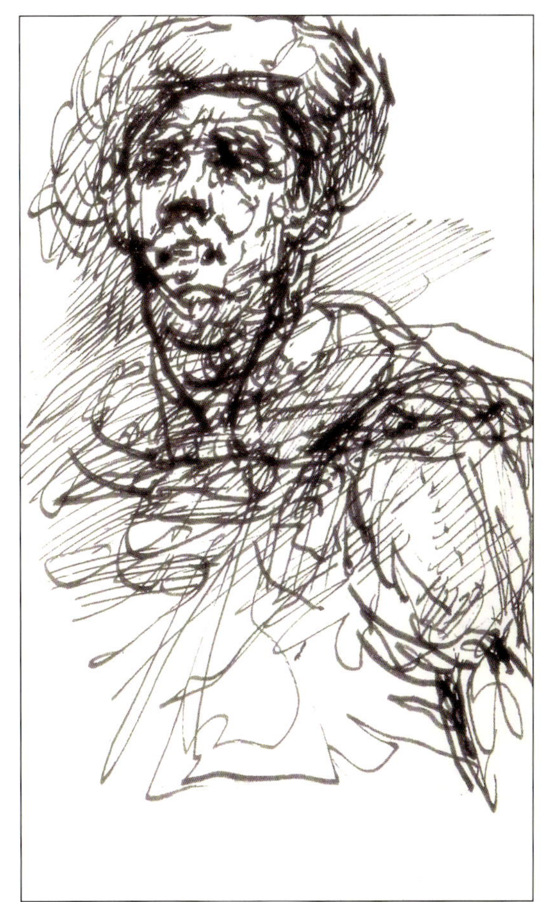
c.

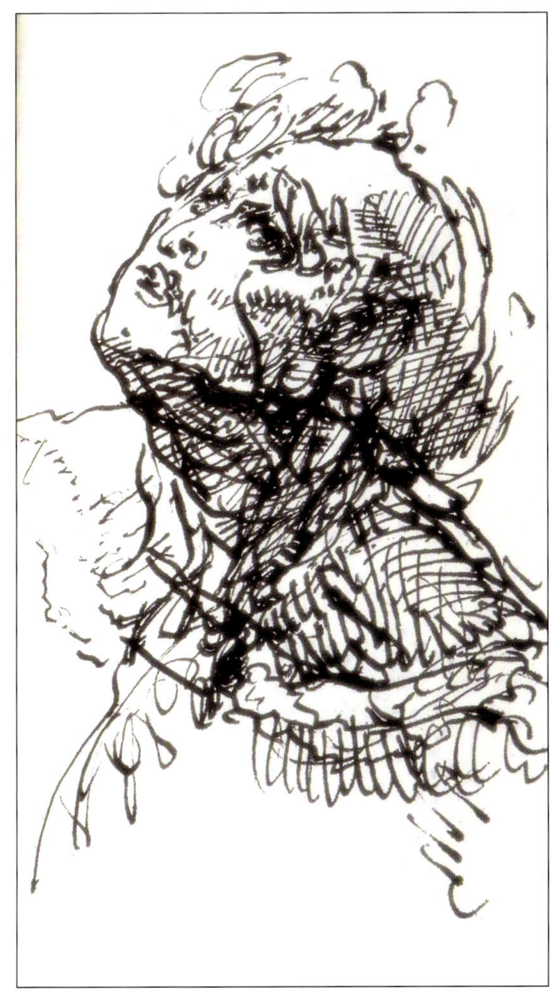
d.

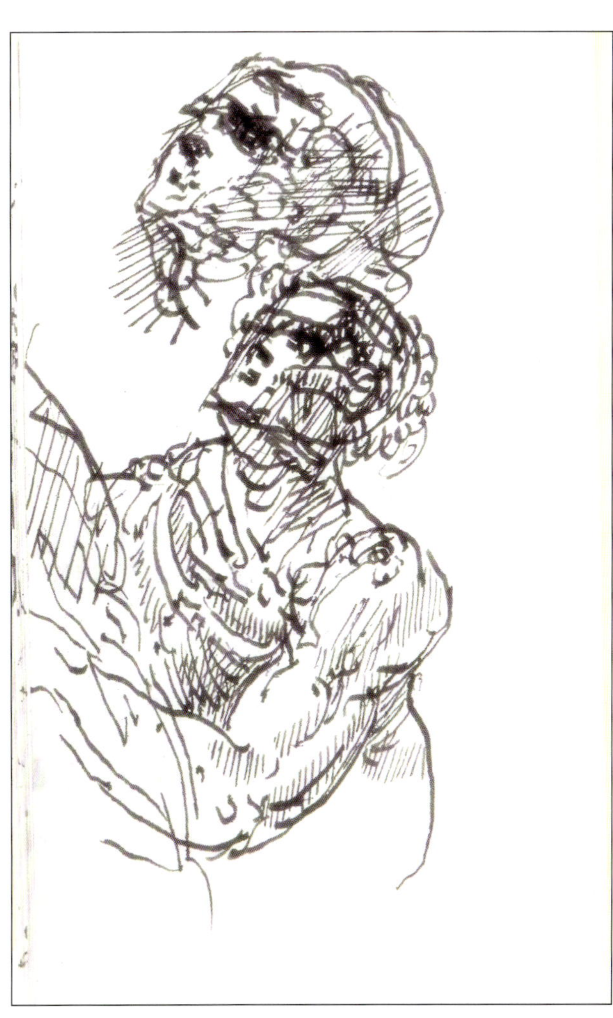
e.

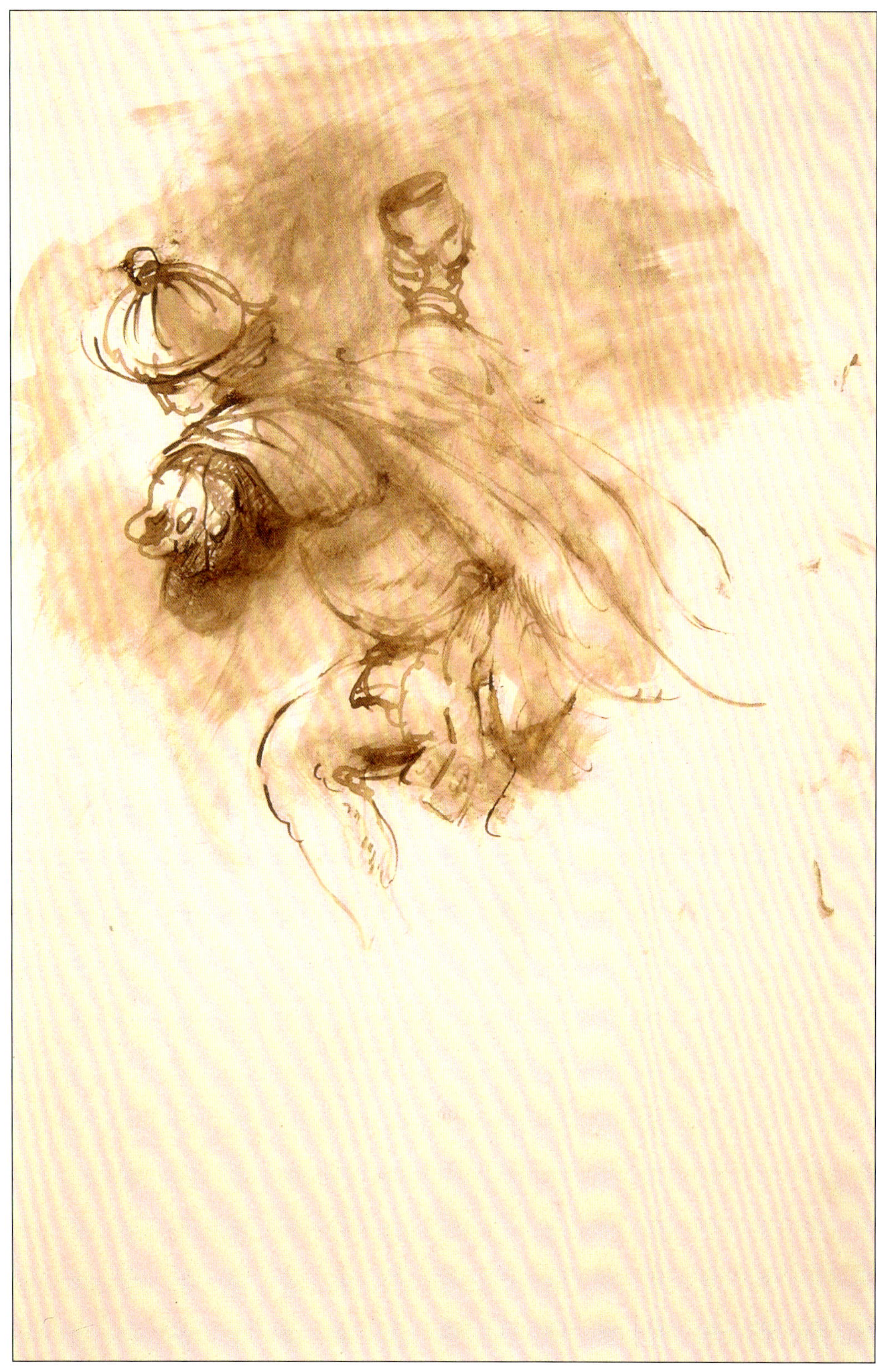

Gambling for the Robe of Christ, 1999
Brown ink wash on cream paper
16 1/4 x 11 in.

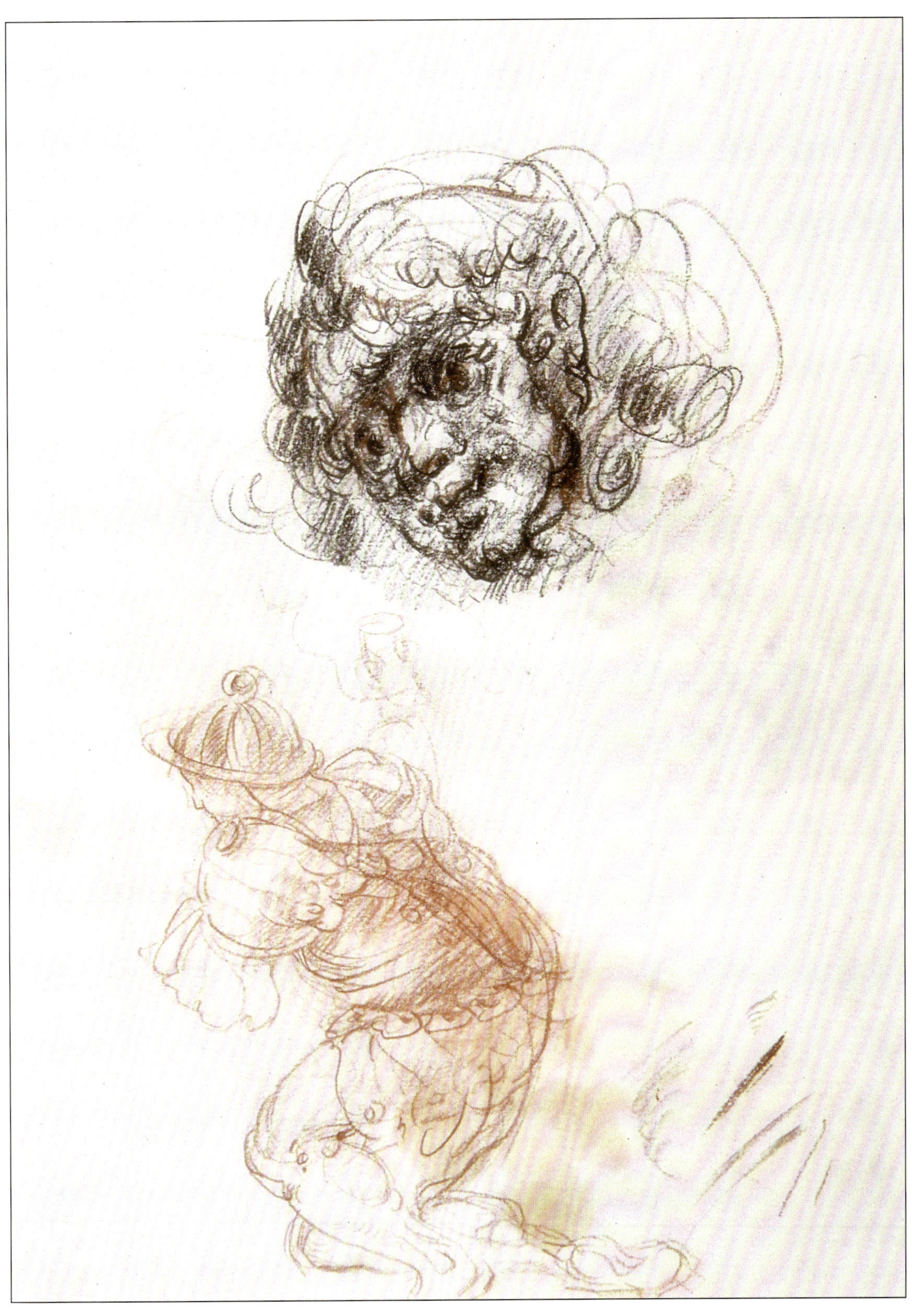

Study for Soldiers, 1998
Red and black chalk on cream paper
14 x 10 1/2 in.

a.

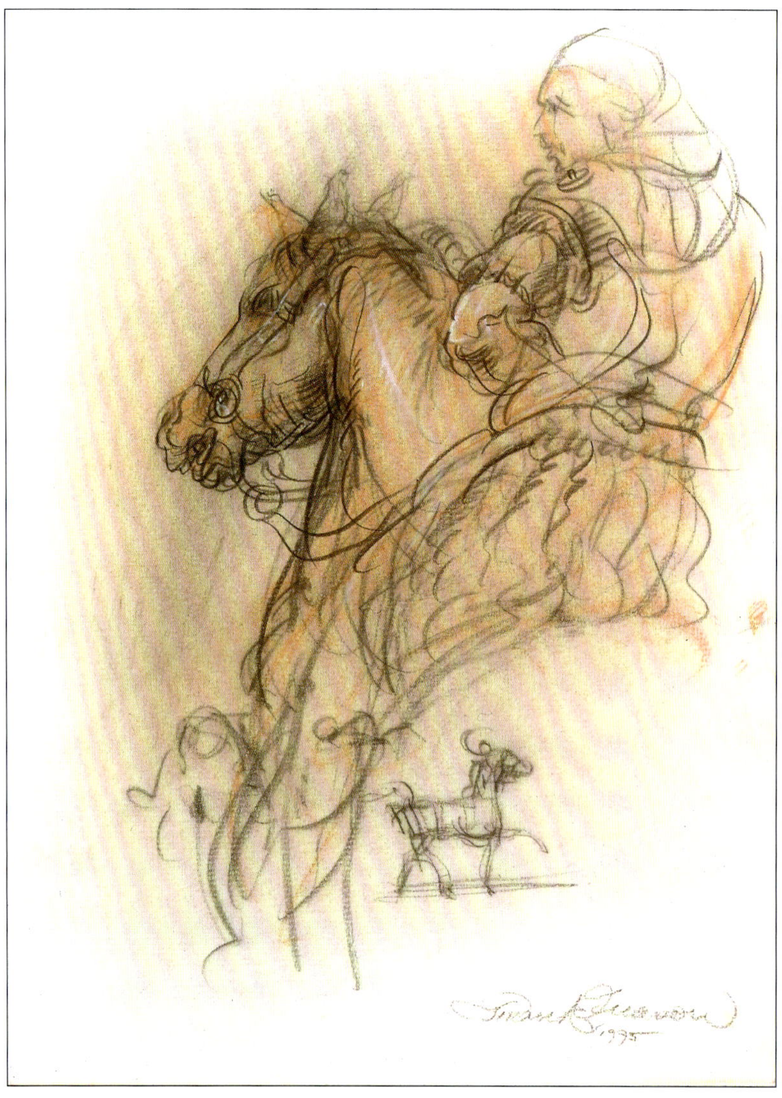

b.

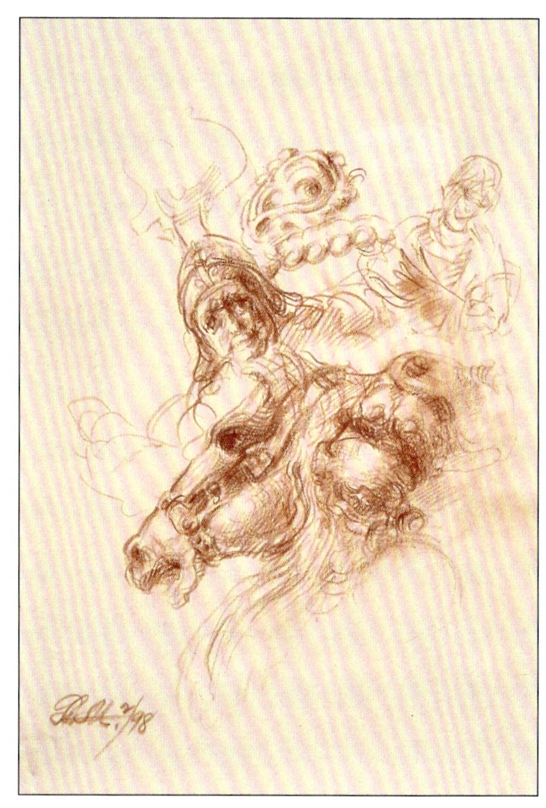

a. *Centurion on Horseback,* 1995
Black and red chalk on cream paper, 11 7/8 x 9 in.

b. *Studies for Centurion and for Horse,* 1998
Red chalk on cream paper, 11 x 8 1/2 in.

c. *Centurion on Horseback,* 1997
Brown ink wash on prepared white paper, 9 1/4 x 6 1/2 in.

d. *My Son Arden Posing as Soldier,* 1997
Oil on panel, 10 x 8 in.

e. *Roman Soldier,* 1995
Black chalk and brown ink wash on tan paper, 9 7/8 x 6 3/4 in.

f. *Back View of Two Soldiers,* 1998
Black chalk on cream paper, 11 x 8 1/2 in.

g. *Back View of Soldier,* 1998
Black chalk and pen and brown ink and wash on cream paper
10 1/2 x 7 3/4 in.

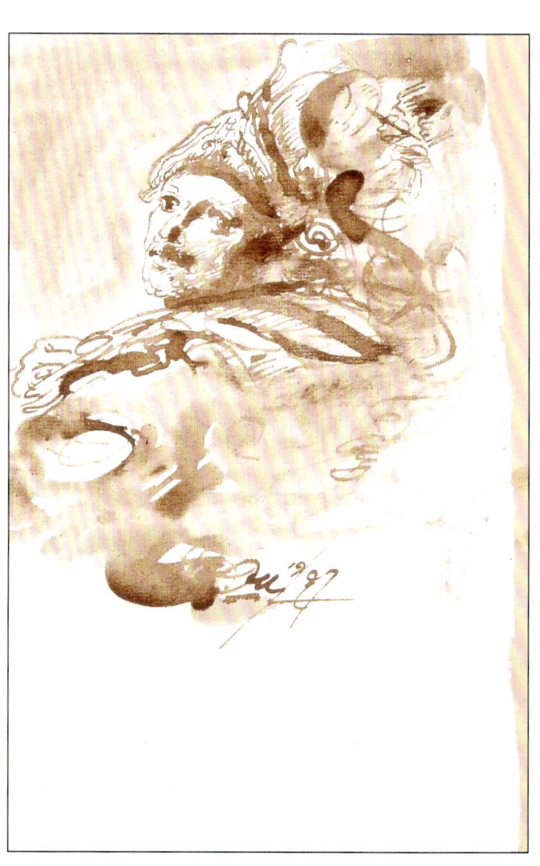

c.

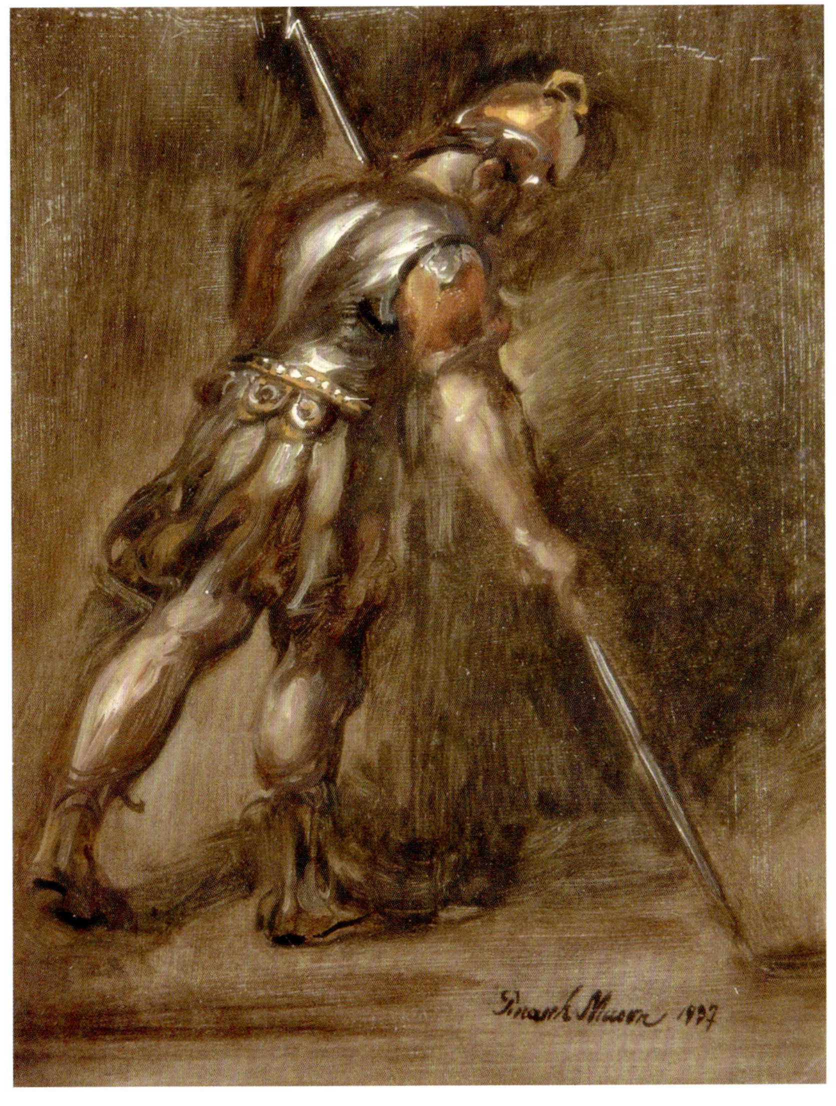

d.

e.

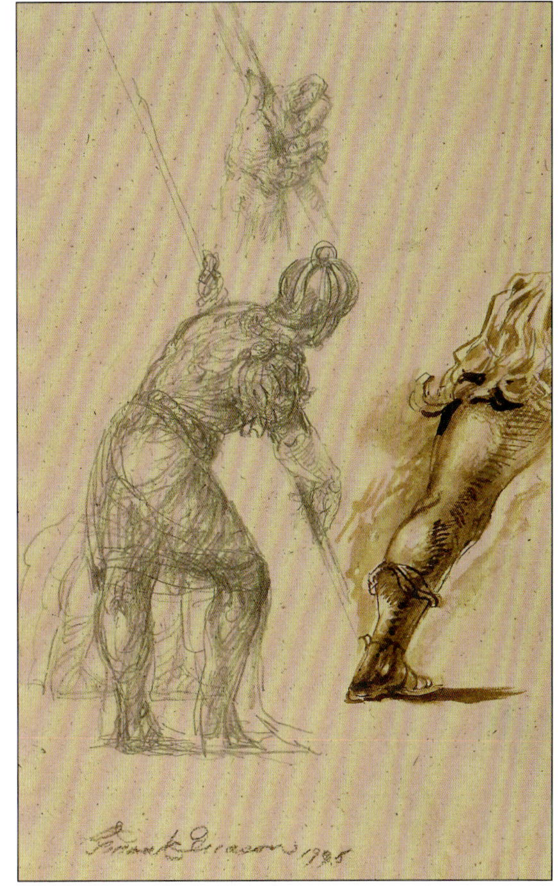

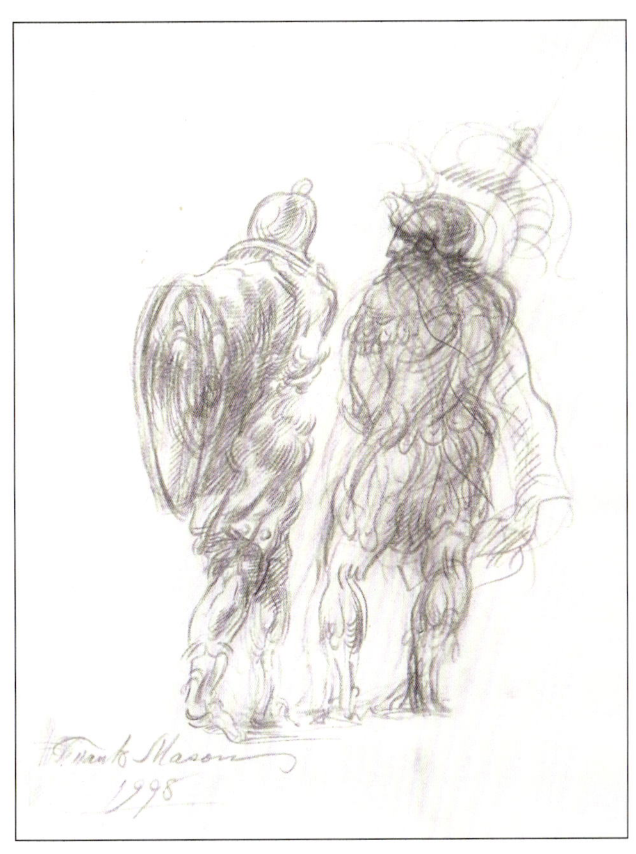

f.

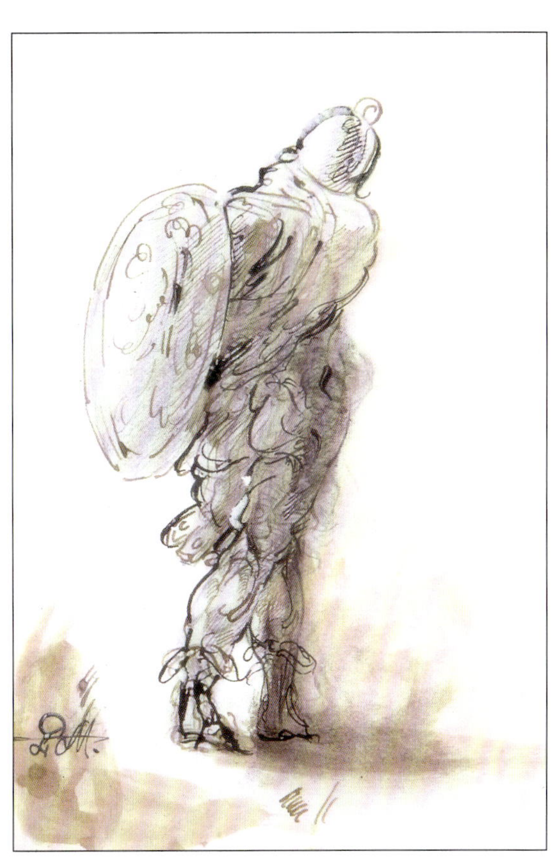

g.

THE RESURRECTION OF CHRIST

IN THE END OF THE SABBATH, AS IT BEGAN TO DAWN TOWARD THE FIRST DAY OF THE WEEK, CAME MARY MAGDALENE AND THE OTHER MARY TO SEE THE SEPULCHRE. AND, BEHOLD, THERE WAS A GREAT EARTHQUAKE: FOR THE ANGEL OF THE LORD DESCENDED FROM HEAVEN, AND CAME AND ROLLED BACK THE STONE FROM THE DOOR, AND SAT UPON IT . . . .AND THE ANGEL. . .SAID UNTO THE WOMEN, FEAR NOT YE: FOR I KNOW THAT YE SEEK JESUS, WHICH WAS CRUCIFIED. HE IS NOT HERE: FOR HE IS RISEN. . .—MATTHEW 28: 1, 2, 5, 6

Commissions from private individuals for portraits are not uncommon, and I have had my share of them. But commissions from churches are another thing. Most artists (and I am one of them) think wistfully of a time when the cathedrals of Europe frequently commissioned specific paintings from the great masters. It helped culture to flourish, it guaranteed an audience for religious paintings, and it filled European churches with masterpieces that continue to provide inspiration. Commissions from European churches are rare today, but I had a great one in 1962 from the Sovereign Military Order of Malta to paint a series depicting the life of Saint Anthony of Padua for the Church of San Giovanni di Malta in Venice. I am proud to say that today these scenes hang alongside a painting by Bellini. Rarer still are commissions from American churches, and I was overjoyed to receive one from Monsignor Marinacci to do a painting of the Resurrection for St. Patrick's Old Cathedral in New York City. It was installed in 1972 behind the high altar. I did several preliminary studies for the painting, usually scenes with several figures—the Roman soldiers asleep on duty near the tomb or Marys encountering their risen Lord—before I arrived at my final interpretation: an heroic figure of Christ alone breaking forth from the tomb. I put into the painting my conviction that the cold, still body in the tomb was fully restored to life. He is not an unearthly spirit presence, but a flesh-and-blood person, a living Christ, truly risen from the dead.

The Resurrection of Christ, 1972
Oil on canvas, 132 x 108 in.
St. Patrick's Old Cathedral, New York, N.Y.

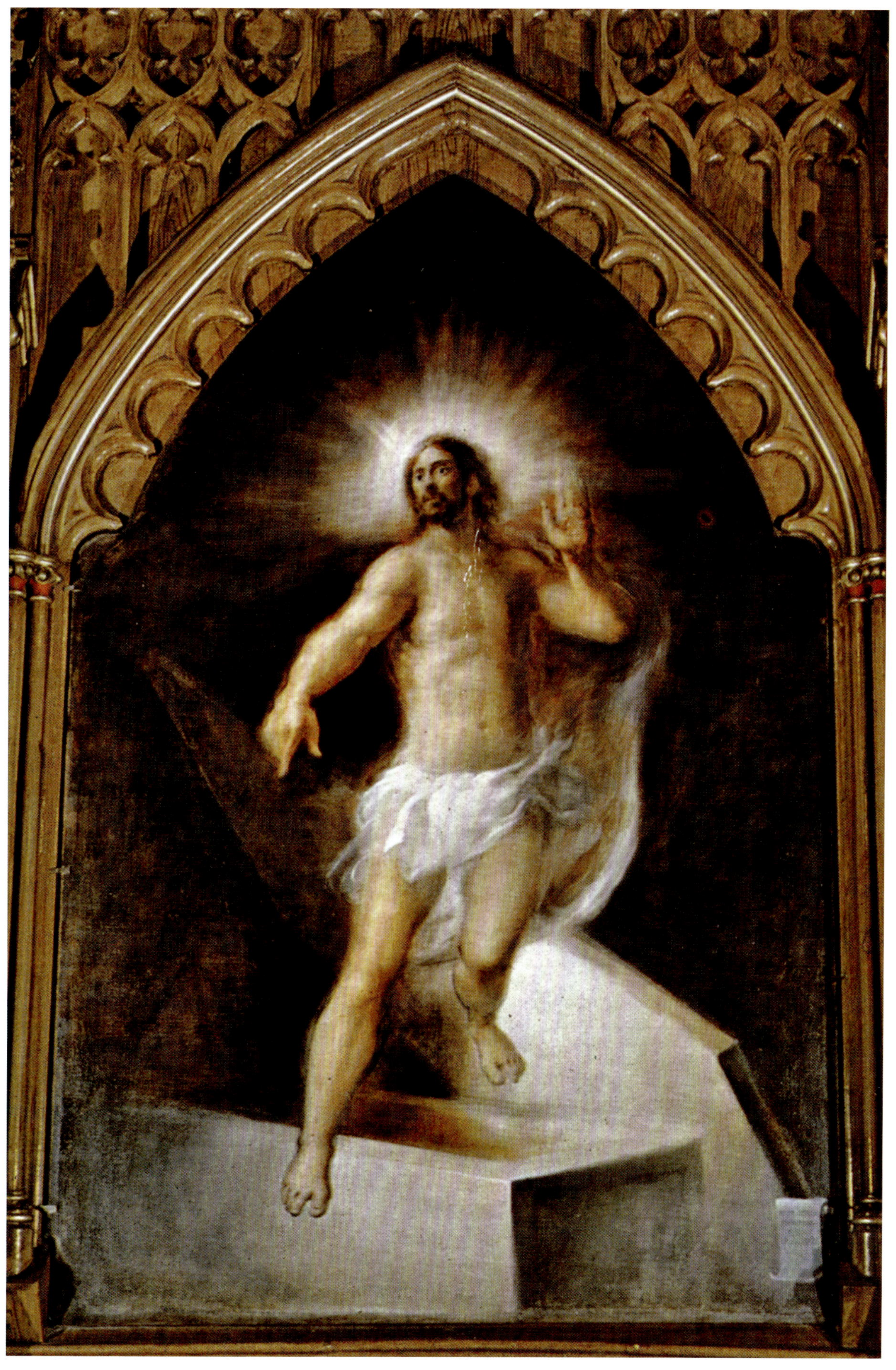

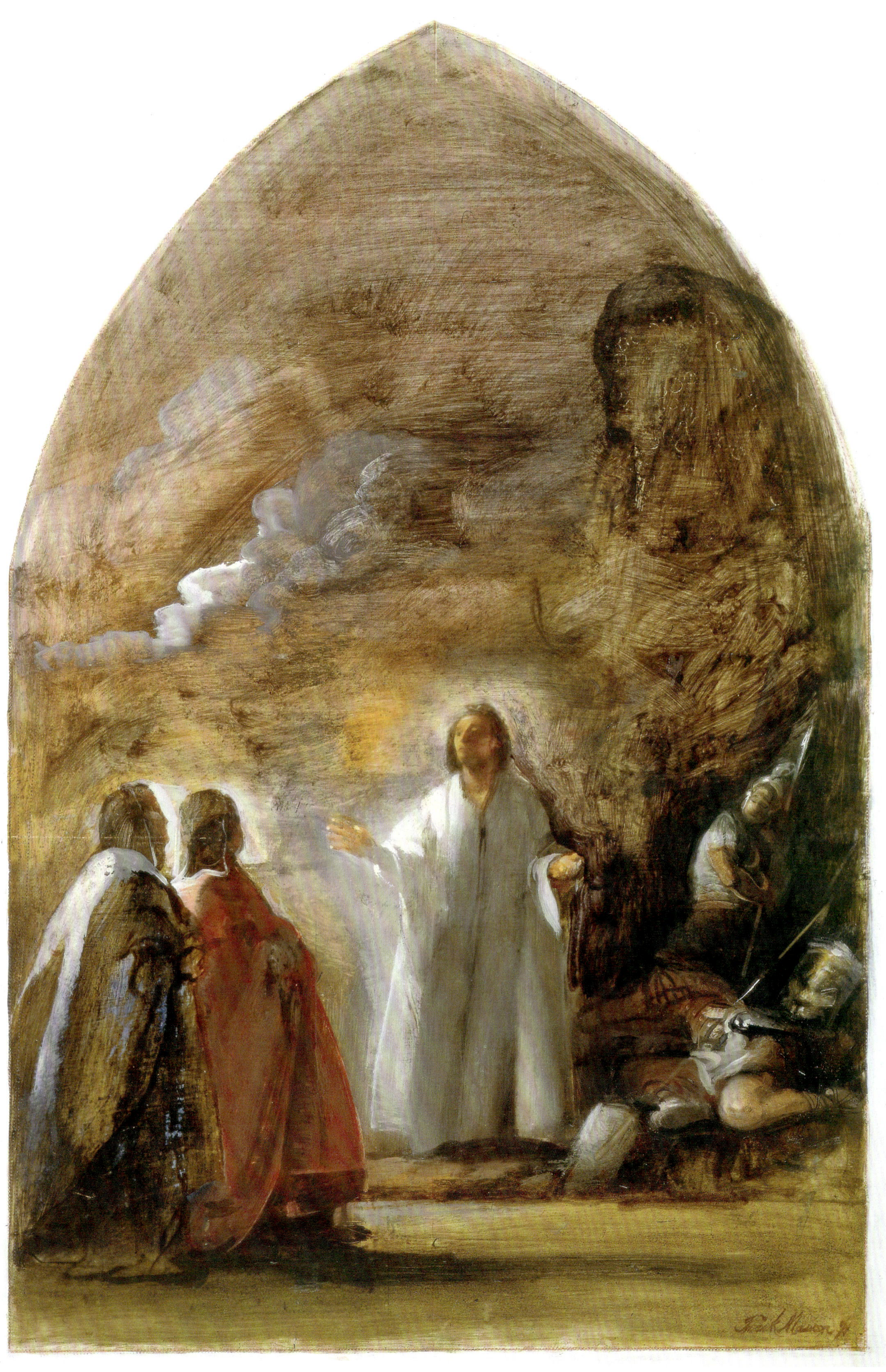

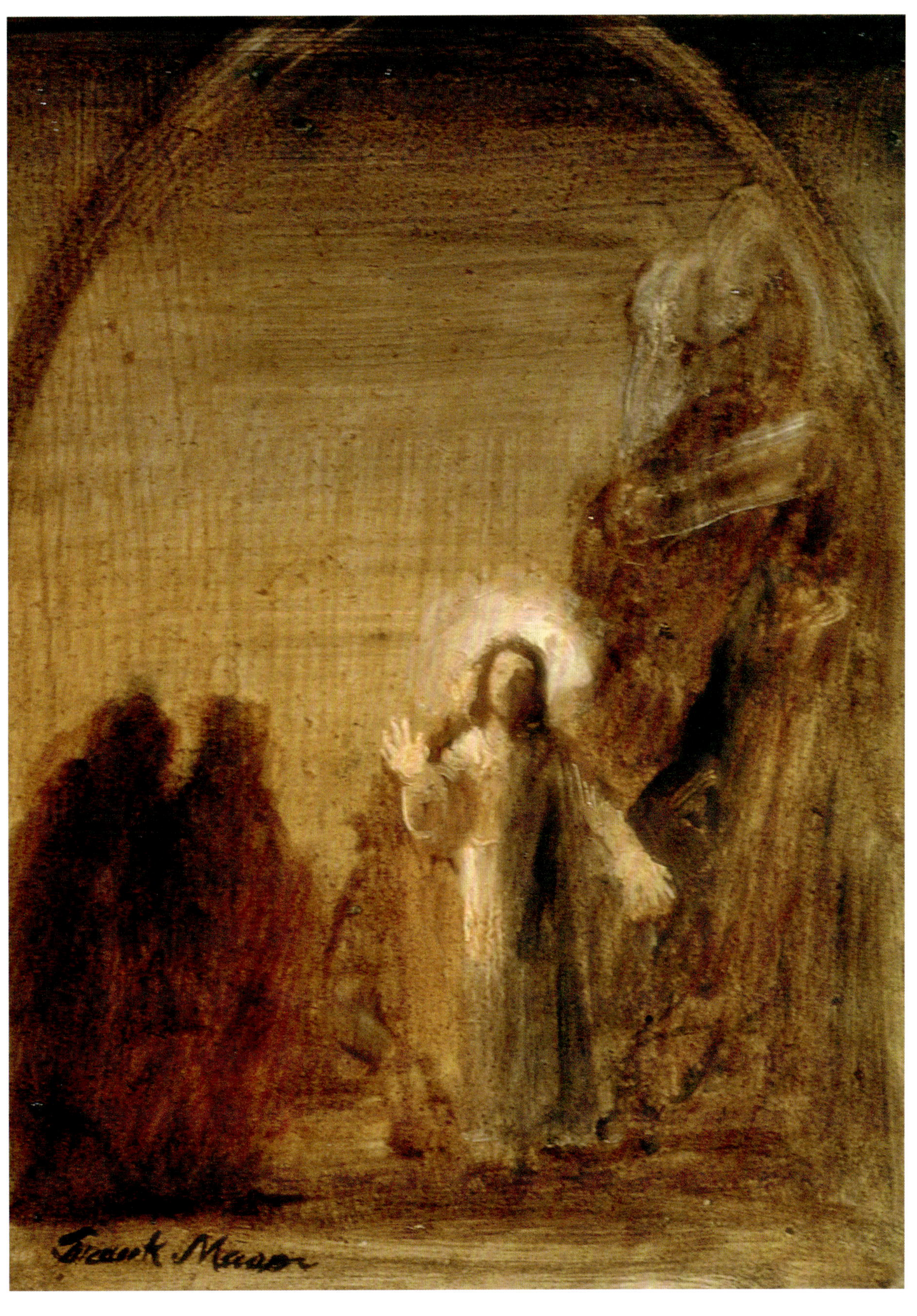

Noli Me Tangere, 1971
Oil on panel, 38 x 30 in.

Noli Me Tangere, ca. 1970
Oil on panel, 12 x 9 in.

a. b.

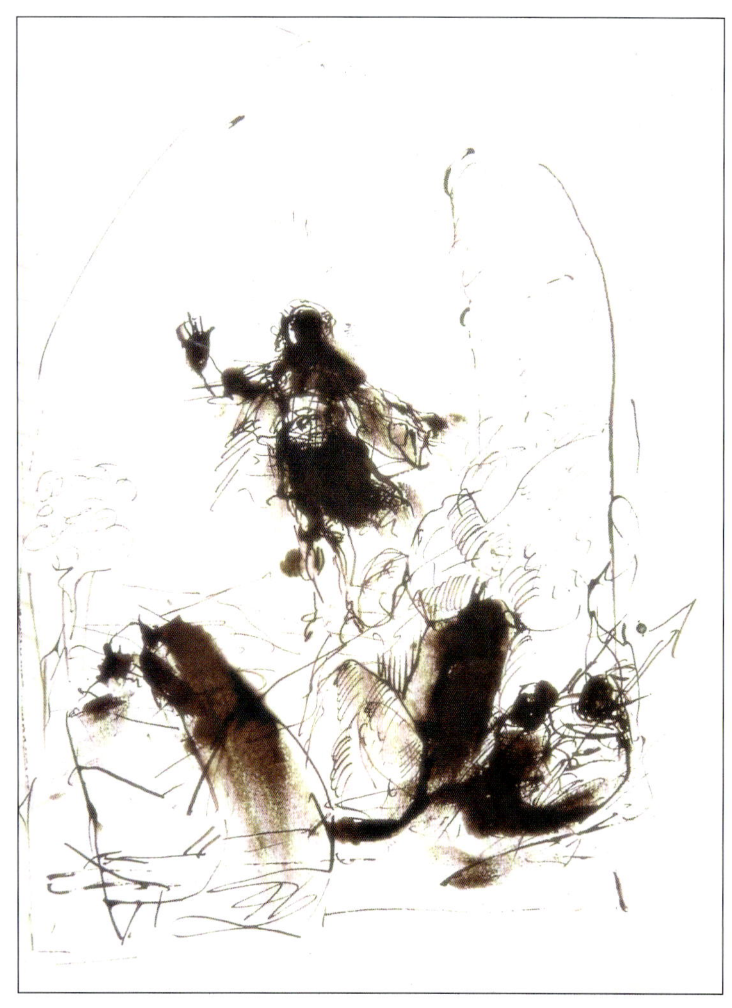

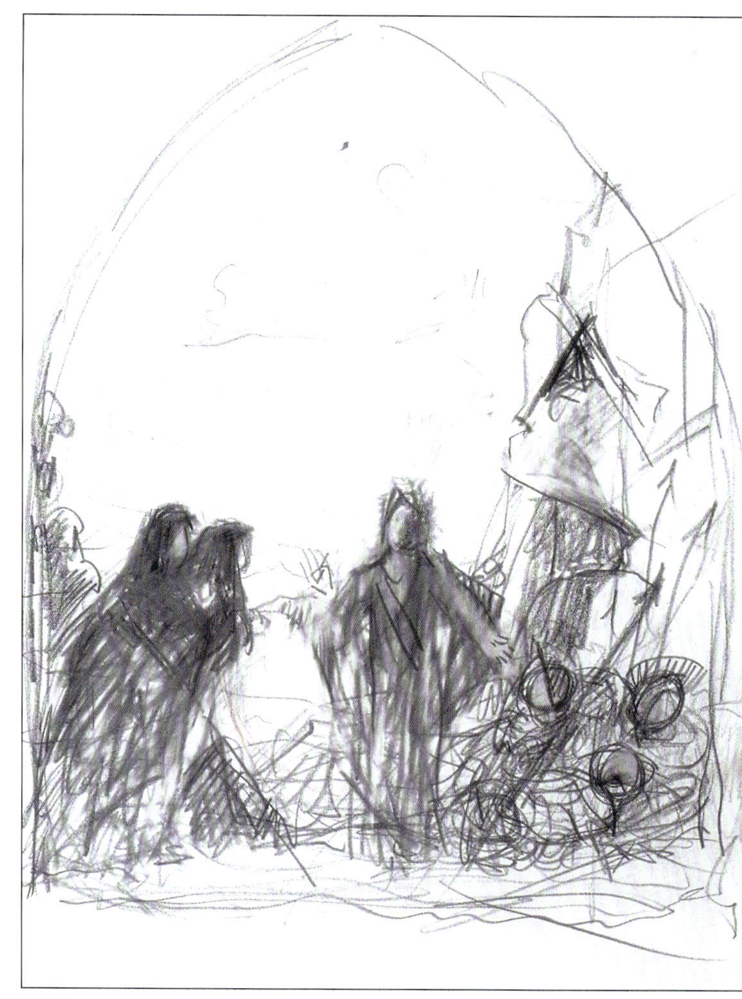

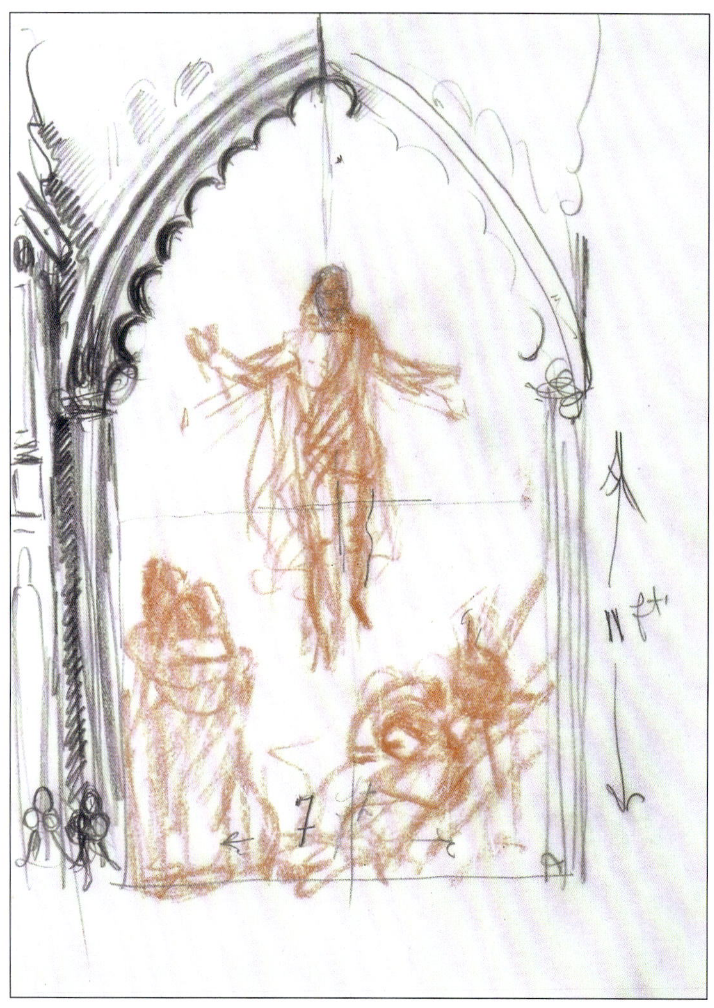

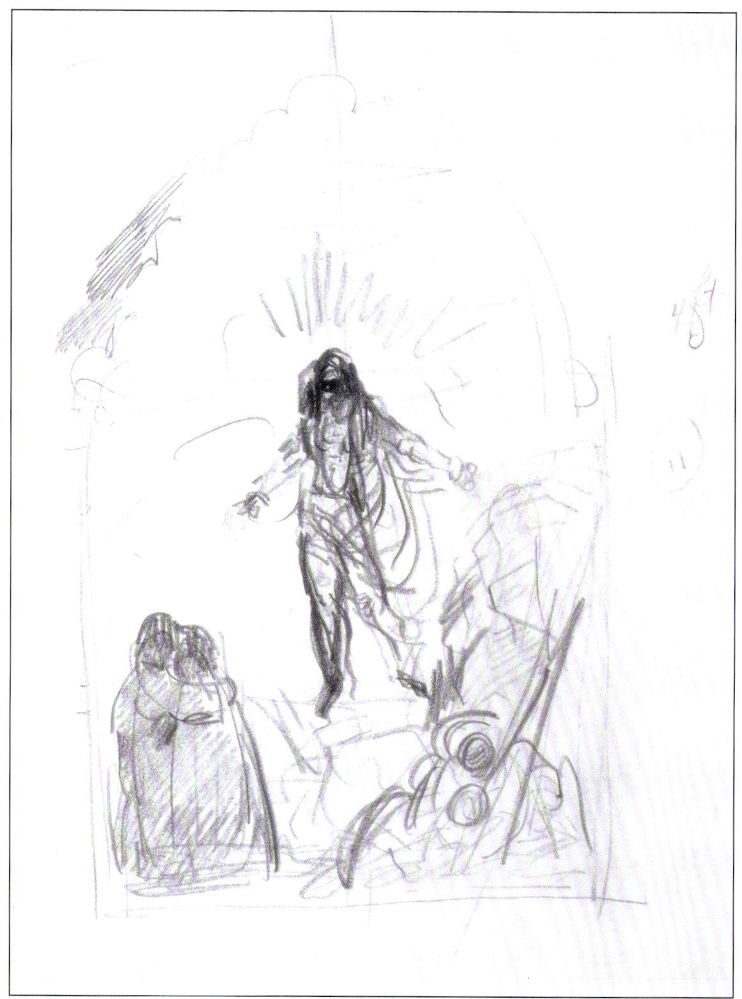

c. d,

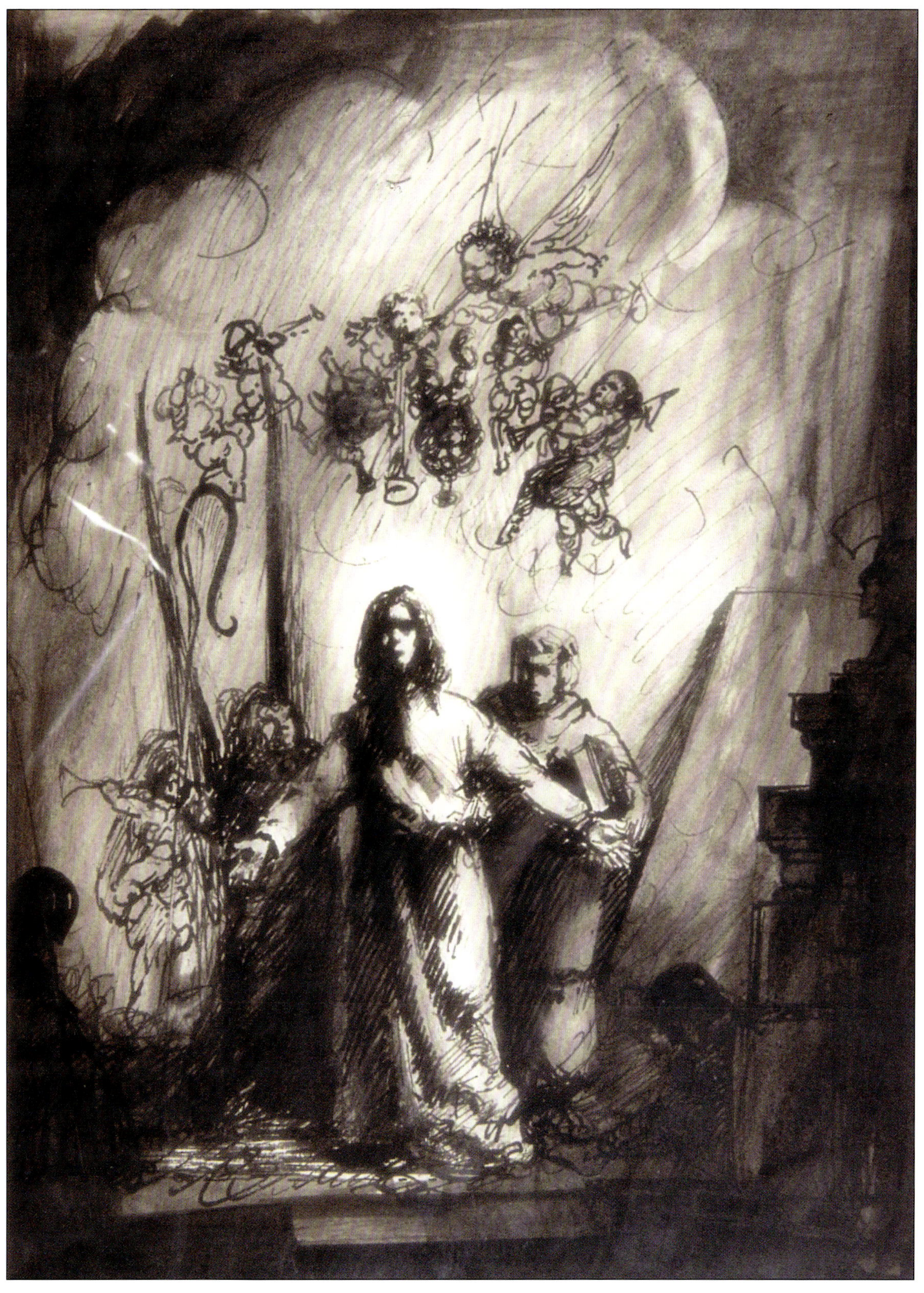

a. *Study for Resurrection,* ca. 1971
Pen and brown ink and wash
on white paper, 11 x 8 in.

b. *Noli Me Tangere,* ca. 1970
Graphite on white paper, 13 5/8 x 11 in.

c. *Study for the Resurrection,* ca. 1970
Red chalk and graphite on white paper
13 5/8 x 11 in.

d. *Study for the Resurrection,* ca. 1970
Graphite on white paper
13 5/8 x 11 in.

e. *Resurrected Christ with Angels,* 1957
Pen and black ink and wash on white paper
12 x 9 in.

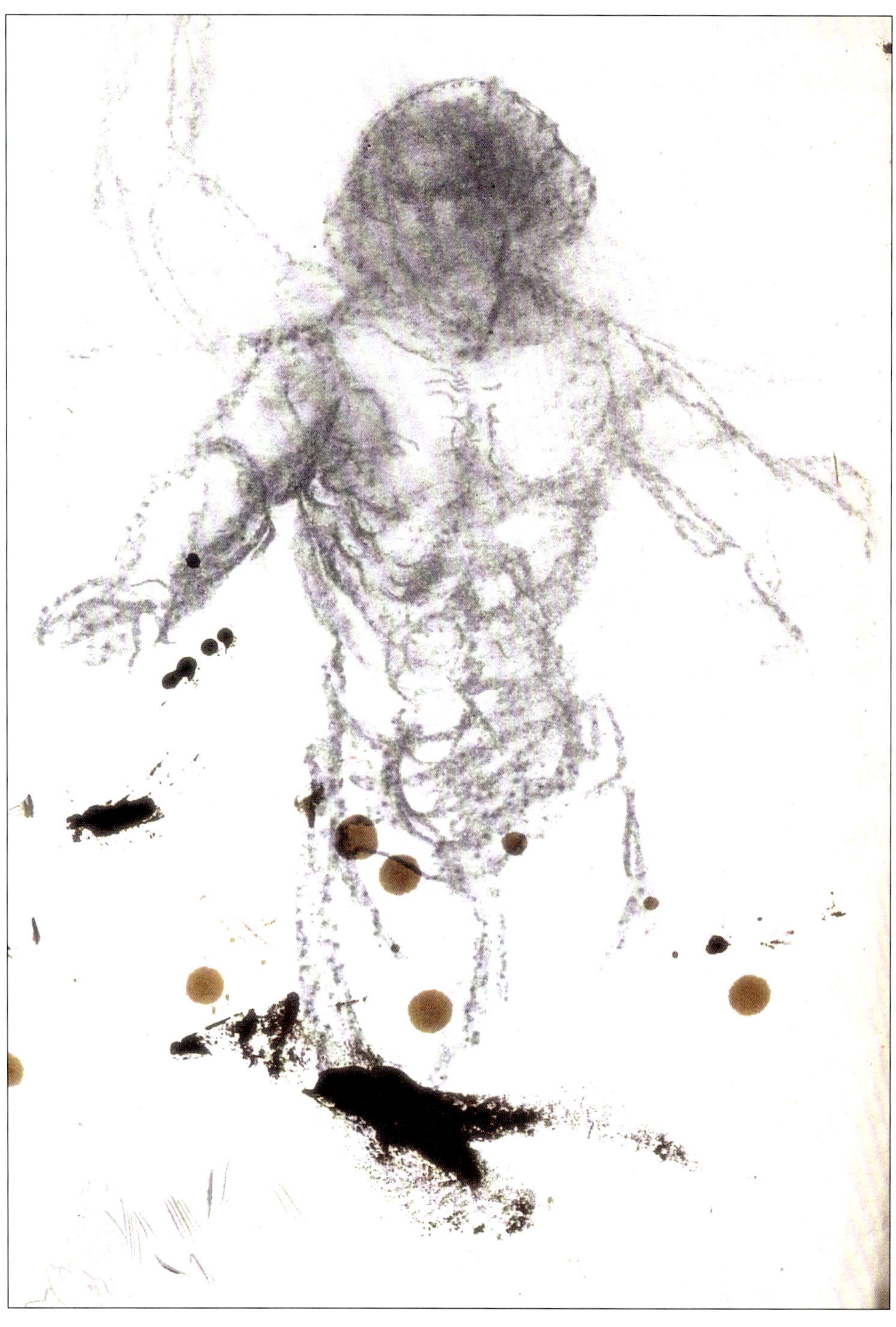

Study of Christ, 1971
Black chalk on cream paper
21 3/8 x 16 1/2 in.

Bozzetto for Resurrection in St. Patrick's Old Cathdral, New York City, 1971
Black chalk on canvas, 30 x 24 in.

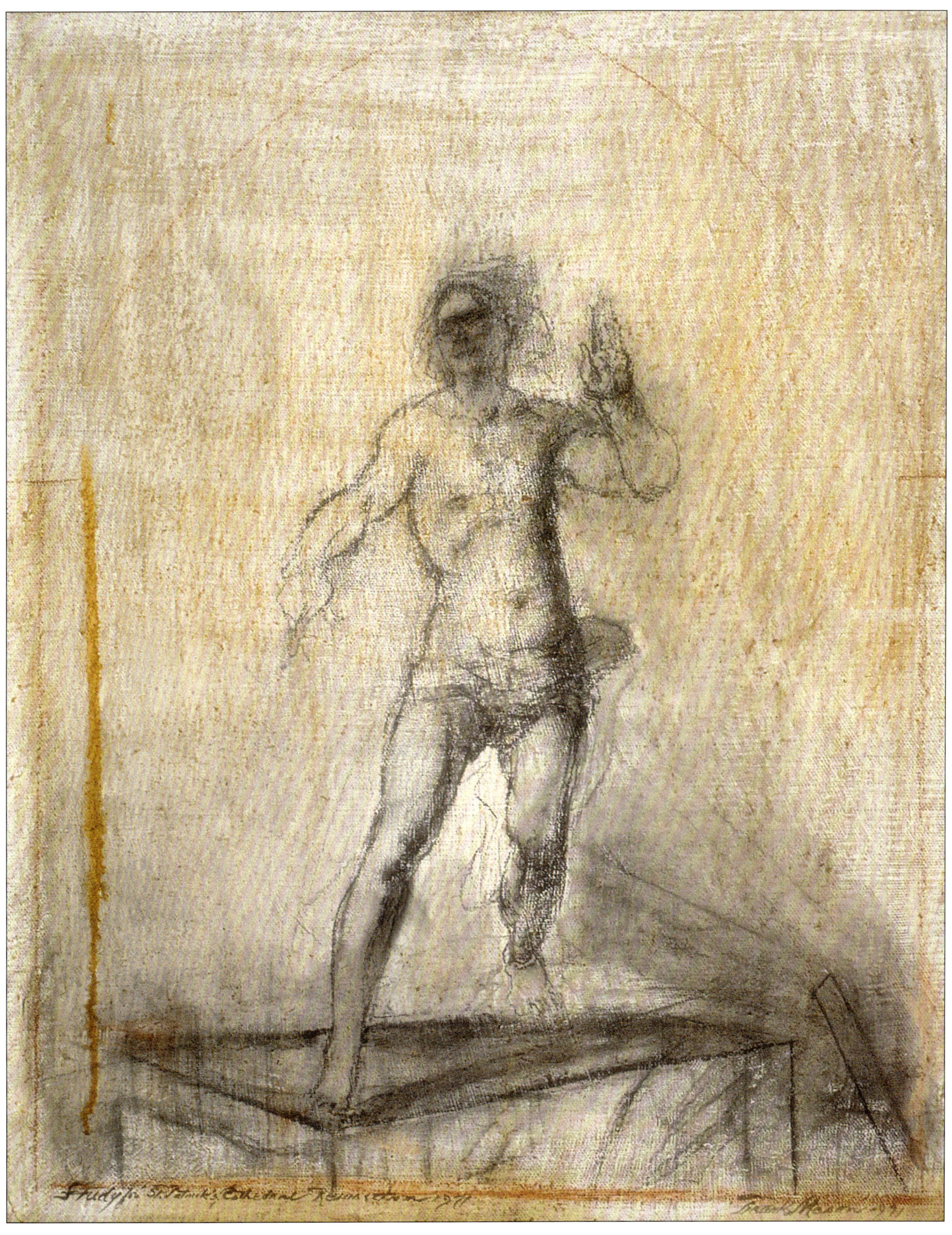

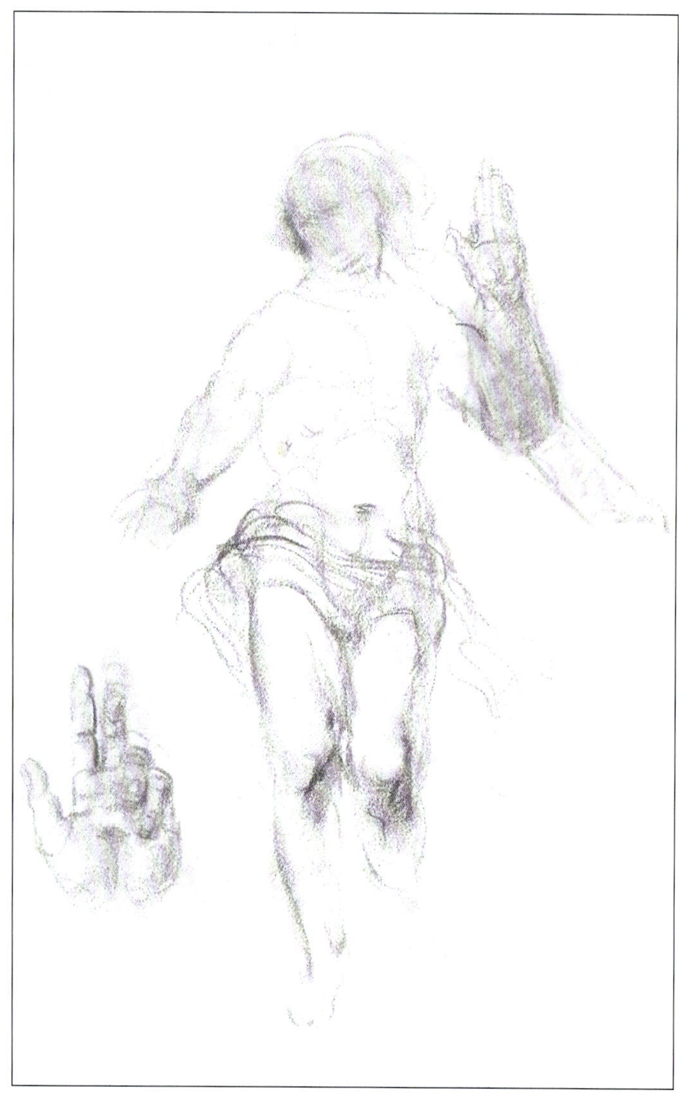

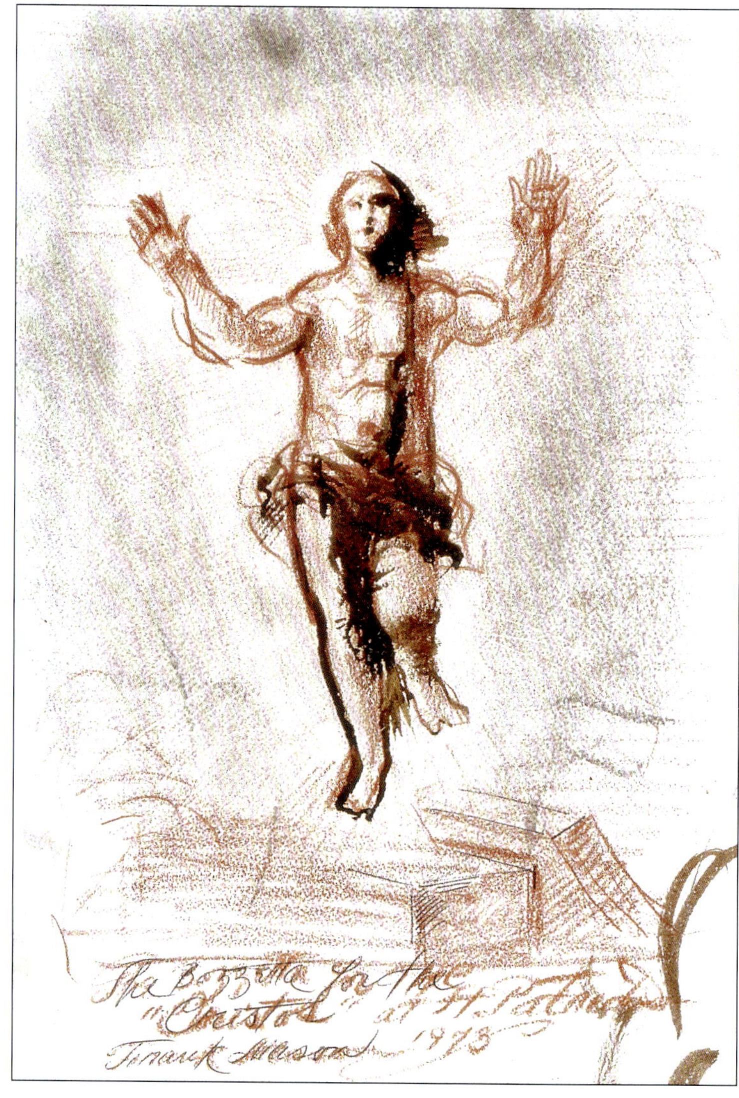

Study for Resurrected Christ, 1971
Black chalk on white paper
22 7/8 x 15 3/8 in.

Bozzetto for the Christos at St. Patrick's, 1973
Red chalk and brown ink wash on cream paper
11 1/2 x 7 3/4 in.

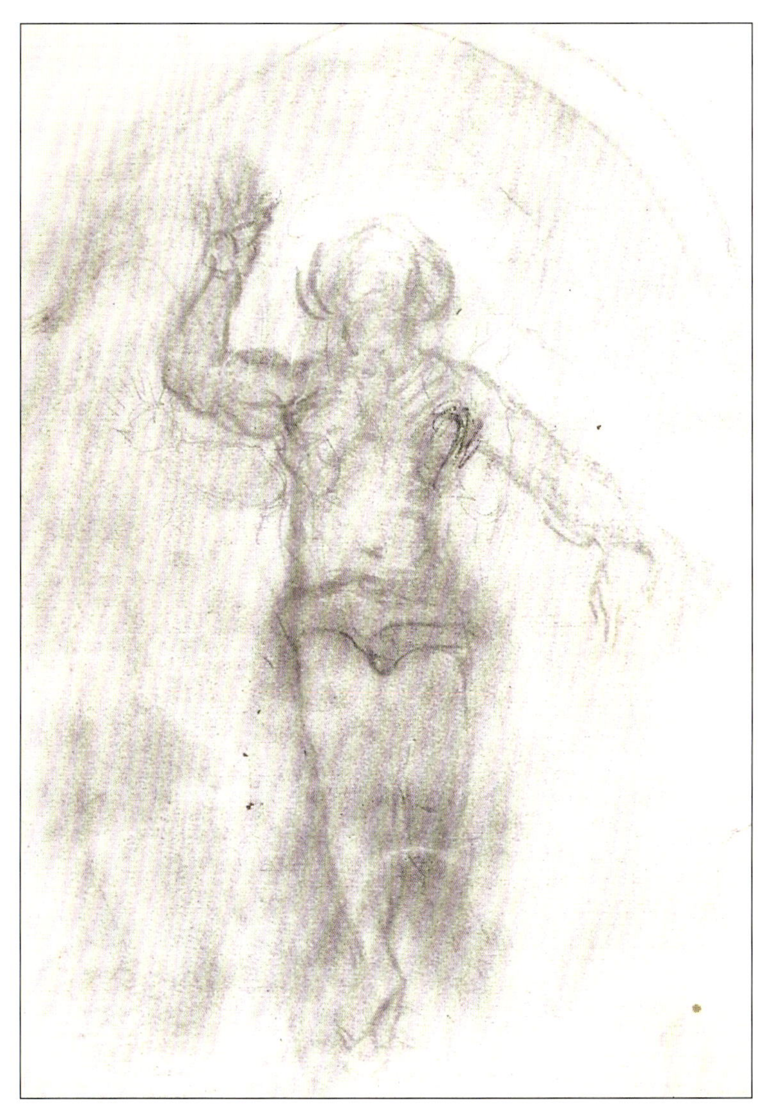

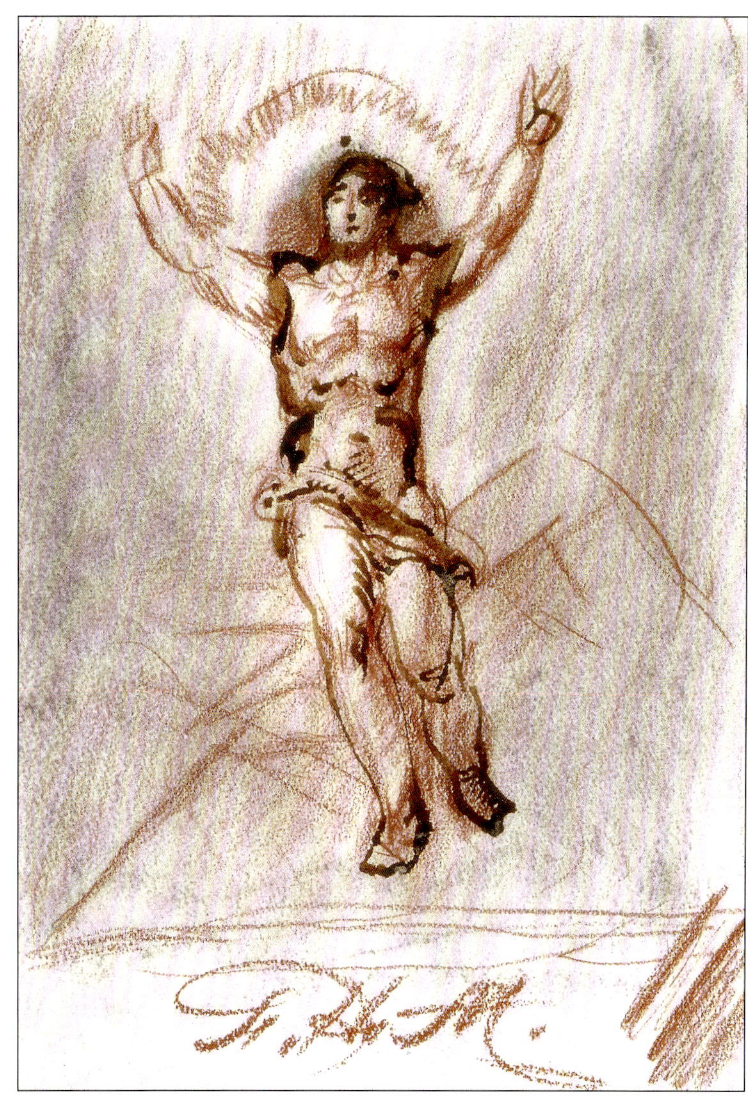

Study for the Resurrection, 1971
Graphite on white paper
14 x 10 3/4 in.

Study for the Resurrection, 1971
Red chalk and graphite and brown ink wash
on white paper, 11 1/2 x 7 in.

Four Studies for Christ, 1971
Pen and brown ink and wash and red chalk on white paper, 13 7/8 x 10 7/8 in.

Studies for Figure of Christ, ca. 1970
Brown ink wash and red chalk on white paper, 13 5/8 x 11 in

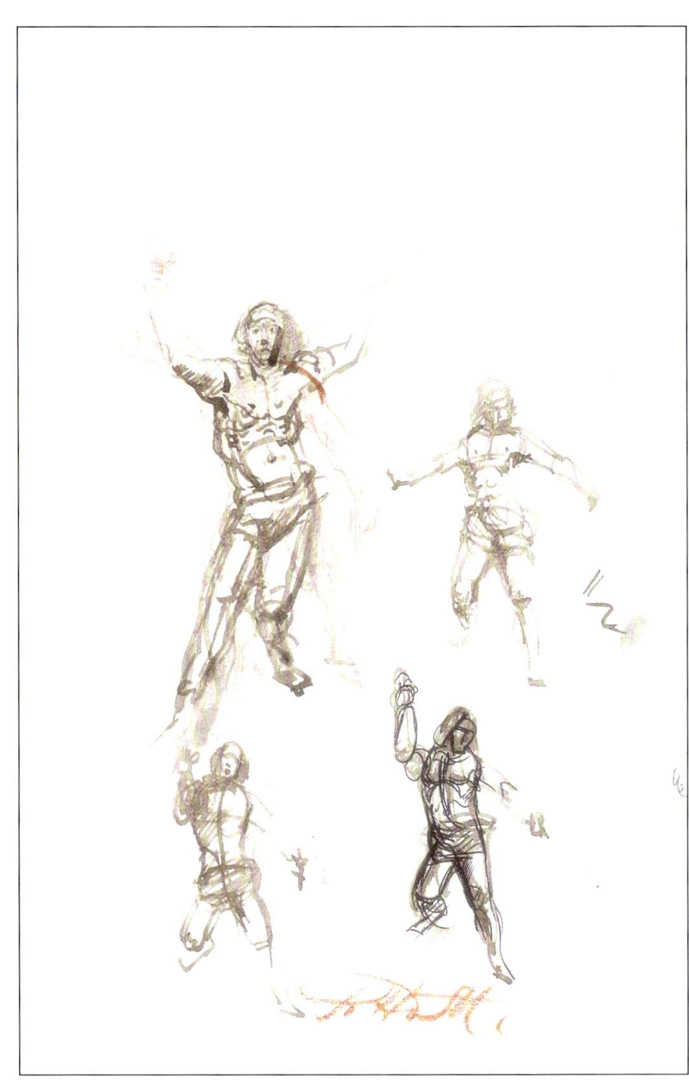

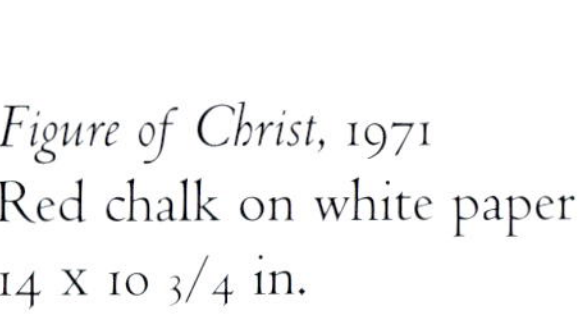

Figure of Christ, 1971
Red chalk on white paper
14 x 10 3/4 in.

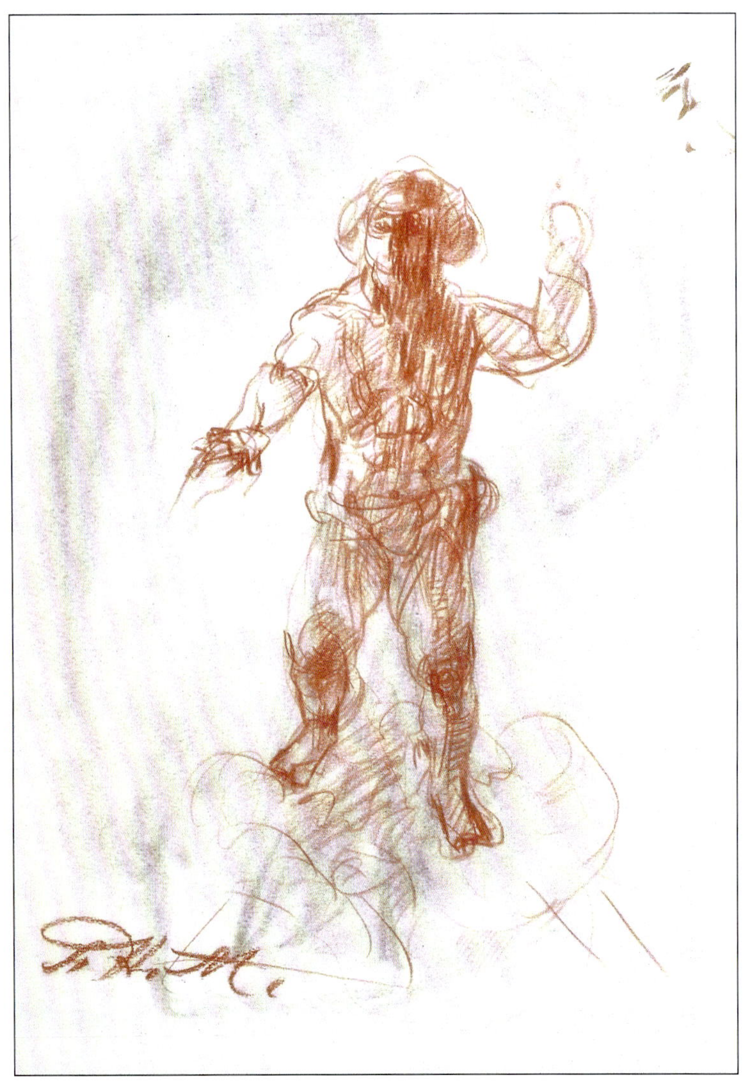

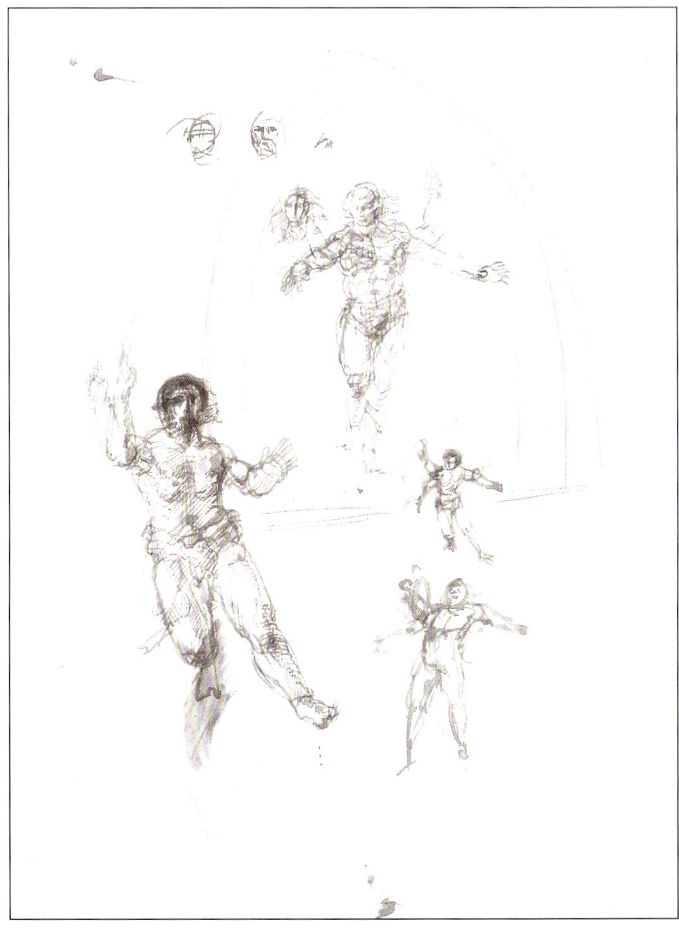

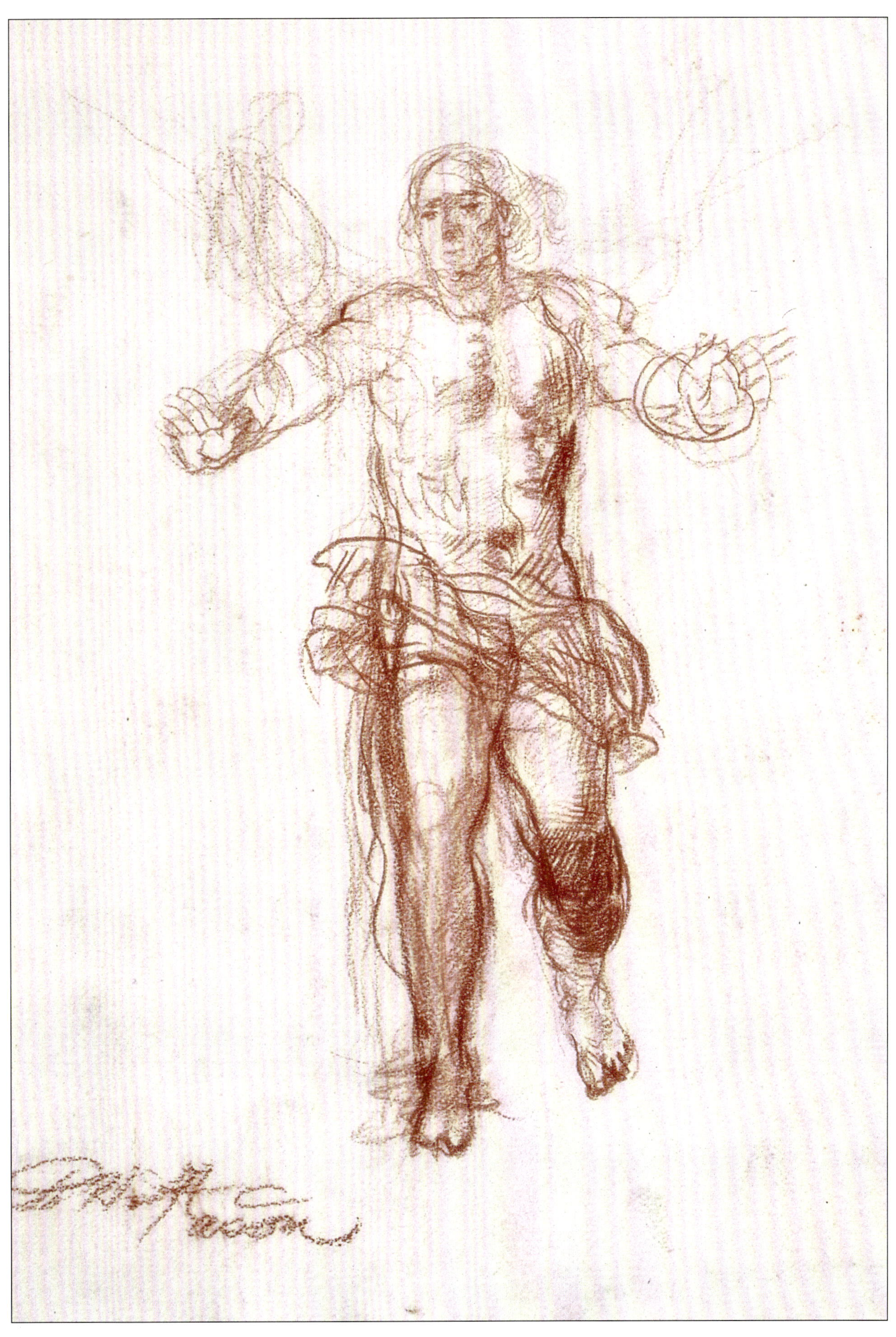

Study for the Resurrection of Christ, 1971
Red chalk on white paper
15 1/2 x 11 1/2 in.

a.

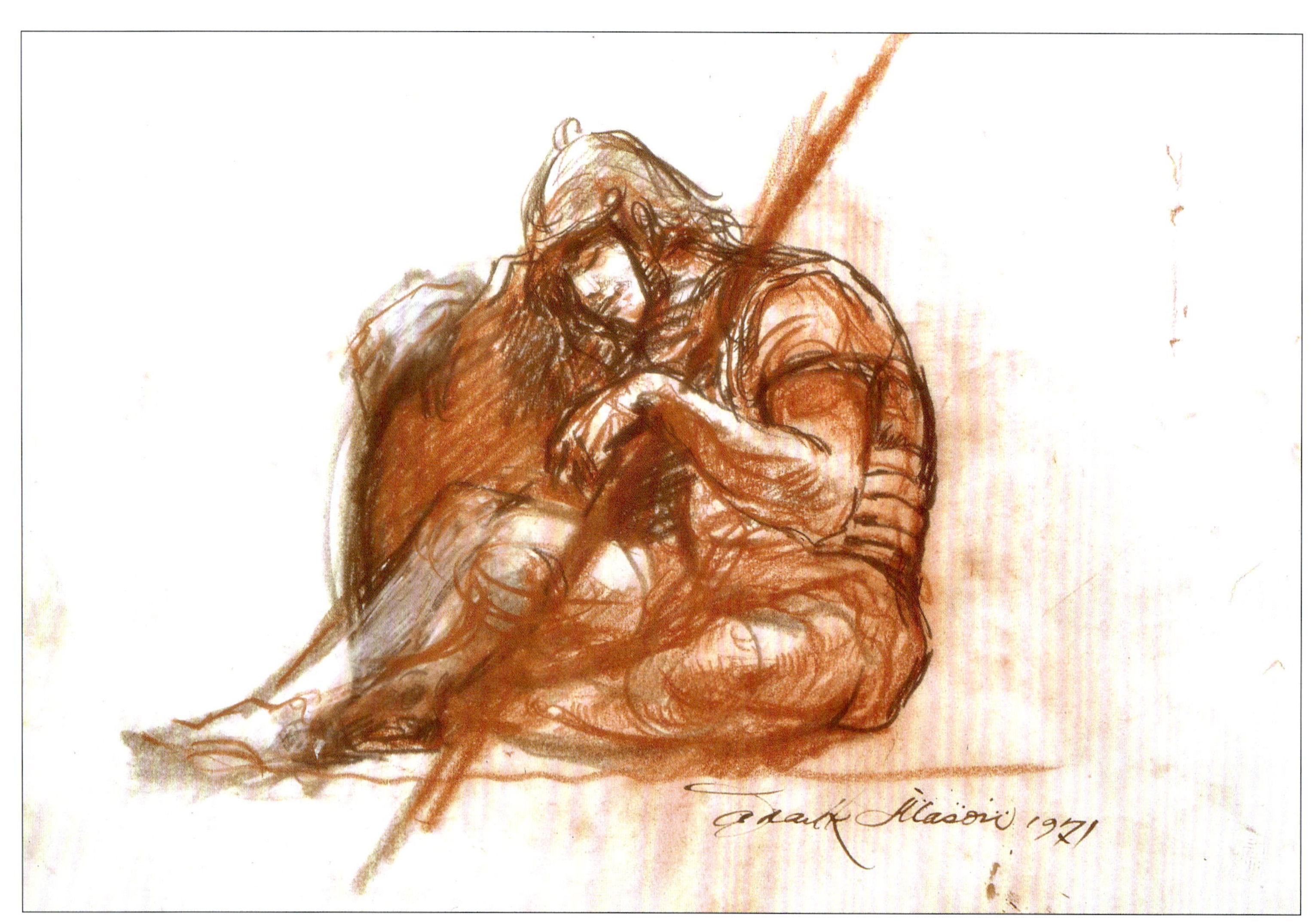

a. *Soldier Asleep at the Tomb of Christ,* 1971
Red and black chalk on white paper
12 x 18 in.

b. *Sleeping Guards at the Tomb,* 1971
Graphite on cream prepared paper
8 x 11 5/8 in.

c. *Sleeping Soldier for Resurrection,* ca. 1970
Red chalk on white paper
11 x 13 5/8 in.

d. *Soldier for the Resurrection,* ca. 1970
Red chalk and graphite on white paper
11 x 13 5/8 in.

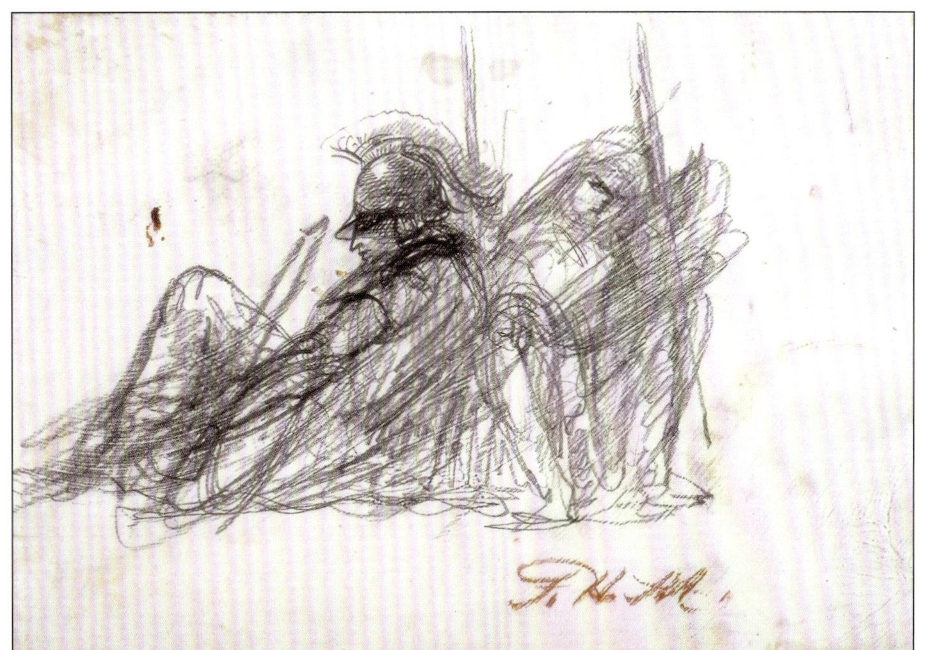

b.

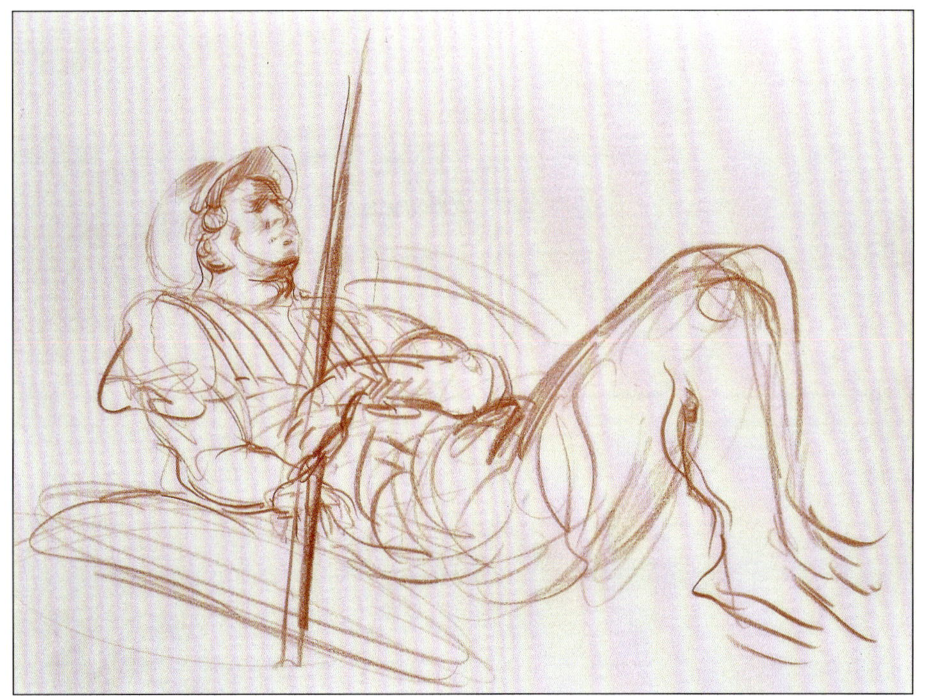

c.

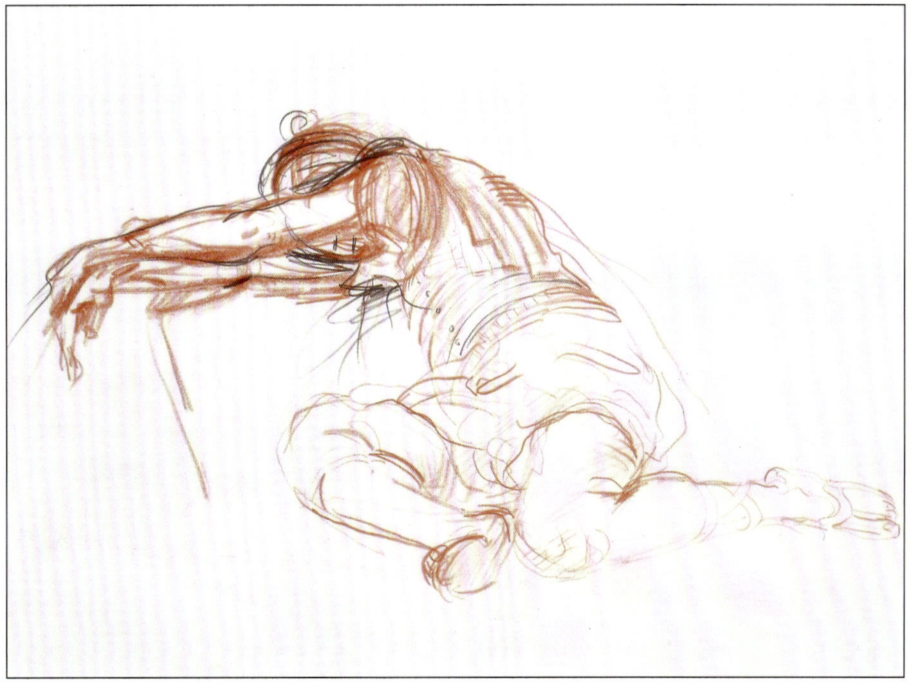

d.

Christ at Emmaus

And, behold, two of them went that same day to a village called Emmaus. . .and they talked together of all these things which had happened. And it came to pass, that, while they communed together and reasoned, Jesus himself drew near, and went with them. But their eyes were holden that they should not know him. . . .And beginning at Moses and all the prophets, he expounded unto them in all the scriptures the things concerning himself. . . And it came to pass, as he sat at meat with them, he took bread, and blessed it, and brake, and gave to them. And their eyes were opened, and they knew him; and he vanished out of their sight. —Luke 24: 13–16, 27, 30, 31

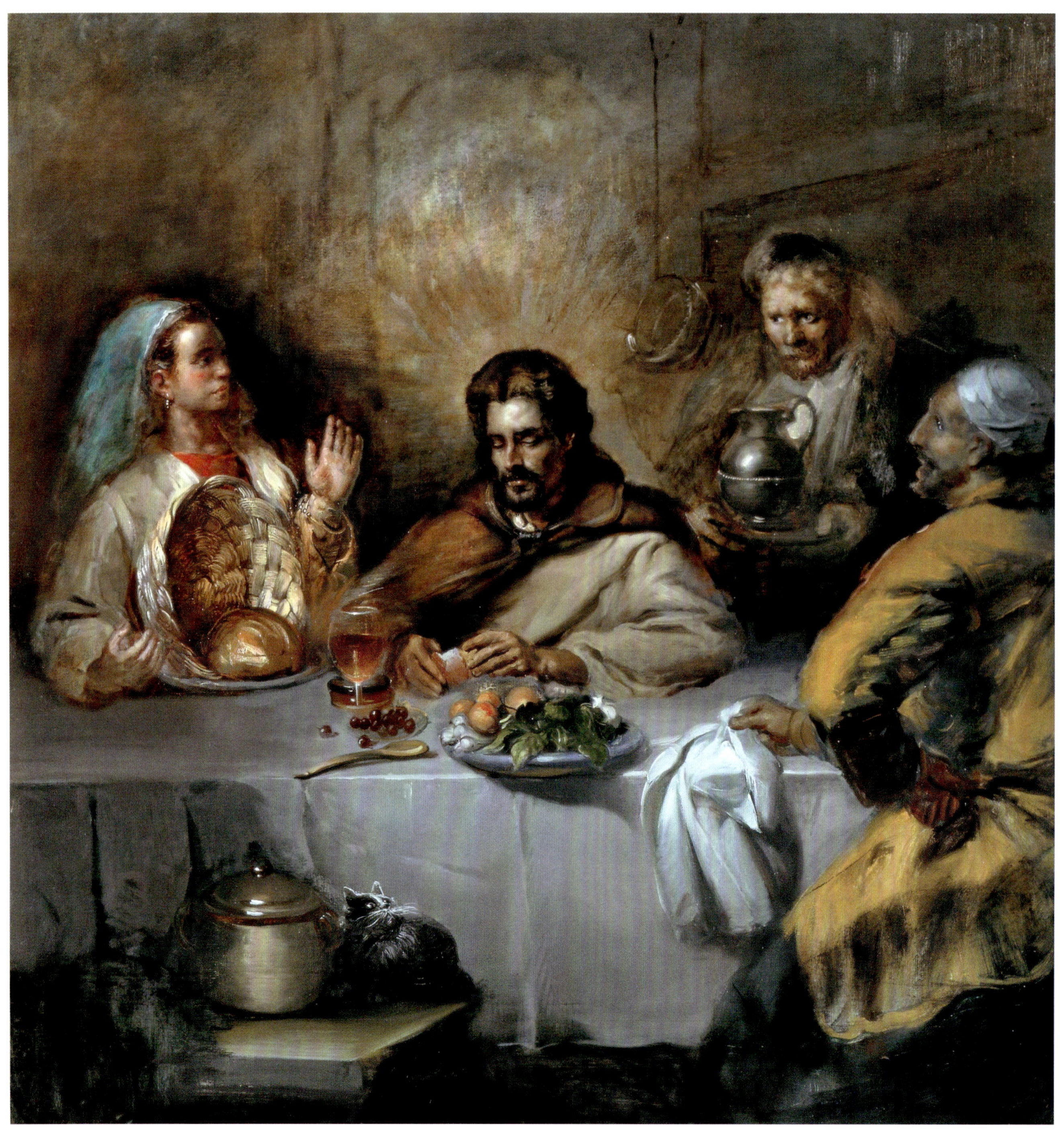

a.

a. *Christ at Emmaus,* 1984
Oil on canvas, 72 x 70 in.

b. *Study for Christ at Emmaus,* 1984
Red chalk on pink paper
9 3/4 x 11 in.

c. *Christ Blessing the Bread at Emmaus,* 1984
Graphite and brown ink wash
on cream paper, 7 1/2 x 9 3/8 in.

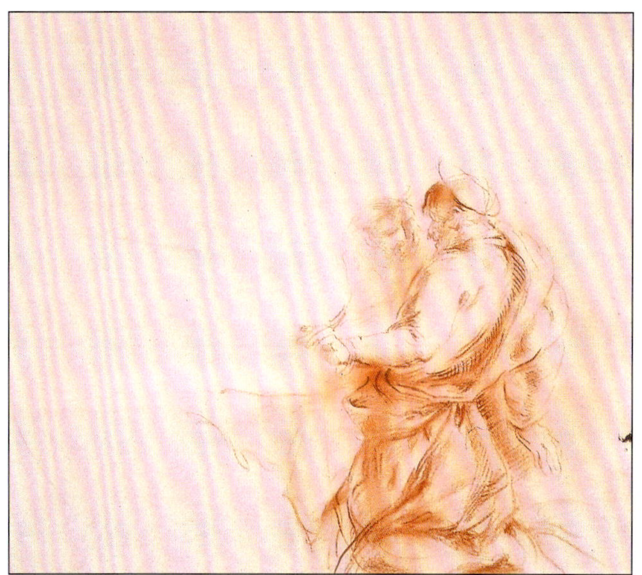

b.

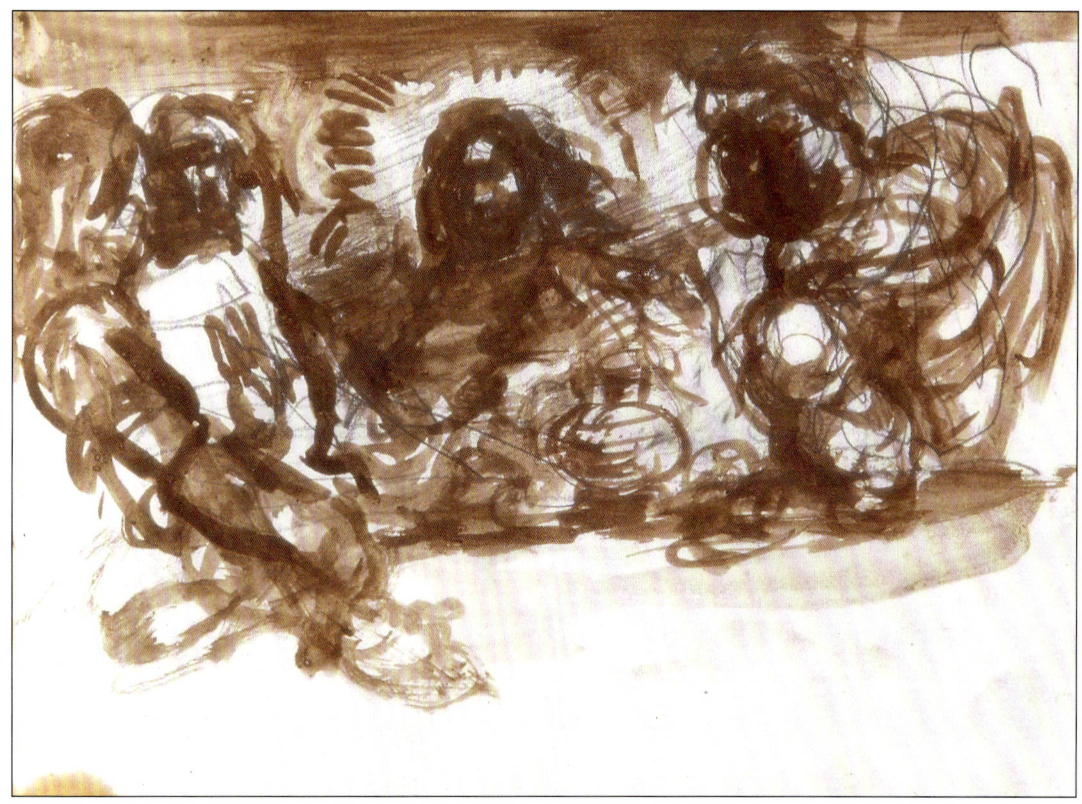

c.

St. Luke tells the marvelous story of the two disciples who travel all day with the risen Christ without realizing who He is. Finally, over dinner that evening, they recognize Him in the breaking of the bread. It is a dramatic scene: Christ at the table in the shadowy inn, the simple meal on the coarse white cloth before Him. The two men, the serving girl, and even the cat fix their eyes on Him in wonder. What a climax to their journey from Jerusalem to Emmaus! I researched carefully for the setting for this painting. I wanted the walls to look like stone because buildings in that area at that time were made with thick stone walls to keep out the heat. The costume worn by the figure of Christ was made by the mother of one of my models out of surplus army blankets. They were the right color and texture; people don't realize that in the hot desert areas the natives wear woolens to keep heat out and moisture in. The apricots—a fruit in season in Israel at that time of year—I found at a wholesale fruit market in lower Manhattan, and the loaf of bread came from the Italian bakery around the corner from my studio. I painted the cat from my imagination.

DOUBTING THOMAS

BUT THOMAS, ONE OF THE TWELVE, CALLED DIDYMUS, WAS NOT WITH THEM WHEN JESUS CAME. THE OTHER DISCIPLES THEREFORE SAID UNTO HIM, WE HAVE SEEN THE LORD. BUT HE SAID UNTO THEM, EXCEPT I SHALL SEE IN HIS HANDS THE PRINT OF THE NAILS. . . AND PUT MY FINGER INTO THE PRINT OF THE NAILS, AND THRUST MY HAND INTO HIS SIDE, I WILL NOT BELIEVE. AND AFTER EIGHT DAYS AGAIN HIS DISCIPLES WERE WITHIN, AND THOMAS WITH THEM: THEN CAME JESUS, THE DOORS BEING SHUT, AND STOOD IN THE MIDST, AND SAID, PEACE BE UNTO YOU. THEN SAITH HE TO THOMAS, REACH HITHER THY FINGER, AND BEHOLD MY HANDS; AND REACH HITHER THY HAND, AND THRUST IT INTO MY SIDE: AND BE NOT FAITHLESS, BUT BELIEVING. AND THOMAS ANSWERED AND SAID UNTO HIM, MY LORD AND MY GOD. JESUS SAITH UNTO HIM, THOMAS, BECAUSE THOU HAST SEEN ME, THOU HAST BELIEVED: BLESSED ARE THEY THAT HAVE NOT SEEN, AND YET HAVE BELIEVED. —JOHN 20: 24–29

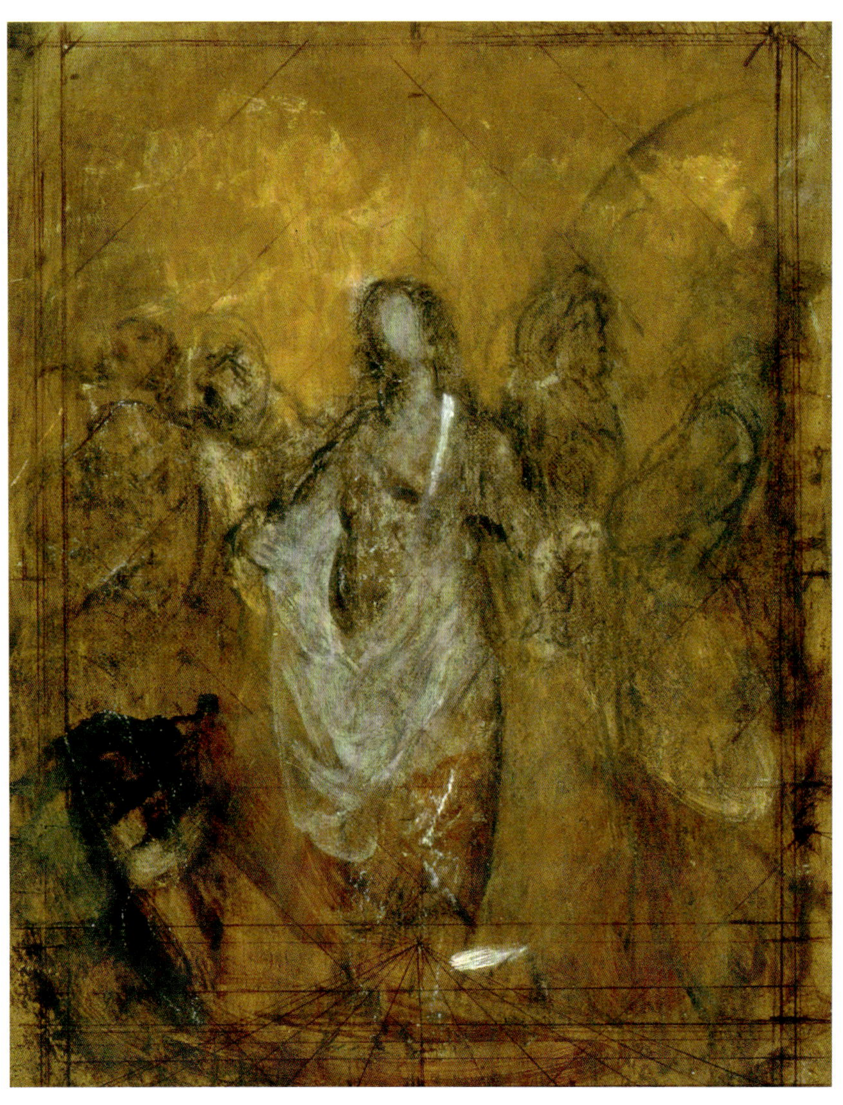

Doubting Thomas, 1995, oil on canvas on panel, 12 x 9 1/2 in.

Thomas has given his name to untold numbers of skeptics down through the centuries. The testimony of the other apostles, who have already encountered the resurrected, living Christ, cannot convince Thomas that their Master has indeed risen. Oh, no; that's not enough for Thomas. He must have tangible proof; he must experience Christ for himself. I wanted to paint the moment when Christ appeared at the table, to show Thomas' astonishment and wonder when at last he is truly convinced. In a way, Thomas was luckier than we are. He did actually see the living Lord. Thomas' story tells me that hearing or reading about Christ is not enough; I must experience Him in my heart with faith and sense His real presence in my daily life. And it's not always an easy thing to do.

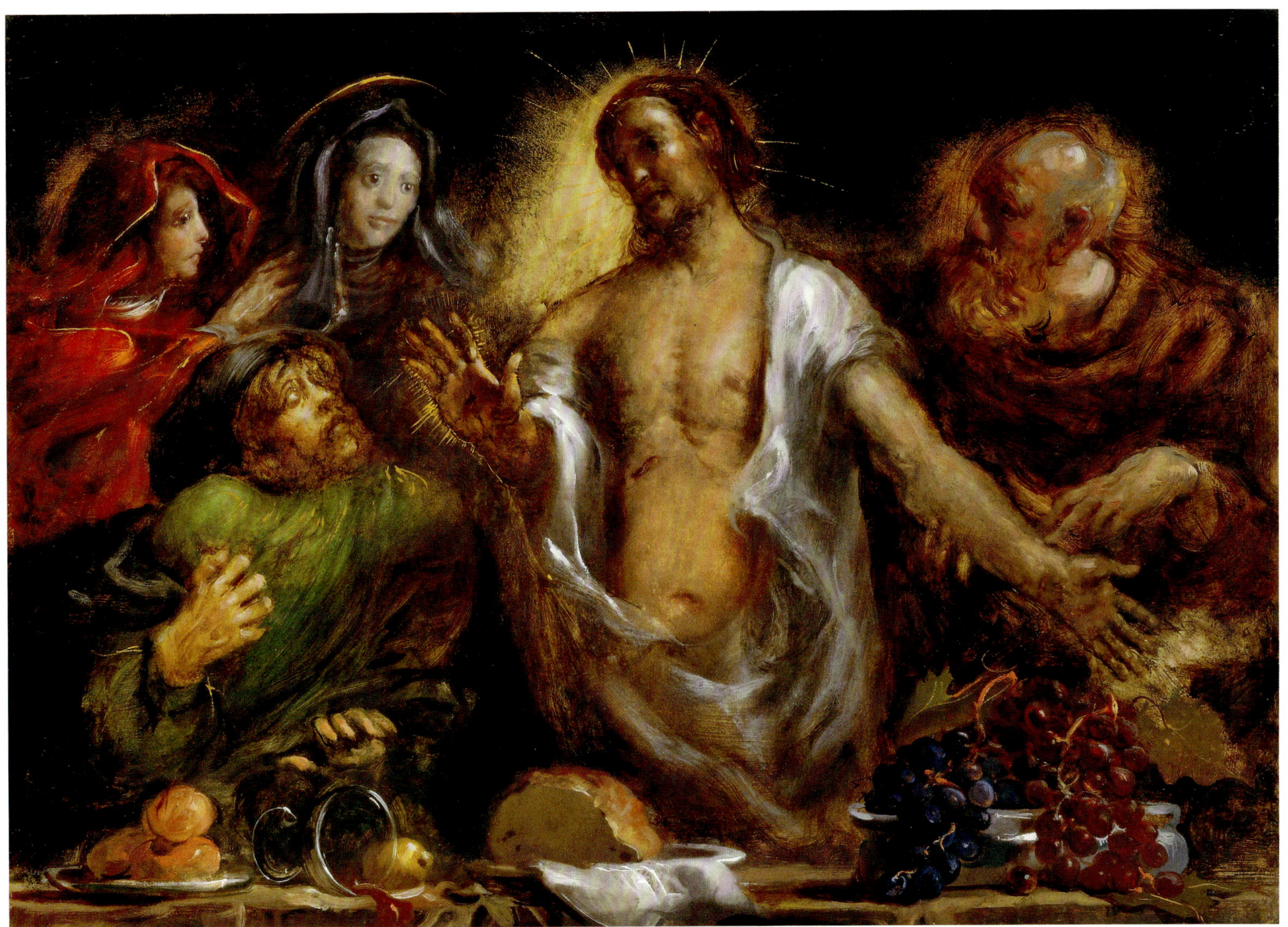

Doubting Thomas, 1995, oil on wood panel, 24 x 34 in.

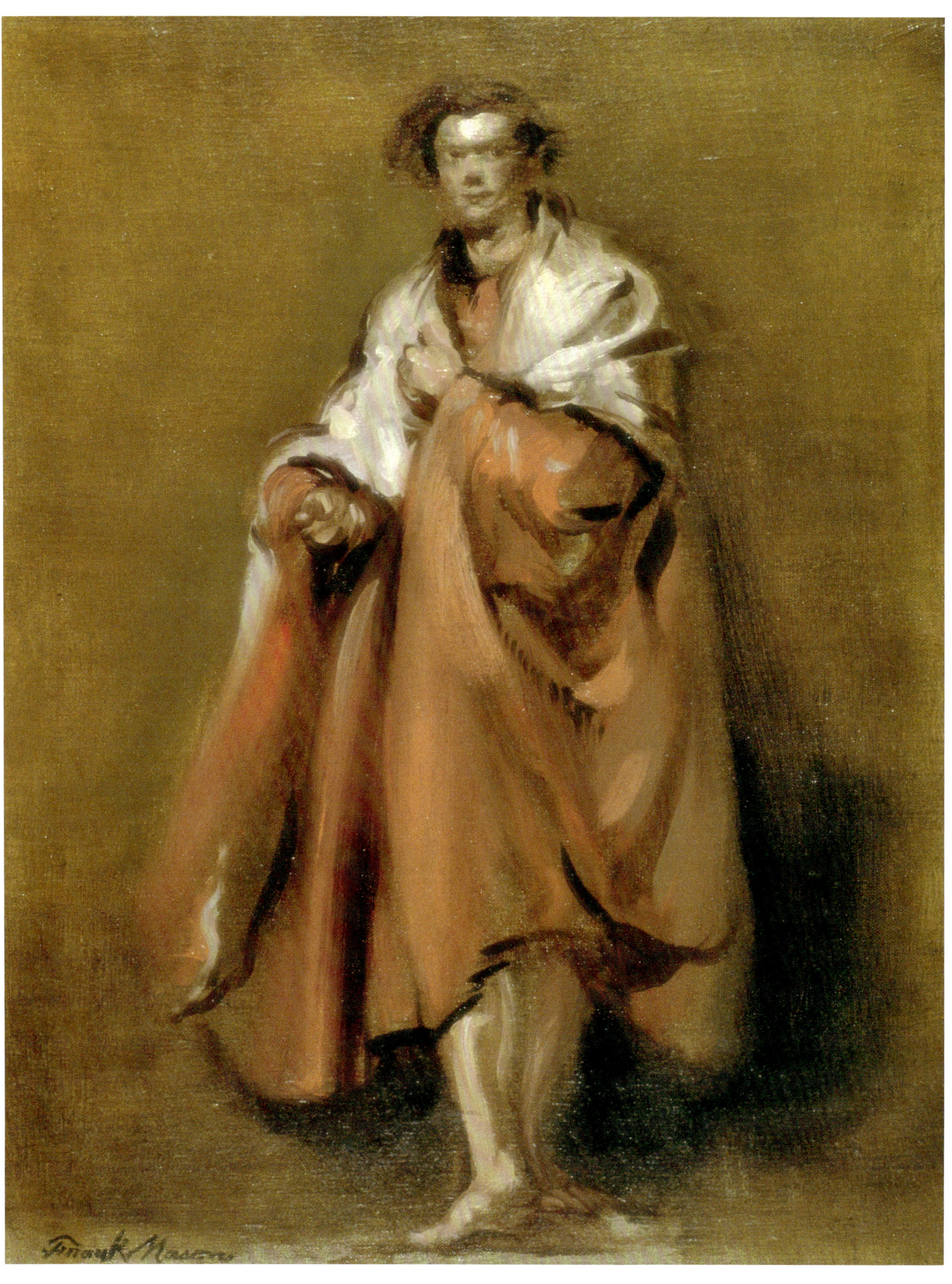
Frank Mason

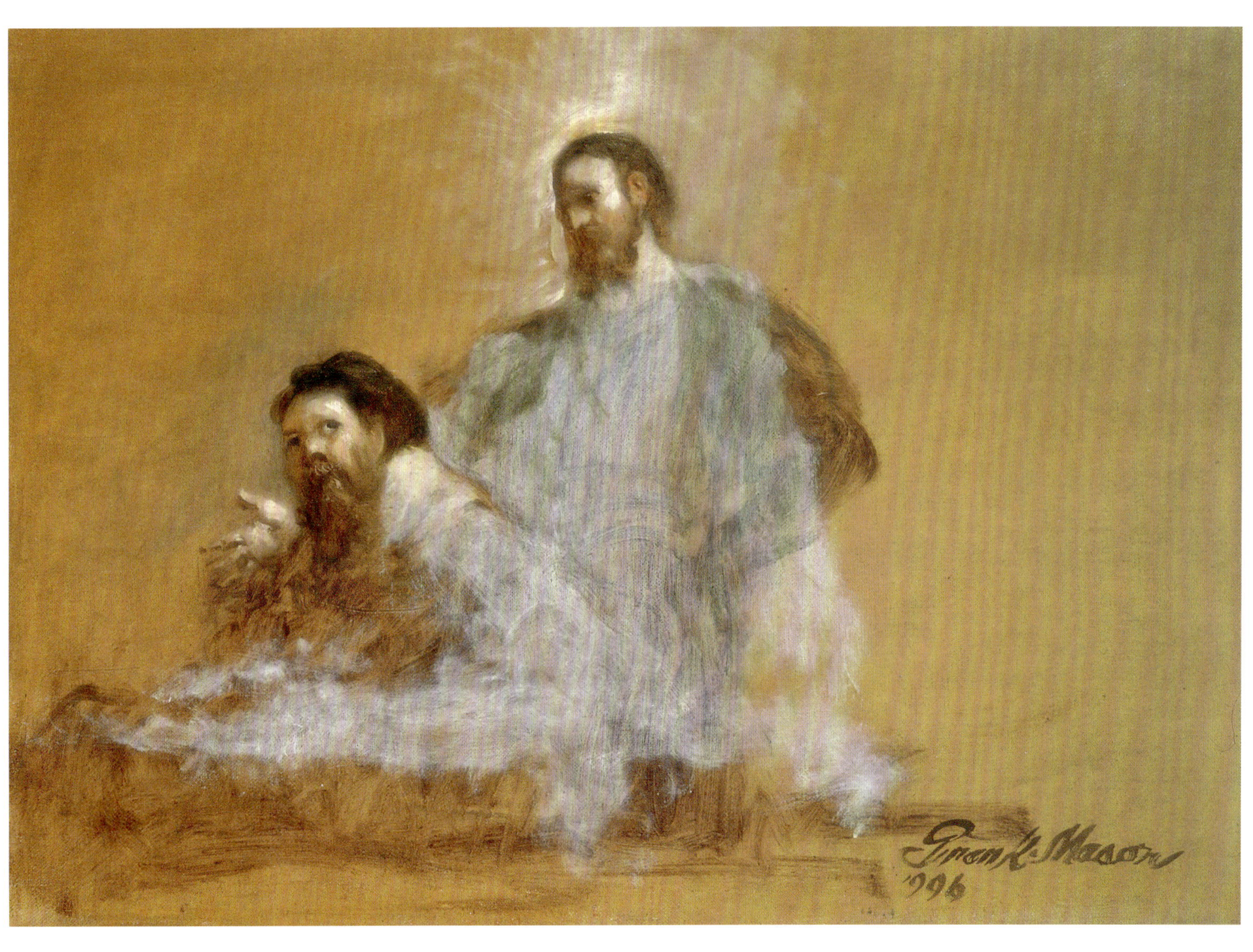

Doubting Thomas, ca. 1975
Oil on canvas, 24 x 18 in.

Artist as Thomas and Christ, 1996
Oil on canvas, 16 x 22 in.

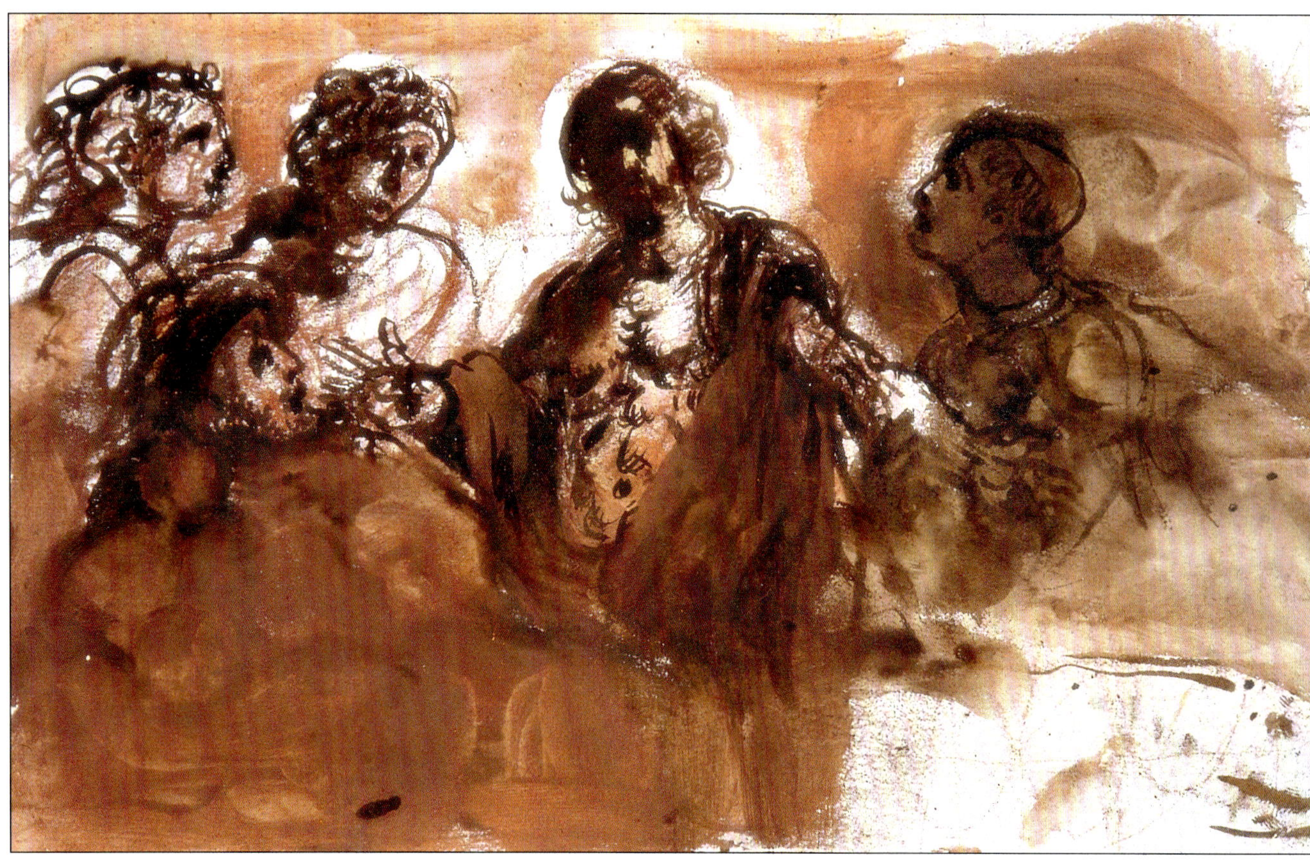

a.

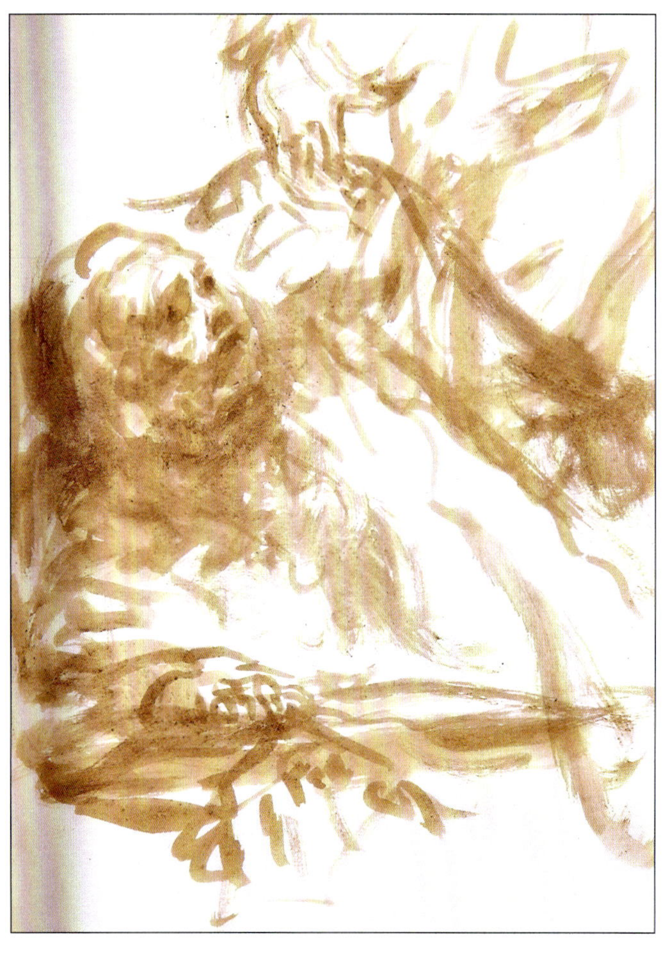

b.

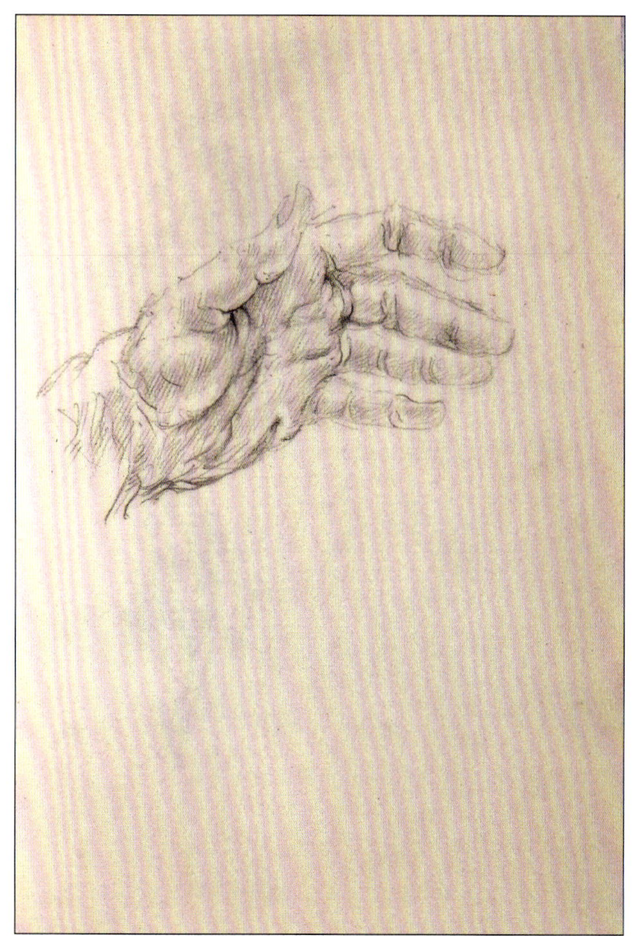

c.

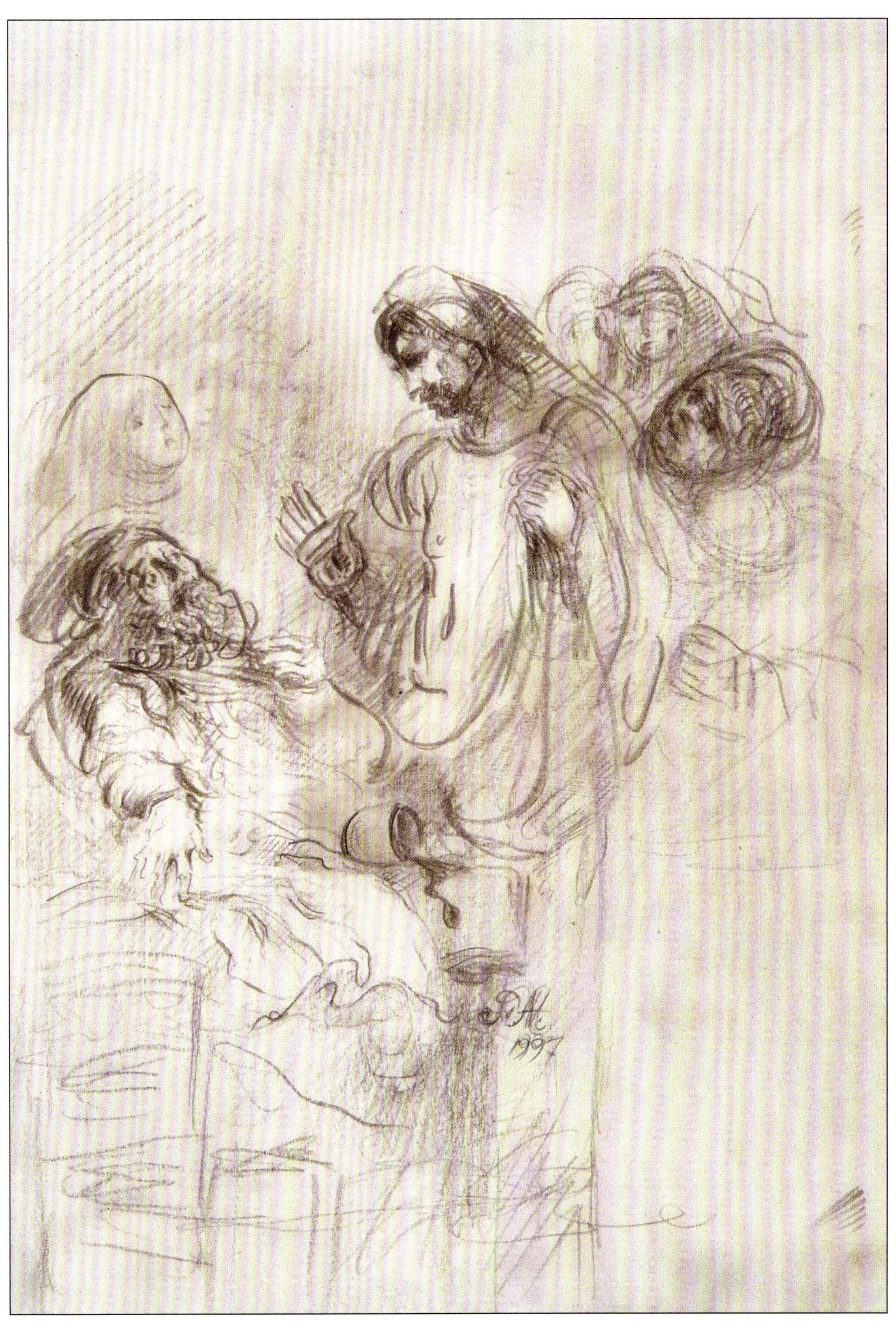

d.

a. *Doubting Thomas with Christ and Disciples,* 1995
Pen and brown ink and wash and red chalk
on prepared buff paper, 6 3/4 x 10 in.

b. *Doubting Thomas at Table,* 1995
Brown ink wash on white paper
10 1/2 x 7 3/4 in.

c. *Hand for Doubting Thomas,* 1995
Black chalk on cream paper
9 1/2 x 6 1/2 in.

d. *Christ and Doubting Thomas,* 1997
Black chalk on white paper
12 x 9 in.

St. Paul on the Road to Damascus

And Saul, yet breathing out threatenings and slaughter against the disciples of the Lord, went unto the high priest, and desired of him letters to Damascus to the synagogues, that if he found any of this way, whether they were men or women, he might bring them bound unto Jerusalem. And as he journeyed, he came near Damascus: and suddenly there shined round about him a light from heaven: and he fell to the earth, and heard a voice saying unto him, Saul, Saul, why persecutest thou me?. . . .And he trembling and astonished said, Lord, what wilt thou have me do? And the Lord said unto him, Arise, and go into the city, and it shall be told thee what thou must do. . . .And he was three days without sight. . .And there was a certain disciple at Damascus, named Ananias. . . .And Ananias. . .said, Brother Saul, the Lord, even Jesus, that appeared unto thee in the way as thou camest, hath sent me, that thou mightest receive thy sight, and be filled with the Holy Ghost. And immediately there fell from his eyes as it had been scales: and he received sight forthwith, and arose, and was baptized . . . .And straightway he preached Christ in the synagogues, that he is the Son of God. —Acts 9: 1–4, 6, 9, 10, 17, 18, 20

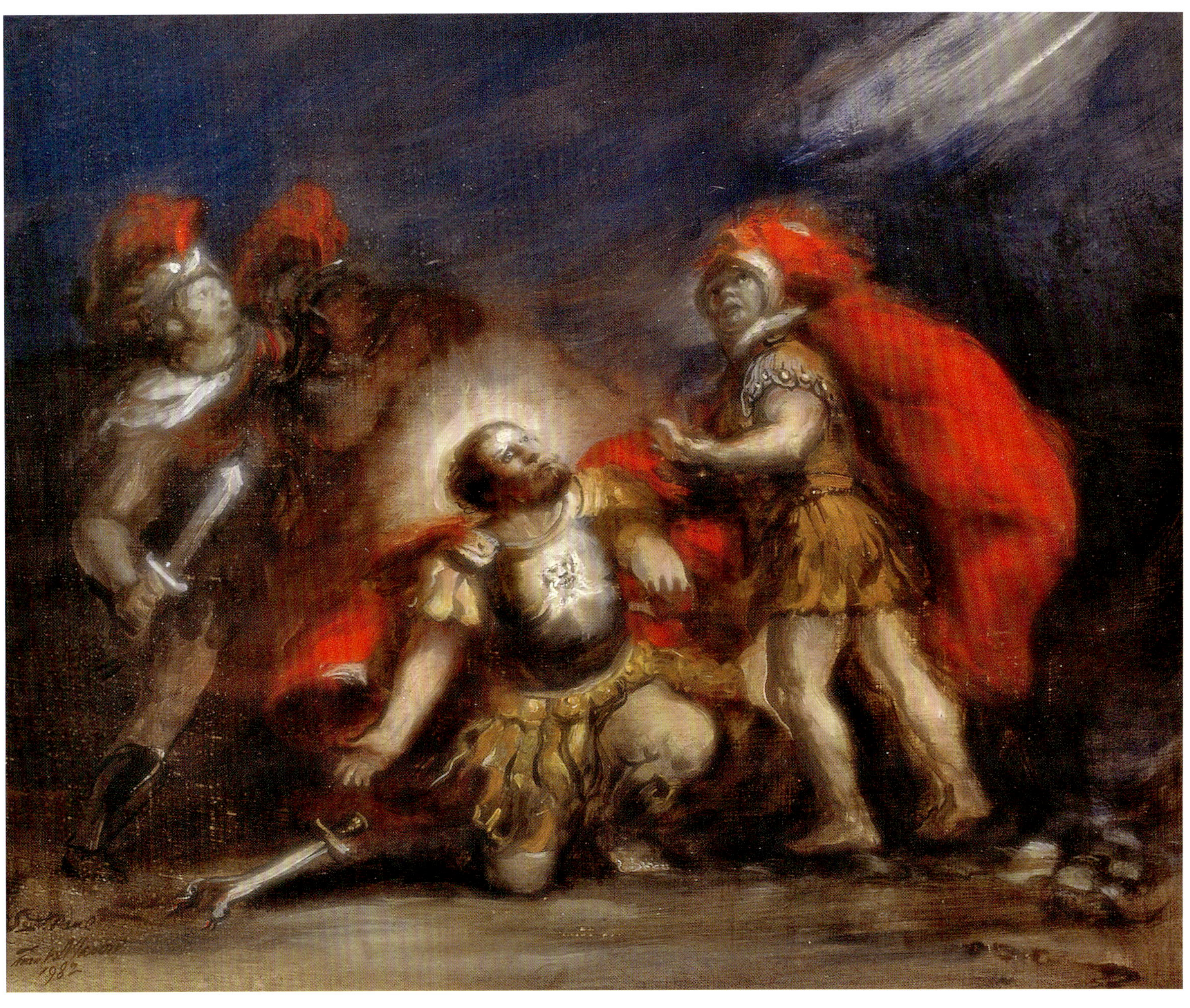

Head of St. Paul, 1980
Oil on panel, 6 x 6 in.

The Conversion of St. Paul, 1982
Oil on panel, 16 x 21 in.

To me St. Paul has always seemed the most important voice in the New Testament, the man who brought the light of Christianity to the Gentiles. From my own research I know that he was an important man in his own day. Known as Saul, he was a lawyer as well as a rabbi, influential with both the Roman and the Hebrew hierarchy. Well-educated, undoubtedly well-to-do, he was also a Roman citizen, a title which conferred great privilege at that time. In all the years I had been thinking about the painting, I had not fixed on a setting—a scene which would reveal the man Saul as he once was and the apostle Paul he was later to become. Then, one night, shortly after Easter, I had a dream that brought my scattered ideas together in sharp focus. The dream showed me a gorgeous sunset with heavy rolling clouds close to the earth and fantastic colors blazing in the sky. In the dream a voice spoke to me clearly, saying, "You're looking the wrong way, Frank. Look over there." When

I looked in the opposite direction, I saw a beautiful clump of trees bathed in light pouring down from the heavens. I was astonished and frightened, knowing that I was in the presence of the Lord of Hosts and realizing that this, THIS was the light Saul had seen on the road to Damascus. Now I had the picture as I had wanted to do it—more than a portrait, a grand view. I remarked to my wife Anne, "I suppose I'll have to go to Israel to paint the landscape where it happened." Anne said, "Nonsense. Make it a Vermont landscape." And I did.

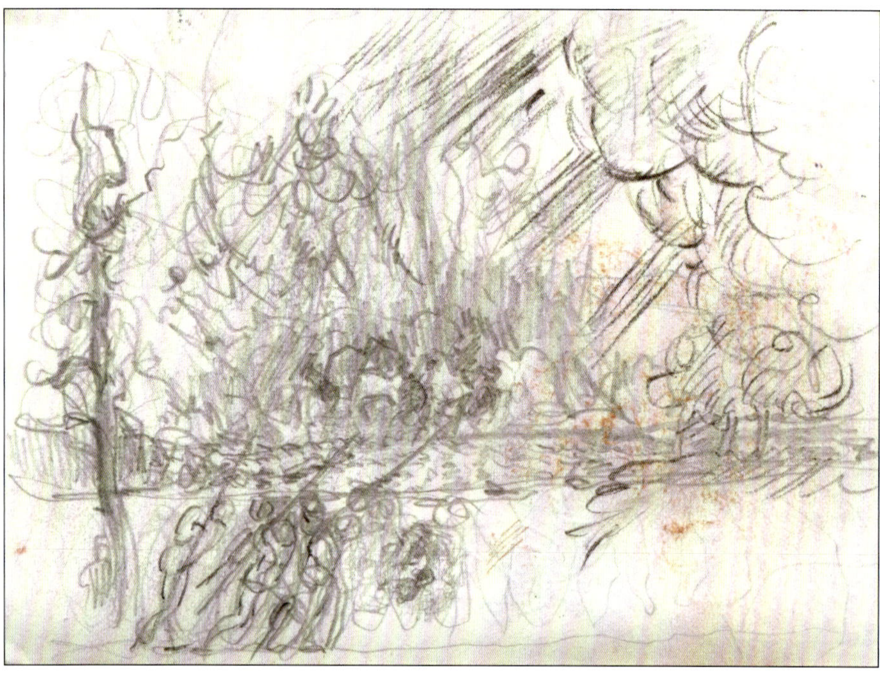

Landscape Vision and Soldiers, Road to Damascus, 1982
Graphite and black chalk on white paper, 4 1/2 x 6 in.

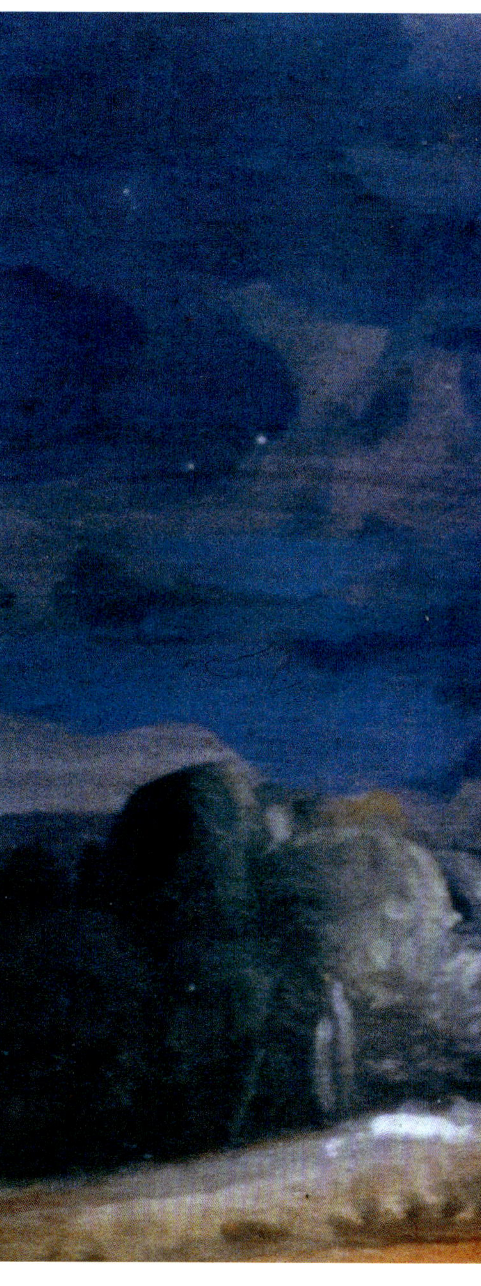

Landscape Vision for St. Paul on the Road to Damascus, 1992
Oil on panel, 8 x 14 in.

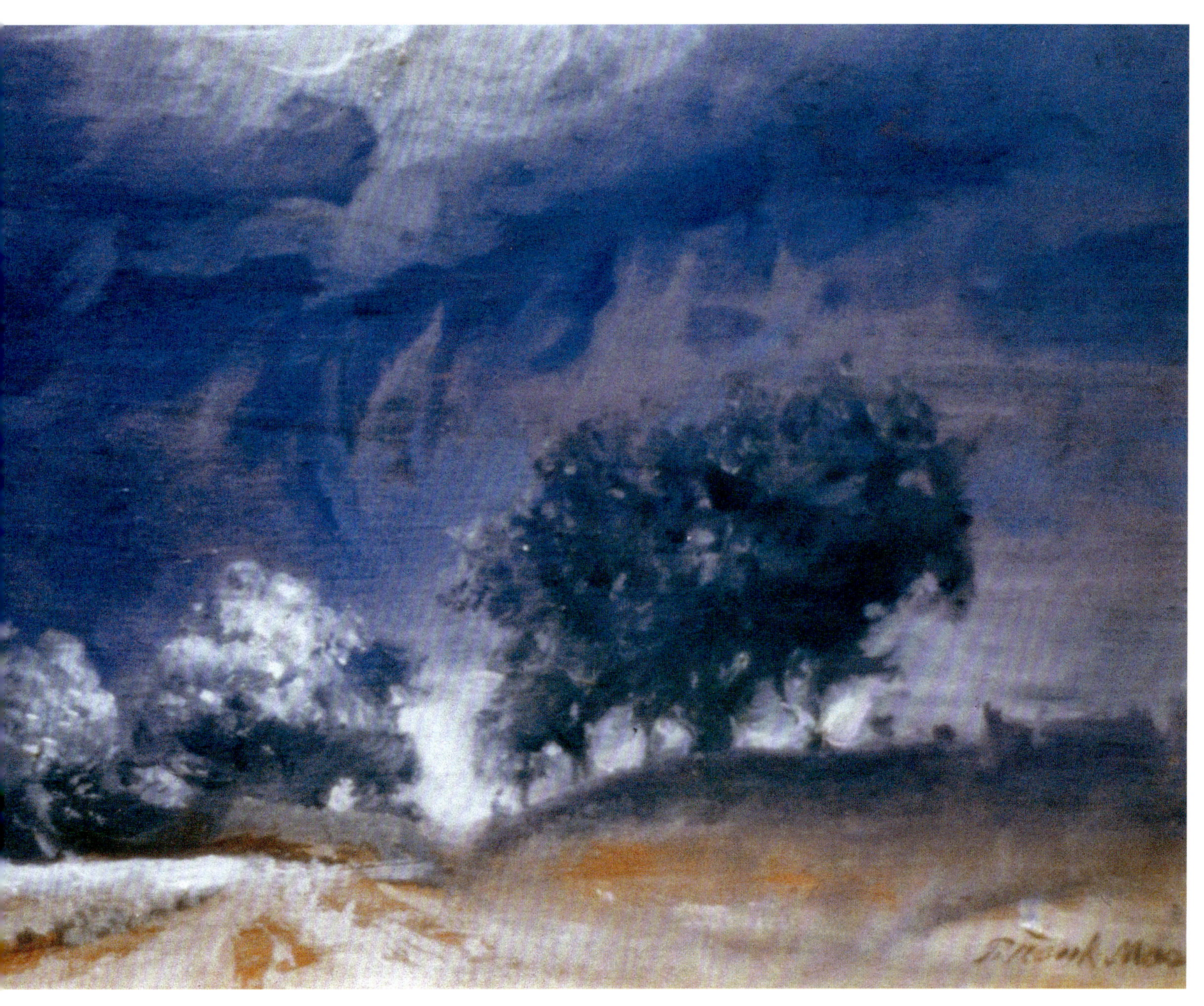

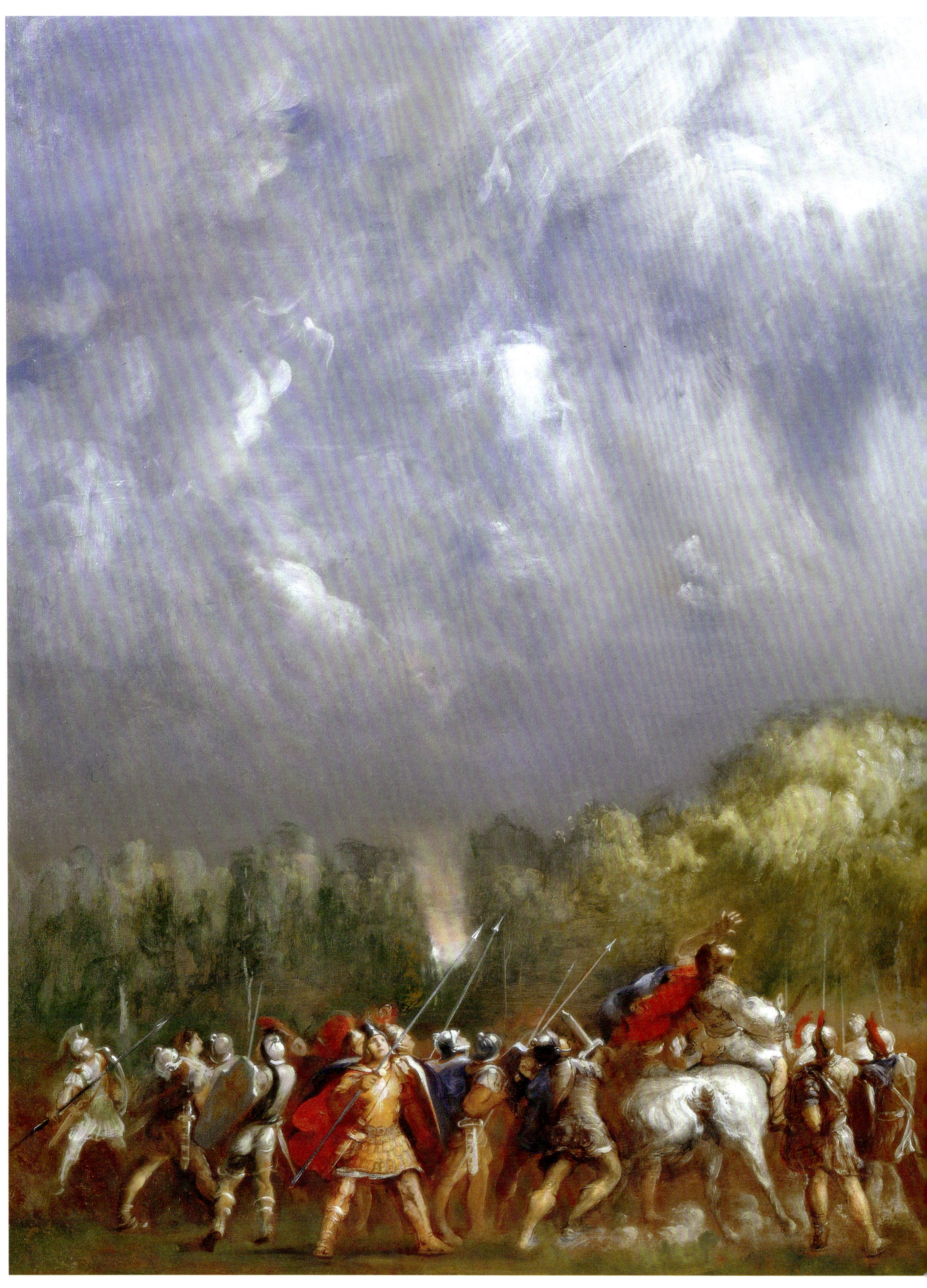

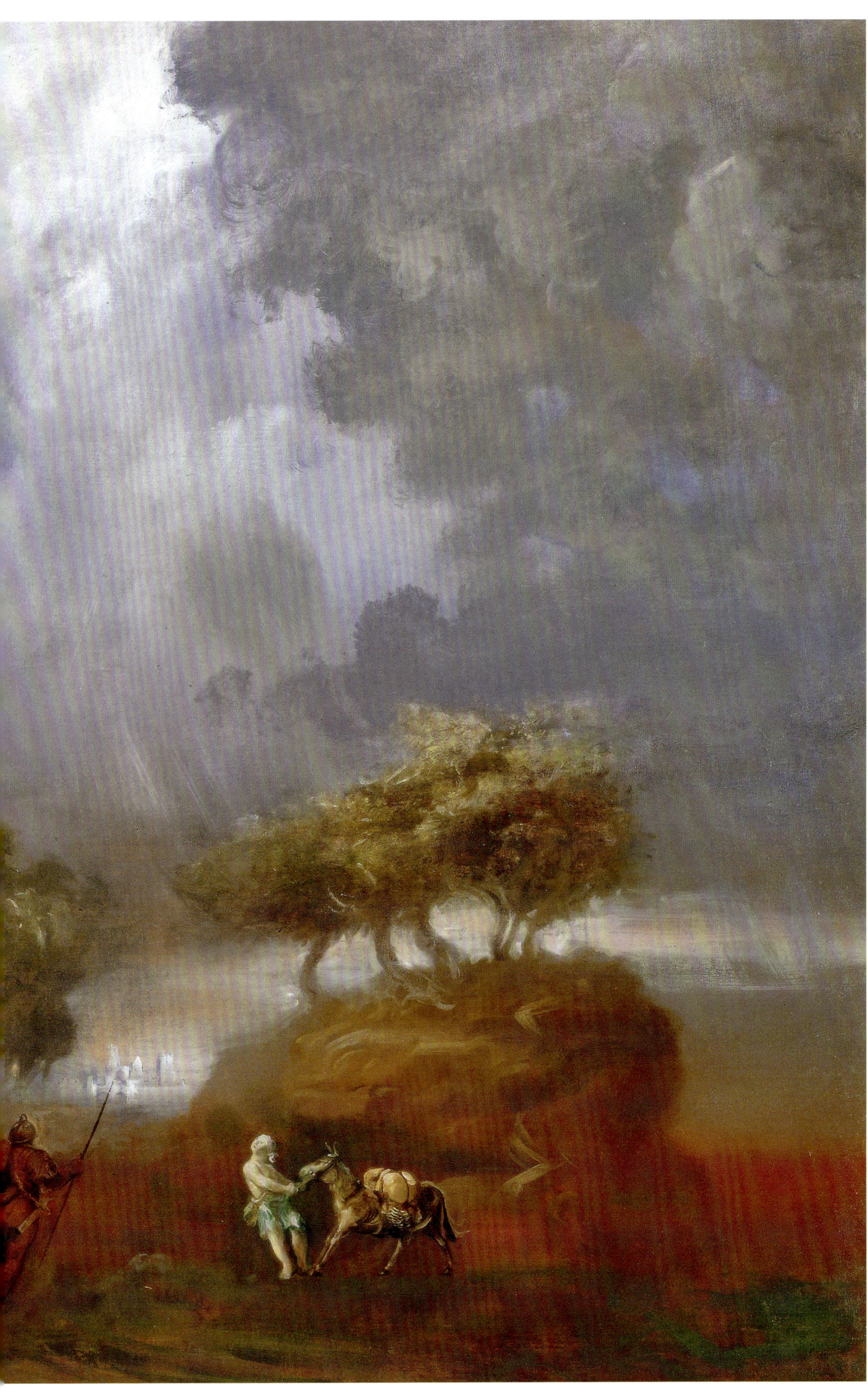

St. Paul on the Road to Damascus, 1992
Oil on canvas
56 x 79 in.

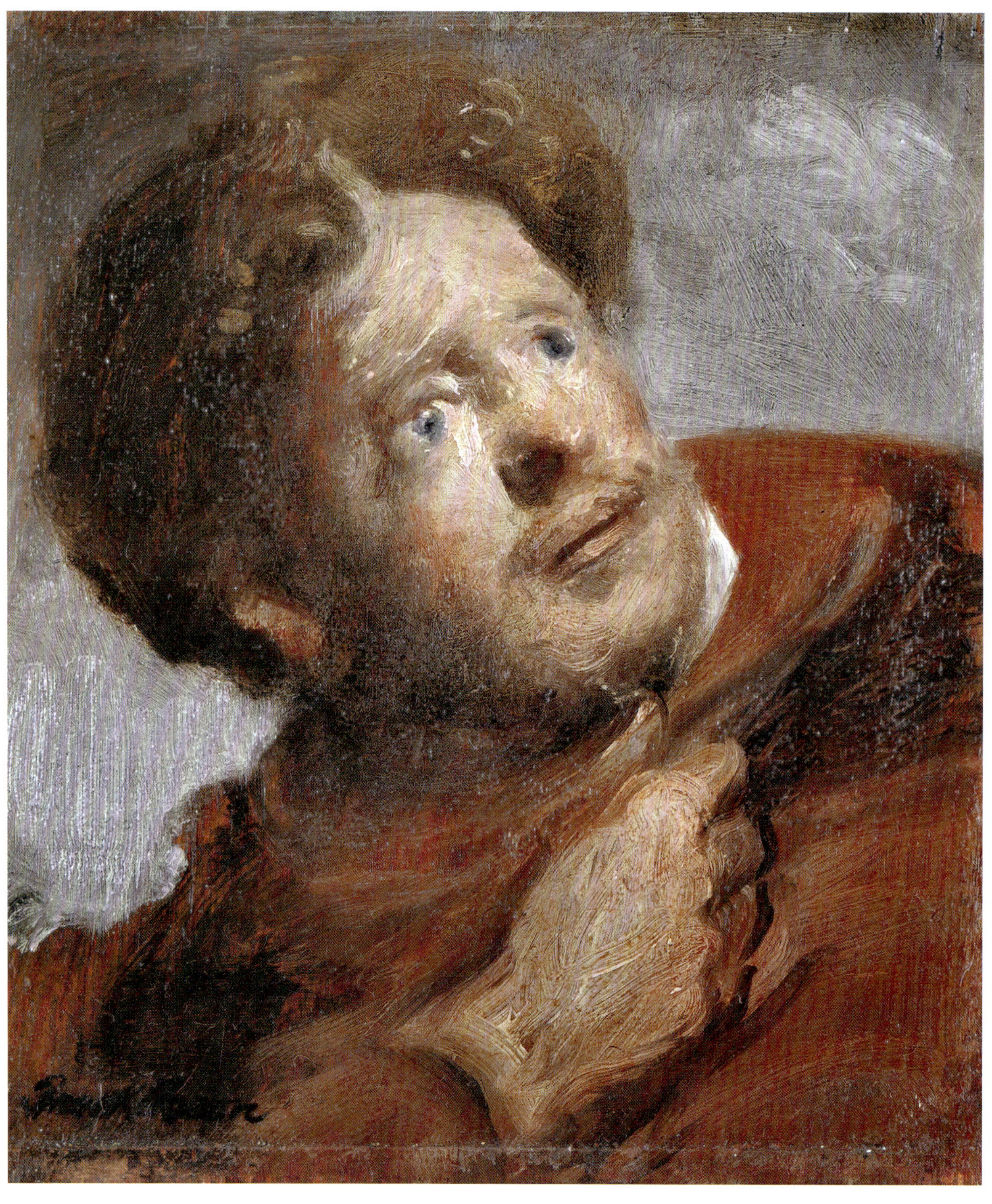

Head of St. Paul, ca. 1978
Oil on panel, 8 x 7 1/2 in.

St. Paul, 1991
Oil on panel, 28 x 24 in.

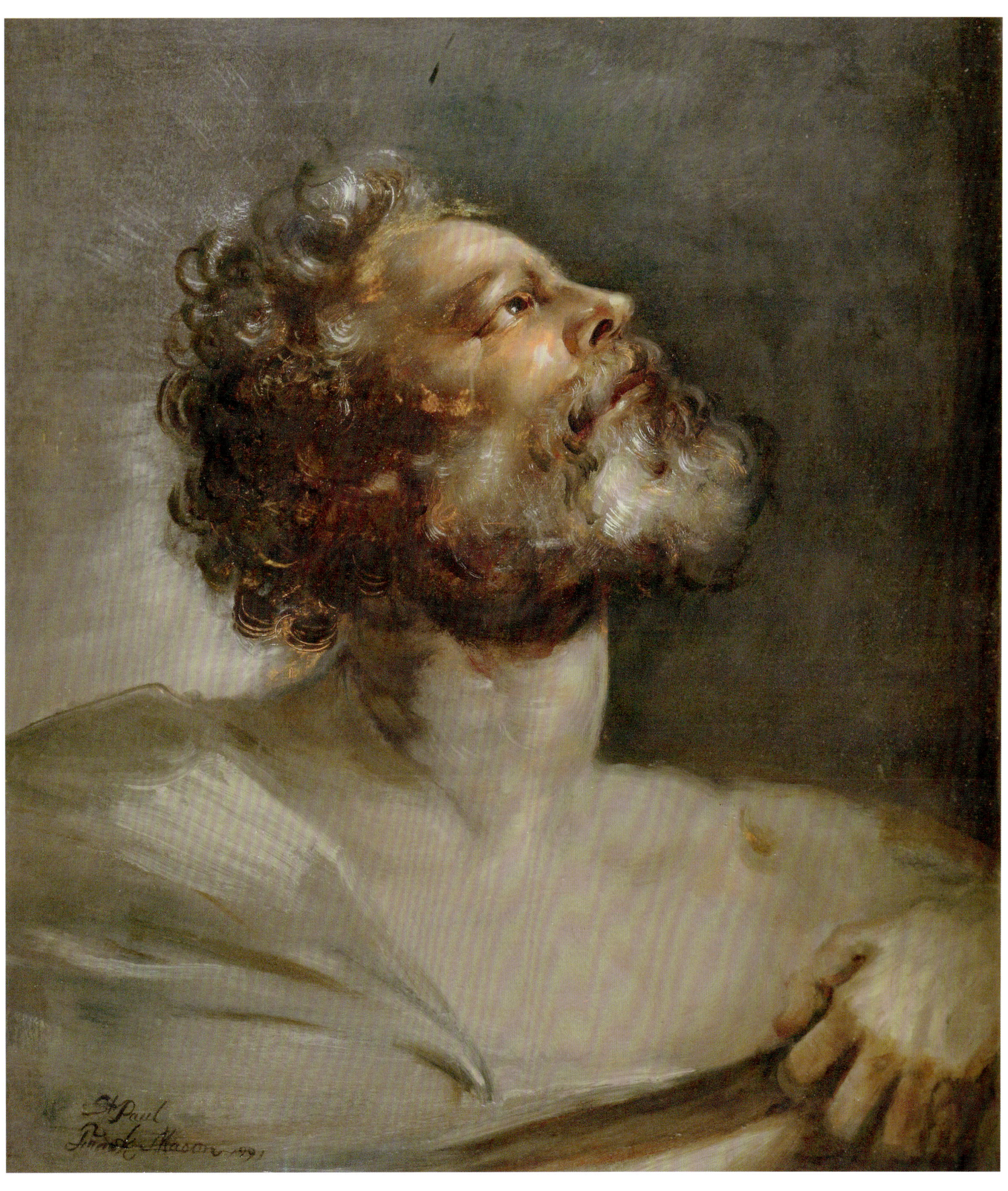
St Paul

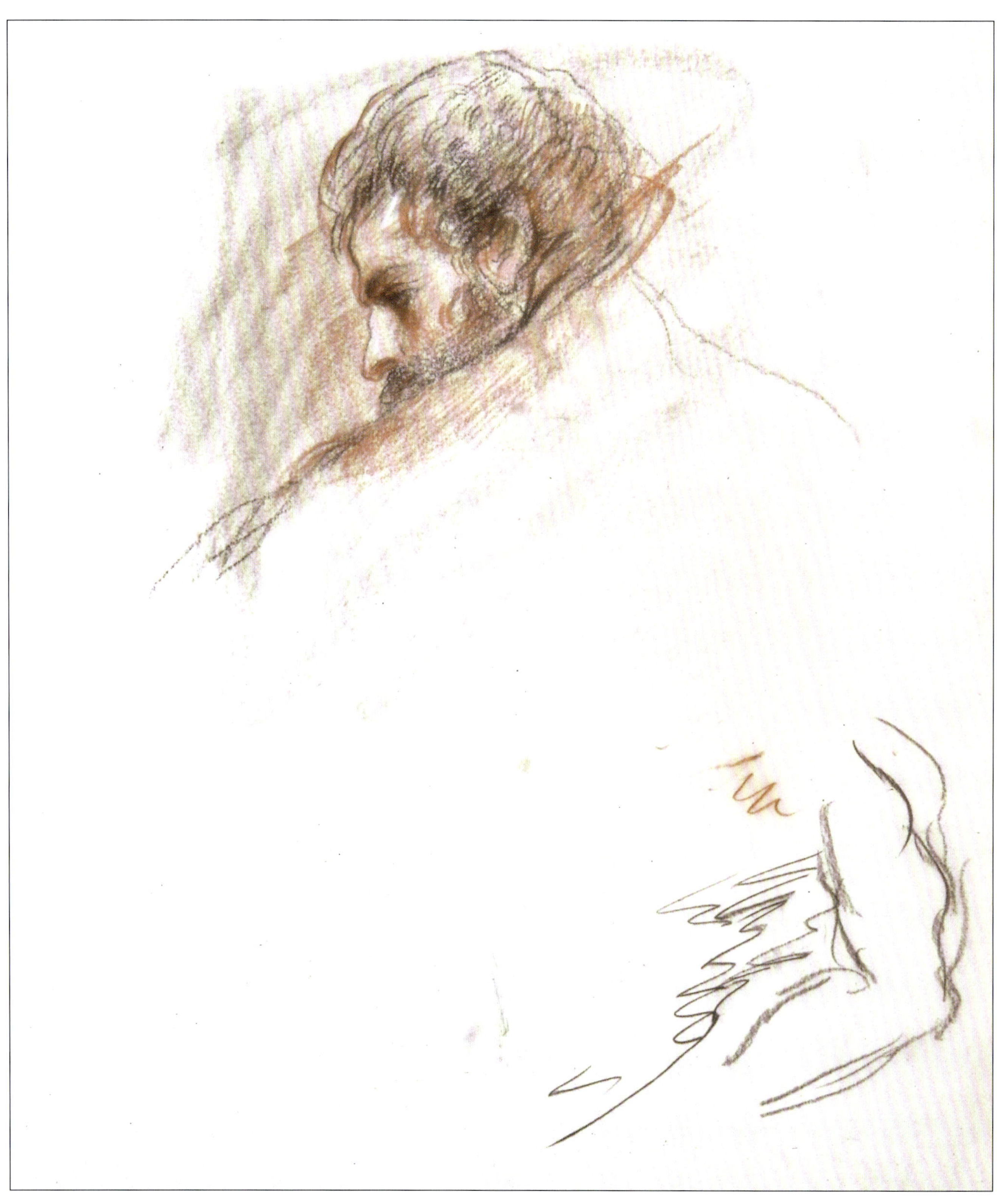

Head of St. Paul, ca. 1980
Red and black chalk on white paper
14 3/4 x 12 1/2 in.

St. Paul, Roman Costume, ca. 1975
Black and red chalk heightened with white chalk on green-gray paper, 10 x 7 in.

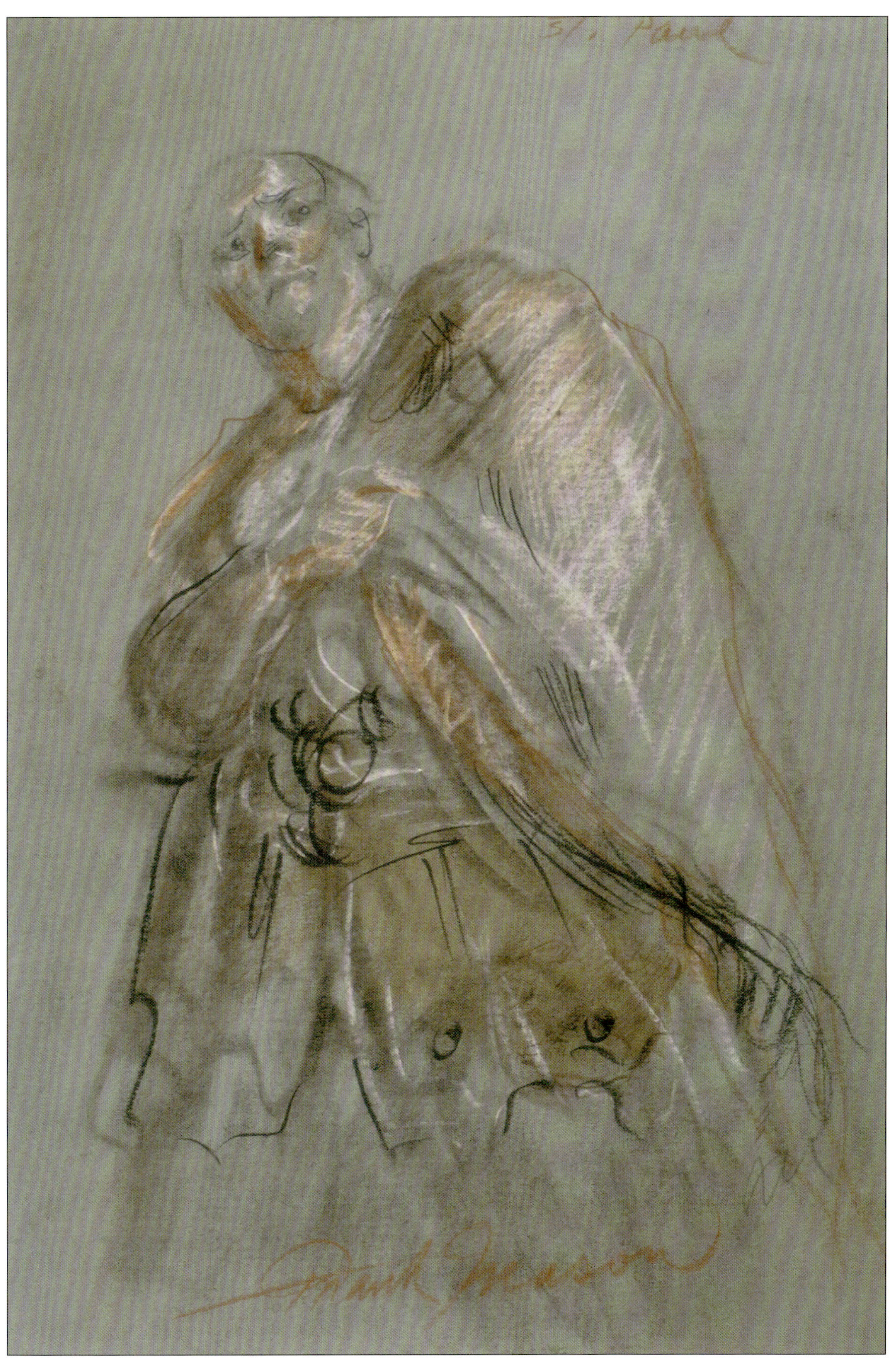
St. Paul
Frank Mason

St. Paul on the Road to Damascus with Soldiers, 2001
Oil on panel, 24 x 18 in.

St. Paul on the Road to Damascus with Soldiers, 1987
Brown ink wash on cream paper, 12 x 9 in.

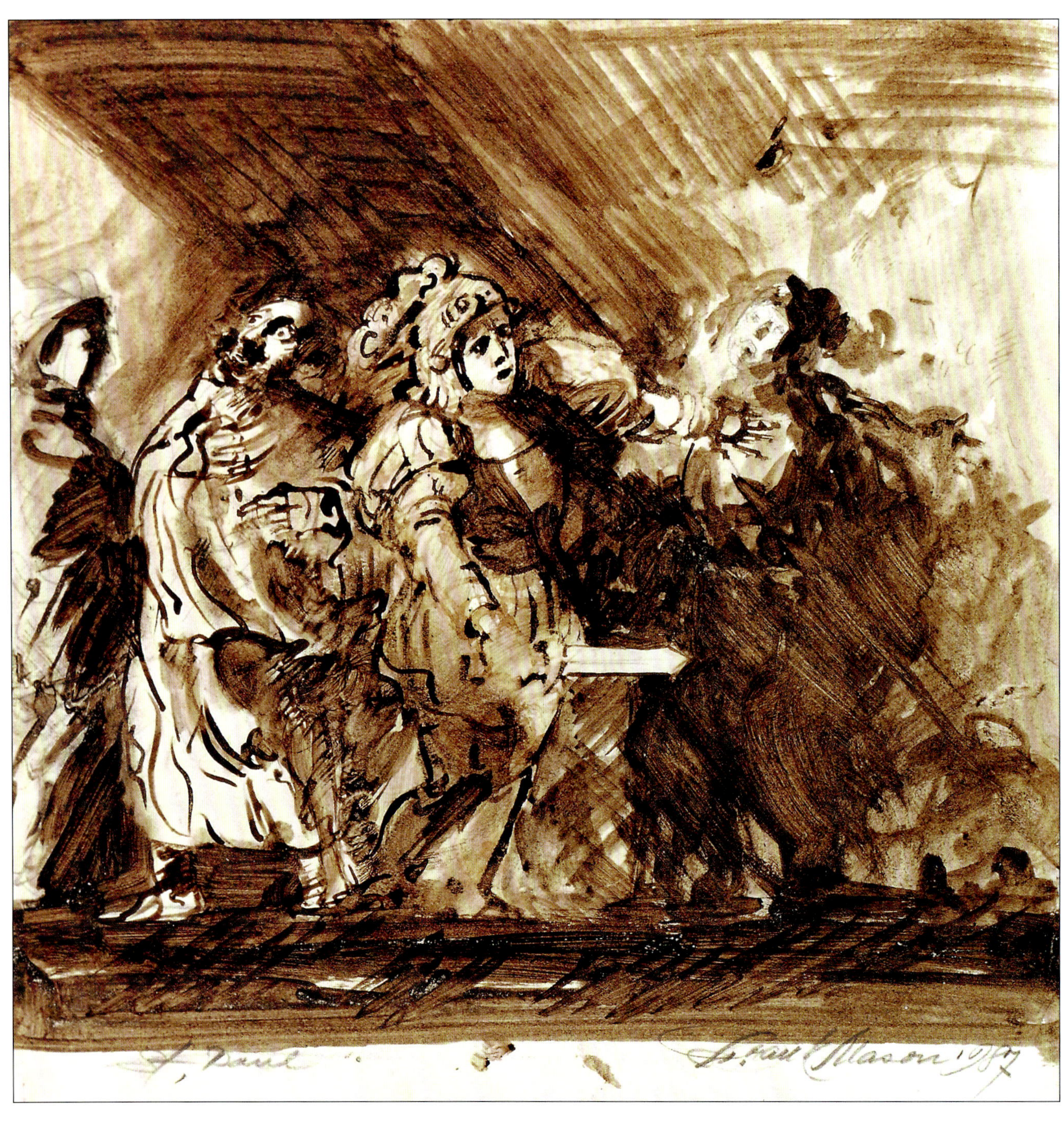

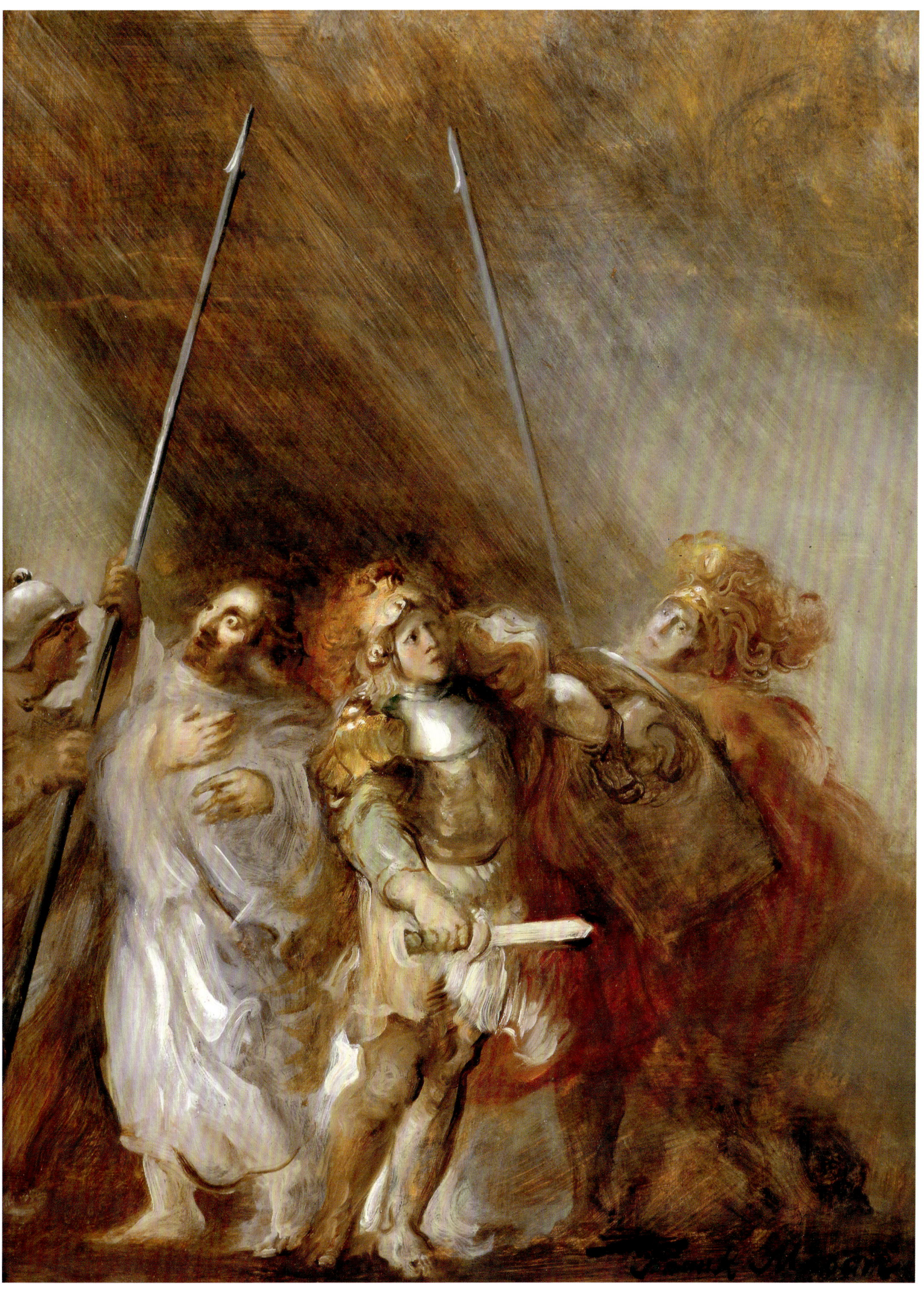

a.

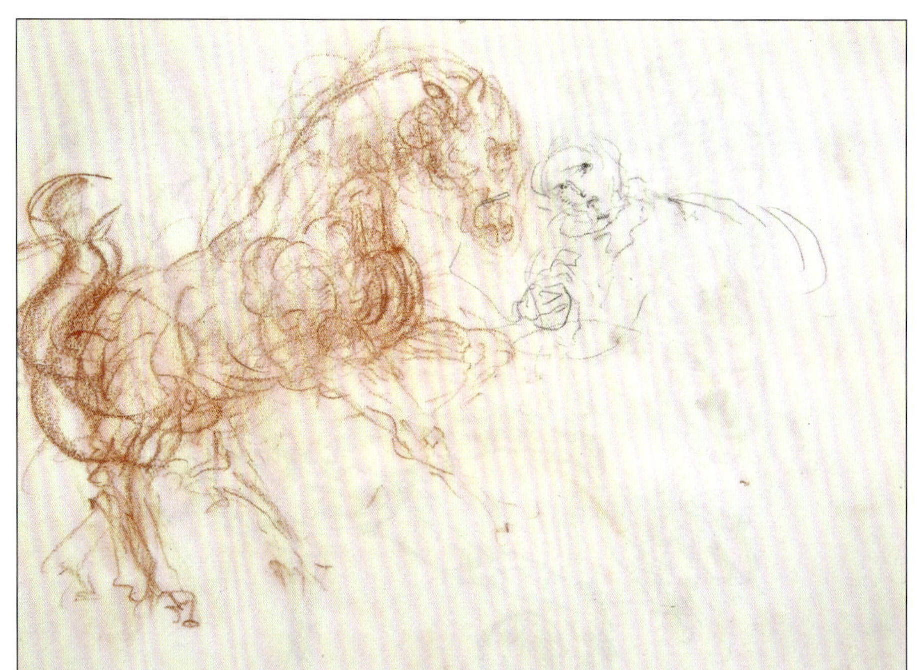

b.

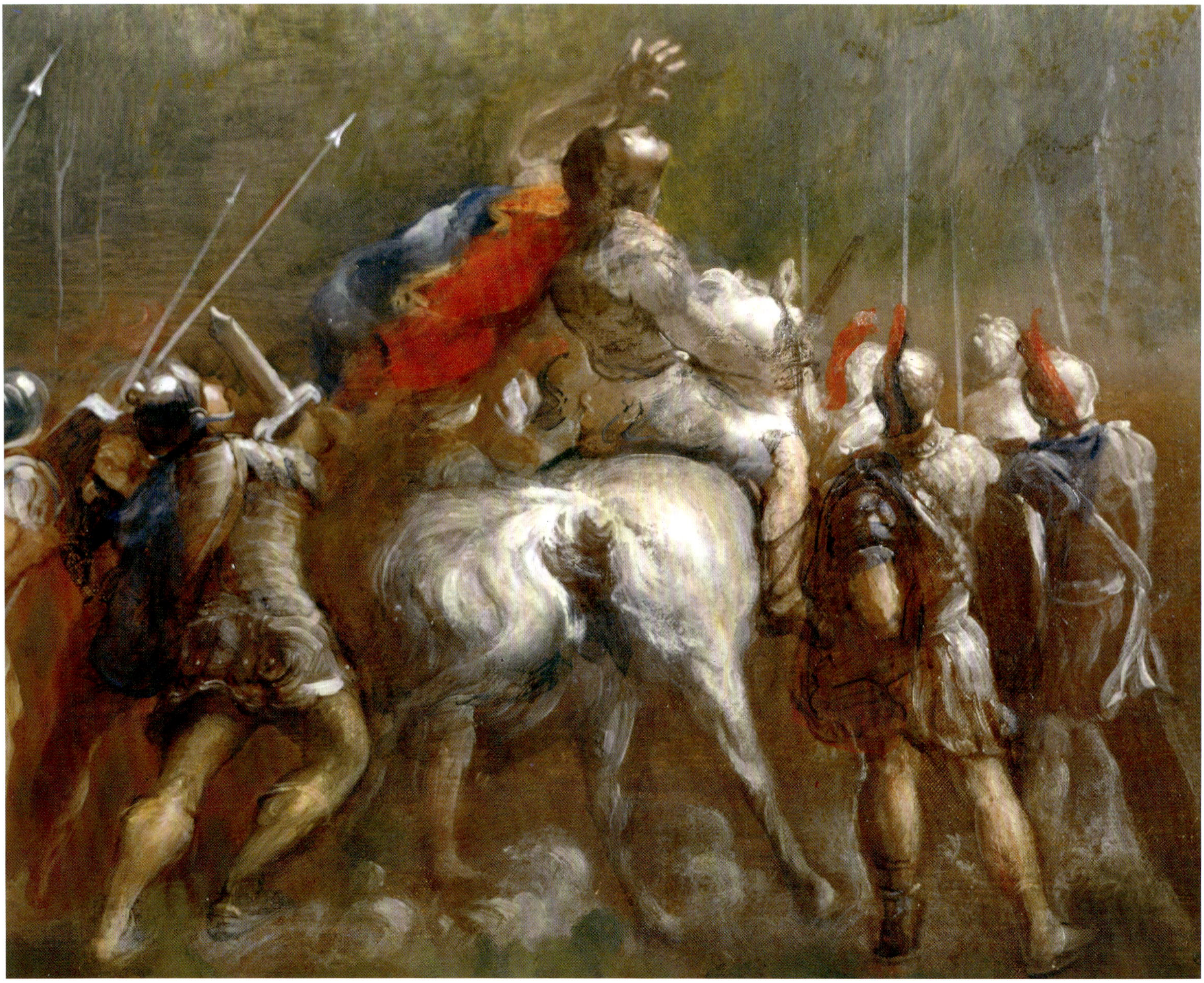

a. *St. Paul with Rearing Horse,* ca. 1980
Red chalk and pencil on white paper
9 1/2 x 12 1/2 in.

b. (Detail) *St. Paul on the Road to Damascus*

c. *Horse for St. Paul,* ca. 1991
Graphite on white paper
6 x 4 1/2 in.

d. *Horse Study for St. Paul on the Road to Damascus,* 1977
Black chalk on white paper
11 x 9 3/4 in.

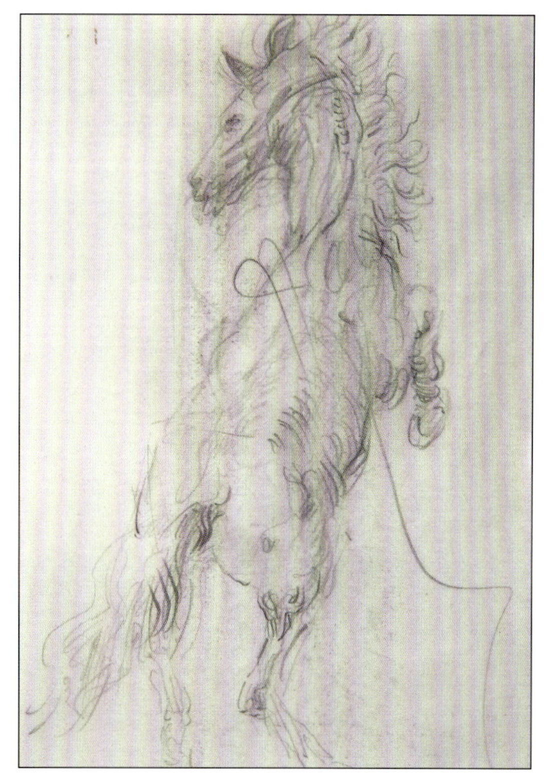

c.

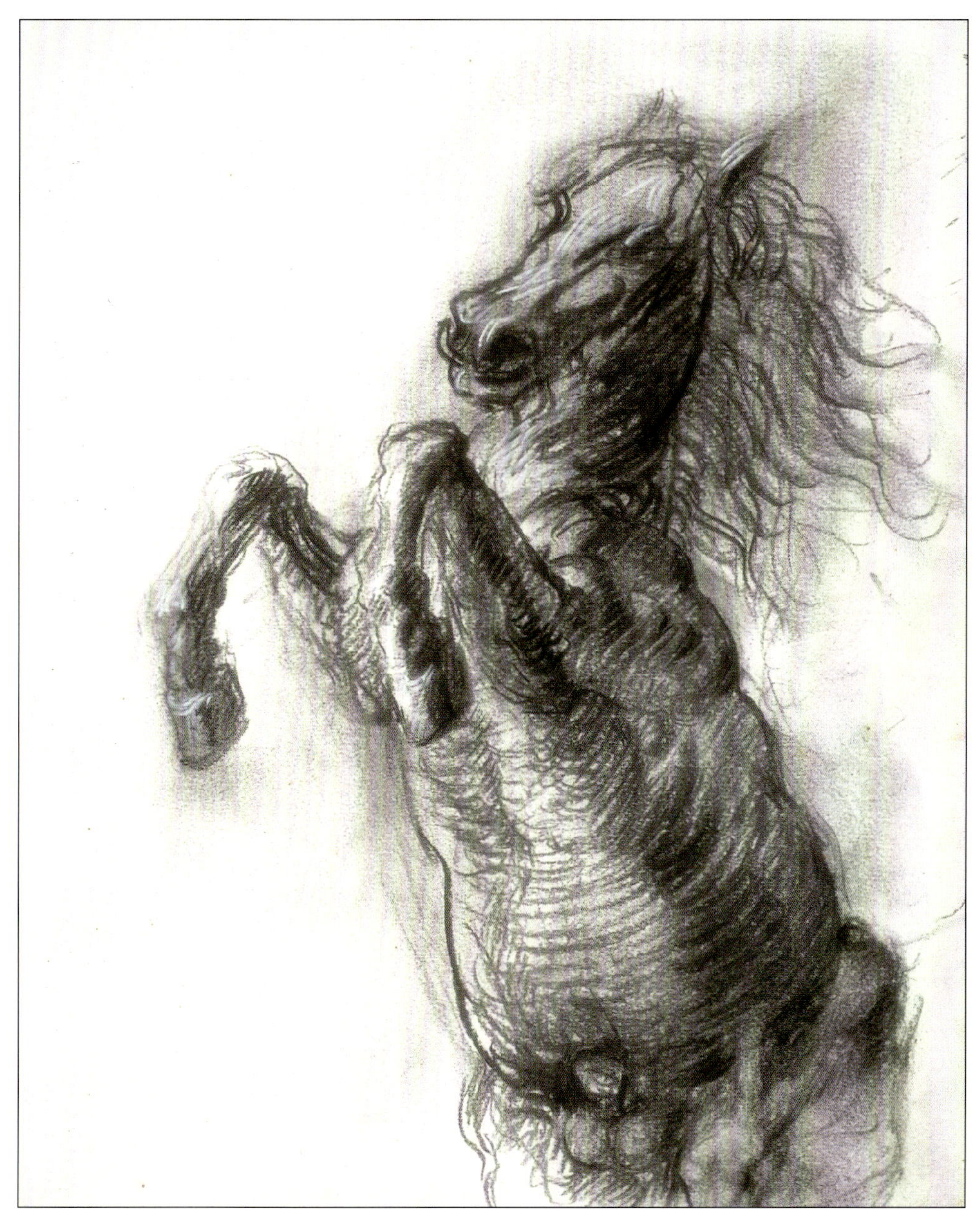

d.

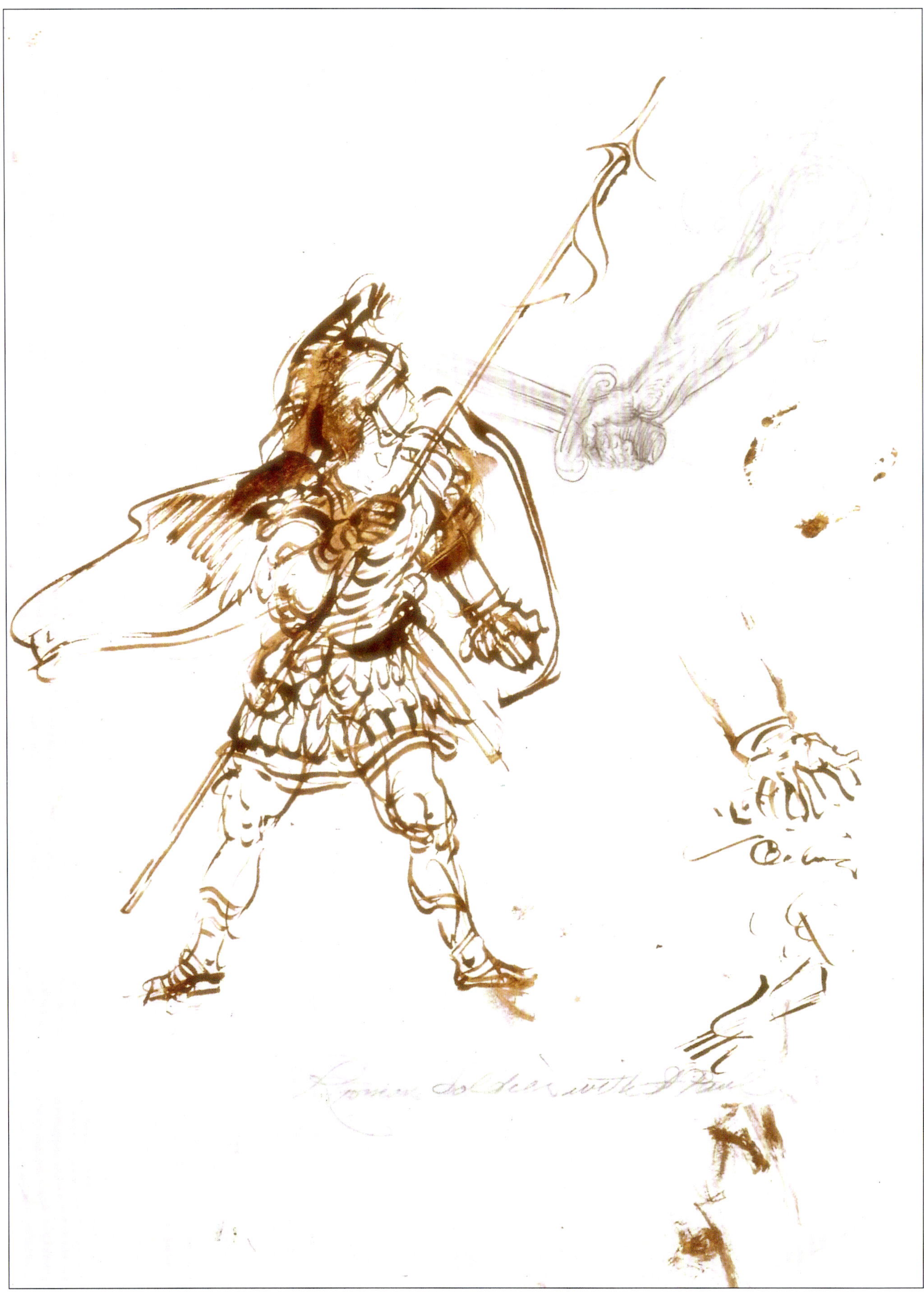

Roman Soldier with St. Paul, 1989
Brown ink and graphite on white paper, 14 x 10 1/2 in.

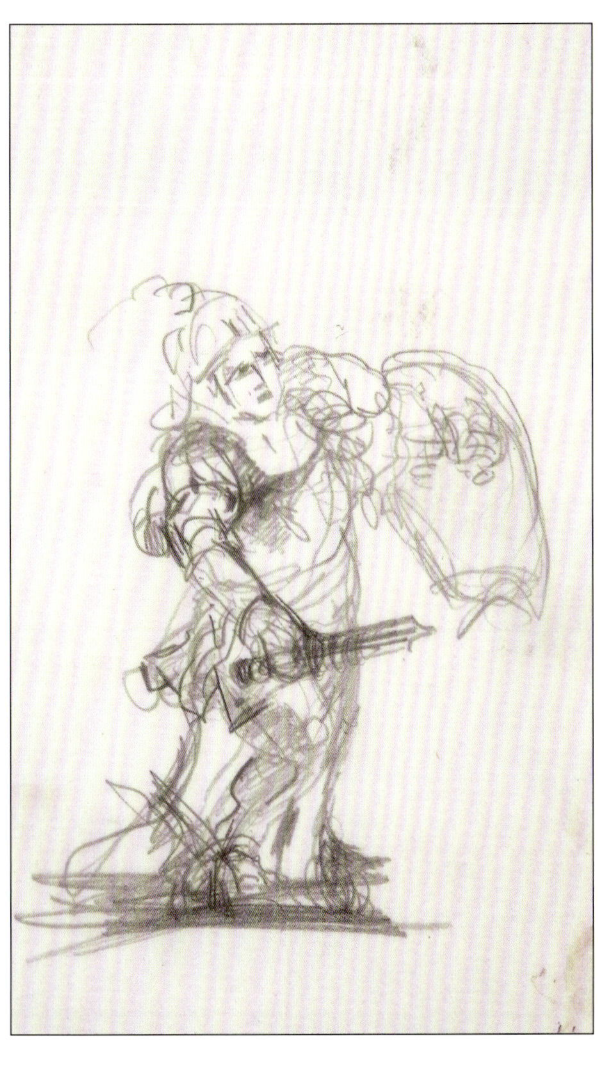

Soldier for St. Paul, 2000
Graphite on white paper
9 1/4 x 5 in.

St. Paul, ca. 1980
Red chalk on gray paper
6 1/2 x 9 1/4 in.

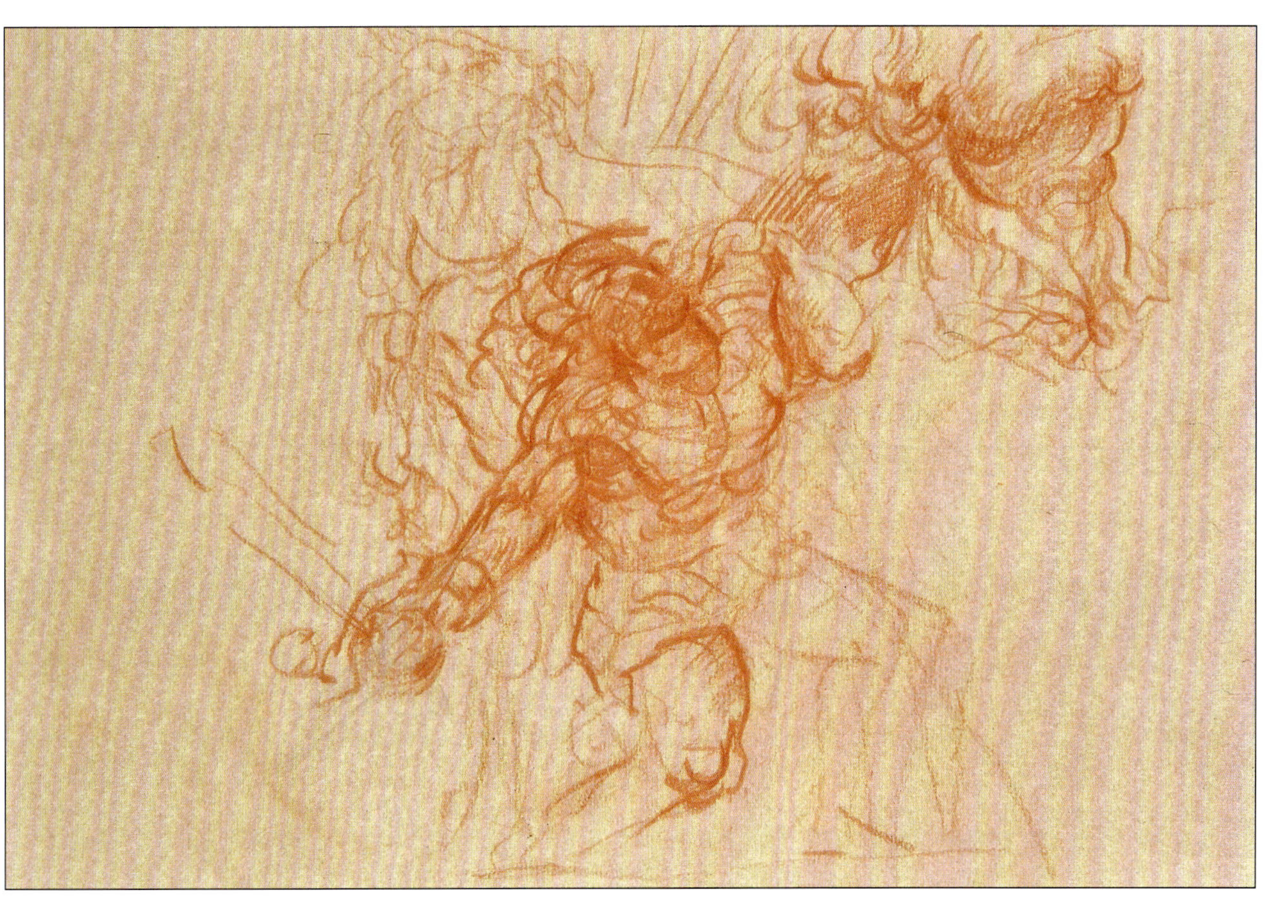

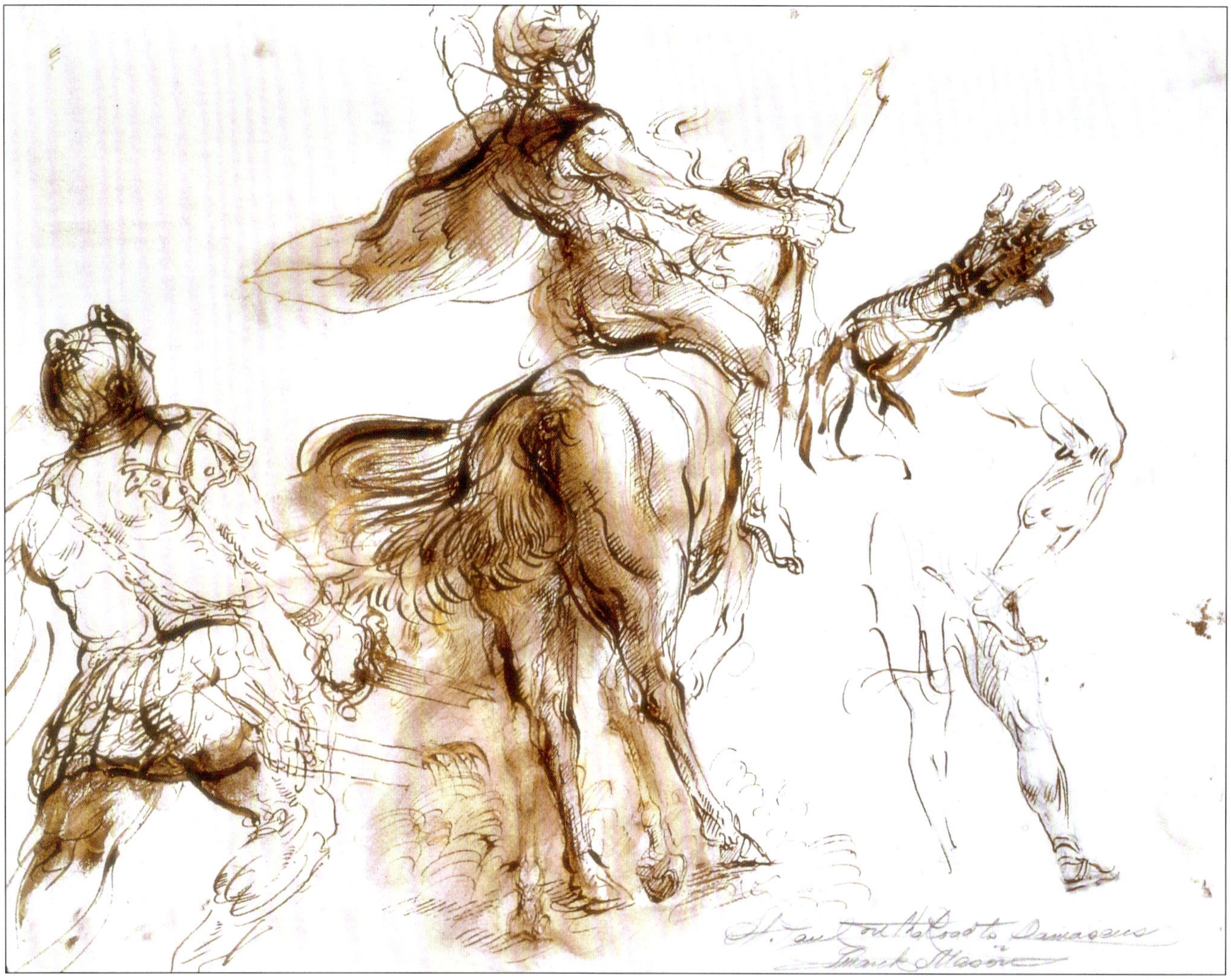

a.

b.

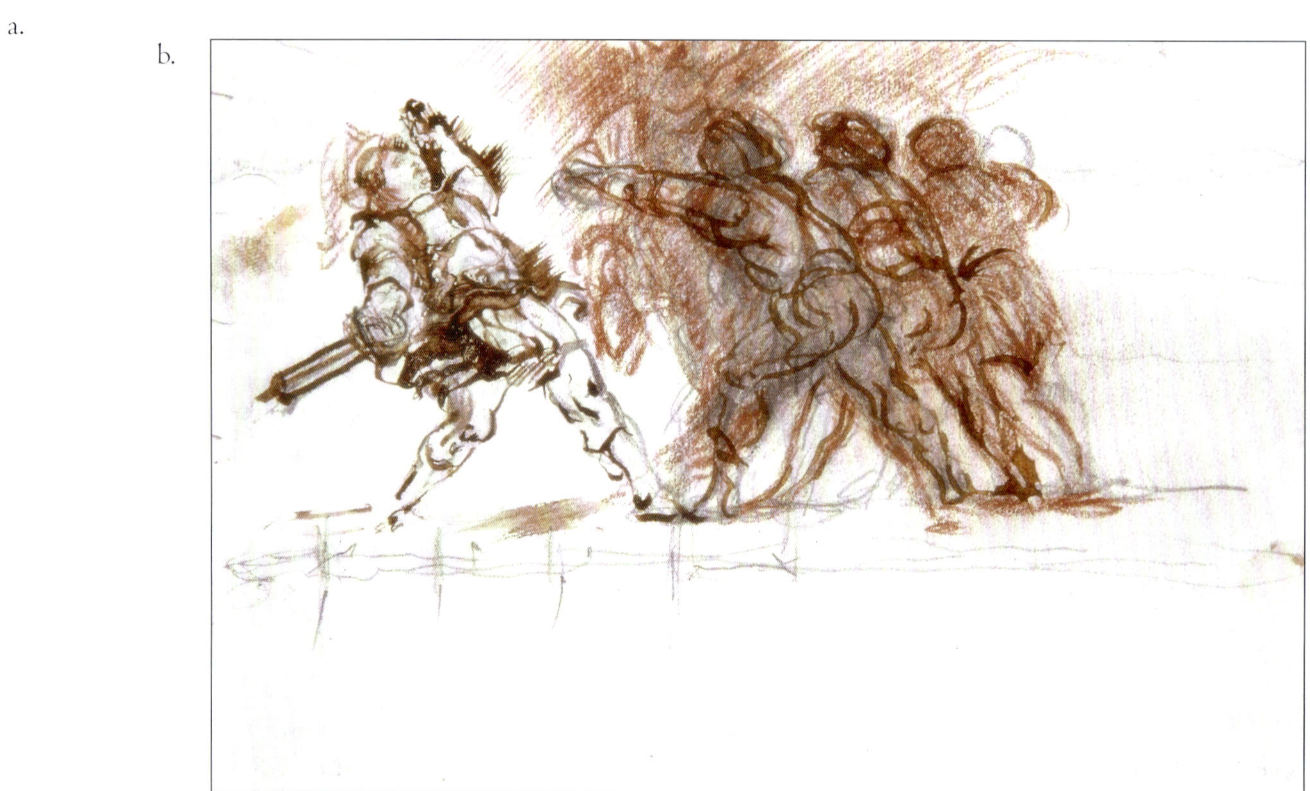

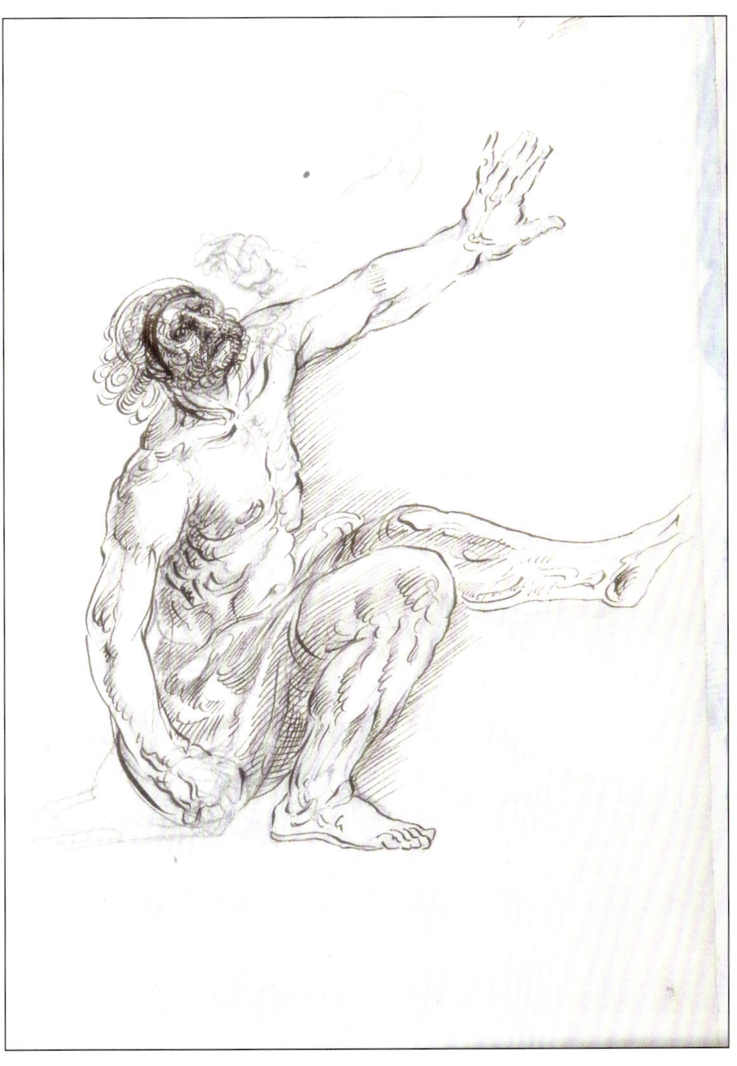

c.

a. *St. Paul on the Road to Damascus,* 1989
Pen and brown ink and wash on beige paper
10 1/2 x 13 3/4 in.

b. *St. Paul and Soldiers,* ca. 1980
Graphite and brown ink wash and red chalk on white paper, 6 1/2 x 9 1/4 in.

c. *St. Paul on Road to Damascus,* 1980
Graphite and pen and brown ink on white paper
12 x 9 in

d. *St. Paul—Figure Group,* ca. 1991
Graphite on white paper, 6 1/2 x 4 1/2 in.

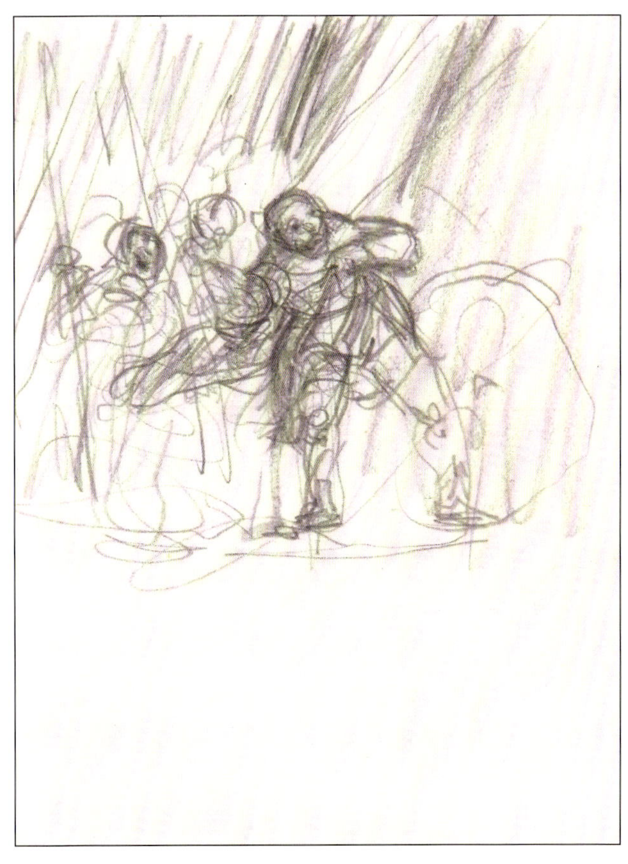

d.

St. Paul, ca. 2000
Pen and brown ink and wash
on cream paper, 5 x 3 1/2 in.

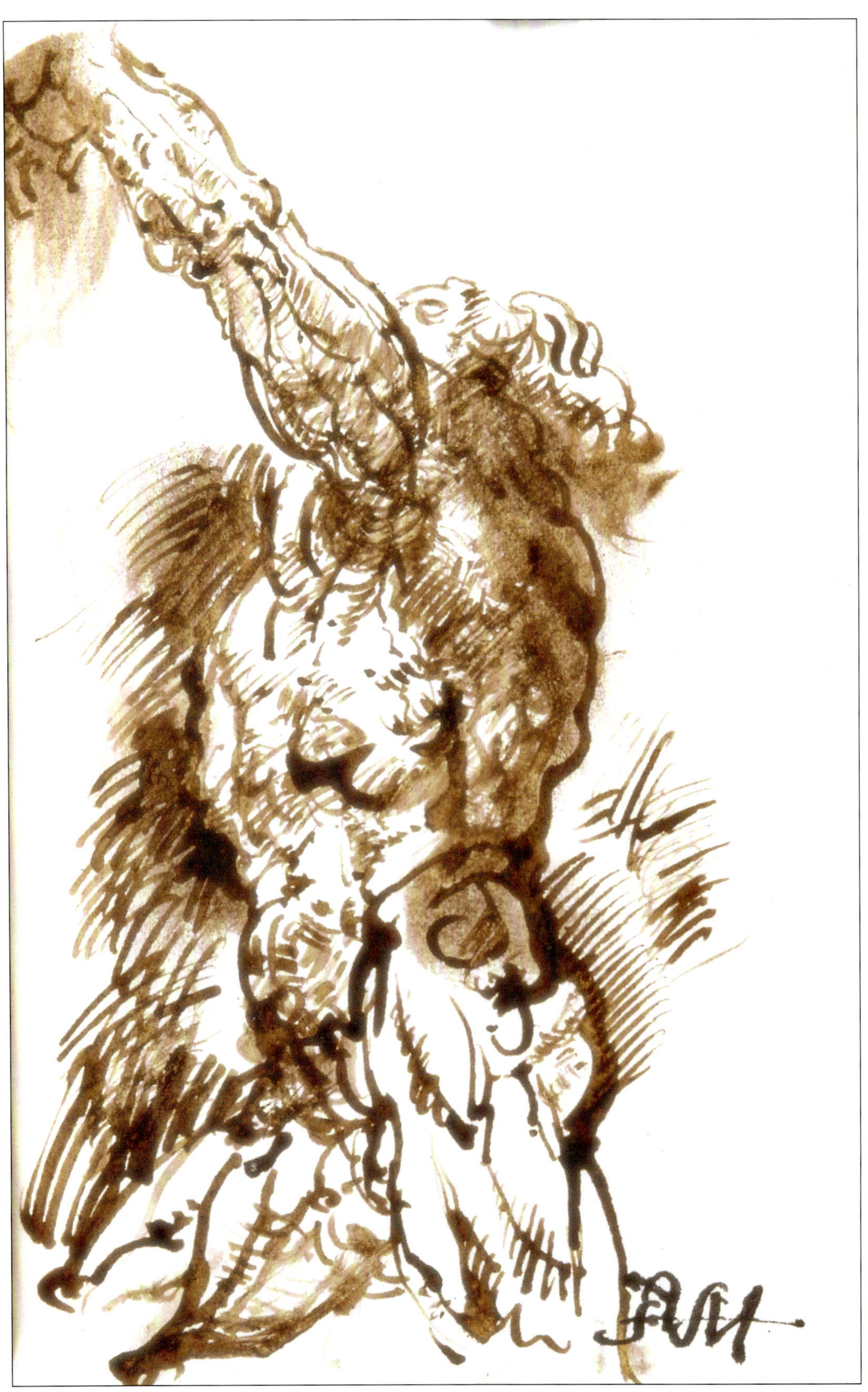

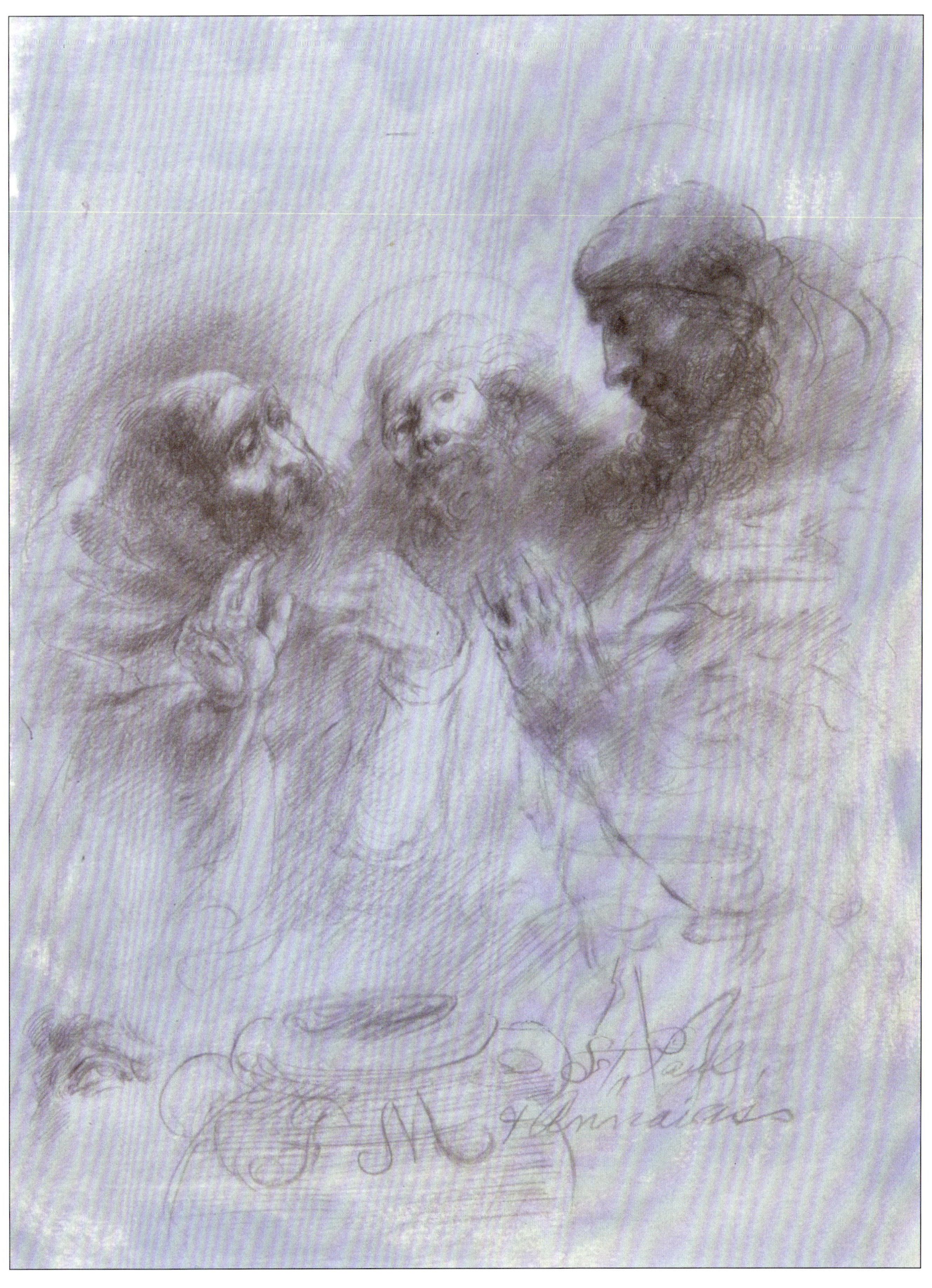

St. Paul and Annaias, ca. 1990
Graphite on blue prepared paper, 14 x 10 1/2 in.

Biography

Frank Mason was interested in the arts at an early age. He often talks about the importance of a supportive home atmosphere for an aspiring young artist. Both of his parents—as well as his older brother, Walter, who bought Mason his first paint box—were in favor of his artistic career and proud of his accomplishments. This familial support also came from his first wife, Phyllis Harriman Connery, also an artist. When the two married, he was happy to include her son, Crispin, in their family. They later had a child of their own, Arden. Both sons live active lives, the older an elected official in Maine and the younger an artist in Connecticut. In 1966, Mason married a second time to Anne Crosby.

The move to New York during Mason's teenage years put him in touch with the Music and Arts High School and the Metropolitan Museum, where he spent hours studying the works of Rembrandt, Hals, and Valasquez. This intense interest in Renaissance paintings was an early expression of Mason's artistic philosophy which includes serious respect for the history of art, a belief that the materials used are crucial to freedom of artistic expression, and a conviction that great art requires hard work. In his teaching, he has grounded the present in the past. He has spent a lifetime researching materials used in the Renaissance to facilitate his own artistic freedom of creativity. And his prodigious efforts—first as a student and then as a professional—have put into practice his belief that the gift of talent is a challenge to be developed to the fullest extent possible through hard work.

Resigning only recently, Mason was an Instructor of Fine Arts at the Art Students league for fifty seven years. He has been described as the artist who carried the torch of Realism through the age of Abstract Expressionism, when the connection between the present and the past might have been lost. Mason says the truth is that he was too naive to know that he was against the tide, as he was simply doing what he loved—painting and teaching the love of beauty.

Protesting against the destruction of classical beauty has been a major facet of Mason's career. He discusses the present lack of understanding of past artistic accomplishments, which has led to a thriving field of restoration that treats paintings of other ages as though they are being created now. The result has been a flattening of paintings that were intended to be three-dimensional. Mason believes the issue to be one of artistic integrity, and his protests have been passionate as well as long-term. Due in part to his many years of protesting the destruction of these precious works, an organization—ArtWatch International—has been formed. Mason is an active member.

Throughout his long career, Mason's fiery pursuit of excellence has led to many awards. In 1999, Mason received the Newington Cropsey Foundation's Award for Artistic Excellence as well as an Arthur Ross Award from Classical America in recognition of his contribution to the art of mural painting in the classical tradition. In 2000, he received the Salmagundi Club Medal of Honor in recognition of extraordinary service in the arts. In 2002, the Artists' Fellowship gave Mason the Benjamin West Clinedinst Annual Memorial Medal. Mason sees these awards not only as recognition of his own accomplishments but also as confirmation that the classical point of view continues to influence the world in the present as in the past.

This collection of paintings and drawings depicting the life of Jesus has been a lifelong labor for Frank Mason. Beginning with the earliest painting completed at age nineteen—*Christ Healing the Man with the Withered Hand*—each work was the result of an inspired moment, supporting Mason's belief that his artistic talent is God-given. He is concerned with the illusion of subject matter in space and atmosphere seen, as he would say, "through the light of God." His work will be known for its life force revealed through form, color, atmosphere, and design—traditional values handed down from the Hellenic Greeks through the Renaissance to the present time. And in that present, the joy of being able to express his deepest beliefs on canvas has been his greatest reward.

Selected One-Man Exhibitions

1955 Ward Eggelston Galleries, New York, New York
1958 Condon Riley Art Gallery, New York, New York
1961 Condon Riley Art Gallery, New York, New York
1962 Phoenix Museum of Fine Arts, Phoenix, Arizona
1962 Wickersham Art Galleries, New York, New York
1964 French and Company, New York, New York
1964 Suffolk Museum, Stony Brook, New York
1966 Arts League of Ligonier Valley, Ligonier, Pennsylvania
1966 Gallery International, Cleveland, Ohio
1967 Harbor Gallery, Cold Spring Harbor, New York
1969 Vendo Nubes Gallery, Philadelphia, Pennsylvania
1971 Harbor Gallery, Cold Spring Harbor, New York
1973 National Arts Club, New York, New York
1974 Mood Gallery, Milan, Italy
1975 Harbor Gallery, Cold Spring Harbor, New York
1979 John Pence Gallery, San Francisco, California
1982 Oldfield Gallery, Pittsburgh, Pennsylvania
1982 Southern Vermont Arts Center, Manchester, Vermont
1983 O'Meara Gallery, Ltd., Santa Fe, New Mexico
1984 John Pence Gallery, San Francisco, California
1984 St. Peter's College, Jersey City, New Jersey
1985 Welton Becket Associates, New York, New York
1986 Casey Gallery, Scottsdale, Arizona
1986 Old Trinity Cathedral, New York, New York
1986 Stehle-Read Fine Art, Midland, Texas
1988 Thornhill Gallery, Old Greenwich, Connecticut
1988 Union League Club, New York, New York
1989 Sweetwater Art Center, Sewickley, Pennsylvania
1992 Monica North Galleries, Pompeii Museum, Saratoga Springs, New York
1993 Art Students League, New York, New York
1996 St. Johnsbury Art League, St. Johnsbury, Vermont
2000 Bondstreet Gallery, Naples, Florida
2001 Bondstreet Gallery, Naples, Florida
2006 Salmagundi Arts Club, New York, New York
2008 The John Hudson Gallery, Poughkeepsie, New York

Group Exhibitions

1967 Mostra d'Arte Internationale, Anticoli Corrado, Italy
1968 International Exhibition, Palais des Congres, Monaco
1968 The Butler Institute of American Art, Youngstown, Ohio
1969 "Professionals Who Teach," Paintings by Instructors of the Art Students League at the Gallery of Modern Art, New York, NY
1974– The Butler Institute of American Art, Youngstown, Ohio
1975 "Caravan of Freedom," Travelling exhibition of the National Society of Mural Painters for the 1981 Bicentennial Celebration, New York, Vermont, North Carolina, Delaware
1979 "From All Walks of Life," Travelling exhibition of the National Academy of Design, New York, NY
1979 "Salute to the Met," National Society of Arts and Letters, Metropolitan Museum, New York, NY
1980 "Art and the Law," Travelling exhibition of the Minnesota Museum of Art, St. Paul, Minnesota
1980 Winter Sports Exhibition, National Art Museum of Sport, Lake Placid, New York
1983 "New York by Artists of the Art Students League," Museum of the City of New York, NY
1983 "The Artist's Studio in American Painting,"National Academy of Design at the Allentown Art Museum of Lehigh Valley, Allentown, Pennsylvania
1988 Visual Individualists United, Iowa State University, Ames, Iowa
1990 The American Academy and Institute of Arts and Letters 42nd Annual Purchase Exhibition, New York, NY
1991 "A Family of Artists," American Fine Arts Society, New York, NY
1991 "Different Voices," Church of St. Ignatius Loyola, New York, NY
1992 "Romantic Realism: Visions of Value," Grand Central Art Galleries, New York, NY
1993 "The League at the Cape," Exhibition of paintings of the Cape by Art Students League members, Provincetown, Massachusetts
1993 "Different Voices," Church of St. Ignatius Loyola, New York, NY
1995 "Freedom of the Arts," Centennial Exhibition of the National Society of Mural Painters, Art Students League, New York, NY
1996, "The Legacy Lives," American Renaissance for the 20th Century, Lever House, New York, NY
1997 "The Legacy Lives," American Renaissance for the 20th Century, Hillsdale College, Hillsdale, Michigan
1998 National Symphony Orchestra Annual Fund Raiser Exhibition, Edes House, Georgetown, Washington, DC
1998 "The Art Students League of New York: Works by the Instructors," Gremillion and Company Fine Art, Inc., Houston, Texas
2000 "The League in Woodstock: 1906-Present," Woodstock School of Art, Woodstock, New York
2001 Art Renewal Center, On Line Museum of 19th and 20th Cenury Paintings, www. artrenewal.com
2002 "Art on Campus: Creative Work by Art Faculty of the Region," Southern Vermont Arts Center, Manchester, Vermont

2002 "The Legacy of Frank Vincent Dumond," Leu Gallery, Belmont University, Nashville, Tennasee

2004 "Seeing People: Paintings from the National Academy of Design," UBS Art Gallery, New York, NY

2005 "Salmagundi Club: An American Institution," New York, New York, National Museum Tour

2008 Landscape Exhibition, Wendt Gallery, Laguna Beach, CA

Selected Collections

Church of San Giovanni di Malta, Venice, Italy

Butler Institute of American Art, Youngstown, Ohio

King Faisal Naval Base, Jidda, Saudi Arabia

St. Patrick's Old Cathedral, New York, New York

Museum of the City of New York, New York, New York

American Embassy, London, England

Springfield Museum of Art, Springfield, Ohio

Phoenix Museum of Art, Phoenix, Arizona

Heinz Hall Collection, Pittsburgh, Pennsylvania

Church of Santa Vittoria, Anticoli Corrado, Italy

Hinkhouse Collection, Stephens College, Columbia, Missouri

Salmagundi Club, New York, New York

Hyram Blauvelt Wildlife Museum, Oradell, New Jersey

Schomberg Center for Research, NY Public Library, New York, NewYork

Hinkhouse Collection, Coe College, Cedar Rapids, Iowa

Robert Hall Fleming Museum, Burlington, Vermont

Duke University, North Carolina

Museum of Anticoli Corrado, Anticoli Corrado, Italy

Westmoreland Museum of American Art, Greensburg, Pennsylvania

Melick-Hinkhouse Collection, Eureka College, Eureka, Illinois

New York State Capitol Hall of Governors, Albany, New York

Fort Belvoir Museum, Alexandria, Virginia

Museum of the Southwest, Midland, Texas

San Antonio Museum of Art, San Antonio, Texas

Art Students League, New York, New York

National Academy of Design, New York, New York

Blaik Gallery, U.S. Military Academy, West Point, New York

Iowa Wesleyan College Art Museum, Mt. Pleasant, Iowa

Lakeview Museum of Arts and Sciences, Peoria, Illinois

Union League Club, New York, New York

Southern Vermont Arts Center, Manchester, Vermont

Thomas Jefferson University, Philadelphia, Pennsylvania

University of Pennsylvania, Philadelphia, Pennsylvania

University of North Carolina, Chapel Hill, North Carolina

Luther College, Decorah, Iowa

South Carolina Museum, Columbia, South Carolina

Selected Awards

1966 Sovereign Military Order of Malta Cross of Merit, Prima Classe, for eight paintings of St. Anthony of Padua, permanently hung in the 11th Century Church of San Giovanni di Malta, Venice, Italy

1968 "Prix d'Amerique du Nord" and Gold Medal from American Artists Professional League, International Exhibition, Palais des Congress, Monaco

1990 Purchase Prize, American Academy and Institute of Arts and Letters, New York, New York

1999 Arthur Ross Award, Classical America, New York, New York

1999 Newington-Cropsey Annual Award for Excellence in the Arts, Newington-Cropsey Foundation, Hastings-on-Hudson, NY

2002 Annual Benjamin West Clinedinst Memorial Medal, The Artists' Fellowship, New York, New York

2000 Salmagundi Club Annual Medal of Honor, New York, New York

2003 Dr. Clifford Wheeler Mills Memorial Award, Allied Artists of America Exhibition, New York, New York

1997 Lee M. Loeb Memorial Award, Salmagundi Club Exhibition, New York, New York

1945 Popular Prize, Associated Artists of Pittsburgh, Carnegie Museum, Pittsburgh, Pennsylvania

1977 Salmagundi Club Award, Audubon Artists Annual Exhibition, New York, New York

1997 St. Michael's Religious Award, Pennational Exhibit, Ligonier, Pennsylvania

2002 Frank C. Wright Medal of Honor, American Artists Professional League Exhibition, New York, New York

2004 Henry Nordhausen Memorial Award, Salmagundi Club Exhibit, New York, New York

1968 + 1973 President's Award, American Artists Professional League Annual Exhibition, New York, New York

2003 Elaine and James Hewitt Memorial Award, Audubon Artists Exhibit, New York, New York

2001 John R. Grabach Memorial Award, American Artists Professional League Annual Exhibition, New York, New York

2003 Macowin Tuttle Memorial Award, Salmagundi Club Exhibition, New York, New York

1992 + 1999 Helen G. Oehler Memorial Award, American Artists Professional League Annual Exhibition, New York, New York

2004 Phillip Isenberg Award, Salmagundi Club Exhibition, New York, New York

2005 Athenaeum Award, St. Johnsbury, Vermont

Professional Activities

Student of Frank Vincent Dumond, Art Students League, New York, New York

Instructor of Fine Arts, Art Students League, New York, New York, 1951–2008

Fellow of the Royal Society of Arts, London, England

ArtWatch International, New York, New York

National Society of Mural Painters, New York, New York

National Academy of Design, New York, New York

Salmagundi Club, New York, New York

American Society of Portrait Artists, Montgomery, Alabama

Artists' Fellowship, New York, New York

American Artists Professional League, New York, New York

Allied Artists of America, Inc, New York, New York

Audubon Artists, Inc, New York, New York

New York Artists Equity Association, Inc, New York, New York

Hudson Valley Art Association, Inc.

Photograph Credits

Tony Mysak
Erik Landsberg
Authenticolor, Inc.
Allan Baillie